making sense of sports

Third edition

- Ellis Cashmore

First published 2000 by Routledge
11 New Fetter Lane, London EC4P 4EE

Simultaneously published in the USA and Canada
by Routledge
29 West 35th Street, New York, NY 10001

Second edition 1996
Reprinted 1998 (twice)
Third edition 2000

Routledge is an imprint of the Taylor & Francis Group

© 1990, 1996, 2000 Ellis Cashmore

Typeset in Times and Futura by Keystroke, Jacaranda Lodge, Wolverhampton
Printed and bound in Great Britain by TJ International Ltd, Padstow, Cornwall

British Library Cataloguing in Publication Data
A catalogue record for this book is available from the British Library

Library of Congress Cataloging in Publication Data
Cashmore, Ernest.
    Making sense of sports / Ellis Cashmore.— 3rd ed.
       p. cm.
    Rev. ed. of: Making sense of sport. 1996.
    Includes bibliographical references (p.) and index.
       1. Sports—Social aspects. I. Cashmore, Ernest. Making sense of sport. II. Title.

GV706.5 .C38 2000
306.4′83—dc21

                                                                          99–058714

ISBN 0–415–23224–4 (hbk)
ISBN 0–415–21383–5 (pbk)

making sense of sports

Sports are more important than ever socially, economically and culturally. As well as embodying cherished values and ideals, sports now reflect many of the worries of wider society. Drugs, racism, corruption and violence are all now major concerns and our experience of sport is increasingly subject to a gigantic industry made up of owners, players, sporting goods manufacturers, television networks and corporate sponsors.

In this newly expanded edition of *Making Sense of Sports*, Cashmore addresses all those issues as well as the more basic questions about the history of sports, its social context and possible future development. Among the new edition's other themes are:

- the body, how it works and why it is more cultural than natural;
- why women continue to be devalued and depreciated by sports;
- Nike, globalization and the sports industry;
- art and how it reflects changing conceptions of sports.

This lively and entertaining textbook will be an indispensable guide for undergraduates in sports studies and for students taking classes in sports and physical education.

Ellis Cashmore has held academic positions at the Universities of Massachusetts, Tampa, Washington and Hong Kong. He is now Professor of Culture, Media and Sport at Staffordshire University, England.

other routledge titles by ellis cashmore

SPORTS CULTURE – AN A–Z GUIDE

THE BLACK CULTURE INDUSTRY

. . . AND THERE WAS TELEVISION

DICTIONARY OF RACE AND ETHNIC RELATIONS

OUT OF ORDER? POLICING BLACK PEOPLE
(*with Eugene McLaughlin*)

BLACK SPORTSMEN

his other books

DICTIONARY OF CULTURAL THEORISTS
(*with Chris Rojek*)

UNITED KINGDOM? CLASS, RACE AND GENDER SINCE THE WAR

THE LOGIC OF RACISM

HAVING TO – THE WORLD OF ONE-PARENT FAMILIES

NO FUTURE: YOUTH AND SOCIETY

RASTAMAN: THE RASTAFARIAN MOVEMENT IN ENGLAND

INTRODUCTION TO RACE RELATIONS
(*with Barry Troyna*)

BLACK YOUTH IN CRISIS
(*with Barry Troyna*)

APPROACHING SOCIAL THEORY
(*with Bob Mullan*)

LONDON AND NEW YORK

contents

acknowledgments

I am grateful to Amy Shepper, of Florida Atlantic University, who has helped me in too many ways to mention, Sheelagh Rowbotham, of Staffordshire University, who has aided my research throughout the production of the book, and Roberto Ferrari, of Florida Atlantic University, who kickstarted the research for the chapter "Through artists' eyes." Erwin Bengry, of Staffordshire University, has assisted me in all sorts of ways, from accessing data to talking through ideas. Mari Shullaw, my commissioning editor, has been a great supporter of *Making Sense of Sports* through all of its editions and her constructive criticism and encouragement have been indispensable.

abbreviations

AA	American Association (baseball)
ABA	American Basketball Association
ABC	American Broadcasting Company
ABL	American Basketball League
ACB	Australian Cricket Board
ADP	Adenosine diphosphate
AFC	American Football Conference
AFL	American Football League
AL	American League (baseball)
ANC	African National Congress
ANS	Autonomic nervous system
ATP	Association of Tennis Professionals
BAF	British Athletics Federation
BBC	British Broadcasting Corporation
BDO	British Darts Organization
BSkyB	British Sky Broadcasting
CBS	Columbia Broadcasting System
CNS	Central nervous system
EPO	Erythropoietin
ESPN	Entertainment and Sports Network
FA	Football Association
FAME	Falk Associates Management Enterprises
FCC	Federal Communications Commission
Fifa	*Fédération Internationale de Football Associations*

HBO	Home Box Office
HRM	Heart Rate Monitor
hGH	Human growth hormone
IAA	Intercollegiate Athletic Association
IAAF	International Amateur Athletic Federation
IBF	International Boxing Federation
ICC	International Cricket Conference
ITF	International Tennis Federation
ITV	Independent Television
MCC	Marylebone Cricket Club
MHR	Maximum heart rate
MLB	Major League Baseball
MLS	Major League Soccer
NABP	National Association of Baseball Players
NBA	National Basketball Association
NBC	National Broadcasting Company
NCAA	National Collegiate Athletic Association
NFC	National Football Conference
NFL	National Football League
NHL	National Hockey League
NL	National League (baseball)
NYSAC	New York State Athletic Commission
PAC	Pan-African Congress
pfc	Perfluorocarbon
PNS	Peripheral nervous system
ppv	Pay per view
RAS	Reticular activating system
RFU	Rugby Football Union
RSPCA	Royal Society for the Prevention of Cruelty to Animals
SANROC	South African Non-Racial Olympic Committee
SARU	South African Rugby Union
TBS	Turner Broadcasting System
T–E ratio	Testosterone to epitestosterone ratio
TNT	Turner Network Television
Uefa	*Union des Associations Européennes de Football*
USATF	USA Track and Field
USTA	United States Tennis Association
WBA	World Boxing Association
WBC	World Boxing Council
WNBA	Women's National Basketball Association
WPBSA	World Professional Billiards and Snooker Association

introduction

why sports fascinate and

captivate us

WHY . . . ?

Question: How many people would willingly sit in front of their television sets for five weeks to watch 64 games between 22 overpaid athletes trying to move an inflated leather ball across a 24-foot line, while another 11 try to move the same ball across another line 100 yards away?

Answer: 37 billion, including 1.7 billion – a quarter of the world's total population – for the final 90 minutes alone.

Rational minds might wonder at this apparent waste of time, of energy, even of brain cells. Yet soccer's World Cup championship of 1998 cast a spell over most of the planet. Even in countries not represented in the championship, daily coverage of the events captivated tv audiences.

It might be easy to assume that the five-week spectacle was highly unusual. After all, the World Cup comes along only every four years. But between them, the tournaments are typically an equally gargantuan summer Olympics, a rugby World Cup, two World Track and Field Championships, 20 tennis Grand Slam tournaments, not to mention four full seasons of baseball, basketball, football, golf, hockey, and a mixed bag of other sports to keep the world captivated. The enthusiasm for sports is truly universal and seemingly unquenchable: no matter how much sports we get, we thirst for more.

And yet, there is no apparent rhyme, less still reason, to the activities that comprise sports. They do not contribute to cures for debilitating diseases or to solutions to military conflicts; nor do they help ameliorate poverty, dysfunctional families, racism, or any of the other seemingly intractable problems that bedevil contemporary society.

Despite this, we spend inordinate amounts of money either to watch or to bet on events; we travel often great distances; in some cases, we even fight – to the death – over sports. We should properly feel at least slightly uncomfortable about this. Challenge is important to the human condition: it is one of the oldest preoccupations. Where obstacles – natural or artificial – exist, we always attempt to surmount them. And, where they don't exist, we invent them. Countless episodes of triumph or folly and, sometimes, disaster, have followed our attempts to conquer obstacles. Witness the yearly catalog of deaths resulting from mountaineering expeditions.

The human tendency to rise to challenges rather than just accept them is no doubt part of our evolutionary adaptation. If we did not rise, we would not have survived as a species. Sports kick in when we have taken on all the challenges germane to our survival and then lust for more: when the challenges no longer exist, we invent them. Sporting competition has everything: the challenge, the confrontation, and the climactic finality of a result. Someone, or something, always wins, loses, or ties. And this goes some way toward understanding our fundamental fascination with sports. But we still need to dig deeper for the sources.

No human institution is immune from critical investigation. Not even ones that provide us with so much pleasure. This is why there are theories of and investigations into art, humor, and, of course, sex. Ask anybody why they like any of these and odds are you will get a stock response along the lines of "because they bring joy," or "they're good fun." Fair comment. But the analyst of sports uses this only as the starting point of his or her examination.

Often, there is resistance to approaching sport on any other terms other than those of the fan, the reporter, or the athlete. Sports practitioners and journalists have warned off those who bring too much intellect to what is, after all, a blessed human activity. Theoretical contemplation is all very well; but sports are for doers, not thinkers. If you intellectualize over an activity too much you lose sight of the basic reason why people like it. That was the jaundiced view once encountered by sports analysts. Now it is changing. Sport as an institution is just too economically big, too politically important, too influential in shaping people's lives not to be taken seriously as a subject for academic inquiry. ("Sport" refers to the entire institution and is preferred in Britain to the plural "Sports" which describes the various activities and organizations and is more popular in the USA.)

Those whose emotions are left undisturbed by sports, are often bewildered and sometimes disgusted by the irrational waste of sports. Readers of this book will probably not be among this group; but they will be looking for explanations: they will want to make sense of what is, on the surface at least, a senseless activity. This book, as its title suggests, tries to do exactly that. In the chapters that follow, we will go beyond surface appearances to reveal new perspectives on sports.

None of what follows denies the validity of the views of the fans, the athletes, the sports journalists, nor indeed the cynics. I will integrate as many different perspectives as necessary in the attempt to make sport comprehensible as an enduring, universal phenomenon. The reader will find contributions from a range of behavioral and physical sciences, such as anthropology, biology, history, psychology, and sociology. None of these disciplines has been able to supply a single unifying answer to the question of why people are so drawn to sports. But, by piecing together various insights, we can assemble a broad understanding.

In the balance of this chapter, I will offer three general observations on the reasons for the existence and longevity of sports. They all begin from the premise that life has deficiencies. Sports are a way of compensating for those deficiencies.

Life is too predictable

"The why of a fan" is the title of an article published in the *North American Review* way back in 1929 in which A. A. Brill argued that "life organized too well becomes monotonous; too much peace and security breed boredom; and old instincts, bred into the very cells of the body . . . still move the masses of normal men" (1929: 431). (Year of publication followed by page numbers quoted appear in parenthesis throughout this book.)

Brill wrote in terms of the "restrictions of modern life" depriving people of their "activity and scope, the triumphs and *réclame*" which were achievable through physical prowess under "more primitive conditions." In explaining the fans' attraction to sports, Brill exposed what he took to be a dark truth about human nature; he described the human being as "an animal formed for battle and conquest, for blows and strokes and swiftness, for triumph and applause" (1929: 434).

As the civilizing process and rise of governing states removed the necessity for physical struggle and modernity brought with it order, stability, and security, so the nasty and brutish qualities were made redundant – but not irrelevant. They were of great use in sports. The sports that began to take shape in the middle of the nineteenth century required physical prowess. Of course, not everyone could excel in physical activities; but the ones who could not were able to identify with those who could.

In Brill's view, this enabled them to recover something resembling their natural state: they could "achieve exaltation, vicarious but real" and be "a better individual, better citizen." Sports, or at least its precursors, actually contributed to building a better citizenry for the modern nation-state.

Improbable as Brill's argument might have been as a total theory of sports, it offered a timeless insight about the drabness and uniformity ushered in by modernity, which is often thought to have begun in the Enlightenment of the eighteenth century and had effects across all facets of society – as we will see. One of the effects of the modern effort to bring shape and coherence to human affairs was that life became more directed, more patterned, and more predictable.

The German social theorist Max Weber used the term "calculability" to capture the ethos of modern bureaucracy; he meant that the workings of the complex organizations that had proliferated all around him (he was writing around 1904–20) strained toward regulation. Their rules and procedures were designed to minimize the intrusion of the personal emotions or whims of those who administered its policies. As a result, the performance of a bureaucracy was highly predictable. (We return to Weber's theories in Chapter five.)

Once the applicable regulations and procedures are known, it is possible to calculate exactly how a bureaucracy is going to deal with a matter and predict the likelihood of a certain kind of outcome. So bureaucracies stabilize a society, order its policies, regulate its citizens, and make it reliably predictable. All this makes for a rational and smooth-running society. It also affects the mentality of the people who live in such a society.

Calculability is an organizing principle in all contemporary societies, apart from those in the throes of upheaval. Spontaneity and randomness may be pleasant diversions but, in large doses, they can prove disruptive and threaten the citizenry's sense of security. Still, there is a residual attraction in the unplanned, surprise happening; everyone knows the pleasant sensation of an unexpected gift or a turn of events that were completely unexpected. On an occasional basis, surprises are fine; were they to invade our working, or public lives, they would lead to disruption and, possibly, disorientation.

In the main, we try to confine the fascination for the unpredictable to our private lives. Office workers can approach their daily tasks with a strangulating regard to rationality and precision. Once out of the office, they might retreat to the tumult of a home where chaos, clutter, and utter confusion reign. One set of the rules for work, but another for home.

The separation of life into public and private spheres is itself a product of the modern age. It has the advantage of allowing the individual to compensate in one sphere for the tensions and frustrations that build up in the other. How many of us have quietly boiled in rage during a lecture or at work? We might keep a lid on it, but explode once we are in a different context. Most of us experience bureaucracies, if only indirectly, and, equally, most of us have been irritated or angered by them; but we typically do not scream or assault people. Instead, we find outlets for these emotions elsewhere – like in sports.

Kicking or throwing balls, riding horses in a circle or inflicting damage on others may look like irrational pursuits. But, that is precisely the point: whether watched or performed, they guide the participant clear of the formal limits of bureaucracies and into areas where the outcome of situations is wholly unpredictable; the opposite of bureaucracies.

For all of the layer-on-layer of organization that sports have acquired, especially in recent years, the actual sporting activity has retained one special nucleus: *indeterminacy*. You can never predict the result with unerring success. That is, unless the result is fixed; but then it ceases to be a genuine sport and becomes a fake or just plain theater. The indeterminate qualities of sports make them constant challenges to the bureaucratic spirit of predictability. The result of a competition can never be determined in advance, even when the odds overwhelmingly favor one party over another. Athletic competition is an area where fairytale endings occasionally do come true. Every underdog has a shot at winning, no matter how small.

In a world in which certainty has become the norm, uncertainty is a prized commodity. And, of course, sports are commodities in the sense that they are packaged as visually moving and colorful displays that excite our senses. Not that they would excite us if their outcomes were known ahead of schedule: contrast the rush of watching an event as it happens to watching a tape delay transmission once the result is known. It is not knowing what will happen that makes sports attractive. They cannot be determined, their outcomes are uncertain and, calculate as we may, the form book will never tell us what is going to happen once the competition begins.

Bureaucracy predominates in most countries where there are organized sports and the shift from goods-producing to service economies promises no significant reduction in organization and standardization. As economies develop, so do sports and, for that matter, religion, education, science, and many of the other important institutions that have been subject to bureaucratic imperatives.

The irony here is that, while sports are exciting because of their separation from other parts of life, the organizations that govern and administer sports have increasingly reflected those other parts. Sports have accumulated their own bureaucracies and some of their policies have resulted in administrative decisions that seem to go against the grain of sports. Boxing champions have had their titles stripped from them without even fighting in the ring;

European soccer teams have been made to play games behind locked doors with no fans allowed in.

We might rail against the rulings, but most sports have become so vast that they need complex, bureaucratic organizations to function effectively and policies to maintain continuity. Imagine the amount of intricate organization and planning that goes into an event like soccer's five-week World Cup championship, or the summer Olympic Games, both of which occur every four years.

Even the day-to-day activities of sports performers have come to resemble those of other workers. Divisions of labor; deadlines; monotonous regimes; computer-enhanced analyses: these are all elements of work that have infiltrated sports. Much of sports today is routine and predictable. But not everything: the uncertainty that hangs over the actual competitive match-up can never be eliminated. Nor can the inspiration, innovation, vision and moments of bravura skill that emerge in the competitive encounter. These are like lightning bolts that interrupt an otherwise continuous skyline. The unpredictability of sports provides an agreeable, perhaps even necessary, divergence from the certainty that prevails in much of our everyday lives.

Life is too civil

The British writer Howard Jacobson has offered a short but provocative account of our fascination with sports. Like Brill, he relies on a primitive model of the human being as engaged in a sort of struggle against the civilizing influences of contemporary life. Sport is an outlet for our lust for killing, "the aestheticization of the will to murder," as Jacobson calls it in his article "We need bad behaviour in sport, it's the way to win" (in the *Independent*, June 6, 1998).

Jacobson appeals to Darwin's theory of natural selection: he believes that life is itself a form of competition, though human society cannot function on a win-at-all-costs principle. So, we have devised manners, customs, protocols, the patterns of restraint by which we live in civil society. "Which is why we have invented sport," writes Jacobson.

Our primary instincts incline us toward competition in order to survive, yet civil society forces us to curb those instincts or at least channel them into "the means whereby we can obey our primary instinct to prevail while adhering to the artificial forms of civilized behaviour." Jacobson goes on: "We watch sport in the hope that we may see someone die, or failing that, humiliated. We give up our weekends to witness rage, violence, unreason . . . to be part of the unrelenting hysteria of species survival, but at a safe distance."

In other words, it is bloodletting by proxy: we let others – the athletes – play out our instinctual impulses. This is why we feel indifferent about some sports performers who are technically good, but "nice," yet we give our hearts to headcases who seem to epitomize the rage we sometimes feel inside us.

On this admittedly extreme view, a pool table or a tennis court, a football field, or a baseball diamond is a symbolic killing field; a refined Roman Coliseum, where real deaths actually did occur. All fulfill the same function: providing a stage on which to mount a ritualized Darwinian survival of the fittest. We the spectators are effectively electing others to do the dirty work for us. This makes for an attractive spectacle; murder rendered aesthetically pleasing for the masses.

Jacobson's perspective is open to many objections, not least because it crudely reduces a complex series of activities to a basic survival impulse. Yet, it provides an intriguing starting-point for discussion: sports as symbolic expressions of an impelling force that has its sources in our survivalist instincts. If we did not have sports, we might be still splitting other people's heads open.

Sigmund Freud explained that civilization is a sort of mutilation that the civilized being never completely accepts; the civilized individual unconsciously tries to recover a natural wholeness. It is the pursuit of this wholeness that endangers himself or herself as well as others. It is a form of primitive death wish.

We stand as privileged citizens of a world that has taken over a millennium to reduce the despotism, poverty, ignorance, and barbarity that were features of primitive cultures. But, on this view, we have renounced some part of our natural selves. We see in later chapters how the conversion from barbarity to civilized culture has formed the basis of more elaborate and sophisticated theories of sport.

Life is too safe

Both perspectives covered so far consider that life has become too organized and too laden with rules for our own good. There is something primeval inside us being stifled by the containing influences of modernity. Complementing this is the view that the massive changes wrought over the past two centuries have made life, not only predictable and rule-bound, but also safe.

Of course, there are road deaths, unconquerable diseases, homicides, fatal accidents and other unseen malefactors lurking in society. But, for the most part, our lives are a lot more secure than they were even 30 years ago, let alone in the days of barbarism. Of course, we also create new perils, like environmental pollution and nuclear energy plant catastrophes. It seems the more we find ways of minimizing danger in some areas, we reintroduce them into others.

The sociologist Frank Furedi argues that, by the 1990s, societies all over the world had become preoccupied, if not obsessed, by safety. Risk avoidance became an organizing principle for much behavior. Safety was not something that people could just have: they needed to work toward getting it. So, human control was extended into virtually every aspect of cultural life: nothing that was potentially controllable was left to chance.

The title of Furedi's book *Culture of Fear* describes an environment in which risks are not so much there – they are created. We started to fear things that would have been taken for granted in previous times: drinking water, the nuclear family, technology; all came to be viewed as secreting previously unknown perils. Furedi despairs at this "worship of safety," as he calls it. The most significant discoveries and innovations have arisen out of a spirit of adventure and a disregard for perils.

While we avoid risks that lie outside our control, we are quite prepared to take voluntary risks. The so-called "lifestyle risks" such as smoking, drinking, and driving are examples of this. But sports present us with something quite different: manufactured risks that are actually designed in such a way as to preserve natural dangers or build in new ones. Horse racing always contains some risk for both jockey and horse, particularly in steeplechases. Lowering fences would reduce the hazard; but the governing associations have resisted doing so.

On the other hand, boxing, especially amateur boxing, has done its utmost to reduce the dangers that are inherent in combat sports. Yet both sports are fraught with risk and both continue to prosper. According to Furedi's thesis, it is probable that they would continue to prosper with or without safety measures. He cites the example of rock climbing which had some of its risks reduced by the introduction of improved ropes, boots, helmets and other equipment. Furedi writes: "The fact that young people who choose to climb mountains might not want to be denied the *frisson* of risk does not enter into the calculations of the safety-conscious professional, concerned to protect us from ourselves."

Furedi is one of a number of writers who have speculated on the rise of what Ulrich Beck calls the *Risk Society* (1992). Beck believes that advances in science and technology have expanded our knowledge not only of how the world works, but of the perils it holds. Many of the perils have actually been fostered by our desire to know more. In other words, many of the anxieties we have, have been produced by knowledge not ignorance.

Author of the book *Risk*, John Adams believes we have inside us a "risk thermometer" which we can set to our own tastes, according to our particular culture, or subculture: "Some like it hot – a Hell's Angel or a Grand Prix racing driver, for example; others like it cool . . . But no one wants absolute zero" (1995: 15). We all want to restore some danger to our lives. How we do it is quite interesting: for instance, the same people who go white-water rafting or bungee-jumping will probably steer clear of a restaurant declared unsafe by state sanitary inspectors.

A game of chess or pool may offer no hint of danger, but skiing, surfing, extreme sports, and all motor and air sports certainly do. Even sitting in a crowd watching these sports carries a sense of danger. And, if the crowd happens to be at a game of soccer, the danger may be not just vicarious. The risk in some sports may be tiny; but its presence is what counts; and where it does not exist, we invent it.

Seekers for the source of our attraction to sports have found its source in the ways society has changed. Complex industrial societies and the maze of bureaucratic rules and procedures they brought stifled our natural spontaneity and made life too boring, according to Brill. Our primitive urges to do battle were suppressed by the development of civility and good manners in Jacobson's view. And, for others, contemporary life has become organized in such a way as to minimize risks. Sports re-inject these missing elements back into our lives. None of us is willing to sacrifice the benefits of an orderly life in which we are relatively safe and can go about our business without having to wonder what tomorrow will bring. At the same time, we need activities that give vent to what some writers believe to be natural impulses.

It seems that humans are bored: they yearn for the uncertainty, risk, and danger, life lived on the basis of instinct and passion. Sport provides an occasion for exhibiting the excesses that are prohibited in other aspects of life. It has parallels with the Potlatch ceremonies in which the peoples of northwest America exchanged gifts in ritualized ceremonies; and in the carnivals of the Middle Ages (in which competitions featured, as we will see in later chapters). Both presented occasions for breaking rules. In particular, the "carnivalesque," written of by Mikhail Bhaktin, presented an occasion for violating rules (1981). The penalties for such offenses would be severe in any other context. The carnival was an escape from ordinary life.

Sports have obviously morphed over the years, but we can still find in them the kinds of escape attempts that inspired early industrial workers in the nineteenth century to enrich their laborious lives by organizing games. Their efforts were gropings toward what we now regard as legitimate sports. Their pursuits were as lacking in purpose as today's sports: they were simple activities enjoyed purely for their own sake. Professionalism has ensured that sports are no longer as simple as that; today's athletes compete for money, gamblers bet for the same reason and there are an assortment of others, including agents, coaches, and owners, whose motives may include a pecuniary element. But, for the overwhelming majority of fans and amateur players, sports still have an *autotelic* quality – the act of competing is the main pleasure. Their function lies in avoiding what we do during the rest of the working week.

Sports, at least those of today, have nothing to do with anything at all, certainly not work. They do not resemble anything, represent anything, and do not actually do anything apart from providing a momentary release from other, less pleasurable, facts of life. We savor sports as ends-in-themselves.

Even sports which appear plain stupid have stood the test of time and measure up to the strict criteria of sport. There has even been a campaign to have melon-seed spitting in the Olympic program: every August in Le Frechou, France, about 50 well-trained competitors line up for this traditional country contest. Before we dismiss it as a huge prank, we should take note that spitters regularly make distances over 30 feet, suggesting that there is technique involved. While on the subject of distances, the world record for cow-dung throwing is 266 feet. Every year in Beaver, Colorado, champion-ships are held and rules applied (like the "chips," as they are known, being 100 per cent organic and non-spherical in shape!). There is even a World Dwarf Throwing Authority that has defied political correctness and still holds its 100-year-old championships in Australia. Wacky they may seem, but they are only as irrational and purposeless as the competitions we take seriously and, in many cases, fight over.

There is a symmetry between our enthusiasm for sports and our embrace of other gestures, displays and even fantasies that have no under-lying reference points. We visit theme parks, like DisneyWorld in Florida and Alton Towers in England, and surround ourselves with artificial articles that have no reality outside themselves. We decamp to fantastic communities where image is everything. Our voyages into cyberspace can also be seen as flights away from the gray mundanity and toward a lusciously unrestricted universe where former identities are swapped for new ones.

At various points in history, sports have held practical value, military, industrial, commercial; now sports beckon as a way of restoring excitement. This makes them no less powerful or compelling than they once were. Far from it: sports are more arresting now. As John Hannigan writes in his *Fantasy City: Pleasure and profit in the postmodern metropolis*: "Sports has become a defining part of our life and culture, infusing a wide range of events, activities and institutions . . . professional sports have taken the role of a com-mon cultural currency" (1998: 142). This cultural currency is exchanged by more people than at any time in history. Sports are watched by more people, turn over more money and probably bear more responsibility for hope and heartache than ever before. The precise reasons for this appear obscure, but we will reveal them in the chapters to come.

Culture of Fear by Frank Furedi (Cassell, 1997) is a strong argument that explains our continuing fascination with danger and may profitably be read in conjunction with Michael Bane's *Over the Edge: A regular guy's odyssey in extreme sports* (Gollancz, 1997), and an interesting study published in the journal *Physician and Sportsmedicine*, "Why do some athletes choose high-risk sports?" by D. Groves (vol. 15, no. 2, 1987).

Risk by John Adams (UCL Press, 1995), while not about sports, is full of insights about how our obsession with security has created as many problems as it solves.

The why of a fan by A. A. Brill is still worthy of serious attention, despite its age. Published in the *North American Review*, in 1929, it retains its relevance to our attempts to explain contemporary sports.

Reviewing the second edition of *Making Sense of Sports*, Timothy Chandler, of Kent State University, wrote: "I was surprised to find that Cashmore had not attempted to make sense of sports as a ritual sacrifice of human energy" (*Culture, Sport, Society*, vol. 1, no. 1, 1998). Make the attempt.

naturals

the role of evolution

NO LIMITS

Bill Reef, the race director of the "Bolder Boulder" event in Colorado found himself at the center of a controversy when he restricted Kenyan entrants to three. Reef's defense was that Kenyans were not as media-friendly as their American counterparts and the race sponsors were concerned about the way in which Kenyans were dominating. In 1996, Kenyans took eight of the first ten places; in 1997, they took seven of the first eight. Reef was insuring against a repetition in 1998.

A single nation has rarely dominated a sport as completely as Kenya did men's middle- and long-distance running in the 1980s and 1990s. The extraordinary capabilities of Kenyans both on the track and cross-country was expressed time and again through two decades, but never more so than in 1997, when an unprecedented seven world records fell in a one-month period, all but one to Kenyan athletes. While Reef did not actually say this, one could almost hear him thinking that Kenyan runners were physically advantaged when it came to running. They seemed as close as anything to "naturals."

There are some athletes who seem to have qualities that suit them ideally for a successful sports career; qualities

13

that might even be seen as wondrous or peculiar, that no amount of training can duplicate in lesser beings. Bernard Malamud's allegorical novel *The Natural* was the story of one such athlete, Roy Hobbes, an invincible baseball player, who brandished his bat like King Arthur's Excalibur. Barry Levinson's 1984 movie of the book emphasizes the mythological aspects of the "natural."

The world of fact is not too far away from the world of fiction. For example, has there ever been a such a complete golfer as Jack Nicklaus, or a tennis player to match Martina Navratilova? Wayne Gretzky was as peerless in hockey as Michael Jordan was in basketball. Juan Manuel Fangio, who was unbeatable in the 1950s, is acknowledged as the best racing driver ever (though, had he lived longer, Ayrton Senna may have challenged him). These performers all seemed to have gifts that made them as naturally suited to their events as Kenyan runners, it seems, are to middle distances.

Yet, we are all "naturals" in one way or another: endowed with some capacity for a sporting activity. Some more than others may possess great mechanical efficiency and skill in performing certain tasks and may even refine these to the point where their expertise appears effortless; so effortless in fact that it appears to be the product of a gift. On closer inspection, a sports performer's command is more likely to be more the result of painstaking training than special inborn ability.

Rejecting the old adage "great sportsmen are born, not made" (and the sexism it implies) takes us so far in explaining why certain consummate performers have risen to the top. They have worked harder, have more determination to succeed and can get focused at precisely the right time in a competition (Joe Montana's remarkable facility for this distinguished him from quarterbacks with better arms). But athletes are simply not born equal: a 5' 4" South Korean, no matter how hard he practices throwing hoops, is not going to prove much of a match for Kobe Bryant. A native of Nairobi who works out over a mile above sea level, will not threaten Alberto Tomba on the ski slopes. In the first case, training will simply not provide what genetics has not. In the second, environment prohibits the development of skills that are integral to some sports.

All human beings have some natural ability: sports express this in exaggerated and often extravagant forms. It provides opportunities to wring from our natural mental and physical equipment behavior that deviates dramatically from normal responses. The deviation has, it seems, no limits. Runners, rowers, and swimmers cover distances faster and faster; gymnasts perform with staggering technical proficiency; tennis players hit with ever-greater velocity.

Those who cannot squeeze such efforts from their bodies are often drawn to watch, admire, and be awed by the efforts of others, efforts that sometimes last for only a few seconds. A Christian Styren dive, spectacular as it may be, takes less than 1.5 seconds. Shaquille O'Neal slam-dunks in two seconds tops. Marion Jones runs 100 meters in the time it takes to start a car. Alex Rodriguez can steal a base while spectators are taking a swig of beer. No matter what the sport, spectators will go to great lengths and pay money to witness a human performance that may well be fleeting.

We learn to appreciate sports performances, just as competitors learn basic techniques and styles on which they later innovate. The sports fan is like the art critic who acquires a knowledge of what to look for, how to evaluate, the meaning of certain properties and so on. The athlete needs not just knowledge, but a physical mastery; in other words, a skill. This involves a lengthy and, sometimes, complex process in which he or she is made to call into service devices, ingenuity, and powers that might have gone undiscovered had the athlete not been urged or even forced to develop them. During this time, a sports competitor changes, physically and mentally: he or she learns how to control bodily movements, in many cases calibrating those movements with inanimate objects, like rackets and balls.

Looked at this way, sports are learnt. But, they are also completely natural: without the basic anatomical and behavioral apparatus, we could not perform even the simplest of operations, let alone the more complicated maneuvers needed for decent sporting action. There are what we might call limiting "givens" in the physical makeup of humans, just as there are in those of other animals. Humans have succeeded in overcoming all manner of limitations set by nature, basically by creating and employing technologies. Not that we are totally alone in this: some other species use rudimentary technologies, though not on anything like the scale of humans.

Technology has assisted sports performance and been integrated into most spheres of sports. As artifacts, technologies are manufactured items that we create and use to assist us. Poles help us vault higher, surfboards help us travel across the ocean surface. We monitor the results and modify the technologies, then pass them on to successive generations. This is not only true in sports, of course: we are constantly passing on information about technologies in the effort to improve life.

Our ability to use technology derives from natural abilities: specifically, a brain large and complex enough to imagine a product, movable limbs and prehensile hands and feet to create and utilize it, and an acute sense of sight to envisage the product and gauge distance. These are not properties unique to humans, but the way in which they are combined in the human species is very particular and is resembled only in other higher primates, namely monkeys and apes. The question is: what is it about the special combination in humans that enables them to develop the potential of their animal nature to levels far removed from those of other species?

> ## Culture
>
> From the Latin *Cultivara (terra)*, meaning land suitable for growth, this is often used in contrast to *nature* and refers to the learned traditions that are acquired socially and appear among mammals – especially primates. Human culture means the lifestyle of a group of people, including their repetitive, patterned ways of thinking, behaving and even feeling. These ways are picked up through learning processes rather than through natural inheritance. The anthropologist Edward B. Tylor, in his classic text *Primitive Culture* (first published in 1871), proposed a definition of human culture that included "knowledge, belief, art, morals and habits acquired by man as a member of society." This is a very inclusive definition and others prefer to restrict the use of "cultural" to refer to rules for thought and behavior and the ways those rules are put into practice.

Sports, as I will argue in detail later, have only been possible because of such advanced developments; other animals engage in activities that look like sports, but are not. Pursuing this logic, not only sports but religion, industry, warfare, education and so on – all conventionally regarded as social institutions – are grounded in our animal origins. The entire discipline of physical (sometimes called biological) anthropology is dedicated to the task of assessing the relative contributions to social life made by heredity and environment.

Social science examines the same things, but in a very different way. It finds the former approach too reductionist in its attempt to break down (or reduce) phenomena into their constituent parts to understand how they work. The sociologist sees the human effort to challenge, manipulate or transcend the physical and biological facts of life giving rise to distinct patterns of thought and behavior. These patterns cannot be explained by reference to biological factors alone. The interaction between human beings and their natural environments results in events and processes that defy explanation in purely biological terms.

Between the two disciplines, there is a whole range of diverse attempts to describe and analyze human behavior, each with its own version of why we do the things we do. In the course of this book, I will consider several of them and assess what contributions they may make to our comprehension of just one element – sports.

SEVEN KEYS

Stripped to their bare elements, human beings are mobile, multi-celled organisms that derive their motive force from eating other organisms. In taxonomic terms, humans are Animalia, as distinct from members of the plant kingdom, bacteria, single-celled organisms, and fungi. So, we have a great many characteristics in common with other animals, especially those with whom we share common ancestors, our closest evolutionary relatives being other primates, a taxon that includes monkeys, apes, lemurs, tarsiers, and others.

There are seven key characteristics of primates that set them apart from the rest of the living world and afford them special advantages for survival. Humans have extra-special advantages, but, for the moment, we will focus on similarities. The seven features are: an ability to grip and control; relatively great strength of limb; stereoscopic eyes positioned at the front of the head; small numbers of offspring; a high degree of interdependence and a corresponding tendency toward living in groups; a use of reliable, efficient communication systems; and a large brain relative to body size. Now, let us deal with each of these key characteristics in more detail.

All primates have prehensile hands and feet: they can catch, grip, and hold, thanks to relatively long, flexible digits. The ability to grip and control is enhanced by opposable thumbs or big toes which make it possible to lock around objects rigidly and so control an object's movement, as a golfer carefully guides the arc of a club's swing. From an evolutionary point of view, the origins of prehensility are not difficult to trace: distinguishing primates from

---

Reductionism

This is a method for analyzing phenomena based on the philosophy that matter is best understood once divided into its component parts. So, human societies can be approached in terms of individual beings, who, in turn, may be reduced to genes, which in turn may be reduced even further and so on. In other words, complex wholes can only be fully understood by isolating their parts. Critics argue that the "sum of the parts" is frequently not the same as the "whole" and that emergent qualities are produced when all the elements come together; these are distinct and need to be analyzed in terms of the whole. "How can one understand something like fashion by reducing it to its constituent parts?" they might ask, adding that it becomes meaningful as fashion only when people act together in a collectivity, however loosely assembled. This approach is known as holism.

other mammals was their tree-dwelling capacity. Prehensile hands and feet were useful for climbing up and down and to and from trees in forests, and additionally for plucking fruits and berries and overturning stones to pick up insects to eat.

The ability to grip is complemented by a strong versatile set of fore-limbs. Suspending full body weight and swinging needs extremely powerful, long arms and legs. The very specialized functions of arms and legs for primates are reflected not only in the size and heavy muscle of the limbs, but in their range of movement: they can flex (bend), extend, and rotate. Combined with the dexterity of the hands and feet this assists fast, multi-directional travel, sometimes over great distances. Gymnasts offer examples of how this ability has not been completely lost despite the human's transition from the trees to the ground.

Related to this mobility is the position of the eyes, which are to the front rather than the sides of the head. Two eyes enable stereoscopic vision, which permits reasonably accurate estimates of distances. The sense of vision is highly developed in primates, as opposed to, say, dogs which see the world in monochrome, but have sensitive snouts and use their acute sense of smell as their chief source of information about their environments. It's no accident that no sport is based on smelling or sniffing ability, whereas a great many are organized around the ability to gauge distance and co-ordinate hand move-ments accordingly, archery and shooting being obvious examples. (It seems feasible to imagine that if humans were sensitive to smell we might have devised a sport in which an acute sense of smell was employed in conjunction with other capacities; a modified form of orienteering perhaps.)

With other primates, humans share a tendency to give birth to one or two infants at a time; larger births are known, of course, but they are deviations from the norm. Mammals that have large litters lose some offspring at, or shortly after, birth. Primates have a smaller number of births, usually after a relatively long pregnancy, and accentuate the role of the mother in caring for and protecting the infant in an environment uncomplicated by the kind of competition that comes from large litters.

One very important consequence of having small families with intense mother–infant contact is that primates learn interdependence. They rely on each other far more than many other species which are abandoned at a young age and learn to adapt and survive individually, or else perish. Primates, by contrast, never learn the skills associated with lone survival. Having a protec-tive mother, the infant has no need of such skills. What an infant does acquire is an ability to co-operate and communicate with others. And this helps explain why primates spend their lives in groups, caring for and co-operating with others.

Individual survival for humans as well as other primates is a matter of communicating effectively in groups. So, all primates are gregarious: they grow and mature socially and not in isolation. Very few sports do not reflect this; most are organized in terms of a club structure with high degrees of inter-dependence and mutual co-operation needed. Even fabled long-distance runners need coaches to plan their training and other competitors to make their racing meaningful.

A lifetime spent in the company of others on whom one has to depend for survival necessitates a high degree of communication. The process of inculcating communication skills begins with the passing of auditory, visual, and tactile (touch) signals from mother to infant. It continues through life; in fact, group life is contingent on the successful storage and transmission of large volumes of information. At its simplest level, the warning conveys perhaps the single most important communication for survival. The human cry of "Fire!" imparts much the same effect as a screech of a panicking baboon. In both cases the first communicator supposes the recipients have some facility for recalling the image of impending danger.

It seems that the necessity of communicating and the ability to do so quickly and efficiently has a connection with the large size of the brain of the primate compared to other mammals. Human beings have the largest brains and are clearly the most adept at communicating. They are, as a direct result, most developed socially. A growth in the size of the human brain can be traced back to two periods. The first, between 1.6 and 2 million years ago, witnessed a rapid expansion in cranial capacity, a change which accompanied the origin of what we now call *Homo erectus* (probably in Africa) and the use of new types of primitive tools. Bipedalism emerged as a result of a transference from the trees to the ground; the change in habitat necessitated a behavioral adap-tation in posture and, eventually, an anatomical change of great significance, particularly in relation to arms and hands which were no longer employed to suspend the body and could be used for many other purposes.

Anthropological evidence suggests that the size of the typical skull then remained stable for about 1.3 million years, before a second, sudden increase in brain size. The appearance of *Homo sapiens* about 0.2 or 0.3 million years ago was followed by a burst of cultural change in the spheres of manufacture, settlement, and subsistence. This is important as there is much contention about the precise relationship between the growth of what is now the human brain and changes in habitat and activity. What is absolutely certain is that there is some form of close relationship, though the direction and way in which it worked is still in dispute.

The idea of a spontaneous expansion is not supportable. More plausible is a scenario in which the actual size of the brain after the advent of *Homo erectus* stayed the same, but the number of brain cells and neural pathways between them continued to increase. This made it possible for *Homo erectus* to become a more effective bipedal hunter and gatherer, operating at the time of day when other predatory creatures (and, therefore, competitors) were sheltering from the intensely hot midday sun. Growing extra brain cells, in this interpretation, was a defense mechanism against the harmful effects of the sun's rays on the brain; that is, the humans grew bigger brains, leaving many of the cells redundant, as mere "failsafe" devices in the tropical heat. (There are other explanations which we will consider in Chapter four.) This might well have established a neural potential for more sophisticated communication and imaginative thought, which, in turn, stimulated a phase of modifying physical environments rather than adapting to them. The phase marks the beginning of sport as we will see later in Chapter three. One often hears of triathletes who swim, cycle, and run for seven hours or more, sometimes in hot atmospheres, described as "mad." Ironically, they may be demonstrating the extraordinary adaptive brilliance of the human brain in acquiring an ability to function effectively all day in extreme climates. The adaptation dates back to *Homo erectus*'s pursuit of game animals.

THE HUMAN EDGE: LANGUAGE

The human brain is the organ that is responsible for the difference between *Homo sapiens* and the rest of Animalia. The enlarged neural capacity introduced the possibility of ever more elaborate forms of communication. The physiology of the human ear and vocal tract meant that audible messages could be sent with a high probability that they would be received with reasonable efficiency. These elements, combined with the enhanced capacity for imaginative thinking, laid the foundations for human language and, by implication, new systems of word-associated thought.

Language assists the accumulation of information to be stored in the brain and confirms the awareness that other humans have similar stores of information. At the blandest level, we might ask how a game of hockey would be possible unless the players were cognizant of the rules and aware that all other players had the same knowledge. Any sport has the same prerequisite. Without language or, at least, some derivative communication system, abstract rules would not be possible; nor, therefore, would sport.

Humans are not alone in being able to pass on knowledge from one generation to another and so perpetuate cultures, but they have the special ability to add to, or recreate, cultures whereas other primates merely inherit and receive. A verbal language, as opposed to sign-based systems of communication, makes this possible. Culture, we should note, refers to anything acquired and transmitted by learning and not by physical inheritance. While other animals most certainly maintain recognizable cultures, even higher apes are quite limited in their capacity to communicate and, as a result, do not pass on a vast amount of experience to new generations. The transmission has to be direct and immediate (for example, modeling and imitation); apes lack the linguistic capability to standardize, encode, classify, and concentrate meanings and experience.

By contrast, humans can transmit sometimes quite abstract meanings through several generations without any significant loss of informational accuracy. Ancient Greeks, as we will see in the next chapter, left a largess of information about themselves in the form of inscriptions, mostly on walls or clay tablets. A comprehension of these inscriptions tells us that the Greeks pursued athletics in a recognizable, rule-governed form more than any other ancient culture. Language which articulates this information is such that we can actually use it to project into the future. A future tense permits the communication of imaginative schemes and the transmission of such activities as sport. The unique elements of human language that provide for this type of knowledge of ancient cultures almost certainly arise from our genetic adaptations related to social co-operation and interdependence and changing patterns of subsistence. We have the neural equipment for picking up language; that much is clear. Less clear is the reason for the bewildering diversity of human cultures. Our biological equipment scarcely changes at all over time and space; languages, customs, religions, laws, etc., vary greatly from society to society and from one time period to another.

The suggestion is that, once acquired, the developed language, and the new styles of thought it ushers in, launches its users into all manner of trajectories. Humans plan and create complex organizations and institutions of a quite different quality and order than those found among other animals. Obviously these elaborate phenomena are ultimately dependent on biological factors; but their accomplishment cannot be exclusively traced to biological equipment and inheritance. The often extraordinary transformations in human performance engendered by an inspirational coach, for example, remind us that we should approach biology as a license not a limit.

My prehensility and neural circuitry make it possible for me to write this book, but there are countless other non-physical influences on my ability and disposition to write – and on your willingness to read. The very concept of a book to be produced and used reflects an extremely sophisticated and unique level of communication. Books are needed for records, and records have been vital to the evolution of sport. Any balanced comprehension of sports clearly needs a range of scientific approaches: one "-ology" isn't enough. We must refer to hereditary nature; equally, though, we must examine environmental life experience, how organisms react to physical conditions surrounding them.

Between the gene and the environment there are all sorts of intervening factors and processes that must be studied if we are to reach an understanding.

The biological characteristics which distinguish humans from other animals – bipedalism, prehensility, large and more complicated brains, and language – are necessary conditions for culture building. Necessary, but by no means sufficient. Yet in recognizing this, we must at least begin our analysis of sports with a scenario: creative human beings striving to satisfy at least the minimal requirements for subsistence while subjected to the physical constraints imposed by their own biology and the material world around them. Their primary needs are to produce food, shelter, tools, and to reproduce human populations. Unless they can complete these tasks, they will have no opportunity to believe in religions and ethics, create political and economic systems, engage in war, or perform any of the other activities associated with culture.

Inspirational coaches

Sports history is full of individuals who seem to be able to inspire athletes to accomplishments beyond what seem to be their natural limitations. They have been able to take ordinary players with seemingly limited natural ability and turn them into great athletes. Among the most inspirational coaches are:

Vince Lombardi, who led the Green Bay Packers from an ailing outfit to two Super Bowl victories in the 1960s and was known to be a strict disciplinarian. His martinetish style was described by one of his players: "Lombardi is very fair – he treats us all like dogs." Contrary to popular myth, Lombardi did not utter the oft-quoted maxim about winning not being everything, but the only thing. His message actually had a very different import: winning, he insisted, "is not everything, but trying to win is."

Brian Clough, who won a total of 12 major titles for English soccer clubs between 1969 and 1993, when he retired, his most notable success being with Nottingham Forest who were twice European champions. In terms of wins only the second most successful head coach (Bob Paisley being number one), Clough achieved his success with limited resources and at unfashionable clubs. He allowed no stars at his clubs, all players being equal parts of one unit; only his status was bigger than that of the team. "His sheer presence transformed players," one of his ex-players wrote of him. An observer reflected on his coaching: "He would be god one day, the devil the next."

Franz Stampfl, an Austrian track coach who, in the 1950s, moved to England where he transformed training methods with his innovative interval training, in which repeated punishing attacks on a specific distance replaced the old notion of trying to improve one's time for the whole distance. He demonstrated that ferocious pace and not mere stamina was the key to middle-distance success. In the process, his charges became accustomed to physical pain. Stampfl's principal success was Roger Bannister's historic 3:59.8 mile, the first under four minutes, but he also guided Chris Chataway, Chris Brasher and a squad that dominated middle-distance running in the mid-1950s.

Emmanuel Steward, who presided over the Kronk boxing gym in Philadelphia, where training was designed to weed out the weak through a grueling ordeal of near-inhuman floor and bag exercises and give-no-quarter sparring. Multiple world champion Thomas Hearns was one of his products, but his supervision of Evander Holyfield, before his tactical win over much-heavier Riddick Bowe, indicated Steward's mastery of strategy as well as conditioning techniques. Commenting on a beaten boxer who had shown little resilience, Steward said: "He wouldn't be allowed to shadow box at our gym."

These activities, almost by definition, depend to some extent on genetically predetermined capacities. It follows that an aesthetic, expressive, and intellectual cultural activity such as sport must be a response to physical constraints and conditions. In the next two chapters, I will approach sport as such a response. Beginning with a breakdown of the physical constraints and conditions, I will address the issue of how sporting performance is physically possible. From "how" I move to "why," specifically asking the reasons for humans' attraction to sporting endeavors. An answer to this first requires us to look at human efforts to survive and subsist in their material environment and how these efforts have effects on their total life experiences.

FURTHER READING

Culture, People, Nature, 6th edition, by Marvin Harris (HarperCollins, 1993) is an introduction to general anthropology and a model of clarity. Harris favors a materialist approach which complements the one taken in this book. His view is that the shaping of thought and behavior is the outcome of adaptations to ecological conditions. Taking a Darwinian starting point, Harris argues: "As a result of natural selection, organisms may be said to become adapted to the needs and opportunities present in their environments." And further: "All individuals are the products of the interaction of their genes and their environment." More extreme versions of materialism would insist that thought and behavior can be understood by studying the constraints to which human existence is subjected; these constraints arise from the need to produce food, shelter, tools, and machines and to reproduce human populations within the limits set by biology and the environment. Harris replies to critics of his approach in *Theories of Culture in Postmodern Times* (AltaMira, 1998).

Tools, Language and Cognition in Human Evolution, edited by Kathleen Gibson and Tim Ingold (Cambridge University Press, 1993), has several pertinent chapters, including "The emergence of language," "The intelligent use of tools" and "Early stone industries and influences regarding language and cognition." The use of tools, in particular spears and bows used for hunting, is seen as one of "the hallmarks of anatomically modern humans."

Human Evolution, Language and Mind: A psychological and archaeological inquiry by William Noble and Iain Davidson (Cambridge University Press, 1996) emphasizes the critical role played by the distinctly human trait of symbol-making in communication; other primates use utterances that are like symbols, but probably not with intentions.

So Human an Animal: How we are shaped by surroundings and events by Rene Dubos (Transaction, 1998) is, as its subtitle suggests, an argument about how human "nature" is something of a misnomer. It contrasts nicely with E. O. Wilson's *Sociobiology: The new synthesis* (Harvard University Press, 1975), a hugely ambitious attempt to explain differences and similarities in living forms by reference to the tendency to optimize reproductive success; the theory has been criticized by many who oppose Wilson's emphasis on biological factors rather than social or cultural ones.

ASSIGNMENT

"Between the gene and the environment there are all sorts of intervening factors and processes that must be studied" (see p. 22). List as exhaustively as possible the factors and processes that contribute to the creation of what we might regard as "natural" sports performers; in other words, the kinds of factors and processes that show that performers learn and develop as much as they inherit.

leading QUESTIONS

q: Is being left-handed an advantage in sports?

a: According to at least two theories, yes.

Considering that, in any given population and at any time, between 8 and 10 per cent of people are left-handed, the number of top-class sports performers seems disproportionately high. Any survey of sports "greats" is bound to include Babe Ruth, Rod Laver, Martina Navratilova, Marvin Hagler and Wasim Akram – all lefties. There are numerous others. To explain this, we need to understand why people are left-handed at all.

The word *sinistral*, meaning a left-handed person, has an interesting etymology, deriving from the Latin for "left," *sinister*, which also means an evil omen (sinister-looking person), or something malignant (sinister motive). Historically, there was little difference: left-handed people were associated with malevolence. As that myth receded, it was replaced by more enlightened empirical research, much of which still suggested some sort of undesirable characteristics or even pathology.

Left-handedness is a distinctly human trait: other animals show no bias or preference in claws, paws, hoofs, fins, etc. Most theories are based on the lateralization of the brain; that is, the degree to which the right and left cerebral hemispheres of the brain differ in specific functions. The human brain is divided into two hemispheres, the left side often being described as the dominant half because that is where the centers of language and speech and of spatial perception are located in most people. Nerves on the two sides of the body cross each other as they enter the brain, so that the left hemisphere is associated with the right-hand side of the body. In most right-handed people the left hemisphere directs speech, reading and writing, while the right half is responsible for emotions.

For years, it was thought that left-handedness was the result of a kind of reversal of the more usual pattern, with the main functions of the brain being on the right. But, in the 1970s, research by J. Levy and M. Reid (in *Science*, vol. 194, 1976) showed that, in fact, most left-handers are still left-brain dominant and have their centers of language, speech and spatial perception in the same place as right-handers.

Two lines of research led to the conclusion that there was a close connection between left-handedness and physical fitness. The most influential theory was that of Geschwind and Galaburda, who, in 1987, proposed that there was an association between left-handedness and immune or immune-related disorders. This stemmed from birth-related problems. Left-handedness was also related to disabilities, such as stammering and dyslexia. Later studies cast doubt on these conclusions.

A second line of research came to light in 1991 in a widely reported article in *Psychological Bulletin* (no. 109). In it, the authors Coren and Halpern claimed that left-handers die sooner than right-handers. The mean age of death for lefties was 66 compared with 75 for righties. Coren and Halpern gave two explanations for this. First, environment: we live in a world that has been designed and built with right-handed people in mind. Door handles, telephones, cars: the construction of these and countless other technological features reflects right-handedness. So, when left-handed people perform even the simplest of functions, they find them slightly more awkward and so have a higher risk of accidents (and accident-related injuries). Several subsequent studies confirmed that lefties were more prone to accidents.

Second, birth problems: referring back to the Geschwind and Galaburda studies, Coren and Halpern hypothesized that exposure to high fetal testosterone at birth may lead to developmental problems for left-handed people. This particular aspect and, indeed, the whole early-death theory did not go unchallenged and other studies both refuted the findings and uncovered others. For instance, Warren Eaton and a research team from the University of Manitoba took one strand of Coren and Halpern's research and argued that: "Indirect evidence for an association between sinistrality [left-handedness] and maturational lag can be found from the fact that males, who are more likely to be left-handed, are less advanced in language and skeletal development than are females" (*Journal of Child Psychology and Psychiatry and Allied Disciplines*, 37/5, 1996). On closer examination, however, direct evidence was not forthcoming.

The research supporting or refuting the relationship between left-handedness and early death, accident-proneness, physical immaturity and other pathologies continues, though little light has been thrown on the exceptional sphere of sports. If, as most of the evidence suggests, lefties are disadvantaged in some way, how come so many of them rise to the top in sports? One interesting theory came from a French biologist, Michel Raymond *et al.*, of the University of Montpellier, who published his views in the *Proceedings of the Royal Society* (December, 1996). Marshaling data about athletes, including both amateurs and world-class professionals, Raymond concluded that, compared to their total size in the population, lefties are over-represented in sports.

The reason for this is: left-handers have an advantage in confrontation sports – those sports in which an opponent is directly confronted, including boxing, fencing, and tennis, as well as team sports such as baseball, cricket, and basketball. There is no over-representation of southpaws in non-confrontation sports, such as track or swimming in which opponents compete alongside each other. Not only are lefties over-represented in confrontational sports, they are especially good at them. And, the closer the inter-action between opponents, the greater the prevalence of left-handers. So, we would expect more southpaw boxers than lefty baseball hitters or pitchers and even fewer left-handed rugby players.

Yet even in sports like baseball and cricket where competitors face each other at several yards distance, there are more than the expected number of lefties. The researchers found that, over a six-year period, about 16 per cent of top tennis players were left-handed and between 15 and 27 per cent of bowlers in international cricket and pitchers in Major League Baseball. For close-quarter sports, the difference is more pronounced: 33 per cent of competitors in the men's world foils championships, increasing to 50 per cent by the quarter-final stage of the competition. Remember: this is a group that represents 10 per cent of the total male population at most. The pattern was less marked for women, though there was still over-representation at the fencing championships.

One tempting thought is that, if left-handed people are disadvantaged in several areas of development and functionality, they may be overcompensated when it comes to sports skills, like hand-to-eye co-ordination, quick reflexes, astute judgment, tactical awareness, or just raw strength. Or, it could simply mean that the sheer fact of favoring one's left arm in a context geared to right-hand biases lends the southpaw a strategic advantage. Because of the frequency of right-handers in any given population, sports performers are habituated in training and in competition to facing other righties. So, left-handers, because of their relative scarcity, have an edge of sorts: they hit, run and move in unexpected ways.

Certainly, sports are full of stories of orthodox (left leg forward) boxers who detest fighting southpaws because of the special problems they pose. These include having to jab along the same path as the opponent's jab and constantly having one's front foot trodden on. Baseball hitters swing at the ball in such a way that their momentum carries their bodies in the direction they want to move to get to first base; saving fractions of a second can be vital in a game where fielding is crisp and accurate. Pitchers, like cricket bowlers, can deliver at unfamiliar angles. Returning serve against left-handers is known to be difficult for a right-hander, especially defending the advantage court; lefties are known for their ability to cut the ball diagonally across the body of the receiver. In basketball, a portsider typically tries to pass opponents on the side they least expect; there is barely time to determine whether the opponent is left handed or not.

The strategic advantage of playing against opponents who are used to a different pattern of play seems to be the answer to the preponderance of them in some sports. In others, where being left-handed counts for little, their prevalence is about the same as in the general population. According to Raymond et al., 9.6 per cent of goal-keepers in soccer are lefties; and left-handed field-eventers account for 10.7 per cent of all competitors. At the top levels of darts, snooker, bowling, and gymnastics, lefties are actually under-represented. Somehow, they gravitate toward the sports in which they possess a natural advantage. There are, of course, notable exceptions: world champion pole-vaulter Stacy Dragila is a lefty – note her unusual grip.

An anonymous journalist with The Economist magazine (in "Left-handedness: Sinister origins," February 15, 1997) adds an evolutionary level to this argument: over the years, the strategic advantage enjoyed by lefties outweighed the other possible disadvantages uncovered by the aforementioned psychological research. Natural selection, of course, favors the best physically-equipped (strongest) species, which survived and were able to pass on their genes to their children. This would account, albeit in a crude way, for the persistence of left-handed people in an environment built largely by and for right-handers and in which social pressures (such as associating sinistrality with wrong-doing) might reasonably have expected to pressure lefties to change their biases.

More questions . . .

- Is left-handedness still an advantage in sports that involve less use of the arms, like soccer or diving?
- How might you set about changing a naturally left-handed child into a right-hander?
- Do left-handers pose particular problems for coaches/managers?

Read on . . .

- Coren, S., *Left Hander: Everything you need to know about left-handedness* (John Murray, 1992).
- Harris, L. J., "Do left-handers die sooner than right-handers? Commentary on Coren and Halpern's (1991) 'Left-handedness: A marker for decreased survival fitness,'" *Psychological Bulletin*, vol. 114, no. 2 (September, 1993).
- Muris, P., Kop, W. J., and Merckelbach, H., "Handedness, symptom resorting and accident susceptibility," *Journal of Clinical Psychology*, vol. 50, no. 3 (May, 1994)
- Pass, K., Freeman, H., Bautista, J., and Johnson, C., "Handedness and accidents with injury," *Perceptual and Motor Skills*, vol. 77, no. 3 (December, 1993).

built for action

the structure and

functions of the human

body

ALL SYSTEMS "GO" – FOR 3 MINUTES 26 SECONDS

July 14, 1998: the body of 23-year-old Moroccan Hicham El Guerrouj breaks onto the track at the Olympic Stadium in Rome, Italy. Less than three-and-a-half minutes later, El Guerrouj breasts the tape, having traveled 1,500 meters an astonishing 1.37 seconds faster than any other human. In 3:26 exactly, El Guerrouj has set in motion processes and mechanisms of immense complexity: his every muscle has contracted, stretched and twisted; his lungs have filled and emptied repeatedly; his heart has pumped at least 20 gallons (76 liters) of blood into all areas of the body. All this has been made possible by the intricate organizing and synchronizing capacity of his brain, which has submitted his entire body to one purpose for the duration of the race: the performance.

Question anyone who has witnessed a sports event first hand, or even on television, and they will be unlikely to disagree that the essence of sports lies in the actual sporting performance – the body in motion. The moment when competitive humans bring to an end their preparations and make visible their self-willed mastery of a particular set of skills is an engaging experience that easily surpasses reading reports, watching interviews, studying form, or any of the other ancillary activities associated with sports. The bodily performance itself occupies center stage in sports. And while the stage itself – its structure, scenery and props, and the audience – will occupy our attention in the pages to follow, we must provide some analysis of the performance before progressing. The body will command a great deal of attention in this book: how our perceptions of it have changed, how it relates to gender and race, how it responds to drugs, how it has been visualized by artists, and so on. We cannot address the questions without at least a basic understanding of how it works.

When we watch sports, we watch bodies move: the peaks of even a chess game are when the players extend their arms to propel pieces across the board. PlayStation, the computer games product, used an advertisement featuring the Dutch soccer player Dennis Bergkamp; under the image of the player and a ball there was a strapline that read: "Obey my feet." The instruction was presumably intended for the ball. All sports performers try to impose their wills; the body is the means through which the imposition is accomplished.

Obviously, we all control our bodies; the sports performer just controls his or hers in a particular kind of way. The more control they have, the better their chances of imposing their wills – and the more likely the chances of success. So, what enables us to control our bodies? It seems a ludicrously obvious question, but one which needs an answer if we are to understand better the complexities of sport.

Imagine El Guerrouj as a series of systems, interacting so as to produce motion. When the starter's gun fires, El Guerrouj's central nervous system receives the signal and very rapidly relays messages to his muscular system which is stimulated to move by electrical impulses. Muscular contractions move his limbs mechanically, this being made possible by the fact that the muscles are attached to the bones of El Guerrouj's skeleton, which is yielding, yet tough enough to withstand the stress of movement without fracturing. Fuel is needed for the athlete to be able to repeat the motion and this comes via breathing, circulation, and digestion; once burned up, the waste matter of fuel has to be disposed of.

Viewed as a lump of matter, El Guerrouj's body is a bundle of about 60 billion living units called cells, each of which has the same basic structure, comprising membrane (which holds the units together), ribosomes (which manufacture proteins), iysosomes (which destroy harmful substances and diseased parts of the cell), golgi complex (which stores endoplasmic substance), reticulum (which transports substances throughout a cell), cytoplasm (which is the liquid in which the other elements float), mitochondria (which are powerhouses, where oxygen and food react to produce vital energy to keep the cell alive), and a nucleus (which contains the chromosomes carrying coded instructions for the workings of the cell). Cells often cluster together to form other substances, such as tissue and muscle (which comprises 50 per cent of cells, being a type of tissue) and these tissues can also work in groups to become organs (heart and lungs, for instance). When organs operate together to perform a particular function, like transporting blood around the body, we usually talk in terms of systems.

For a middle-distance runner like El Guerrouj to perform at his maximum, all his systems need to be working maximally and synchronously. For our purposes we will probe the body as if it were a series of systems acting interdependently. A logical first step is to ask how a runner, or indeed any living animal, is able to move at all and here we are drawn to an examination of the skeletal and muscular systems.

MOVING THE SKELETON

The skeleton isn't just a framework, an elaborate coat-hanger on which we drape skin and muscle. It's a rather elaborate, living structure that serves four important functions: protection, support, storage, and movement. Structurally, it has two aspects: the axial comprises the skull, backbone, ribs and sternum; the appendicular refers to appendages (legs and arms), the pelvic girdle (to which the legs are attached), and the pectoral girdle (to which the arms are connected). In total, there are over 200 bones.

The human brain is disproportionately large compared to those of other mammals and, together with the spinal cord, controls in large part the movements of the whole body.

As a complex, yet delicate, piece of equipment, it needs maximum protection: ergo the skull (or cranium), a resilient helmet composed of plates of bone fused together to form a hard casing around the brain. The interstices between the bones are called sutures and allow growth in the size of the brain until around the age of 20, after which they weld together. The skull affords sufficient protection for the brain in most activities, although motor sports, hang-gliding and other sports in which the risk of direct collision is high (e.g. football, cricket, and cycling) utilize headgear for additional protection.

The other main part of the central nervous system, the spine, also needs the protection of bone; in this case a long, flexible column of vertebrae separated by discs of cartilage. In functional terms, the spine represents a remarkable adaptation, affording protection to a sensitive cable of nerves that runs from the brain to all areas of the body. The spine is articulate so as to permit the movement and flexibility so necessary to survival. This flexibility is bought at a cost, for in certain parts of the back the spine has little or no support. Hence weightlifters strap broad belts around their waists so as to maintain rigidity in and give support to the vulnerable areas of their lower back when it is likely to be exposed to stress. Some other sensitive organs, like the lungs and heart, are also given skeletal protection, but, unlike some vertebrates (armadillos and tortoises), humans have discarded external physical protection and rely more on the wit and ingenuity that derive from the large brain, and the fleetness of foot made possible by bipedalism to protect themselves.

The conventional notion of the skeleton as a means of support is true for the majority of bones. But this needs qualification. The bony material itself is not solid, but is a composite of collagen protein fibers and inorganic mineral crystals ordered in a meshwork of cylindrical layers. This honeycombed arrangement prevents brittleness and gives bone some degree of elasticity: should stress be applied, bone distributes it to prevent a concentration. Excessive stress will cause cracks or breaks, of course, but bone's yielding capacity, or "give," reduces the danger of breakage. These qualities make it ideal as a supporting apparatus because it combines tensile strength with the yield needed for a wide range of motions.

As a rule, the heavier the load a bone must bear, the greater its diameter must be. Human thigh bones, or femur, are large, as are tibia and fibula connecting the knee to the foot; they are responsible for supporting the upper body weight. But, while the femur has some protection from the quadriceps, the tibia and fibula are exposed and may need artificial cushioning from direct knocks in sports like soccer and hockey.

The skeleton can support effectively only if it grows in correspondence with the rest of the body. And bone does grow; it receives food and oxygen from blood vessels. New layers of tissue encircle existing material and form new bone, thus increasing the diameter (growth in length ceases before the age of 20). Bone grows in response to force, as does muscle. Bend, twist, compress, load, or combine these and, over time, the bone will grow to meet its task and fulfill its function, within limits of course. It will react to certain pressures or movements by fracturing, breaking, or shearing. (When this happens, cells in the outer layer of the bone – the periosteum – multiply and grow over the break, joining the two parts together.)

At the other extreme, bone will lose mass if deprived of function. Stored inside bone are the minerals calcium and potassium which are delivered to the cells by blood (and which give bone its hardness) and marrow, a soft jelly-like tissue that produces red and white blood cells. The fourth major function of the skeleton – and the most important for our purposes – is that of providing mechanical levers for movement. Bones are connected to each other at joints which serve as axes for rotation. For instance, the forearm, the upper-arm bone or the humerus, acts as a fulcrum, and the radius and ulna as a lever. The elbow joint, which is a hinge, makes possible a simple range of movement; flexion (bending) and extension (stretching). Other joints, like the biaxial (between forearm and wrist and at the knee), the pivot (at the wrist), and the ball-and-socket (at the shoulder and hip) are more complicated arrangements and permit multiple movements in different planes and directions.

Were the joint a manufactured piece of equipment, the articular surfaces would grind together and need the addition of lubricants. The human body takes care of this by interposing a film of lubricating fluid between opposing bone surfaces (in which case, they are called synovial joints), or by sandwiching a tough pad of gristle between articulating bones (cartilaginous joints). An engineer would love this natural bearing which reduces friction.

Cartilage belongs to a class of connective tissues which, as the name suggests, joins or ties together the various parts of the body and makes movement smooth. Its capacity is not limitless, however, and cartilage can wear out. Ligaments, which are flexible collagen bands that connect and support joints, are also liable to wear-and-tear, especially amongst sports performers, such as throwers or shot putters, who maximize the intensity or repetition of stresses on shoulder and elbow joints and are therefore prone to sprains (torn ligaments) and dislocations of joints.

Perhaps the most troublesome connective tissue for sports competitors is tendon, which is basically a collagen cable that joins muscle to bone and so transmits the pull, which makes the bone move. Tendons make it possible to use a muscle to move a bone at a distance. In the case of fingers, which are clearly vital in dexterous activities (e.g. ping pong, darts, and spin-bowling in cricket), we need muscular control of the fine movements without the invasive presence of muscles at the immediate site. Were the necessary muscles attached directly to the finger bones, the size of the digits would be so large that catching, holding, or even forming a fist would be a problem. Without the action permitted at distance by slender tendons, primate prehensility would be severely restricted. Special nerves in the tendon are designed to inhibit over-contraction, but tears do occur often when co-ordination is impaired by fatigue or poor skill. Tendon tears may be partial or complete and, although any muscle tendon is at risk, those subjected to violent or repetitive stresses, such as the Achilles tendon and shoulder tendons, are most frequently involved.

The way the skeleton is framed and its levers fitted together gives the body the potential for a great variety of movement through all planes. But we still need to analyze the source of its motion. Plainly stated, muscle moves our bones; it does so with two actions, contraction and relaxation. Usually, the arrangement features tendons connecting bones to one or more muscles which are stimulated by nerves to contract, causing the tendons to tighten and the bone to move. (Some muscles appear to be attached directly to bone, obviating the need for tendons, but motion is accomplished by basically the same process.)

Muscle use is present in every sporting activity, right from sprinting where muscles are maximally in use, to playing chess where muscles function perhaps only to position eyeballs in their sockets or to move a finger by inches. The various types of muscle present in humans differ in structure and properties, but the striated muscle, which acts as the motor of the skeleton, is our chief concern. Striated muscle is under our control in the sense that we voluntarily induce its contraction and hence movement. Other types of muscles contract in the absence of nerve stimulation: cardiac (heart) muscle, for example, contracts independently of our will and has the property of "inherent rhythmicity" (we will return to this).

Skeletal muscle consists of fibers, which are long tubes that run parallel to each other and are encased in sheaths of the ubiquitous collagen. Each fiber is made up of strands called myofibrils, which are themselves composed of two types of interlocking filaments. Thick filaments are made of a protein called myosin and thin ones of actin, and they are grouped in a regular, repeated pattern, so that, under the microscope, they give a striated, or streaky, appearance. The lengths of myosin and actin filaments are divided into units called sarcomeres, the size of which is recognized as the distance between two "Z-lines" (the structures to which the actin filaments are attached).

Although the filaments cannot change length, they can slide past each other to produce the all-important contraction. We will see later how messages from the central nervous system are taken to muscles by nerve impulses. When such an impulse reaches a muscle fiber with the instruction "Move!" energy is released in mitochondria and the filaments move closer together, shortening the muscle. As they pass, a chemical reaction occurs in which: (1) calcium is released from storage in the tubular bundles; (2) in the calcium's presence, myosin molecules from the thicker filaments form bonds with the actin filaments; (3) the myosin molecule is then thought to undergo a change in shape, yanking the actin filaments closer together; (4) the contraction of the muscle fiber ends when the calcium ions are pumped back into storage so as to prevent the formation of new chemical bonds.

The effect of the contraction is a pull on the bones to which the muscles are attached and, as the four phases take no more than a few thousandths of a second, we are capable of mechanical movements at very high speed. The flexion and extension of boxer Roy Jones's famous left hook was timed in terms of hundredths of a second. Such a punch, which had a concussing effect, required a great force of movement, so many fibers would have been required to contract together at speed. Golfer Jose Maria Olazabal's putt, by contrast, would involve fewer fibers.

In both instances, opposing, or antagonistic pairs of muscles would be working to allow free movement. For the hook or the putt, biceps muscle

Mitochondria

These are the power-stations of a cell where glucose and oxygen react together to create energy which converts the chemical adenosine diphosphate (ADP), which is like a flat battery, to charged-up adenosine triphosphate (ATP). This then supplies the rest of the cell with power. As its energy is used up, the ATP reverts back to ADP and returns to the mitochondria for recharging. ATP is most likely the supplier of energy for every activity in animals and plants. Energy, of course, is needed for muscular movements, but also for nerve conduction and other functions.

would contract to bend the elbow, which its opposing member, the triceps, would relax. To straighten the arm in the action of a shot-putter the triceps need to contract, while biceps relax. Muscles are equipped with special receptors that let the brain know the extent of contraction and the position in three-dimensional space without our having to look constantly to check. We can close our eyes, but know the movement and position of our limbs.

The 206 bones of the adult skeletal system form a protective casing for the brain and the spinal cord, a sturdy internal framework to support the rest of the body, and a set of mechanical levers that can be moved by the action of muscles. All of these make the human body a serviceable locomotive machine for walking, running, and, to a lesser degree, swimming, climbing, and jumping. But, like other machines, the body depends on fuel supply for its power, a method for burning the fuel, and a system for transporting the waste products away. Again, the human body has evolved systems for answering all these needs.

NOT BY FOOD ALONE: ENERGY

As a living organism, the human being depends on energy. Plants get by with light and water; animals need food. In particular, humans need protein (built up of chemical units called amino acids), carbohydrates (comprising sugars which provide most of our energy), lipids (or fats for storage and insulation), vitamins (about 15 types to assist various chemical processes), minerals (like iron and zinc), and water (to replace liquids). These provide raw energy sources that drive the machinery of the body; that is, making the compounds that combine with oxygen to release energy, and ensure the growth and repair of tissues. (The combination with oxygen will be dealt with later on.)

Obtaining food is of such vital importance to survival that the entire plan of the human body is adapted to its particular mode of procuring food. Sports, as I will argue later, reflects our primitive food-procurement even to this day. For the moment, we need to understand not so much the way in which food is obtained, but how it is used. In their original forms, most of the above substances are unusable to human beings. So we have evolved mechanisms for rendering them usable as energy sources. Processing food is the function of the digestive system, which consists of a long, coiled tube, called the digestive tract, and three types of accessory glands.

Typically, food is introduced to the body through the mouth where it is chewed, pulped, and mixed with saliva in a process of ingestion. After being formed into lumps, it is swallowed and drops into the pharynx (throat) and, then, to the epiglottis, which is a small valve that closes off the windpipe. Water falls under the force of gravity, but food is ushered along by a wave of muscular contractions called peristalsis. Fibers in the wall of the esophagus tube (gullet) push the food downwards to the stomach (which explains why cosmonauts can still eat in the absence of gravity).

From here, the food passes into the stomach, a sausage-shaped organ which can expand to about a two-pint capacity. At this stage, a churning process starts in which the food is mixed with mucus, hydrochloric acid, and enzymes (chemical substances that speed up processes – in this instance, the breaking up of protein). The effect of this is to liquefy the food, so that after between three and four hours the churned-up mass (called chyme), which now resembles a cream soup, gets transferred, via peristaltic waves, to the stomach's exit point and then to the duodenum which is the first chamber of the small intestine. Contrary to popular belief, it is here rather than the stomach, where most of the chemical digestion gets done: bile from the liver and enzymes from the pancreas are released. (An exception is alcohol, which is readily absorbed in the stomach and does not pass through.)

A note here about the role of the brain in regulating the discharge of naturally secreted juices that aid digestion: seeing, smelling, tasting, or even thinking about food can stimulate the brain to send messages to the glands in the mouth and stomach to release a hormone called gastrin that is quickly absorbed into the blood and then to glands where it triggers the release of gastric juice. Hence sports competitors who chew gum to enhance their concentration are usually doing a disservice to their stomachs by producing gastric juices when there is no food. Gastric juices have enough acidity and protein-splitting capacity to burn human flesh. The stomach has natural protection against this, although resistance can be lowered by alcohol or aspirin and by overproducing the juices when no food is available.

Lymph

From the Latin *lympha*, for water, this is a body fluid derived from the blood and tissue and returned to the circulatory system in lymphatic vessels. At intervals along the vessels there are lymph glands which manufacture antibodies and lymphocytes that destroy bacteria. The lymph system has no pump like the blood system and the movement of lymph is brought about largely by pressure from contracting skeletal muscles, backflow being prevented by valves. The lymph system doubles as the body's immune system in that it produces proteins called antibodies, lying at the surface of certain white blood cells (lymphocytes). When needed, antibodies and cells rush into the bloodstream and "round up" the harmful bacteria and viruses. While the lymph system can make thousands of antibodies, its vital adversaries are constantly mutating so as to find ways of defeating it, as the Aids pandemic indicates.

A possible result is an open sore in the wall of the stomach, or a duodenal ulcer.

Basically, the idea is to reduce the parts of the food that can be profitably used by the body (the nutrients) to molecular form and allow them to seep through the cells lining the long digestive tube, through the minuscule blood or lymph vessels in the stomach wall and into the blood or lymph. All the cells of the body are bathed in a fluid called lymph. Exchanges between blood and cells take place in lymph. Lymph is derived from blood, though it has a kind of circulatory system of its own, filtering through the walls of capillaries, then moving along channels of its own (lymphatics), which join one another and steer eventually to the veins, in the process surrendering their contents to the general circulatory system. Food is absorbed through the wall of the intestine which is covered in villi, tiny absorbent "fingers" that give the tube a vast surface area. Not all food passes directly into blood vessels: the lymphatics are responsible for collecting digested fats and transporting them to the thoracic duct which empties into one of the large veins near the heart.

Once absorbed the nutrients are carried in the blood and lymph to each individual cell in the body where they are used up; that is, metabolized. The residue of indigestible or unabsorbed food is eliminated from the body by way of the large intestine. En route, bacteria in the large intestine feed on the vestiges and, in return, produce certain vitamins which are absorbed and used. Some of the unwanted water is converted to urea and passed out via the bladder. The body has precise control over what it needs for nutrition, growth, and repair. One of the many functions of the liver is to store surplus nutrients and release them together to meet immediate requirements. This large abdominal organ receives digested food from the blood and reassembles its molecules in such a way as to make them usable to humans. Different cells need different nutrients, so the liver works as a kind of chef preparing a buffet for the blood to carry around the rest of the body.

A supply of glucose is needed by all body and especially brain cells, particularly as they have no means of storage. If, after a sugar-rich meal, the body has too much glucose in the blood, the liver cells remove it and store it, later pushing it back into the blood when the glucose level drops. After a carbohydrate-rich meal, the level may increase briefly, but the liver will take out the surplus for later use. Muscle cells are also able to store large amounts of glucose molecules, packaged as glycogen, which is why endurance-event competitors, like marathon runners, try to pack muscle and liver cells with stored glycogen prior to competition in the expectation that it will be released into the blood when levels fall. After the glucose is used up, liver cells start converting amino acids and portions of fat into glucose and the body shifts to fat as a source of fuel.

Metabolism refers to all the body's processes that make food usable as a source of energy. The success of these depends on how effectively the body can get the nutrients and oxygen it requires to the relevant parts of the body and, at the same time, clear out the unwanted leftovers like carbon dioxide. The substance employed for this purpose is blood, but it's actually more than just a convenient liquid for sweeping materials from place to place. Cells, cell fragments, platelets, proteins, and small molecules float in a liquid plasma,

Muscle-packing or muscle-loading

Carbohydrates (carbs) provide most of our energy and can be ingested in many forms, after which they are reduced to simple sugars before being absorbed into the bloodstream. Carbs are an economical source of fuel. Liver and muscles store carbohydrates in the form of glycogen, which converts rapidly to glucose when extra energy is needed. Mindful of this, endurance performers sometimes seek to "pack" or "load-up" their muscles with glycogen by consuming large amounts of carbo-hydrate foods such as bread, cereals, grains, and starchy products for about 72 hours preceding an event. The idea is to store as much glyco-gen as possible, making more glucose available when energy supplies become depleted.

which is mainly water (and makes up about 60 per cent of the blood's composition). The plasma contains red and white blood cells; the latter are capable of engulfing bacteria and combating infections with antibodies. Red cells are more numerous and contain hemoglobin, a chemical compound with a strong affinity for oxygen.

Hemoglobin allows blood to increase its oxygen-carrying capacity exponentially. Long- and middle-distance runners have exploited the advantage of having more hemoglobin in their blood by training at high altitudes, where there is less oxygen naturally available in the air. Their bodies respond to the scarcity by producing a chemical that triggers the release of larger numbers of red cells in the blood. After descending to sea level (or thereabouts), the body will take time to readjust and will retain a high hemoglobin count for some weeks, during which an athlete may compete and make profitable use of a generous supply of oxygen to the muscles (blood doping, as we will see in Chapter nine, involves extracting hemoglobin-packed blood during altitude training, saving it, and administering a transfusion to the athlete immediately prior to a race). At the other extreme, excessive bleeding or an iron-deficient diet can lead to anemia, a condition resulting from too little hemoglobin.

So, how do we manage to circulate this urgently required mixture throughout the body? The internal apparatus comprises the heart, blood vessels, lymph, lymph vessels, and some associated organs, like the liver. These form a closed system, meaning that the blood that carries the vital substances all over the body is confined to definite channels and moves in only one direction, rather than being left to swim about. It travels in three types of vessels. The thickest are arteries in which blood moves at high pressure from the heart to the body's tissues. These arteries divide over and over again to form microscopic vessels called capillaries that spread to every part of the body.

A single capillary is only about half a millimeter long and a single cubic meter of skeletal muscle is interlaced with 1,400 to 4,000 of them. Laid end-to-end, the length of all the body's capillaries would be about 60,000 miles, or 96,500 kilometers – twice the earth's circumference. While coursing around, oxygen- and nutrient-rich liquid, plasma, seeps through the ultra-thin walls of the capillary. At the same time, capillaries, like vacuum cleaners, suck up waste products from cells. Gradually, capillaries merge together to form larger vessels that turn out to be veins; these keep blood at a lower pressure as they deliver it back to the heart.

A fist-sized muscle weighing less than a pound, the heart is a four-chambered pump that pushes blood into the arteries, gets it back from all parts of the body (except the lungs), pumps it out of the lungs, takes it back from the lungs, then returns it to the body. The chambers of the right side of the heart consist of one atrium and one ventricle. Connected to the right atrium are two large veins, one of which brings blood from the upper body and one from the lower. Blood flows from the right atrium into the right ventricle via a one-way valve; it leaves this chamber through a pulmonary artery that branches and services the lungs. Another valve stops any backflow. Blood returns from the lungs via pulmonary veins which drain into the left atrium and, then, to the left ventricle.

From here, the blood is squeezed into the aorta, the single largest artery of the body, which runs into several other arteries connected to the head, arms, and the upper chest, and, later, to abdominal organs and body wall. In the pelvis, the aorta branches and sends arteries into the legs. Blood returns to the right atrium of the heart through veins. The direction of the blood is ensured by a series of valves (blood, controlled by the valves, moves in one direction only). We call the movement away from ventricles systole and its opposite diastole. At any one time, there are about 1.5 gallons of blood in the mature human body. It takes less than a minute for the resting heart to pump out this amount and considerably less for the exerting sports performer, who can push out as much as 6.6 gallons (25 liters) per minute when active.

As mentioned before, the heart muscle has inherent rhythmicity and the pump acts independently of our volition. It will (given a suitable atmosphere) pump even outside the body, and with no stimulation; this makes heart transplants possible. Not that the heart is indifferent to outside influences; a sudden shock, for example, can cause sufficient stimulation to slow down, or skip, the heartbeat.

During exercise or competition the action may accelerate to over 200 beats per minute. The heart muscle itself would stretch and automatically increase its strength of contraction and flow of blood. Athletes work at increasing blood flow without increasing the corresponding heartbeat. The extra blood flow results in a heightening of the pressure of blood in the arteries of the chest and neck, which are detected by special sensory cells embedded in their walls. Nerve impulses are sent to the brain, resulting in impulses being relayed back to the heart, slowing its beat rate and lowering potentially harmful blood pressure levels. So, the brain has to monitor and feed back what is going on during intense physical activity.

The rate of heart action is also affected by hormones, the most familiar in sports being adrenaline which causes an immediate quickening of the heart in response to stressful situations. The reaction is widespread; among other things, blood vessels in the brain and limbs open up, and glycogen is released from the liver. In this type of situation, the skeletal muscles might receive up to 70 per cent of the cardiac output, or the total blood pumped from the heart. Under resting conditions, the liver, kidneys, and brain take 27, 27, and 14 per cent respectively. Immediately after eating, the digestive organs command great percentages (to carry food away), thus reducing the supply to the muscles. So, activity after a meal tends to be self-defeating; you cannot get as much blood to the muscles as you would if you waited for three hours or so.

> ### Heart Rate Monitor (HRM)
>
> A device comprising a chestband transmitter and a wrist-worn receiver that indicates how fast the heart is beating. The principle of exercising within a certain percentage of maximum heart rate has been known for years; but only with the advent of the HRM has the ability to apply those benefits been available to athletes. It is necessary to know the maximum heart rate (MHR) of the athlete and the threshold heart rate, the point at which exercise moves from aerobic effort to anaerobic. By exercising at slightly below the threshold, one can gradually force it up. Olympic 4,000-meter pursuit cycling champion, Chris Boardman, used an HRM in competition as well as training: in setting the world hour distance in Bordeaux in 1994, he had to cope with severe heat – which makes the heart beat faster – so adjusted to ride at six beats faster than he had planned.

I mentioned before that food alone does not give the body energy, but needs the addition of oxygen, which is, of course, inhaled from the surrounding air, taken to the lungs, and then transferred to all parts of the body via the blood. Once it arrives at cells, the oxygen reacts with glucose, supplied by courtesy of digested carbohydrates, and produces energy at the mitochondria sites. During this process of respiration, unwanted carbon dioxide and water are formed in the cells. Exhaling gets rid of them. Lungs and windpipe make up the respiratory system, though the actual process of breathing is controlled by the contractions of muscles in the chest, in particular the diaphragm muscle beneath the lungs and the muscles between the ribs.

Space in the lungs is created by the diaphragm moving down and the ribs expanding. Air rushes in mainly through the nostrils where it is filtered, warmed, and moistened, and then into the lungs via the windpipe, or trachea. To reach the lungs, the air travels along tubes called bronchi which, when inside the lungs, divide into smaller and smaller tubes, ending in small bunches of air sacs called alveoli. Oxygen seeps out of the alveoli and into surrounding capillaries which carry hemoglobin, a compound which, as we noted, readily picks up oxygen. While oxygen leaves alveoli, carbon dioxide, produced by the body cells, enters ready to be exhaled, a motion initiated by a muscular relaxation of the diaphragm and ribs. Air rushes out when we sigh "Phew!" to denote relief and relaxation; the ribs close in and the diaphragm lifts up.

The motions are more pronounced during continuous physical exertion; the body makes a steady demand for more oxygen, and to meet this we breathe more deeply and more fully. The heart responds by pumping the oxygen-rich blood around the body faster. The process involves sustained use of oxygen in the breakdown of carbohydrates and, eventually, fats to release in the mitochondria of cells where the raw fuel Adenosine triphosphate is energy charged up as Adenosine triphosphate. This is why the name aerobic (meaning "with air") is applied to continuous activities, such as cycling, swimming, and running over distances. In contrast, weight-lifting, high jumping, and other sports requiring only short bursts of energy are anaerobic. In this case, food is not broken down completely to carbon dioxide and water, but to compounds such as alcohol or lactic acid. An incomplete breakdown means that less energy is released, but what is released can be used immediately.

"Oxygen debt" affects many sports competitors, particularly ones whose event requires explosive bursts, but over a reasonably sustained period. Four-hundred-meter runners often tie up in the home straight; they cannot get the oxygen and glucose round their bodies fast enough, so their muscles use their own glycogen stores for releasing Adenosine triphosphate anaerobically (without oxygen).

The product of this process is lactic acid, which needs oxygen to be converted into carbohydrate to get carried away. As runners need all the oxygen they can process for the release of energy they "borrow" it temporarily, allowing the lactic acid to accumulate in the muscles and cause fatigue. After the event, the debt has to be repaid, so rapid breathing invariably carries on. Shorter-distance sprinters also incur oxygen debts, but the build-up of lactic acid in their muscles is not usually great enough to hinder contraction. Longer-distance performers tend to get second winds: an increase in heart beat rate and breathing enables the runner to take in enough oxygen to convert and dissipate the lactic acid without over-extending the oxygen debt.

COMMUNICATIONS AND CONTROL

Let us return to Hicham El Guerrouj for a moment. We now have an idea of how his movements are possible: how the supporting scaffold of his skeleton is urged into motion by the contraction of muscles; how those muscles are fed a supply of fuel to turn into energy; and how that fuel, in the form of food and oxygen, is pushed to its destination by blood which, at the same time, picks up waste products to dispatch. Although we have examined these processes separately, in actual performance, of course, all the processes are closely connected and dependent on each other.

The digestion of food, for instance, would be of no value without a bloodstream to absorb it and to distribute the products; release of energy in a contracting muscle would cease if the lungs failed to supply oxygen via the circulatory system; a contracting muscle has to be connected to articulated

---

Hyperventilation

Carbon dioxide (CO_2) is a waste product and needs to be flushed out of the blood. Even a small increase in the CO_2 content of the blood stimulates deep and, later, more rapid breathing to reduce the CO_2. The action is brought about involuntarily, usually during physical activity because of the fast breakdown of carbohydrates to release energy (impulses are sent to the medulla, resulting in increased breathing). Occasionally, this can lead to an over-reduction and a loss of consciousness. When this happens, hyperventilation is said to occur.

---

bone to get a movement. The workings together of these is no haphazard affair. During strenuous activity, when muscles need to lose excess carbon dioxide and take in more glucose and oxygen, the rate of breathing increases automatically and the heart beats faster, so sending a greater amount of oxygen rich blood to the muscles.

Crudely stated, the information we receive about the environment arrives by way of cells called receptors, which respond to changes in, for example, light and sound. They produce pulses of electricity which travel along nerves to the brain, which quickly interprets the meaning of the changes and issues instructions to the relevant other parts of the body (e.g. "loud noise – cover ears"). Some of the information received by the brain is stored for future use, a facility of crucial importance in the acquisition of skill, which involves the capacity to react in precisely the same way to similar stimuli time after time.

The two components of the whole nervous system are: (1) the central nervous system (CNS), comprising the control center of the brain and its message conduit, the spinal cord; and (2) the peripheral nervous system (PNS), which is the network of nerves originating in the brain and spinal cord and which is responsible for picking up messages from the skin and sense organs (sensory nerve cells) and carrying messages from the CNS to the muscles (motor nerve cells).

Nerves are spread throughout the entire body; each one consists of a bundle of minute nerve fibers and each fiber is part of a nerve cell, or neuron, of which there are about 100 billion woven into each body in such a way as to bypass the packed body cells. To do this, the network needs a shuttle service provided by connector neurons which carry signals back and forth. Further physical facts about signals are, first, that the nerve fibers that pick up sensations from receptors and deliver them to the CNS, do so with electrical impulses that are chemically charged; changes in the balance of the minerals sodium and potassium in the cells cause the impulse. Second, the speed of the impulse varies from fiber to fiber and with environmental conditions. And third, fibers covered in sheaths of myelin (a fatty substance) conduct impulses faster than naked fibers.

Perhaps the clearest way of depicting the role of the nervous system is by tracing its stages. Suppose you are a gun marksman (or woman); you must use primarily the senses of sight and touch when focusing on the target and aligning the gun and make adjustments to these environmental factors. A first step is made by bringing the target into focus: the eyes are, of course, sense organs (i.e. an assembly of receptors) and their surface, known as the retina, will react to rays of light by changing its chemical structure; this triggers off an electrical impulse that travels along nerve cells, or neurons, to the brain.

There are no direct connections between neurons, so the impulse may have to travel a circuitous route. The tiny gaps between neurons are synapses and these are bridged by a chemical neurotransmitter that takes the impulse across the synapse to the next neuron. The points of connection with the next neuron are called dendrites, which are in effect short, message-carrying fibers. One long fiber, called an axon, carries messages away from one neuron to the dendrites of the next. It takes only fractions of a second for the impulse to make its way through the synapses and neurons to the brain.

The fine web of nerves running through most of the body pale beside the densely complex mesh of neurons in the brain. Senses gleaned from our contact with the environment provide inputs which are sent to the brain; this processes the information before sending out instructions to muscles and glands. Most of our behavior in and out of sports is controlled in this way. A fast pitcher in a baseball game may choose to do many different things on the basis of his sense impressions, mostly picked up by his vision and touch. He may notice a shuffle in the hitter's gait; he may feel moisture rising in the air that may affect the trajectory of his ball. His brain sends messages to his muscles so that he deliberately pitches a fast, high delivery.

But not all of our behavior is produced by such a process: the receiving hitter may not expect the fast ball which zips sharply toward his head, prompting him to jerk his head away almost immediately to protect it from damage – as we would withdraw a hand inadvertently placed on a hot iron. This type of reflex action is controlled by the spinal cord section of the CNS. The nervous impulse defines an arc that short-circuits the brain, so that the message never actually reaches it. The behavior resulting from the reflex arc is sudden and often uncoordinated because all the muscle fibers contract together to avoid the danger. A boxer drawing away from a punch, a goalkeeper leaping to save a short-range shot, a volleyball player blocking an attempted spike; all these suggest automatic responses that need not involve conscious will for their successful completion. We hear much about reflex movements in sports and, clearly, sports in which fast reaction is crucial do exhibit such responses. But most sports action is governed by the brain and, for this reason, we need to look in more detail at the structure and functions of this most vital of organs.

While the brain itself is an integrated unit which, like any other living organ, needs a continuous supply of food and oxygen to produce energy, it can be seen in its component parts, each of which has specific functions. The medulla, for instance, controls involuntary activities that we cannot control consciously, but which are essential for survival (such as breathing and heart rate). Also of interest for sporting performance is the cerebellum which receives messages from the muscles, ears, eyes, and other parts and then helps co-ordinate movement and maintain balance so that motion is smooth and accurate. Injury to this component does not cause paralysis, but impairs delicate control of muscle and balance; for instance, the ability to surf or skate would be lost. All voluntary and learned behavior is directed by the cortex, the largest portion of the brain; this forms the outer layer of the area known as the cerebrum lying at the fore of the brain.

The cerebrum is divided into two halves, or hemispheres, each of which is responsible for movement and senses on its opposite side. Nerves on the two sides of the body cross each other as they enter the brain, so that the left hemisphere is associated with the functions of the right-hand side of the body. In most right-handed people, the left half of the cerebrum directs speech, reading, and writing while the right half directs emotions; for left-handers, the opposite is true. So, Goran Ivanisevic's service would have been controlled by the right side of his brain, while his emotional racket-busting outbursts would be associated with the left. Physical movement is controlled by the motor area; motor neurons send impulses from this area to muscles in different parts of the body. The more precise the muscle movements, the more of the motor area is involved; so a hammer-thrower's actions would not use up much space while a dart player's would, as he or she would be utilizing fine movements of the fingers.

The only other zone of the brain I want to note at present is the thalamus, which is where pain is felt. Pain, of course, is principally a defensive phenomenon designed to warn us of bodily danger both inside and outside the body. Impulses originating in the thalamus travel to the sensation area so that a localization of danger can be made. This is a mechanistic account of our reactions to pain: it is actually affected by all manner of intervening factors, including self-belief. In other words, if people do not believe they will feel pain, they probably will not – at least under certain conditions. There are also cultural definitions of pain: we learn to interpret pain and react to it and the thresholds may differ from culture to culture.

> ### Brain types
>
> Concept derives from the theories of Jon Niednagel, who believes there
> are inherited designs to brains which affect our mental and physical skills
> and predispose us to certain events. By knowing what sort of brain type
> sports performers have, it is proposed that they can be matched to training
> schedules that will allow them to excel. Those dominated by the right-hand
> side of the brain are represented by P and by the left J; extroverts by
> E and introverts by I. Those whose dominant functions are sensing
> and feeling are SFs and those who rely on sensing and thinking are STs.
> NFs have intuition and feeling, while NTs are both intuitive and intelli-
> gent. Sports performers are grouped by their brain-type characteristics.
> For example: Martina Hingis INTJ; Dennis Rodman ENFJ.

Such is the nature of competitive sports nowadays that few concessions
to pain are allowed. Inspirational coaches encourage performers to conquer
pain by developing what is often called "mental toughness," just ignoring
pain. Chemical ways of "tricking" the brain have been developed. Some
drugs, for example, cause nerve cells to block or release a neurotransmitter
(the chemical that carries nerve impulses across synapses to the dendrite of
the adjacent neuron), the idea being to break the chemical chains linking
brain to cell. We will look at the use of drugs more closely in Chapter nine.
The point to bear in mind for now is that the CNS generally, and the brain
in particular, play a central role, not only in the process of movement, but in
the delicate sensory adjustments that have to be made in the operation of
all sports, even those such as power lifting, which seem to require pure brawn.
The lifter's cerebellum enables him or her to control the consequences of
the lift; without this, initiation might be possible but corrective feedback
co-ordination would be absent. In short, there would be no balance and
no instruction to the opposing (antagonistic) muscles to make a braking
contraction on the lift's completion. The whole operation would collapse.

While we exert a large degree of control over our bodies through the
CNS, many vital activities, such as heartbeat, peristalsis, and functioning
of the kidneys simply cannot be controlled voluntarily. Handling these is a
secondary system of nerves called the autonomic nervous system (ANS).
Many of the cell bodies of the ANS lie outside the brain and spinal cord and
are massed together in bunches, each bunch being a ganglion. These ganglia
receive information from receptors in the various organs of the body and then
send out the appropriate instructions to muscles, such as the heart, and

glands, such as salivary glands. The instructions are interesting in that they are twofold and antagonistic.

Unlike skeletal muscle which is either stimulated to contract or not (it needs no nerve impulse to relay), cardiac muscle and the smooth (as opposed to striated) muscle of other organs must be stimulated either to contract more than usual or to relax more than usual. To achieve this, the ANS is divided into two substrata: the sympathetic system (more centrally located) and the parasympathetic system (more dispersed). The parasympathetic system constricts the pupils of the eyes, increases the flow of saliva, expands the small intestine, and shrinks the large intestine; the sympathetic system has the opposite effect. Impulses are propagated continuously in both systems, the consequences of which are known as tone – a readiness to respond quickly to stimulation in either direction.

Tone is rather important in certain sports: for instance, a panic-inducing visual stimulus will cause an increase in sympathetic impulses and a decrease in parasympathetic impulses to the heart, eliciting a greater response than just a sympathetic stimulation. Impulses from the two systems always have antagonistic effects on organs. The name autonomic nervous system implies that it is independent and self-regulated, whereas, in fact, the centers that control ANS activity are in the lower centers of the brain and usually below the threshold of conscious control. The appeal of bringing ANS functions under conscious control is fascinating; yogi have for centuries been able to slow heartbeat quite voluntarily, with corresponding changes to the entire body. The potential for this in sports, particularly in the areas of recovery and recuperation, is huge.

In sports, responses to change in the environment have usually got to be swift and definite. Consequently, our treatment of the nervous system has focused on its ability to direct changes and issue instructions to the relevant parts of the body in order that they react quickly. The quickest communication system is based, as we have seen, on electrical impulses. But the body's response to an internal change is likely to occur over a period of time and be brought about by chemical adjustments. The substances involved are hormone molecules and they are manufactured by a group of cells called endocrine glands, the most important of which is the pituitary attached to the hypothalamus on the underside of the brain. This produces a growth hormone by regulating the amount of nutrients taken into the cells. Hormones themselves are messengers, secreted into the blood in which they travel to all body parts, interacting with other cells and effecting a type of fine-tuning.

Because some hormones have very specific effects – many of them local rather than body-wide – they have been of service to sports performers seeking to enhance performance (as we will discover in later chapters). The male testes secrete the hormone testosterone, which regulates the production of sperm cells and stimulates sex drive. Testosterone has been produced chemically and the synthetic hormone introduced into the body of competitors. Among the alleged effects are an increase in muscle bulk and strength and a more aggressive attitude.

Adrenaline is another example: as we have seen, it pours into the blood, stimulating the release of glycogen from the liver, expansion of blood vessels in the heart, brain, and limbs, and contraction of vessels in the abdomen. Fatigue diminishes and blood coagulates more rapidly (which is why boxers' seconds apply an adrenaline solution to facial cuts). Competitors pumped-up with adrenaline will usually have a pale complexion, on account of their blood being diverted from skin and intestine, and dilated pupils; hearts will be pounding and the breathing will be fast. The muscles will have the capacity to contract quickly and effectively either for, as the expression goes, fight or flight. This is an unusually fast hormonal change and most influences are long term, concerning such features as growth and sexual maturity. When they pass through the liver, the hormones are converted to relatively inactive compounds which are excreted as waste product, or urea, by the kidneys; this is why urinalysis is the principal method of detecting proscribed substances – it determines hormonal products in urine.

The chemical fine-tuning of the body is extensive and, in the healthy body, works continuously to modify us internally. Sweat glands are largely responsible for our adjustment to heat and, as many sports activate these, we should recognize their importance. The glands' secretions cover the skin with millions of molecules of water and they begin rising to the surface (epidermis) when external temperatures exceed about 25°C/77°F, depending on weight of clothing or the rigor of the activity performed. When blood reaching the hypothalamus is 0.5–1°C/35°F above normal, nerve impulses conveyed by the ANS stimulate sweat glands into activity.

Fluid from the blood is filtered into the glands and passes through their ducts so that a larger amount of moisture is produced on the skin surface. As it evaporates, the heat in the molecules escapes, leaving coolness. The internal temperature of the body is kept within acceptable limits, as long as the sweat continues to take away the heat. (When temperatures drop, a reflex action is to shiver, which is a spasmodic muscular contraction that produces internal heat.) Most, but not all, sweating results from the eccrine glands; secretions around the armpits and nipples of both sexes and the pubic area of females come from apocrine glands, which discharge not only salt and water, but odorless organic molecules that are degraded by skin bacteria and give off distinct smells. In mammals, the smell has a sexual function, though the lengths to which humans go in trying to suppress or disguise the smell suggests that the function has been discarded in our species.

A general point here is that sweat is not just water but a concentration of several materials and profuse sweating may deprive the body of too much salt. Heat prostration and sunstroke are curses to marathon runners and triathletes and their efforts to conquer them include swallowing salt tablets before the race, drinking pure water at stages during the race, and taking Gatorade or other solutions of electrolytes (salt and other compounds that separate into ions in water and can therefore help in the conduction of nerve impulses and muscle contraction). Problems for these athletes multiply in humid climates where the air contains so much vapor that the sweat cannot evaporate quickly enough to produce a cooling effect; instead, it lies on the skin's surface forming a kind of seal. The result is known as heat stagnation. Even more dangerous is the situation when, after prolonged sweating due to activity in hot atmospheres, sweat production ceases and body temperatures soar to lethal levels.

Sweat glands perform a vital compensatory function in minimizing the effects of heat during physical activity and, under instruction of the brain, try to stabilize body temperature at around 37°C/86°F. But their thermostatic powers have clear limitations when tested by athletes, for whom 26 miles is but the first station of the advance toward the boundaries of human endurance.

The journalist who coined the now-clichéd term "well-oiled machine" to describe some highly efficient football team actually, and perhaps unwittingly, advanced a rather accurate description of the collection of trained and healthy individuals in question. Machines in the plural would have been more correct because, when examined in one perspective, that's what human beings are: a functioning series of systems made of cells and based on principles that any engineer, biologist, or chemist would find sound. But this is a partial and inadequate description and this chapter has merely set up a model; now it must be set in context and seen to work. We now have a grasp of the basic equipment and capabilities of the body; we still know little of its properties and motivations. Sport as an activity derives from natural faculties, but the particular form or shape it has taken and the way it has been perpetuated and mutated over the centuries is not understandable in purely biological terms. It needs explanation all the same and this will be the task of the following chapters.

FURTHER READING

The Biophysical Foundations of Human Movement by Bruce Abernathy, Vaughn Kippers, Laurel Mackinnon, Robert Neal and Stephanie Hanrahan (Human Kinetics, 1997) takes a multidisciplinary approach to biophysics, integrating contributions from functional anatomy, exercise physiology and other disciplines. *Physiology of Sport and Exercise* by Jack Wilmore and David Costill (Human Kinetics, 1994) reviews the major body systems and examines the body's response to exercise; its strength is in emphasizing the role of the environment in affecting how the body responds – as such it complements the approach taken in this book.

Biomechanics of Sport and Exercise by Peter M. McGinnis (Human Kinetics, 1999) takes an original approach by including self-experiments in a program of active learning designed to improve understanding of human activity. *Practical Skills in Biology*, 2nd edition, by Allan Jones, Rob Reeves and Jonathan Weyers (Longman, 1998) is a similarly interesting approach to the understanding of the human body, providing practical laboratory-based exercises and field studies.

ASSIGNMENT

In the seventeenth century, the French philosopher René Descartes tried to explain living processes like digestion, growth, and reproduction in terms of a mechanical model, i.e. the human as a machine. Repeat the exercise: break the human body down into its component parts and analyze the relations between them as if you were studying a machine, then do a specification sheet (rather as car manufacturers do), incorporating dimensions, safety ratings, replacement parts, insurance, maintenance costs, unique features, etc.

Finally, create some copy for a possible advertisement, for example: "Beneath the sleek contours of its outer shell is an engine incorporating all the latest technological advances – from electronic microchip management systems controlling fuel injection and timing through to the latest 16-valve system with turbo charger and intercooler together with 170-brake horsepower. With an acceleration of 0–60 mph in seven seconds and a top speed of 140 mph the machine runs well without adjustment on unleaded or leaded fuel. The fully independent multi-link suspension, disc brakes on all wheels, power steering, and electronically controlled four-wheel antilock brake system combine to offer precise handling."

animal spirits

a history of sports

THE ORIGINS OF COMPETITION

Can we recognize anything in the following activity that merits description as a sport? Time: early 1800s. Place: Birmingham, England. Players: a tethered bull and a ferocious dog.

> Sometimes the dog seized the bull by the nose and "pinned" him to the earth, so that the beast roared and bellowed again, and was brought down upon its knees ... The people then shouted out "Wind, wind!" that is, to let the bull have breath, and the parties rushed forward to take off the dog ... However, the bulls were sometimes pinned between the legs, causing [them] to roar and rave about in great agony.

The passage is from Richard Holt's book, *Sport and the Working Class in Modern Britain*, which is full of other lurid details of what passed as sports in the eighteenth and nineteenth centuries (1990: 16). As well as bull-baiting, as the above activity was known, there was cock-fighting, which involved pitting two highly trained cocks together, and dog-fighting, which goes on in Britain and the USA today, albeit illicitly. Legislation made such contests illegal, though cruelty to animals has by no means disappeared. The persistence of fox-hunting in the face of protests confirms this.

These types of activities in which animals were made to fight, maim, and often kill each other, were regarded as sports. Before the reader rushes to deny any connection between such barbaric contests and what we now recognize as sports, consider some of the similarities. *Competition* for no reason apart from competition itself: unlike animal fights in other contexts, there were no evolutionary functions (such as "survival of the fittest") served by the fights. *Winning* as a sole aim: spectators were interested in a result rather than the actual process of fighting, and animal contests typically ended with one either dead or at least too badly injured to continue. Holt adds to his description of the Birmingham bull bait that, "blood would be dropping from the nose and other parts of the bull" (1990: 16).

Spectators: the tournaments were set up with an audience in mind – in specially dug pits around which a crowd could stand, in barns, or other public places where the action was visible to spectators. *Gambling*: the thrill of watching the contest was enhanced by wagering on one of the animals and money frequently changed hands among the spectators. *Animals* were trained and used: although the contests were unacceptably cruel by today's standards, we still train and employ animals in sports, such as horse- and dog-racing, pigeon-racing, polo, and (though repugnant to many) bull-fighting. Perhaps the most remarkable legacy is the Iditarod, a 1,149-mile race through Alaska featuring packs of huskies pulling a person in a sled. The original trail was

Blood sports

Recreational pursuits that involved inflicting harm on animals were of three types, all very popular between 1780 and 1860 and modestly popular beyond. Baiting involved chaining, tethering, or cornering an animal and setting trained dogs to torment or attack it: this was favored by the British and American plebeian, or working class. Typically, a bull would be brought by a butcher or farmer who would be paid to have it secured to a post while specially trained dogs were allowed to snap at and bite it. The bull, having been ripped by the dogs, would be slaughtered and its meat sold. Badger-baiting involved releasing dogs down a badger's set to chase it out. Fighting consisted of goading trained dogs or cocks into fighting each other until one rendered the other unable to continue. This was a more commercialized activity followed by the English aristocracy, according to Holt. Hunting for amusement was also popular in the period, the quarry being ducks, cats, and bullocks, among other animals. Some of these activities persist to the present day.

forged by dog-sleds carrying freight to miners and prospectors; the latter-day contest recreates the hunger and exhaustion of driving for eight days and nights at temperatures of minus 60°F. Competitive and recreational fishing remains one of the world's most popular pursuits.

All these elements are present in human cultures that extend far beyond the Industrial Revolution of the late eighteenth and early nineteenth centuries, which is the conventional starting-point for studies of sport. True, the distinct shape or form of sport developed in that crucial period and the organizational structure that distinguishes sport from mere play was a product of the industrial age. But I believe we can go back much further: in fact, given the right conceptual approach and historical direction, it is possible to trace the origins of contemporary sports back to primitive matters of survival; which is precisely what I intend to do in this chapter.

The methods we once used for getting nutrition have been reshaped and refined, but are still vaguely discernible. Track and field events such as running and throwing are virtually direct descendants of our ancestors' chase of prey and their attempts to stun or kill them with missiles; some events still consciously model themselves on the disciplines and aptitudes associated with hunting, modern pentathlon (riding, fencing, shooting, swimming, and running) being the clearest example. More advanced tool use, which enhanced the ability to survive and improved nutrition, also generated a new adaptation that we see reflected in current sport. Tools that were once used for killing or butchery have been transformed into symbolic instruments like bats, rackets, and clubs and used in a fashion which disguises the functions of their predecessors. The origins of others, such as epées, are more transparent. The purpose of this chapter is to provide an account of the beginning of sports and its subsequent development up to the last century.

In the perspective I choose to view sport, the entire phenomenon has human foundations that were established several thousand years ago. It follows that any chronicle must track its way back through history to discover the reasons for the human pursuit of what are, on analysis, mock hunts and battles and the purposes they serve at both individual and social levels. The latter point will be answered in the next chapter, but the immediate task is to unravel the mystery of ancestry: how did sports begin? It's a question that requires an ambitious answer, one which delves deep into history for a starting-point.

Homo sapiens first appeared 100,000 to 200,000 years ago. In evolutionary terms, this is an eyeblink. Several discoveries of remains have undermined efforts to trace what used to be called the "missing link" – the creature that was more intelligent than apes but had not yet become the finished article. In all probability, such a creature did not exist at all. The more we know, the less simple it seems.

Every new find indicates that there is no single line of descent with a few evolutionary dead-ends branching off it. For hundreds and thousands of years, a bewildering number of different species and subspecies of ape-like and then human-like animals adapted, migrated, and then perished. Only one thing is clear: the species we call human beings came out of Africa, not in a single process of migration, but after a series of waves of migration.

The popular image of humans emerging from their caves before progressing to ever-higher levels of civilization has given film makers some wonderful raw material. Kevin Connor's *The Land That Time Forgot* (1974), featuring marauding ape-men, and Don Chaffey's *One Million Years BC* (1966), made memorable by a young Raquel Welch clad in an animal skin bikini, are two of several films that have capitalized on appealing but erroneous premises. Our species developed in a series of relatively sudden lurches. Traveling on two legs is one of them; tripling of brain size is another.

Between 1.5 and 2 million years ago, *Homo erectus* arrived on the scene in East Africa and, later, spread to Asia and Europe. A highly successful creature in evolutionary terms, *Homo erectus* survived up to about 100,000 years ago and instituted some significant adaptations. According to some theories of evolution, *Homo erectus* evolved into the earliest members of our species *Homo sapiens*, who were succeeded in Africa by the anatomically modern *Homo sapiens sapiens* and in Europe by *Homo sapiens neanderthalensis*, or Neanderthals.

Homo erectus was a respectful and cautious scavenger, though much evidence points to males banding together in predatory squads and becoming proficient hunters of large animals like bears, bison, and elephants and using equipment such as clubs and nets. Layers of charcoal and carbonized bone in Europe and China have also suggested that *Homo erectus* may have used fire. Physically, the male of the species might have stood as tall as 5 feet 11 inches (1.8 meters) and, while the brain was smaller than our own, the animal had enough intelligence to make primitive tools and hunting devices.

About 2.5 million years ago, in East Africa, a small-brained hominoid who walked on two legs became the first butcher: using stone tools, *Australopithecus garhi* cut meat and crushed bones. It is unlikely that the species used language or fire.

Neanderthals, who were well-established in Europe by 70,000 BCE, certainly had sufficient intellect to use fire on a regular basis and utilized a crude technology in making weapons which, as predatory creatures, they needed. As their prey were the large and mobile bison, mammoth, and reindeer, they made good use not only of physical weapons but also of tact, or stealth. They would hunt in packs and allocate assignments to different members. Other hints of social life are found amongst Neanderthals. Evidence of burials, for example, indicates an awareness of the significance of death; ritual burials are not conducted by species other than humans.

There is also something uniquely human about the rapport with other species: the relationships humans have with other animals is an unusual one and Neanderthals may have been the first to forge this special link. It is possible that Neanderthals attempted to domesticate as well as hurt other species. The cartoon depiction of Fred Flintstone adorned in bearskins is a bit more accurate than it seems: it's quite probable that the wearing of skins was thought to invest the wearer with some of the animal's qualities (such as strength of the mammoth or speed of the deer). The close association between many sports and animals is undoubtedly connected to this type of belief.

Some see Neanderthals as distinct from and having no breeding with *Homo sapiens*, while others see them gradually replaced by *Homo sapiens* after long periods of genetic mixing. Whether or not they were replaced or just became extinct, two facts are clear: one is technological, the other social. Neanderthals exploited raw materials for tool manufacture and use; they also displayed collective behavior in the division of labor they used to organize and co-ordinate their hunts. Related to these two activities is the fact that the reciprocal obligations systems used in hunting were carried over into domestic life. Neanderthals were cave dwellers and so used a home-base arrangement; this leads to the suggestion that they most probably constructed a stable pattern of life, possibly based on role allocation.

Homo sapiens shared these features: they used tools, hunted in groups, and had division of labor at the home base and especially in the hunting parties. Accepting responsibility for specific duties had obvious advantages for survival: co-ordinating tasks as a team would have brought more success than pell-mell approaches. Signals, symbols, markers, and cues would have been important to elementary strategies. Complementing this was the sharing of food at the central home base. Maybe this awakened humans to the advantages of pair-bonding and the joint provisioning of offspring: the mutual giving and receiving, or reciprocity, remains the keystone of all human societies.

The hunter-gatherer mode of life is central to our understanding of the origin of sports. It began with foraging and scavenging as much as 3 million years ago; hunting as a regular activity followed a period of feeding off carcasses or spontaneous picking. Including more meat in the diet brought about nutritional changes, but also precipitated the invention of more efficient means of acquiring food. The response was to hunt for it – and this had widespread behavioral repercussions, not only in terms of social organization but also in physical development. Covering ground in pursuit of quarry required the kind of speed that could only be achieved by an efficient locomotion machine. The skeleton became a sturdier structure able to support the weight of bigger muscles and able quickly to transmit the force produced by the thrust of limbs against the ground. Lower limbs came to be more directly under the upper body, so that support was more efficient in motion; leg bones lengthened and the muscles elongated, enabling a greater stride and an ability to travel further with each step. The human evolved into a mobile and fast runner, and, though obviously not as fast as some other predators, the human's bipedalism left upper limbs free for carrying.

Where quarry was near enough to be approached, but also near enough to be disturbed, hunters would need short bursts of explosive speed, an ability to contract muscles and release energy anaerobically. In short, they needed the kind of power which modern sprinters possess. Hunts might take up an entire day and would demand of the hunter stamina, endurance, and the capacity to distribute output over long periods – precisely the type of aerobic work performed by middle-distance and marathon runners, not to mention triathletes.

Effective synthesis of Adenosine triphosphate from Adenosine diphosphate and the removal of waste lactic acid was enhanced by respiratory evolution. Ribs expanded and the muscles between them developed to allow the growth of lungs, which permitted deeper breathing to take in more and more air. Since the sustained release of energy depends on a supply of glucose and other foods, the hunter's diet was clearly important. While we cannot be certain exactly what proportion of the diet was taken up by meat, we can surmise that this protein-rich food source played a role in balancing the daily expenditure of energy and providing enough fats and proteins for tissue repair.

Habitual meat-eating was not unqualified in its advantages; it introduced the very severe disadvantage of bringing humans into open competition with the large mammalian carnivores and scavengers like hogs, panthers, and tigers which roamed the savannas looking for food. Ground speed was, in this instance, a requisite quality for survival, the clawless, weak-jawed biped being ill-equipped to confront the specialist predators. In time, evolution yielded a capacity to make and use not only tools but also weapons like clubs and stones, which at least evened up the odds. The physical clash with other animals continues to fascinate elements of the human population, a fact witnessed in such activities as bear-baiting, boxing kangaroos, and the type of man *vs* horse races in which Jesse Owens performed during the undignified twilight of his career (as we will see in Chapter six). A momentous and rapid change in the period, as we have noted, was the increase in the human's most important asset.

Compared to body size, our brain is a truly exceptional organ; it is one of the most obvious physical features that distinguishes us from the rest of the animal world. How did we acquire our large brains? One theory holds that cooking our food enabled us to digest nutritionally rich vegetables with thick skins that could not be eaten raw. Cooking food made it more easily available, cracking open or destroying physical barriers such as thick skins or husks, bursting cells and sometimes modifying the molecular structure of proteins and starches; all of which gave us the extra calories necessary for brain growth – food for thought, so to speak.

This view opposes the more traditional view of meat as the trigger behind brain development. The larger brain, with its larger neurons and denser, more complex circuitry of dendrite branches, may well have been related to the long days spent beneath the hot sun, hunting in comparative safety while the bigger predators sought shade and rest. As carnivores, we would scavenge what the big cats left behind. The meat gave us energy and the effect of the sun on our heads caused the brain to swell.

Obscure as the relationship between brain growth and behavioral change may remain, we should at least recognize that neither are independent of the environment in which the processes take place. For instance, survival success would have depended on the ability to identify in the surrounding environment things that were needed: rocks for tools and weapons, tracks of game and competitive predators, sources of vegetable foods. The need to discriminate perceptually encouraged larger brains and better communication skills, which in turn occasioned bigger and better brains; these more complicated organs needed nourishment in terms both of food and social stimulation, and this would have been reflected in subsistence methods and social arrangements. The process had no "result" as such, for the brain constantly developed in response to behavioral change but at the same time led to new thoughts that were translated into action: a continuous feedback motion.

Hunting, gathering, and, to a decreasing degree, scavenging were the main human adaptations. Among their correlates were division of labor, basic social organization, increases in communication, and, of course, increase in brain size. Slowly and steadily the species evolved ways of satisfying basic biological drives and needs: food supply, shelter against the elements and predators, sex and reproduction. In the process a prototype emerged: "man the hunter" (and I choose the phrase with care, as evidence suggests that the more robust males assumed most responsibility in catching prey). The species' greater brain capacity gave them the advantage of intellect, an ability to devise methods of tracking and capture, to utilize cunning and stealth as well as force. Concentration became important; intelligence enabled our ancestors to ignore distractions and fix attention on the sought-after game. Hunts, especially for large animals, would be more effectively performed in squads and these required a level of co-ordination, synchronization, and communication. Co-operation and reciprocity were qualities of great utility in hunting and at the home base, where the spoils would be shared.

The accumulated experience of the hunt itself would impart qualities – like courage in the face of dangerous carnivores who would compete for food. Risks were essential to reproductive success; if they had not been taken the species would still be picking fruit. Among the specific skills refined in this period would have been an ability to aim and accurately deliver missiles, a capacity to judge pace in movement, and to overwhelm and conquer prey when close combat was necessary. We might also take note of the fact that humans became impressively good swimmers and divers, evolving equipment and functions that aided deep diving and fast swimming; this aquatic adaptation may have been linked to hunting for fish.

All these features are responses to the manner in which the species procured its food: this is essential to life and so has a strong, if not determining, effect on every aspect of both lifestyle and personality. If an existing method of obtaining food does not yield enough nutrition, then bodies suffer and the species either perishes or makes new adaptations, perhaps formulating alternative methods. In the event, what seems to have happened in the case of *Homo sapiens* is that they hit upon a novel way of guaranteeing a food supply which eliminated the need for many of the activities that had persisted for the previous 2 million years or more, and had carved deeply the features of human character and capacities. As recently as 10,000 years ago, *Homo sapiens* devised a way of exploiting the food supply which was to remove the necessity of hunting and release humans to concentrate on building what is now popularly known as "civilization."

Paleolithic age

From *palaios*, the Greek for ancient times, and *lithos*, meaning stone, this describes the period in which primitive stone implements were used. Beginning probably 2 million years ago when our ancestors put an edge on a stone, pressed its thick end against the palm of the hand and realized its power to strike and cut, this age saw the arrival of the hunter-gatherer, as opposed to the simple forager cultures. It ended as recently as 10,000 years ago, when the domestication of animals and cultivation of plants started.

Instead of exploiting natural resources around them, the species began to exploit its own ability. In short, the ability to create a food supply. This was accomplished by gathering animals and crops together, containing them in circumstances that permitted their growth and reproduction, then picking crops or slaughtering animals as necessary, without ever destroying the entire stock. In this way, supply was rendered a problem only by disease or inclement weather. The practice of cultivating land for use, rather than for mere existence, gave rise to farming.

RECREATING THE HUNT

Although now open to debate, the beginnings of agriculture are seen in orthodox teaching to coincide with the end of what is called the paleolithic age. The transition was seen by some as swift and dramatic, though the view has been challenged by others who accentuate the uneven process of development over periods of time. For example, in Europe, following the recession of the ice age, there appears to have been an interlude in which certain animals, especially dogs, were domesticated, some cereals were harvested, and forms of stock management were deployed, but without the systematic approach of later agriculturists.

Obviously, regions differed considerably ecologically, and the period characterized by the transition from hunter-gatherer to farmer was neither smooth nor uniform. But it was sudden – in evolutionary terms, that is. Only as recently as 10,000 years ago do we see the systematic domestication of animals – a process central to agriculture. It may have taken the form of controlled breeding or just providing fodder to attract wild herds, but the insight was basically the same: that enclosing and nourishing livestock was a far more effective and reliable way of ensuring food than hunting for it.

Complementing this discovery was the realization that planting and nurturing plants and harvesting only enough to meet needs so that regrowth was possible was an efficient exploitation of natural resources compared to the cumbersome and less predictable gathering method. The breakthroughs spawned all manner of toolmaking and other technologies that added momentum to the agricultural transformation that is loosely referred to as the neolithic age (from the Greek *neo* meaning new and *lithos* meaning stone: a period when ground and polished tools and weapons were introduced).

What we need to remind ourselves of is that hunting and gathering had been dominant for more than 2 million years before. During that period the lifestyle and mentality it demanded became components of our character. Chasing, capturing, and killing with their attendant dangers were practiced features of everyday life. The qualities of courage, skill, and the inclination to risk, perhaps even to sacrifice on occasion, were not heraldic but simply human and necessary for survival. What we would now regard as epic moments were in all probability quite "ordinary." The coming of farming made most of these qualities and features redundant. The hunting parties that honed their skills, devised strategies, and traded on courage were no longer needed. Instead, the successful farmer needed to be diligent, patient, responsible, regular, and steadfast. A farmer was more interested in breeding animals than in hunting them. The switch was bound to introduce strains.

Hunting and gathering affected us not only socially but perhaps even genetically, so long and sweeping was its reign. No organism is a product purely of hereditary nature or of environmental experience. Humans are no different in being products of the interaction between genes and the environment. But the kind of evolutionary change we are interested in proceeded at different levels: the human way of living changed, but not in such a way as to incur an automatic switch in human beings themselves. After all, even rough arithmetic tells us that the 10,000 years in which agriculture has developed represents at most 0.5 per cent of the period spent hunting and gathering. Sport, in this scenario, is the evidence that we are still catching up with the changes. It is as if cultural evolution sped ahead of biological evolution: we did not completely change from one type of organism into another as quickly as the cultural pace required. There was still too much of the hunter-gatherer in us to permit an easy settling down to breeding animals and sowing crops.

One response to this strain was to re-enact the hunt: imitate the chase, mimic the prey, copy the struggle, simulate the kill, and recreate the conditions under which such properties as bravery and resolution would be rewarded. It was a fairly minor but important adaptation in which the customary skills, techniques, and habits were retained even when their original purpose had disappeared. It made far more sense to enclose, feed, and domesticate animals than to hunt them, as it did to sow crops rather than gather wild fruits and grains. It was perfectly possible to acknowledge this, while craving the thrill the hunts used to bring. How could the spirit of the hunt be recaptured?

The answer was: let it continue. Hunt for its own sake rather than for food. No matter that hunting served no obvious purpose any longer, let people engage in it for the sheer pleasure or excitement it generated. In this way, people played at hunting: they did not direct their efforts to meeting the immediate material needs of life, or acquiring necessities. Hunting became instead an autotelic activity, having no purpose apart from its own existence.

Autotelic

From the Greek *auto*, meaning by or for itself, and *telos*, meaning end. An autotelic activity is one which has an end or purpose in itself and is engaged in for its own sake.

Once it became detached from the food supply, the activity took on a life of its own. When survival no longer depended on killing game, the killing became an end; what was once an evolutionary means to an end became an end in itself. The new hunt no longer had as its motive the pursuit of food but rather the pursuit of new challenges. Although in behavioral terms much the same activity as hunting, the new version was an embryonic sport or at least an expression of the drive or impulse underlying sports right to the present day. Stripped of its original purpose, the processual aspects of the activity came to prominence. Team co-ordination, stealth, intelligence, daring, physical prowess, and courage in the face of danger were valued more than the end product and, over time, these became integrated into a series of activities, each in some way mimicking the original activities.

It sounds trite to say that the roots of sports lie in our primeval past when so many of today's sports operate not in response to survival but as adjuncts to commercial interests. At the same time, we should recognize that the impulses that make sports attractive enough to be commercially exploited are part of our evolutionary make-up. Sport was the result of the attempt to reintroduce the excitement and thrill of the hunt into lives that were threatened with mundane routines in unchallenging environments. As such it was and remains both precious and profound. It may owe nothing to the hunt nowadays; but it still owes a good deal to the attempts at replacing the hunt with something comparably as exciting.

So, there is perfect sense in Gerhard Lukas's claim that "the first sport was spear throwing," or *speer worfen* (1969). Darts, blowguns, and bows and arrows were modifications of the basic projectile and unquestionably featured in mock as well as genuine hunts. The use of the bow is interesting in that it stimulated the construction of an artifact, the target, the bull's-eye, which, as its name implies, represented the part of the animal to be aimed at. Archery, as a purely autotelic behavior, actually had the quality of compressing a symbolic hunt into a finite area and allowing a precise way of assessing the results. As such, it had potential as an activity that could be watched and evaluated by others, who would not participate except in a vicarious way (that is, they might experience it imaginatively through the participants – which is what most sports spectators do, even today). This vicariousness was, as we now realize, absolutely crucial to the emergence and development of sport.

The facility for bringing the rationality and emotion of a hunt to a home base made it possible to include dozens, or hundreds, of people in the whole experience. Just witnessing an event offered some continuity, however tenuous, within change: spectators could "feel" the drama and tension of a supposed hunt from another age, through the efforts of the participants. The obvious acknowledgment of this came with the custom-built stadia. These came with the clustering together of human populations and the creation of city-states. Irrigation was crucial to farming, of course, so most of the earliest known civilizations had their urban centers near rivers, as in China, India, and the Near and Middle East. Richard Mandell, in his *Sport: A cultural history*

(1984), urges caution in gleaning evidence of what we now call spectator sports in ancient civilizations. But he does show that the Mesopotamians, for example, left traces of evidence that suggest physical competitions. These might have been tests of strength and skill; though they may also have been more military training regimes than amusements for the masses.

The seminal Egyptian civilization of some 5,000 years ago left much material in the form of documents, frescos, tombs, and bric-a-brac. In these we find depicted one of the most essential, enduring, and unchanging activities, and one which we will consider in the next section: combat.

State

An organized administrative apparatus in which a single government is empowered to rule. Governments may change, but the bureaucracy stays essentially intact, giving a stability and continuity to the state and its main institutions. See Chapter fifteen for an analysis of the contemporary state's intrusion in sport.

IN PURSUIT OF *AGŌN*

At some stage in ancient history, the idea of rivalry seems to have struck chords. The straightforward drive of the hunt, in which packs pursued game, acquired a provision. The object was not merely the climax of a kill, but in administering the kill faster or more effectively than others. Competition between individuals or groups added a new and apparently appealing dimension to an already perilous activity, turning it into a game with some semblance of organization and a clear understanding of what constituted an achievement. The amusement value, it seems, was boosted by the introduction of a human challenge and by spectatorship.

It is probable, though undocumented, that physical combat activities between humans and perhaps animals co-existed with the autotelic hunts. We need not invoke the Cain and Abel fable to support the argument that intra-species fighting, for both instrumental and playful purposes, existed throughout history. It is one of the least changeable aspects of *Homo sapiens*. Combat has many different forms, ranging from wrestling to fencing; stripped to its basics, it expresses the rawest type of competition. As such, it seems to have held a wide appeal both for participants seeking a means to express their strength and resilience and for audiences who to this day are enraptured by the sight of humans disputing each other's physical superiority.

The hunt, or at least the mimetic activity that replaced it, would have satisfied a certain need for those closely involved, but the actual behavior would have been so fluid and dispersed that it would not have been closely observed, certainly not as a complete and integrated action. Spectators would have been much more easily accommodated at a home base where fighting could be staged in much the same way and with a similar purpose to mock hunts: to break up tedious routines and raise emotions with brief but thrilling and relatively unpredictable episodes of violent action. The emphasis may well have fallen on animal fighting, unarmed human combat and, possibly, armed humans pitched against large animals such as bears or tigers. Given the purpose of this type of combat, some loose structure or framework governing the fight was likely; combatants fighting to kill or disable an opponent in order to save themselves in any way possible would be warring rather than engaging in a sport.

A fresco excavated from the tomb of an Egyptian prince and dated to about 4,000 years ago looks similar to a modern wall chart and shows wrestlers demonstrating over a hundred different positions and holds. Mandell suggests that there may have been professional wrestlers in the Egyptian civilization. Artwork shows fighters also using sticks about one meter long; even today, stick fighting persists in parts of Egypt, though in a more ritualized form. It is quite possible that the proximity to the Nile encouraged competitive swim ming and rowing. In the plains of the Upper Nile region, hunting of large game, including elephants, was commonplace, the chariot being an effective vehicle for this purpose. Pharaoh Tutankhamun (14th century BCE) is shown on one fresco hunting lions from his chariot. Amphibian Nile dwellers like crocodiles and hippopotamuses were also hunted. Crete (to the south of Greece in the Aegean Sea) had trade contacts with Egypt and some kind of cultural cross fertilization is possible.

Certainly, Cretans were avid hunters and their relics suggest they were combat enthusiasts also, though the form of fighting they favored seems more akin to boxing than wrestling. According to J. Sakellarakis: "One finds in Crete, the first indications of the athletic spirit which was to evolve and reach a high pitch in subsequent centuries" (1979: 14). The games that had been played in Egypt and to the East developed into more exacting performances with set rules. We also have evidence of a version of bull-fighting, and a type of cattle wrestling that resembles the modern rodeo in the United States. Bull-leaping was a dangerous game that involved grasping the horns of an onrushing bull and vaulting over its body. Bull games are still popular today, of course.

The mythical and the mundane are intertwined in our knowledge of Greek civilization, popularly and justifiably regarded as the first culture to incorporate sports or, more specifically, competition, into civic life. The compulsion to pursue public recognition of one's supremacy through open contest with others was known by the Greeks as *agōn*. Athletic excellence achieved in competition was an accomplishment of, literally, heroic proportions. Myths of Hercules sending discuses into oblivion and Odysseus heaving boulders are important signifiers of the high value Greeks placed on physical feats, but the less spectacular evidence shows that they approached, organized, and assessed the outcomes of activities in a way which is quite familiar.

"The spirit of competition and rivalry extended to every area of Greek life," writes Manolis Andronicus in his essay "Essay and education: The institution of the games in ancient Greece" (1979: 43). The Greeks' approach was to win, and here we find the almost obsessional drive for success that characterizes contemporary sport: winning was quite often at any cost and scant respect was paid to such things as "fairness." Some may argue that the search for supremacy is a primordial competitive instinct. It is more likely that particular social arrangements in which inequality and distinct strata are key components encourage individuals to strive hard and "better themselves" by whatever means they can. Athletic prowess was one such means in the ancient civil society of Greece – the *polis*. Victors could acquire *arete* (excellence), the ultimate attainment. Greeks were also very keen on physical perfection and part of the purpose of athletic competition was to display the brawny bodies of men, but not women. One of the ideals embedded in Greek games was *kalos kagathos*, meaning the "good and beautiful man."

In terms of organization, Greeks created events which exist today without major modification. They are credited with being the first organizers of sports on a systematic basis, the Olympic Games, which began in 776 BCE, being the clearest expression of this. This event integrated sports into a wider festival, drawing disparate competitors and spectators together at one site every four years in an effort to convince themselves they were in some sense united. Greeks were also influential in their attempts to determine outcomes. Despite aphorisms about competing being more important than winning, victory was crucial and systems were designed to ensure accurate assessment of performance.

Exact distances were measured and staggers were introduced on racing circuits. Tallies of points were kept in multidiscipline events like the pentathlon (the Greek *āthlon* meant award, or prize, from which came the noun *athlētēs* to describe those who competed for the award). Records of performances were kept (each Olympiad took the name of the victorious sprinter at the previous festival). The games may have been less important as a spectacle than they were as a focal point around which to organize training. Physical fitness, strength, and the general toughness that derives from competition were important military attributes, and so the process was tuned to producing warriors as much as sports performers.

Sparta is the best-known city-state in this context: it was a site of phalanx training in which youths would be taken from their families and reared in an austere garrison where they would be honed for combat. There was also a religious element to competition, for the Greeks believed that athletic victory indicated that the victor would be favored by the capricious gods in whom they believed.

Whatever the motivation in striving to achieve, we can be sure that the Greeks went to great lengths in their preparations and so provided something of a prototype for what we now call training. Spartans in particular used a cyclical pattern of increasing and decreasing the intensity of preparations which is used in most modern sports. The very concept of preparation is important: recognizing that excellence does not spring spontaneously but is the product of periods of heavy labor and disciplined regimes prompted the Greeks to provide facilities. So, in the sixth century BCE, we see a new type of building called a *gymnasium* (meaning, literally, an exercise for which one strips).

By the time of the Greeks' refinements, sports had undergone changes in purpose and, indeed, nature. While the content showed clear lines of descent connecting it with more basic hunting and combat, the functions it served were quite novel: it was seen as a military training activity, as a vehicle for status-gaining, or what we might now refer to as social mobility, and as a way of securing divine favor. This does not deny that the impulses associated with hunting and gathering were present, but it does highlight the autonomy of sport once separated from its original conditions of creation and growth. The Greek adaptation was a response to new material and psychic requirements.

Powerful Greek city-states needed defense against outside attacks and they ensured this by encouraging and rewarding warriors. Accompanying the development of the *polis* was the growth of the state's control over human expressions of violence; sophisticated social organization and internal security were impossible without some regulation of violence. The state's response was to obtain a legitimate monopoly over violence and establish norms of behavior which discouraged the open expression of aggression by citizens and encouraged saving such energy for the possible repulsion of attacks from outside powers. Contests, challenges, and rivalries were ways in which the impulse could reassert itself, but in socially acceptable forms.

The value of athletic competition earned it a central place in Greek civilization and the importance of this is reinforced by writers such as Johann Huizinga and Norbert Elias, who stress that the process of becoming civilized itself implicates a culture in controlling violence while at the same time carving out "enclaves" for the "ritualized expression of physical violence." We will return to the theory in Chapter five, but should note the basic observation that sport serves as a legitimate means through which primitive, violence-related impulses and emotions can simultaneously be engendered and contained. Much of what the ancients would have regarded as expressions of civilization would be seen as barbarous from the standpoint of the late twentieth century.

Gouging, biting, breaking, and the use of spiked fist thongs were all permissible in Greek combat. But these were occasions for the exhibition of warrior-like qualities and mercy was not such a quality. While victory was a symbolic "kill" it was also, at times, a quite literal kill.

Much of the glory and honor that Greeks had invested in athletic competition was removed by the Romans. For the Romans, who conquered Greece, part of the appeal of sports lay in the climax of killing. One of their innovations of Greek sports was in establishing preparatory schools exclusively for gladiators, who would sooner or later be publicly fêted or slaughtered. The actual events would be staged in hippodromes, cavernous stadia where spectators would joyously witness the death of one human being either by another or by a beast.

Influenced by some Greek activities, Romans held foot races, chariot races, and many types of one-to-one combat in the centuries either side of the start of the Christian era. They were also aware of the immense military advantages of having a fit, disciplined, and tempered population. It was expensive to train gladiators, especially if they were all to be killed, so convicted prisoners and slaves were virtually sacrificed.

Adding to the extravagance was the cost of importing animals: wild beasts from throughout the world were captured, transported, and nourished. For five or more centuries, hundreds of thousands of beasts were brought into the Coliseum and other stadia and, watched by massed audiences, pitched against each other or against humans. Death seems to have been an accepted part of this activity. There was nothing curious about the Romans' apparent lack of fascination when it came to hunting (no artifacts to suggest much interest). They had no need to leave their cities: the hunts were effectively transferred to the stadia where audiences could satisfy their appetites for violence, or their "blood lusts," as some might say. Gladiatorial conflicts featuring wild animals were comparable to the primitive hunts; the comparisons between human combat and today's fighting sports are clear.

Nowadays, there are few deaths to observe in sporting combat, and when tragedy does strike it leads to a period of earnest self-reflection as well as attacks from medical authorities on the "barbaric" nature of such activities. The fact remains: audiences are amused and excited by the prospect of human combat, as they are by animal conflict – about which there is far less restraint, as the slaughter in bull-fighting, cock-fighting, and hare-coursing suggests. The threshold of tolerance has dropped, but this is largely a function of the cultural forces that emanate from civilization: the human proclivity to watch, enjoy, and appreciate the infliction of damage during combat does not seem to waver. Perhaps we are not so dissimilar to our Roman ancestors who wallowed in the bloodletting and cheerfully pointed their thumbs to the floor to answer the question, life or death.

The gladiatorial schools finally closed after Christian opposition in the year 399 of the Christian Era. In the following century, the combat grew less deadly and was superseded as an entertainment by less expensive chariot racing, which was arguably the first mass spectator event, drawing crowds of up to 250,000 to the Circus Maximus. Chariot racing required teams, each team wearing different-colored uniforms and the winners receiving prize money as well as garlands. It has been argued that Roman sports assumed a political character in this period. With no genuinely democratic means of representation, the populations may well have grown restive and demanded change were it not for the diversionary effect of the combat and racing.

The entertainment that drew crowds in their hundreds of thousands diverted their attention, if only temporarily, from their grievances and so served the function of maintaining the status quo. Masses were distracted and amused. The theme was updated in the Arnold Schwarzenegger movie *The Running Man* (directed by Paul Michael Glaser, 1987) set in a totalitarian future in which "have-nots" are kept docile by a competition in which convicted criminals are pursued through a maze by "stalkers" – athletes trained to kill. "The public wants sports and violence," observes the competition's MC. "We give them what they want." We will consider the scholarly attempts to portray today's sports in a similar way later.

THE RUSH OF THE SPECTACLE

Beside the civilizations of Egypt, Greece, and Rome, other cultures emerging in the pre-Christian Era had activities resembling sport, though in this historical context we should observe Mandell's caveat that "the boundaries that we moderns use to separate 'sport' from other areas of human endeavor have been indistinct or not worth noticing in other cultures" (1984: 93).

So, we cannot be certain that the swimming, diving, and combat, armed and unarmed, practiced by inhabitants of South Asia around 2,500 years ago approached what we would recognize as sport; they may have had a more specific traditional significance, possibly bound up in the caste system. Similarly, the equestrian pursuits of the Chinese, together with their competitive archery, may have been based less on recreation or amusement and more on military training. Yet, as with Greeks and Romans, the activities themselves have been adapted to suit changing circumstances. For example, the sport we call polo may have started life as a method of target practice in ancient Persia (now Iran). Many of China's martial exercises, which could be used competitively, were functional and were used to maintain a high level of fitness amongst the working population. Japanese industries have successfully adopted this ancient policy, holding exercise sessions before work in today's factories.

The Chinese were probably the first to employ a ball effectively, though there is evidence that the Egyptians experimented. In northern China there was a primitive kicking game. The Chinese invented a projectile that was the forerunner of the shuttlecock and, presumably, propelled it by means of some sort of racket or bat.

The military importance of the horse, especially fast and maneuverable breeds, is obvious and the Japanese perhaps more than any other population recognized this in their sporting traditions. Their competitive shows of speed and intricacy have clear counterparts in today's horse-oriented events, including dressage. Japan's legacy of martial arts is large and well known; combat in the feudal age of the samurai was based on several ancient disciplines and included the mastery of horses, weapons, and unarmed conflict.

Many of the skills survive, though with modifications. The pattern that emerges in Japan as elsewhere is the use of sport as a military exercise as well as a pursuit to retain interest and capture enthusiasm while preparing its participants for the more practical discipline of defense. Wherever we find a cavalry, we almost invariably discover some form of competitive endeavor involving the horse. Typically, the competitors would be something of an elite, with resources and possibly patronage enough to compete and serve; they may well have been lionized as Greek heroes were. Certainly in medieval Europe, armed knights were the basis of the continent's supremacy and glory. The knights would be served by peasants and would enjoy status, though in material terms they may not have been much better off.

Practice fights between mounted knights gave rise to a form of combat known as jousting and, as modern fans are drawn by sparring sessions or exhibition games, spectators stood in line as the combatants galloped toward each other, lances extended. The object was to tilt the lance at the adversary in an attempt to unseat him. As the jousts gained popularity in the fifteenth century, they were surrounded by pomp, pageantry, and ritual, and formal tournaments were lavish affairs attended and heavily patronized by nobility. Jousting became an expensive pursuit quite beyond the reach of the peasantry, and indeed beyond all apart from the wealthy landowners whom the jousters served. Peasants would merely look on as the often huge and elaborate tournaments unfolded.

The combat was frequently along territorial lines, as in a 1520 tournament in northern France between King Henry VIII of England and King Francis I of France. A truly "international" event, it was spread over three weeks and attended by dozens of thousands. As well as the equestrian contests, tournaments might also have included sword fights and more theatrical displays of acrobatics and horsemanship – in the age of chivalry, women were strictly spectators.

Jousting, as with the many other forms of combat, had the military purpose of keeping knights in good fighting shape, but may have been transformed into an alternative to warring. Disputes could be settled less expensively and more enjoyably by tournaments than by costly internecine battles. From the twelfth to sixteenth centuries, tournaments became more organized and orderly, as did European society as a whole. Accommodation was made for spectators, scaffolds and stands being built as the jousts grew more popular and attracted large crowds in Italy, France, Germany, and other parts of Europe.

After the sixteenth century, the grand tournaments faded and rural events emerged, though tilts were often at targets, not humans. The tournaments gradually changed character from being hard-edged and competitive; "from sports to spectacle" is how Allen Guttmann describes the change in his book *Sports Spectators* (1986). The process is familiar to anyone who has witnessed the transmutation of wrestling after it became a popular spectator "sport."

Hunting and archery co-existed with jousting and outlasted it, though never attracting comparable numbers of spectators. Archery survived virtually intact and is today an Olympic event; the old longbows have been considerably modified, of course. Civic festivals were organized around competitions and were grand occasions, drawing vast crowds to pageants all over Europe. The stag- and fox-hunts were direct predecessors of the modern fox-hunts, with the rich amusing themselves by setting free their hounds and giving pursuit; the poor would amuse themselves by pursuing them all.

Cock-fighting

This probably has origins in ancient China and Persia. Greeks may have become aware of it after their victory over Persia at Salamis in 480 BCE and, in turn, introduced it to the Romans. For Greeks, the courage of fighting birds was regarded as exemplary: youths were encouraged to watch and emulate the birds' tenacity and valor in combat. Later, it became a mere source of entertainment, especially for gamblers. It first appeared in England in the 12th century, though its popularity waxed and waned until the 16th century when Henry VIII built a royal cockpit at his palace. In the 18th and 19th centuries, cocks were bought and sold, bred and trained in a more organized way, one trainer, Joseph Gulliver, acquiring quite a reputation. Cock-fighting was banned in 1835 in England but is known to persist in the USA and Britain.

Hunts and other "blood sports" continued to enjoy popularity among lower classes, whose penchant for watching tethered bears prodded with sticks and then set upon by fierce dogs is similar to that of the spectators who gathered at the Roman Coliseum centuries before. Cock-fights, which have almost universal appeal, were held in England from about the twelfth century and attracted audiences from the various classes. As we saw from the description at the beginning of this chapter, the activities frequently ended in dead, dying, or seriously hurt animals.

Hugh Cunningham, in his *Leisure in the Industrial Revolution*, relates a Sunday morning meeting in London in 1816 at which several hundred people were assembled in a field adjoining a churchyard. In the field, "they fight dogs, hunt ducks, gamble, enter into subscriptions to fee drovers for a bullock." The rector of the nearby church observed: "I have seen them drive the animal through the most populous parts of the parish, force sticks pointed with iron, up the body, put peas into the ears, and infuriate the beast" (1980: 23).

Although condemned systematically from the eighteenth century, blood sports persist to this day, most famously in the Spanish bull rings and in the streets of Pamplona. England's Bull Ring, in Birmingham, reminds us that such events were not always confined to Spain; bull-running ceased in England in 1825, a year after the founding of the Royal Society for the Prevention of Cruelty to Animals (RSPCA). The same organization brought pressure against cock-fighting, which was banned in 1835, only to go "underground" as an illicit, predominantly working-class pursuit.

The decline of cock-fighting, bull-baiting, and the like coincided with cultural changes that brought with them a range of alternative leisure pursuits. The whole spectrum of changes was part of what some writers have called the civilizing process – which we will cover in more detail in the next chapter.

But, before we are tempted into assuming that barbaric tastes and activities have completely disappeared, we should stay mindful of Richard Holt's caution: "The tendency by members of all social classes to maltreat animals for excitement or gain is by no means dead even today" (1990: 24). Dog-fighting in particular persists in the West to this day and dogs are bred for the specific purpose of fighting. In the early 1990s, amid a panic over the number of ferocious breeds proliferating, the British banned the import of American pit bulls (such animals are required to be registered in Britain under the Dangerous Dogs Act, 1991; there are about 5,000 unregistered pit bulls trained for fighting rather than as pets). And, as if to remind us of our retrograde thirst for blood, a police operation in County Durham, north-east England, in 1995 yielded six arrests, the recovery of 14 dead cockerels and 40 live birds and implements, including sharpened spurs (probably imported from the USA), weighing machinery and a board that listed names, weights and betting odds on the birds.

Blood sports in general and fox-hunting in particular are seen as having central importance by Norbert Elias and Eric Dunning in their book *Quest for Excitement*. The "civilizing" of society demanded greater personal self-control and a stricter constraint on violence, but the process of hunting or just observing allowed "all the pleasures and the excitement of the chase, as it were, mimetically in the form of wild play" (1986). While the passion and exhilaration associated with hunting would be aroused, the actual risks would be absent in the imagined version (except for the animals, of course) and the effects of watching would be, according to Elias and Dunning, "liberating, cathartic."

Mimetic

From the Greek *mimesis* for imitation, this describes an activity that imitates or resembles another, and which is carried out especially for amusement. A child may mimetically play cowboys-and-indians or adult members of Round Table organizations may imitate battles, albeit in a mock way.

The comments could be applied without alteration to all of the activities considered so far. They are products of a human imagination ingenious enough to create artificial situations that human evolution has rendered irrelevant. But, once created, they have seemed to exert a control and power of their own, eliciting in both participants and audience a pleasurable excitement that encapsulates the thrill or "rush" of a hunt, yet carries none of the attendant risks.

History shows that activities which at least resemble sports are rarely purely autotelic and can be augmented with other purposes. From ancient to medieval ages, the tendency was to imbue supposed sporting activities with a military purpose, often encouraging qualities within participants that were of obvious utility in serious combat. We also find a subtheme in sports history in which many of the main roles were occupied by privileged or elite groups who performed, while most of the supporting roles were played by peasantry or plebeians who watched. The public provision of entertainment by the powerful had a latent political function in diverting attention away from *realpolitik* and animating sentiments and emotions that were not challenging to the established order of things.

Human relationships with other animals have been peculiarly ambivalent. Dogs, for instance, have been domesticated and cared for, and used to hunt other more vulnerable creatures and to retrieve birds which have been killed. Many other animals have simply been used as expendable prey, an observation that gives credence to the view that, while the hunt as a survival mechanism has receded, the violent impulses that it once fostered remain. Animal abuses very gradually declined in the long period under review and, though they were under pressure during the twentieth century, they certainly have not disappeared. Animal uses, as opposed to abuses (though the distinction may not be acceptably clear-cut for everyone), are still very much with us, as dog-racing and horse-racing remind us. The previously mentioned Iditarod in which packs of huskies pull a sled for between six and eight days and nights in temperatures of minus 60°F is an organized competition in which the driver talks to, becomes as tough as, and even sleeps with his dogs, according to Gary Paulsen, in his *Winterdance* (1994).

This close relationship with animals suggests a continuity in sports and one which, if traced back, has its origins in the transition from hunter-gatherer to farmer. While the connecting thread appears at times to be only tenuous, we can infer that there is surely some human property that elicits a desire for a form of autotelic enterprise based on competition. The way in which it manifests itself differs from culture to culture, and so far in this chapter I have pulled out only fragments from history to illustrate the general argument. The impression is still clear enough to draw a plausible scenario and one in which a basic impulse continues to operate in widely different contexts. In most of these contexts, some spectacle was made of violence.

Despite the ostensibly civilizing forces at work, physical cruelty and the infliction of damage on others continued to attract and entertain people. But, in the nineteenth century, very sharp and dramatic changes took place, particularly in Europe, that were to affect the sensitivity to, and public acceptance of, violence, and this was to have an impact on the entire shape and focus of sport. It was also to establish the framework of what would now legitimately pass for sports.

TENOR OF LIFE, TEMPO OF WORK

One of the fashionable haunts of the nobility and upper classes in the early eighteenth century was James Figg's amphitheater in London. Figg, himself a swordsman and all-round fighter, opened the venue in 1719 and attracted large crowds to watch displays of animal-baiting as well as human contests, featuring swords, fists, and staffs. No sexism here: Figg held contests between and among men and women. Figg's cachet brought him appointments as a tutor to the gentry, instructing in the "art of self-defense," which was regarded in those days as very much a gentleman's pursuit.

There was very little gentlemanly restraint in the actual contests, which were bare-knuckle affairs without either a specified number of rounds or a points-scoring system. A match was won when one fighter was simply unable to continue. Three- and four-hour contests were commonplace, with wrestling throws, kicks, and punches all permissible. Such types of combat were rife in England in Figg's time (he died in 1734) and drew on what was ancient tradition, as we have noted. No doubt similar forms of combat took place in other parts of the world in the eighteenth century though, in England, fighting was to undergo a special transformation.

At about the same time as Figg's venture, another combat activity was gaining popularity, at least in parts of Britain. Ball games such as "hurling" and "knappan" were loosely organized according to local customs rather than central rules and were played with an inflated animal bladder. Ancient Greeks and Romans also used pig or ox bladders, though they tended to fill them with hair and feathers, more suited to throwing than the fast kicking games that became popular much later. In the intervening centuries ball games were always peripheral to activities such as combat, racing, or archery, but in the nineteenth century they seemed to take off.

I describe ball games as different to "combat activity" although it seems that at least some variants of what was to evolve into football allowed participants to complement their delicate ball-playing skills with cudgels and other instruments that Mr. Figg and his associates would have been adept at using. Meetings would have resembled an all-out struggle much more than a practiced, rule-bound game with clearly defined goals and final results.

But violence was popular and the rough and wild "folk games," as Eric Dunning and Kenneth Sheard call them in *Barbarians, Gentlemen and Players* were "closer to 'real' fighting than modern sports" (1979). The authors suggest that football's antecedents reflected the "violent tenor of life in society at large" and also the low threshold of repugnance "with regard to witnessing and engaging in violent acts." Sometimes, the distinction between witnessing and engaging became blurred and spectators would join in the action.

It's rather synthetic to link these pursuits of the eighteenth century with today's boxing or wrestling and types of football; first, because of the regional variations and, second, because of combinations of rules and characteristics that made any systematic differentiation of games impossible. Yet, somehow, the essentials of both activities have dropped into the stream of history and arrived in the twenty-first century as well-ordered, highly structured, and elaborately organized sports. I use the two examples because they embody currents and changes that have affected the entire assortment of activities that have become contemporary sports. The decline in spontaneity and open brutality in sports mirrored trends in society generally.

The new rules of prize-fighting, instituted in 1838, introduced some measure of regulation, including a "scratch" line which was a mark in the center of a 24-foot square ring which competitors had to reach unassisted at the start of each round, or else be judged the loser (that is, "not coming up to scratch"). It was a small but significant modification that removed the necessity of a beating into submission or a knockout to terminate a bout. In 1867, Queensberry Rules were devised to reduce the degree of bodily damage possible and to increase the importance of skill as a decisive factor in the "noble art."

Far away from Figg's boxing ring and the raucous folk ball games, another set of forces were helping shape sports; they came from Britain's public (independent) schools, which were strictly for the children of the aristocracy or very affluent. Despite the popular beliefs that public schools in the nineteenth century were upholders of the virtues of sports, they actually echoed many of the sentiments of the Puritans, who disapproved utterly of any activity that seemed frivolous, including dancing, blood sports, and wagering (betting). Such entertainment was seen by Puritans as the mindless pleasure of *flâneurs* and, of course, such idlers were ripe for the devil's work. In the fifteenth and sixteenth centuries, Puritans suppressed any activity resembling a contest in their attempts to create an atmosphere of strict moral discipline. The universities of Oxford and Cambridge banned ball games in the sixteenth century.

Public school masters initially tried to prevent the development of soccer in particular, believing it to be disruptive of order and morally debilitating. There was also the feeling that it was demeaning for the sons of the upper classes to practice activities that were, as one headmaster of the day described them, "fit only for butcher boys ... farm boys and laborers" (quoted in Dunning and Sheard 1979: 47). Gentlemen scholars became the new Corinthians in sharp contrast to the laboring commoners.

Corinthians

From the Ancient Greek city of Corinth, site of the Isthmian Games, which was known for its wealth, luxury, and licentiousness, Corinthians being its inhabitants. In the early 19th century, this took on sporting connotations when it was appropriated by wealthy gentlemen amateurs, who could afford to ride their own horses, sail their own yachts and pursue sports for no financial gain – in contrast to the professional players. The self-styled Corinthians believed they embodied the true spirit of sport for its own sake.

Intellectual trends in Germany and France were influenced by the philosopher J. J. Rousseau whose treatise *Emile* (first published in 1762) argued that physical training and competitive sport would yield positive results in the overall education of a child. Ideas drifted across to English public schools, so that, by the 1850s, two main revisions were made to the original ideas on sports. Expressed by Peter McIntosh in his *Fair Play*: "The first was that competitive sport, especially team games, had an ethical basis, and the second was that training in moral behaviour on the playing field was transferable to the world beyond" (1980: 27).

Together, the ideas formed the core of "Muscular Christianity." Unselfishness, justice, health: these were the type of ideals that were manifest in sport, but also in any proper Christian society. Public schools, influenced by the doctrine, began to integrate a program of sport into their curricula. Team games were important in subordinating the individual to the collective unit and teaching the virtues of alliances. It was often thought that England's many military victories were attributable to the finely honed teamwork encouraged by public schools. Again, we glimpse the notion of sport as a preparation for military duty: the playing fields of public schools were equated with battlegrounds (Eton and Waterloo, for example). Thomas Hughes's classic, *Tom Brown's Schooldays*, is full of allusions to the role of public schools in producing populations suited to rule over an empire.

Muscular Christianity

The term was first used in 1857 by a reviewer of *Tom Brown's Schooldays*. It became applied to a doctrine about the positive moral influence of physical exercise and sport, which had its intellectual roots in the philosophy of J. J. Rousseau in France and Gutsmuths in Germany, and which was approvingly adopted by the public schools of England in the late 19th century. See Tony Money's *Manly and Muscular Diversions: Public schools and the nineteenth-century sporting revival* (1997).

The physically tough and toughening version of football, as practiced by Rugby School under the headship of Thomas Arnold and his assistant G. E. L. Cotton, gained acceptance in many public schools. Its toughness was useful in sorting out those fit enough to survive and perhaps later prosper in positions of power. The frail would either strengthen or perish. Its appeal to the prestigious public schools bent on turning out "great men" was soon apparent as the sport of rugby spread through the network and, in time, to a number of "open" clubs in the north of England (which admitted nouveaux riches and working-class members).

Exporting its sports has been a major trade for England over the decades. Versions of the football played at Rugby and other public schools were popular among college students at North America's principal universities in the 1880s. The throwing and passing, as opposed to kicking, game was played at a competitive level. As early as 1874 there is a record of a game between Harvard and McGill. Interestingly, Wilbert Leonard documents a game of soccer between Rutgers and Princeton back in 1869 (Harvard refused to play soccer and Yale responded accordingly).

Muscular Christianity was also instrumental in carrying the other principal variant of football to the working class. Soccer was encouraged by churches. A quarter of today's English clubs were founded and, for a while, sustained by churches eager to proselytize in urban centers which by the 1880s were humming with the sound of heavy machinery. Industry itself was not slow to realize the advantages of possessing a football team comprising members of its workforce. Places like Coventry, Stoke, and Manchester can boast enduring soccer clubs that were originally works outfits. Arsenal was based at Woolwich Arsenal, a London munitions factory. Games which were only played on designated holy days and other festive occasions became more and more regular, routine, and organized.

In a similar way, many North American professional football franchises started as factory teams. The Indian Packing Company, of Green Bay, Wisconsin, had its own team in the first decade of the twentieth century; as did the Staley Starch Company, of Decatur, Illinois. Players were paid about $50 per week and given time off to train. In 1920, both companies affiliated their teams to a new organization that also had teams from New York and Washington. The teams evolved into the Packers, Bears, Giants, and Redskins respectively.

We might stretch the point and describe the early works teams as "para-industrial": organized much as an industrial force and intended to supplement the strictly industrial. It was a very deliberate policy pursued by factory owners. In some ways, sport was a foil for industrial order; a potent instrument for instilling discipline in the workforce. But, if sport was an instrument, it had two cutting edges for as well as carving out new patterns of order it was also responsible for outbreaks of disorder. Work and leisure were cut in two by the imperatives of industry. The more fluid way of life in which the manner in which one earned a living blended imperceptibly with the rest of one's life disappeared as the factory system issued its demands, which were a workforce ready to labor for a set amount of time at a specific site.

During that time workers operated under virtual compulsion; outside that time they were free to pursue whatever they wished (and could afford).

Sport was a way of filling leisure time with brief, but exhilarating periods of uncertainty: the questions of who or which team would win a more-or-less equal competition was bound to prompt interest and speculation, as, it seems, it always has. The spell of physically competitive activity, far from being broken, was strengthened by the need for momentary release from a colorless world dominated by the monotonous thuds and grinds of machinery. Competitions, whether individual combats, ball games, or animal baits, drew crowds; but public gatherings always carried the potential for disruption.

Public gatherings and festivals, and other staged events attracted a working class which was in the process of becoming industrialized but which had not yet done so by the mid- to late nineteenth century. It was still adjusting to what John Hargreaves in *Sport, Power and Culture* calls the changes in "tempo and quality of industrial work" (1986). Hargreaves argues that the English church's efforts in building football clubs had the effect of controlling the working class so that it would be more pliant for ruling groups. In fact, Hargreaves's entire thesis revolves around the intriguing idea that sport has helped integrate the working class into respectable "bourgeois culture" rather than struggle against it.

But the integration was never smooth and police or militia were regularly called to suppress riots and uprisings at football matches, prize fights, footraces, cock-fights, and so on, as large groups spontaneously grew agitated and unruly. Boxing events to this day employ whips who are promoters' chargés d'affaires responsible for most of the minor business. But, as the etymology suggests, the original whips were employed to encircle the ring, cracking their whips or lashing at troublesome members of the audience (ancient Romans were the first to employ whips at their gladiatorial contests). Local laws were enacted, prohibiting meetings in all but tightly policed surroundings, sometimes banning sports completely. The rise of the governing bodies within individual sports represents an attempt to absorb working-class energies within a formal structure, thereby containing what might otherwise have become disruptive tendencies.

The same forces affecting combat helped reshape football, taking out some of its ferocity and establishing sets of rules in what was previously a maelstrom. In 1863, the Football Association was formed to regulate the kicking form of the sport (the word soccer probably derives from "assoc," an abbreviation of Association). The version that stressed handling was brought under the control of the Rugby Union, which was created in 1871. *Rugby's Great Split*, as Tony Collins calls it, into distinct amateur and professional organizations came in 1895, the latter being known as Rugby League, which remained confined to the northern counties of England where it was favored by the working class. The other major change in rugby came in North America, where, in 1880, the addition of downs to replace the to-and-fro of rugby and a straight line of scrimmage instead of the less orderly scrummage gave American football a character all of its own (the forward pass rule was introduced in 1906).

Baseball's governing body has its origins in 1858 when the National Association of Base Ball Players was formed. The game was played for many years before, probably evolving out of the English games, baseball and rounders, in which players struck a ball with a bat and ran through a series of bases arranged in a circle, or a "round." Baseball was the first fully professional sport in America, charging admissions to ballparks and attracting a predominantly blue-collar fandom.

The changes in the organization of sports were responses to demands for orderliness and standardization. England and, later, North America metamorphosed into an industrial society where the valued qualities were discipline, precision, and control. Sports not only absorbed these qualities, but promoted them, gradually influencing perceptions and expectations in such a way as to deepen people's familiarity with the industrial regimen.

Industrialization drew populations to urban centers in search of work; not work quite as we know it today, but uncomfortable, energy-draining activities performed for long hours often in squalid and dangerous conditions. This type of work needed a new mentality. People were expected to arrive at work punctually and toil for measured periods of time. Their labors were planned for them and their efforts were often highly specialized according to the division of labor.

Behavior at work was subject to rules and conditions of service. Usually, all the work took place in a physically bounded space, the factory. There was also a need for absoluteness: tools and machines were made to fine tolerances. Underlying all this was a class structure, or hierarchy, in which some strata had attributes suited to ruling and others to being ruled. The latter's short-comings were so apparent that no detailed investigation of the causes was thought necessary: their poverty, or even destitution, was their own fault.

All these had counterparts in the developing sports scene. Time periods for contests were established and measured accurately thanks to newer, sophisticated timepieces. Divisions of labor in team games yielded role-specific positions and particular, as opposed to general, skills. Constitutions were drawn up to instill more structure into activities and regulate events according to rules. They took place on pitches, in rings and halls – in finite spaces. Winners and losers were unambiguously clear, outright, and absolute. And hierarchies reflecting the class structure were integrated into many activities. Captains of teams, for example, were "gentlemen" from the upper echelons. The sense of order, discipline, location, and period which sport acquired helped it both complement and support working life. *Homo faber* and *Homo ludens* were almost mirror images of one another. As the form and pace of sport imitated that of industry, so it gained momentum amongst the emergent working class seeking some sporadic diversion from its toil, something more impulsive and daring than the routine labors that dominated industry. While sport was assuming a symmetry with work, it still afforded the working class an outlet, or release from labor; it was pursued voluntarily, at leisure.

Homo faber/homo ludens

From *homo*, the zoological name of the human genus; *faber* being the Latin for work, *ludens* for play. These describe two images of the supposed natural state of humans. In *homo faber*, work is the primary activity and the human existence is based on productive activity; humans express their creativity through the objects they make. Marx's stress on the liberating potential of unfettered labor did much to popularize this. The Dutch historian Johann Huizinga opposed this view, advancing the concept of *homo ludens*, in which irrational play is a primary human capacity that is often stifled by the demands of work, especially in contemporary society. Self realization comes through free, perhaps frivolous, play.

As the nineteenth century drew to an end, most sports took on a much more orderly character: both participants and spectators came to recognize the legitimacy of governing organizations, the standards of conduct they laid down and the structures of rules they observed. The whole direction and rhythm of sport reflected the growing significance of industrial society. In his *Sport: A cultural history*, Richard Mandell writes: "[L]ike concurrent movements in law and government, which led to codification, and rationalization, sport became codified, and civilized by written rules which were enforced by supervising officials (the equivalent of judges and jurors)" (1984: 151).

The reasons for concentrating on nineteenth-century England are: (1) it is here we find something like a factory's smelter shop where rationalized, organized sport appears as an extract from the molten historical trends; (2) the English experience radiated out amongst the imperial colonies and ex-colonies, including North America, with sports, as well as trade, "following the flag"; and (3) it is this period of history that has excited many writers sufficiently to produce theories of the rise of sports in modernity. In the next chapter, I will consider five theoretical approaches that shed light on the reasons for the rapid growth of sports in the late nineteenth and early twentieth centuries and, indeed, for their persistence into the twenty-first.

FURTHER READING

The Eternal Olympics: The art and history of sport, edited by Nicolaos Yaloris (Caratzas Brothers, 1979) is a large-format book, packed with pictures of artifacts and reproductions of artwork, many from the pre-Christian Era. The text comprises a series of essays on the history and development of the ancient Olympic Games.

Sports in America: From wicked amusement to national obsession, edited by David Wiggins (Human Kinetics, 1995) collects 19 essays organized into five parts: (1) Pre-1820; (2) 1820–70; (3) 1870–1915; (4) 1915–45; (5) 1945–Present. The third part, dealing with industrialization and urbanization, is especially relevant; in this, various writers focus on the period 1870–1915.

History of Sport and Physical Activity in the United States, 4th edition, by Betty Spears and Richard A. Swanson (Brown & Benchmark, 1995) is one of the most respected and durable histories of North American sport and should be read in conjunction with *Sports Spectators* by Allen Guttmann (Columbia University Press, 1986) which is densely packed with historical detail on the emergence of sport. Guttmann's focus is far wider than that implied by the title and actually provides a basis for understanding sport. "We are what we watch," writes Guttmann toward the end of the book which captures how sports can be used as a barometer of historical change and one which should be read by any serious student of sport.

Crossing Boundaries: An international anthology of women's experiences in sport, edited by Susan Bandy and Anne Darden (Human Kinetics, 1999) is a collection of materials on the largely undisclosed history of women in sports.

Richard Holt's books, *Sport and the Working Class in Modern Britain* (Manchester University Press, 1990) and *Sport and the British* (Oxford University Press, 1989), examine what now seem to be crude forms of sports and reveal the links between these and today's versions. Older activities gradually faded as industrialization encroached and cultural patterns changed, but Holt emphasizes the continuities and "survivals" from old to new. Complementing these is Hugh Cunningham's *Leisure in the Industrial Revolution* (Croom Helm, 1980).

Combat Sports in the Ancient World by Michael Poliakoff (Yale University Press, 1987) describes in fine detail the early forms of combat, such as the Greeks' *pankration* ("total fight") and Egyptian wrestling. "The will to win is a basic human instinct, but different societies give varying amounts of encouragement (or discouragement) to the individual's attempt to measure himself against others," observes Poliakoff in his chapter entitled "The nature and purpose of combat sport." Elliott J. Gorn's *The Manly Art: Bare-knuckle prize fighting in America* (Cornell University Press, 1986) updates the argument.

Sport History Review, edited by Don Morrow (Human Kinetics), is a biannual journal that concerns itself with sports history.

ASSIGNMENT

Cock-fighting and boxing: these are two sports that have deep historical roots, but which have aroused controversy. Cock-fighting is illegal; and both American and British Medical Associations lobby for a ban on boxing. Despite its illegality, cock-fighting persists underground. Defenders of boxing argue that, if banned, boxing would also go underground, making it more dangerous. But, one might contend that drug-taking is a widespread underground activity and that does not mean we should legalize it. Compare boxing and drug-taking, taking into account that both cost lives, yet both are engaged in by young people on a voluntary basis. If one is legal, should the other be?

leading QUESTIONS

q: How old are sports?

a: 4,000 years, if you accept the theories of Yaloris, who detects evidence of what he calls "true athletic spirit" as long ago as the second millennium Before the Christian Era (BCE).

Others date sports much more recently. It depends on how you define "sports." Most historians tell us to guard against exaggerating the similarities between ancient and medieval contests and contemporary competitions. The actual activities may resemble what we now recognize as sports, but the cultural milieux were completely different and the meanings given to the activities quite unlike today's.

The boundaries we use to separate sports from other areas of life "have been indistinct and not worth noticing in other cultures," writes Mandell. Ancient Greeks, for example, believed winners of events were chosen by gods and the competitions they held were of profound religious importance; as such, athleticism was all-pervasive. Pre-Meiji (before 1868) Japan held archery and equestrian contests, but these were linked to military purposes rather than being purely athletic competitions.

By combining the efforts of various historical scholars, it is possible to construct a timeline that allows us to trace the existence of athletic activities. The dates are, of course, approximate and indicate the time of the first appearance of the activities. The places are often vague, referring to regions rather than the countries as we define them nowadays.

BEFORE THE CHRISTIAN ERA (BCE)

4000	**Mycenae, Hellas (Greece)**. Horse racing.
3000	**Mesopotamia, Sumeria**. Chariot racing. Archery contests. Stick fighting. Paramilitary athletic training.
2300	**Indus River region (Pakistan, India)**. Horse and chariot races. Combat contests.
2000	**Crete, Hellas**. Athletic competition with rules. Bull-leaping, combat contests linked with religious festivals. Throughout Hellas (Greece). Gloved combat contests; foot races, chariot races. Athletic training. Emphasis on victory. **Egypt**. Ball games, staff and knife contests.
2000	**Egypt**. Wrestling contests.
1600	**Minoa**. Combat sports using thonged fists.
1360	**Egypt**. Hunting on Nile.

1200	**Olympia, Hellas**. Beginning of Hellennic Middle Ages. Jumping events, discus, spear throwing, foot and chariot racing, armed combat contests. Funeral games to honor the dead.
776	**Olympia, Hellas**. Inaugural Olympic Games. Foot races only.
708–680.	Pentathlon, wrestling, boxing, *pankration*, horse races added to Olympic program.
600	**Hellas**. Integration of athletics and education. Physical and moral courage intertwined. Healthy body, healthy mind. Rivalries valued in all cultural spheres, including musicians, poets, sculptors etc. Competition for excellence, fame and honor, i.e. *agōn*.
576	**Sparta, Hellas**. Specialized physical training with specialized role of trainer. Athletics part of military education.
400	**Hellas**. Purpose-built athletic stadium. Professional athletes receive subsidies from cities to train full-time.
146	**Greece** subjugated by Romans. Athletics continue, but with increasing emphasis on killing sports, e.g. gladiatorial contests (featuring slaves), *pankration*, archery.

CHRISTIAN ERA (CE)

300	**China**. Equestrian sport. Competitions with military utility, including archery, boxing, wrestling and paramilitary gymnastics.
393	**Rome**. Christian Roman ban on all pagan festivals, including Olympic Games.
410	**Rome**. Fall of Rome. Beginning of Dark Ages → 10th/11th century.
500	**Middle East**. Horse racing.
646	**Japan**. Archery. Equestrian events, including dressage.
900	**Europe**. Equestrian sports. Jousting.
1000	**Japan**. Ball games, possibly adapted from Chinese versions. Sumo.
1100	**Rheinland Pfalz (Germany)**. Tournament attended by 40,000 knights.
1150	**England**. Archery contests.
1400	**Europe** (especially Burgundy, Brabant). Tournaments with equestrian events (including jousting), fencing and sword duels.
1450	**Scotland**. Early forms of golf/hockey ("driving").

1500	**Europe**. International tournaments featuring archery, swordfights, jousts, and other contests.
1555	**Europe**. Ball games, e.g. *calcio* in Italy, *Faustball* in Germany and elsewhere (earlier) among Aztecs, Inuet, Japanese, and Maoris.
1570	**Japan**. Paramilitary sports. Equestrian events. Archery. Swordfighting. Spear-throwing. Shooting. Martial arts, principally competitive jujitsu.
1600	**England**. Rural hunting. Hounds, horses. Prey included boars, wolves, and red deer.
1600	**Europe**. Animal baiting. Dog pits, bear pits, cock pits etc. Rise in gambling. Rural horse racing.
1660	**Germany** and elswhere in Europe. Formal competitive dueling.
1787	**England**. Marylebone Cricket Club (MCC) formed.
1836	**Japan**. Weight-lifting.
1800	**England**. Horse racing in enclosures, early in century.
1858	**USA**. National Association of Base Ball Players (NABP) formed.
1863	**England**. Soccer and rugby divide into distinct sports with own federations.
1867	**England**. Queensberry Rules instituted in boxing.
1870	**Europe, North America, Japan**. Rationalization of sports. Training and trainers appear, growth of organizations to codify and regulate activities and record results. American football acquires its own rules (as distinct from rugby).
1880	**USA, Europe**. Cycling craze among women and men.
1891	**USA**. Basketball invented at YMCA training college in Springfield, Massachusetts. James Naismith credited with being originator.
1896	**Greece**. Modern Olympics (amateur) created. Baron Pierre de Coubertin credited with being originator.

Sources: Coombs (1978); Kühnst (1996); Mandell (1984); Poliakoff (1987); Vandervell and Coles (1980); Yaloris (1979).

More questions . . .

- Is there such a thing as a "competitive instinct"?
- Why were Roman contests so different from Greek athletics?
- Is it fair to describe ancient competitions as "sports"?

Read on . . .

- Kühnst, P., *Sports: A cultural history in the mirror of art* (Verlag der Kunst, 1996).
- Mandell, R. D., *Sport: A cultural history* (Columbia University Press, 1984).
- Poliakoff, M. B., *Combat Sports in the Ancient World: Competition, violence, and culture* (Yale University Press, 1987).
- Yaloris, N. (ed.), *The Eternal Olympics: The art and history of sport* (Caratzas Brothers, 1979).

the hunt for reasons

how theorists have explained sports

ELIAS AND THE FIGURATIONAL APPROACH

"Sportization" is how Norbert Elias refers to the process in which precise and explicit rules governing contests came into being, with a strict application to ensure equal chances for competitors and supervision to observe fairness. He acknowledges that this took place in the nineteenth century and accompanied the English Industrial Revolution. Yet, he is wary of theories that explain one in terms of the other. "Both industrialization and sportization were symptomatic of a deeper-lying transformation of European societies which demanded of their individual members greater regularity and differentiation of conduct," he writes in "An essay on sport and violence" (1986: 151).

The "transformation" had roots as far back as the fifteenth century and involved the gradual introduction of rules and norms to govern human behavior and designate what was appropriate conduct in a given situation; it also involved the rise of impersonal organizations to maintain rules. These reflected a general tendency in Europe toward interdependence: people began to orient their activities to each other, to rely less on their own subsistence efforts and more on those of others, whose tasks would be specialized and geared toward narrow objectives. In time, chains of interdependence were

formed: a division of labor ensured that each individual, or group of individuals, was geared to the accomplishment of tasks that would be vital to countless others. They in turn would perform important activities, so that every member of a society depended on others, and no one was an "island."

The pattern of relationships that emerged is called a *figuration*. For this kind of system to operate with reasonable efficiency, people would have to be discouraged from pursuing their own interests and whims in an unrestrained way. There had to be a method of control over emotions and behavior, particularly violent behavior. The need for control grew more acute in eighteenth-century England, where, in the aftermath of civil strife, many people feared a recurrence, according to Elias and Dunning (1986: 171). The state was the central authority responsible for internal orderliness and overall organization and planning. With the formation of state control came what Elias calls a "civilizing spurt."

Figuration

While, in a general sense, figuration refers to the form, shape, or outline of something, Elias has applied it to interdependent relations between people and used it to represent "chains of functions" between them. Some have found in the concept a new approach to study, while others, like Bauman (in *Sociology*, vol. 13, 1979) have found it reminiscent of more orthodox notions, like "pattern" or "situation," and question the value and originality of the concept.

Here we come across Elias's more general historical account, *The Civilizing Process* (1982), which describes a sweeping trend, or even evolution, in which human societies have controlled the use of violence and encouraged an observance of manners. The two aspects are part of one general tendency. So, for example, the decline of dispute settlements through violence and the rise of social prohibitions on such things as spitting and breaking wind are not unconnected in Elias's scheme. They both represent new standards of conduct in changing figurations. The level of acceptable violence drops as the emergent state takes over the settling of disputes and monopolizes the legitimate use of violence. As rules and conventions develop, they spread to all areas, so that standards are imposed, both externally and internally as well as being controlled by the state; individuals control themselves according to accepted or "correct" codes of conduct.

Since the days of the Ancient Greeks, which is Elias's starting-point, civilization has progressed with the state's power and therefore control over violence within the family and between neighbors, clans, and fiefdoms, increasing at a pace roughly equivalent to our internal controls over emotions and behavior; in other words, self-restraint. (The similarity to Freud's conception of society taming our more primitive urges through the super-ego is quite pronounced here.)

The civilizing process is a vast world trend, but not a completely linear one: there are phases in history when a figuration may "decivilize" and regress to barbarism, tolerating a higher level of violence and ungoverned behavior. This is described by Elias as a "reverse gear." Equally, there is allowance for sharp accelerated movements "forward," such as in the civilizing spurt Elias believes is so crucial to our understanding of modern sport.

While it would caricature the civilizing process to equate it with changes in self-control this particular aspect of the wider development acted as an agent in generating "stress-tensions" which, in turn, agitated the need for organized sport. How does Elias see this happening? First, an abstract observation from Elias's introduction to *Quest for Excitement* (co-edited with Eric Dunning): "In societies where fairly high civilizing standards all round are safeguarded and maintained by a highly effective state-internal control of physical violence, personal tensions of people resulting from conflicts of this kind, in a word, stress-tensions, are widespread" (1986b: 41). Next, most human societies develop some countermeasures against stress-tensions they themselves generate and, as Elias writes in the same introduction, "these activities must conform to the comparative sensitivity to physical violence which is characteristic of people's social habits (customs and dispositions) at the later stages of a civilizing process" (1986b: 41–2).

So, the ways in which people "let off steam" must not violate the standards that have become accepted by society at large. Watching humans mauled by wild animals might have provided stimulating and enjoyable release for the ancient Romans, as might burning live cats or baiting bulls for the English in the nineteenth century. But, the civilizing process, according to Elias, changes our threshold of revulsion for enacting and witnessing violence, so that, nowadays, some cultures in the West find a sport like boxing – relatively mild in historical terms – intolerably violent. The methods we choose to discharge tension closely reflect general standards and sensitivities.

Fox-hunting is Elias's favorite example. Once synonymous with the word "sport," fox-hunting is now an anachronism and pressure against it would have no doubt prompted its demise were it not a pursuit practiced by England's landowning elite. Developing in the late eighteenth century, this peculiarly English sport was quite unlike the simpler, less regulated, and more spontaneous forms of hunting of other countries and earlier ages where people were the main hunters and foxes were one amongst many prey; boar, red deer, and wolves being others. Fox-hunting (itself an example of a figuration) was bound by a strict code of etiquette and idiosyncratic rules, such as that which forbade killing other animals during the hunt. Hounds were trained to follow only the fox's scent, and only they could kill, while humans watched.

The fox itself had little utility apart from its pelt; its meat was not considered edible (not by its pursuers, anyway) and, while it was considered a pest, the fields and forests were full of others which threatened farmers' livestock and crops. The chances of anyone getting hurt in the hunt were minimized, but each course in the wall of security presented a problem of how to retain the immediacy and physical risk that were so important in early times. Elias believes that the elaboration of the rules of hunting were solutions. The rules served to postpone the outcome, or finale, of the hunt and so artificially prolong the process of hunting. "The excitement of the hunt itself had increasingly become the main source of enjoyment for the human participants," argue Elias and Dunning (1986: 166).

What had once been foreplay to the act of killing became the main pleasure. So the fox-hunt was a virtual "pure type" of autotelic hunt: the thrill for participants came in the pace and exhilaration of the chasing and the pleasure of watching violence done without actually doing the killing.

But, the influence of the civilizing spurt is apparent in the restraint imposed and exercised by the participants. The overall trend was to make violence more repugnant to people, which effectively encouraged them to control or restrain themselves. Elias stresses that this should be seen not as a repression but as a product of greater sensitivity. The fox-hunters did not secretly feel an urge to kill with their own hands; they genuinely found such an act disagreeable, but could still find pleasure in viewing it from their horses; what Elias calls "killing by proxy."

Despite all attempts to abolish them, hunts persist to this day, probably guided by appetites similar to those whetted by the sight of humans being masticated by raptors. Hundreds of millions of *Jurassic Park* fans can attest to the enjoyable tension provided by the latter, albeit through the medium of film. While Elias does not cover contemporary hunts, we should add that their longevity reveals something contradictory about the civilizing trend and the impulse to condone or even promote wanton cruelty.

To ensure a long and satisfying chase, and to be certain that foxes are found in the open, "earth stoppers" are employed to close up earths (fox holes) and badger sets in which foxes may take refuge. Many hunts maintain earths to ensure a sufficient supply of foxes through the season (foxes used to be imported from the continent). The hunt does not start until after 11 a.m. to allow the fox time to digest its food and ensure that it is capable of a long run. During the course of a hunt, a fox may run to ground and will either survive or be dug out by the pursuant dogs, a virtual baiting from which even the dogs emerge with damage. New hounds are prepared by killing cubs before the new season, a practice observed and presumably enjoyed by members of the hunt and their guests.

In Elias's theory, fox-hunting was a solution to the problems created by the accelerating trend toward civilization and the internal controls on violence it implied. The closing up of areas of excitement, which in former ages had been sources of pleasurable gratification (as well as immense suffering), set humans on a search for substitute activities and one which did not carry the risks, dangers, or outright disorder that society as a whole would find unacceptable – "the quest for excitement."

The English form of fox-hunting was only one example of a possible solution, but Elias feels it is an "empirical model," containing all the original distinguishing characteristics of today's sport. Other forms of sport, such as boxing, football, cricket, and rugby showed how the problem was solved without the use and abuse of animals; the first two of these were appropriated by the working class. All evolved in a relatively orderly manner, well matched to the needs of modern, bureaucratic society with its accent on organization and efficiency and ultimately in line with the general civilizing process.

The explanation of sport is but one facet of Elias's grand project which is to understand the very nature and consequences of the civilizing process. It follows that critics who are not convinced by his general model are certainly not by his specific one. The actual idea of a civilizing process has the tinge of a theory of progress in which history is set to proceed through predetermined stages which cannot be altered. Elias's mention of the irregularity of the process and the "reverse gear" are rather peripheral to the main thesis which suggests that, as Paul Hoggett puts it, "civilization seems to march onwards fairly straightforwardly without any collapsing back into barbarity" (1986: 36).

Many modern observers of sport might want to argue that "collapses" are quite commonplace and point fingers in the direction of soccer stadia, once the sites of open, almost ritualistic, violence between rival fans. Elias and his devotees would recommend a more detailed examination of history to appreciate that violence has for long been related to soccer; only the media's amplification of it has changed. Presumably the same could be said about fox-hunting which continues unabated today. But, this response is only partially satisfactory, as many other sports have developed violent penumbra quite recently and it is hard to establish any historical connections with, say, boxing, cricket, and rugby, all of which have experienced major crowd disorder over the past few decades.

It is interesting that the nucleus of Elias's model has not been attacked. A basic proposition is that "pleasurable excitement . . . appears to be one of the most elementary needs of human beings," as Elias puts it in his "An essay on sport and violence" (1986a: 174). Yet, Elias never documents the sources of such "needs" and, considering that the entire theoretical edifice rests on them, one might expect some expansion. This is mysteriously absent. Is it a biological drive? Part of a survival instinct? A deep psychological trait? Elias's treatment seems to suggest that the need for "pleasurable excitement" is of a similar order to the need for food, shelter, sex, and other such basic needs. I agree that it appears as basic as these, but I would want to look closely at the changing contexts, social and ecological, in which such needs manifest themselves.

This may seem a small quibble with what is after all a hugely ambitious attempt to illuminate the nature and purpose of modern sport by connecting its changing character to the civilizing transformation of the past several centuries. Far from being an autonomous realm separated from other institutions, sport is totally wrapped up with culture, psyche, and the state. Human "stress-tensions" are linked to large-scale social changes. Yet the analysis still seems caught in a time warp; as Vera Zolberg concludes, it does "not devote adequate attention to one of the most striking features of sport in modern society, that of the business of sport" (1987: 573). The way in which sport has been seized upon by commercial organizations in recent years has tended to show Elias's theory as adequate at a certain level, but unable to cope with the developments imposed on sport by the pressures of professionalism in recent years. The state may once have played a key role in precipitating organized efforts to satisfy basic needs for excitement, but private business has become a powerful force. Alternative theories have tried to link the two.

MARXISM I: THE NARCOTIC EFFECTS OF SPORTS

Sport is a remarkably ironic thing, its chief characteristic being that it provides an entertaining relief from work while at the same time preparing people for more work. This is the central insight of a group of theorists who have, in one way or another, been influenced by the work of Karl Marx. Although Marx himself did not write about sport, his theories have been interpreted by others in a way that provides insights into the political and economic utility of sports.

Marx wrote in the mid-nineteenth century and his focus was modern capitalism, an economic system based on a split of the ownership of the means of production (factories, land, equipment, etc.). Owners of the means of production are bosses, or bourgeoisie, in whose interests capitalism works and who are prepared to milk the system to its limits in order to stay in control. The working class, or proletariat, are forced to work for them in order to subsist. As the system does not work in their interests, they have to be persuaded that it could if only they were luckier, or had better breaks, or worked harder. In other words, the system itself is fine; it's actually the workers who need to change for the good. As long as workers are convinced of the legitimacy of economic arrangements, then capitalism is not under threat. So the system has evolved methods of ensuring its own survival. And this is where sport fits in.

Because Marx's own thought was subjected to so many different interpretations, it was inevitable that no single analysis would emerge that could claim to be "what Marx would have written about sport had he been alive today." When theories of sports bearing Marx's imprimatur began to surface in the early 1970s, they were far from uniform, their only linking characteristic being that sports were geared to the interests of the bourgeoisie, or middle class, had the effect of neutralizing any political potential in the working class and contributed in some way to the preservation of the status quo. Sports were, in other words, to be criticized, not just analyzed.

The principal scholars claiming to work with a Marxist approach were the American Paul Hoch, Jean-Marie Brohm, a French writer, and the German theorist, Bero Rigauer. Other commentators, such as Richard Gruneau, John Hargreaves, Mark Naison, Brian Stoddart, and William Morgan later contributed toward what has now become a respectable body of Marxist literature on sports. The work of Hoch, Brohm, and Rigauer is informed by the spirit of the Frankfurt School, and which we can summarize as Critical Theory. The second takes as its starting-point the theories of the Italian Marxist Antonio Gramsci, whose central concept of hegemony has provided a focus for studies of sport and which we will cover in the next subsection.

Sports serve four main functions for capitalism, according to John Hargreaves. First, organized sport helps train a "docile labor force": it encourages in the working class an acceptance of the kind of work discipline demanded in modern production; hard work is urged in both sport and work. We have noted before how the organization and tempo of industry became reflected in sport and Hargreaves sees the congruence as almost perfect. In his *Sport, Culture and Ideology*, Hargreaves compares the features of sport and industry: "A high degree of specialisation and standardisation, bureaucratised and hierarchical administration, long-term planning, increased reliance on science and technology, a drive for maximum productivity, a quantification of performance and, above all, the alienation of both producer and consumer" (1982: 41).

Major events, like the Olympic Games and Super Bowl, are given as examples of the final point. Second, sport has become so thoroughly commercialized and dominated by market forces that events and performers are treated as – or perhaps just are – commodities that are used by capitalist enterprises: "Sport is produced, packaged and sold like any other commodity on the market for mass consumption at enormous profits" (1982: 41).

The trading or transfer of players typifies the "commodification." The third area in which sport fits in is in "expressing the quintessential ideology in capitalist society." What Marxist theorists have proposed here is that sport works in subtle ways at indicating qualities or imperatives in people; all these qualities have counterparts in society at large. Aggressive individualism, ruthless competitiveness, equal opportunity, elitism, chauvinism, sexism, nationalism: all these are regarded as admirable. Their desirability is not questioned in sports and the uncritical approach to them is carried over to society. Fourth, there is the area of the state: this bureaucratic administration represents capitalist interests. It follows that every intrusion into sport by the state must be seen as some sort of attempt to link sports participation with the requirements of the capitalist system.

Four areas, then, but hardly a theory; they are really only the lowest common denominators for all those favoring a Marxist conception of sport. Beyond these, there are a variety of theories all taking their lead from Marx in the sense that they see the split over the means of production as central. In other words, sport has to be analyzed in terms of class relations. In 1972, Paul Hoch published his *Rip Off the Big Game: The exploitation of sports by the power elite*, in which he advanced one of the most acerbic Marxist critiques of sport, which he likened to the mainstream religions about which Marx himself wrote much. Religion was regarded as little more than a capitalist convenience, absorbing workers' energies and emotions and supplying a salve after the week's labors.

Sport has much the same significance. Both religion and sport work as an opiate that temporarily dulls pain and gives a false sense of well-being, but which is also a dangerous and debilitating narcotic that can reduce its users to a helpless state of dependence. The attraction of sport is as compelling as that of religion and its effects are comparable: it siphons off potential that might otherwise be put to political use in challenging the capitalist system.

The title of Jean-Marie Brohm's book indicates his position on contemporary sport: *Sport: A prison of measured time* (1978). By this, Brohm means that the institutional, rule-governed, highly organized structure of modern sport has been shaped by capitalist interest groups in such a way as to represent a constraint rather than a freedom. Sport is in no sense an alternative to work, less still an escape from it "since it removes all bodily freedom, all creative spontaneity, every aesthetic dimension and every playful impulse" (1978: 175).

The competitor is merely a prisoner, whose performances are controlled, evaluated, and recorded, preferably in quantitative terms. Capitalism as a system stifles the human imagination and compresses the human body into mindless production work; and as sport is but one part of that system, it can do little more than reproduce its effects. It just obeys the "logic" of the system. As Richard Gruneau writes in his *Class, Sports and Social Development*: "For Brohm, capitalism has shaped sport in its own image" (1983: 38).

Others, like Bero Rigauer, in his *Sport and Work*, agree with the basic assumptions and emphasize how corporations have penetrated, or completely taken over sport. It is as if sport has been appropriated by one class and used to bolster its already commanding position in the overall class structure (1981). For Rigauer, sport has aided the economic system by improving the health of workers and so minimizing the time lost at work through illness.

Like Brohm, he sees a "technocratic" take-over of sport, with performances being subject to rationalization and planning, and training becoming more time-absorbing and important than performance itself. Initiative and creativity are stifled, rendering the human performer as the "one-dimensional man," so called by the Marxist philosopher Herbert Marcuse (from whom Brohm and Rigauer draw insights). In all accounts, the human beings are depicted as passive dopes, pushed around by factors beyond their control. But are humans just like hockey pucks? Do they really respond so readily and easily? Those who think not find the work of Hoch and Brohm rather too deterministic – all thoughts and behavior are determined by outside forces emanating from the capitalist system. Sport is but one tool for maintaining the domination and exploitation of the working class.

In contrast, other writers prefer to see the working class playing a more active role. Certainly, there is a complementarity between the way in which modern sport is organized and the functions it fulfills on the one hand, and the requirements of capitalism on the other. But this does not deny that different groups (classes) are involved in different sports and at different levels at different stages in history. Sport is not, as Hargreaves puts it, "universally evil." Its meaning and significance have to be investigated more closely. Other Marxist writers, including Gruneau and Hargreaves himself, have attempted to do this. All would go along with the more orthodox Marxist approach, but only so far.

Sport is much more multifaceted than the others acknowledge. It may give substance to wider ideologies and slough off working-class energies, but it can also be useful as a builder of solidarity within working class groups which are brought together with a common purpose. "It is precisely this type of solidarity that historically has formed the basis for a trenchant opposition to employers," observes Hargreaves (1986: 110).

Public gatherings at sports events have always generated a potential for disorder and have attracted the state's agents of control. Some writers have even inferred a form of political resistance from the exploits of soccer hooligans. So, involvement in sport can actually facilitate or even encourage challenge rather than accommodation. Far from being a means of controlling the masses, sport, on occasion, has needed controlling itself. On the issue of sport as a preparation for work, Hargreaves reminds us that not all sports resemble the rhythms and rationality of work. Fishing and bowling provide relaxation and relief in very stark contrast to work.

Hargreaves (1986) argues against a firmly negative view of sport as providing only "surrogate satisfactions for an alienated mass order ... perpetuating its alienation" and instead argues for a more flexible, spontaneous interpretation. Sport may perform many services in the interests of the status quo, amongst them a belief in the ultimate triumph of ability ("if you're good you'll make it" – in sport or life generally). It also helps fragment the working class by splintering loyalties into localities, regions, etc. But it can also provide a basis for unity and therefore resistance to dominant interest groups: "Part mass therapy, part resistance, part mirror image of the dominant political economy," as David Robins puts it (1982: 145).

MARXISM II: CULTURAL POWER

Even those who stick valiantly to Marx's first principles are embarrassed by the literalism of this type of approach: staying true to Marx and applying his class-based formula to virtually any phenomenon is like trying to vault with a pole made of timber: not only is it heavy, but it's rigid. Other writers have opted for more flexibility, taking basic Marxist ideas as they have been reinterpreted by later theorists, in particular Antonio Gramsci. Hegemony theorists wanted to restore the role of the human being to that of an agent, someone who was active and could intervene in practical matters rather than just respond to the logic of capitalism.

According to hegemony theory, there is nothing intrinsic to sports that make them conservative or subversive: they have no essential qualities. Under capitalism, sports have been supportive to the existing order of things; but there is no necessary reason why, given different circumstances, they could not have a liberating effect. But, for Gruneau in particular, as sports become more structured in their institutional forms, they constrain and regulate much more than liberate their participants. The kind of liberating features of sport he has in mind are spontaneity, freedom of expression, aesthetic beauty. Politically, sports can yield the kind of solidarity that contributes toward the women's movement, civil rights campaigns and other types of protests against injustice and inequality. In sports, there are opportunities to mobilize against the status quo, not just comply with it.

Historically, this has not been the case and the enthusiasm for sports, particularly among the working class, has bolstered the social order. Flocking

---

Hegemony

From the Greek *hegemon*, meaning leader, this refers to leadership, supremacy or rule, usually by one state over a confederacy, or one class over another. It has been used in a specifically Marxist way by Antonio Gramsci, who sought to understand how ruling, or leading, groups in a capitalist society maintain their power by indirect rather than direct economic or military means. They do so by creating a culture that is shared by all but which favors one class over another, usually the most deprived. It is a domination, but of intellect or thought rather than body, though ultimately there is a relation because the labor of subordinate groups is exploited. It is important to appreciate that hegemony is not some artificial contrivance: it is a genuinely felt set of beliefs, ideas, values, and principles, all of which work in a supportive way for the status quo and hence appear as common sense. According to Gramsci, an entire apparatus is responsible for diffusing ideas that complement and encourage consensus. These include the Church, education, the media, political institutions, and, if Stoddart, Naison and others are to be accepted, sports.

---

to sports as amusement, the working class assimilates its values and principles, most of which dovetail perfectly with those of the wider society. Fair play and the opportunity to go as far as one's ability allows are sacrosanct in sports: meritocratic ideals are important in society too. One legitimates the other. Forgotten is the fact that, in any capitalist system, there are gross, structured inequalities in the distribution of income, wealth, and prestige and that these are replicated one generation after the next through an inheritance system that favors rich over poor. For hegemony theorists, it is important that those at the poorer end of the class structure regard this as commonsensical; that they are not constantly questioning the legitimacy of a system that consigns them to also-rans. Sports encourage this by promoting the good of meritocracy and the equality of life chances that seem to be available to everyone, but, in reality, are not.

Two oft-neglected writers, Mark Naison and Brian Stoddart, have offered studies of sports that draw on Gramsci's concept of hegemony and its role in supporting empires. Naison's early article, "Sports and the American empire" (1972) and Stoddart's analysis of the "Sport, cultural imperialism, and colonial response in the British empire" (1988) advance our understanding of the economic and political utility of sports in stabilizing what might otherwise be disruptive colonial situations. Both writers acknowledge the work of C. L. R. James, whose historical analysis of cricket showed how the values supposedly embodied in the sport were disseminated throughout the Caribbean and how these were of enormous benefit to a colonial regime endlessly trying to manage the local populations.

Sport for both Naison and Stoddart is a means of cultural power, not direct political power as suggested by the others. "Athletic events have increasingly reflected the dynamics of an emergent American imperialism," writes Naison (1972: 96). "As the American political economy 'internationalized' in the post-war period, many of its most distinctive cultural values and patterns, from consumerism to military preparedness, have become an integral part of organized sports." And Stoddart: "Through sport were transferred dominant British beliefs as to social behavior, standards, relations, and conformity, all of which persisted beyond the end of formal empire" (1988: 651).

By participating in sports, populations who came under American and British influences were taught teamwork, the value of obeying authority, courage in the face of adversity, loyalty to fellow team members (especially the captain) and, perhaps most importantly, respect for rules. Stoddart writes of cricket, though it could be applied to any sport: "To play cricket or play the game meant being honest and upright, and accepting conformity within the conventions as much as it meant actually taking part in a simple game" (1988: 653).

Ruling over colonies in far-flung parts of the globe could have been achieved by military force; indeed, it was initially. But coercion is not cost-effective, especially so when the geographical distance between the metropolitan centers and the peripheral colonies was as great as it was, particularly in the British case. But, if a population could be persuaded that the colonial rule was right and proper, then this made life easier for the masters. Sport provided a way of inculcating people with the kind of values and ideas that facilitated British rule and a "vehicle of adjustment to American imperialism, its popularity an index of America's success in transmitting adulation of its culture and values" (Naison 1972: 100).

None of this suggests a passive acceptance of the rule of America or Britain. As Thomas Sowell writes in his *Race and Culture: A world view*: "Conquest, whatever its benefits, has seldom been a condition relished by the conquered. The struggle for freedom has been as pervasive throughout history as conquest itself" (1994: 79).

By exporting institutions as strong as sport it was possible to create shared beliefs and attitudes between rulers and ruled, at the same time creating distance between them. Organized sports, remember, were products of the imperial powers, most of the rules being drawn up and governing bodies being established between the 1860s and 1890s, exactly the period when the imperialism was at its height. The rulers, having experience with sport, were obviously superior and this reinforced the general notion they tried to convey – that they were suited to rule, as if by divine appointment.

The rules of sports were codified at a central source, transferred to all parts of the vast imperial web, then adhered to by people of astonishingly diverse backgrounds. The colonial experience in general was not unlike this: ruling from a center and engineering a consensus among millions. Impoverished groups over whom Americans and British ruled were introduced to sports by their masters. When they grew proficient enough to beat them, that posed another problem. West Indian cricketers became adept at repeatedly bowling fast balls which were virtually unplayable. South Africa developed a style of rugby that made it almost invincible. Australia beat England regularly at cricket. The problem as it was seen on British soil was that such achievements might be "interpreted as symbolic of general parity," as Stoddart puts it (1988: 667). Baseball was "popularized by the increasing number of American corporate and military personnel" in Puerto Rico, the Dominican Republic, Venezuela, Mexico, and elsewhere, writes Naison (1972). Now, many players from those countries play in US leagues.

The concept of sport as a purveyor of imperial culture is a powerful one, especially when allied to a Marxist analysis of the role of ideas in maintaining social structures. Sport, in the eyes of critics like Naison and Stoddart, is not the blunt instrument many other Marxists take it to be. For them, its value to ruling groups is in drawing subordinate groups toward an acceptance of ideas

---

Imperialism

From the Latin *imperium*, meaning absolute power or dominion over others, this refers to the political and economic domination of one or several countries by one other. The union of the different countries, known as colonies, is the empire. There is an unequal relationship between the ruling sovereign country, sometimes known as the metropolitan center, and the peripheral colonies which are reduced to the status of dependants rather than partners. Technically, the USA's colonial dependencies have been few compared to, say, Britain or those of other European powers in the 19th and early 20th centuries. But its indirect political influence and its economic pre-eminence over a vast network of other countries have convinced many that there is a North American imperialism.

that are fundamental to their control. This was appropriate in the empires of America and Britain, where orders and directives came from a central source; just like the rules of any sport.

For theorists influenced by Marxism, sports can never be seen as neutral. They can be enjoyed; indeed they must be enjoyable to be effective. If we spotted the surreptitious purposes of sports, we could hardly be gratified by them at all. For them to work, sports must be seen as totally disengaged from the political and economic processes. In the colonial situation, it was crucial that sports were enjoyed and transmitted from one generation to the next. Yet, according to Marxism, this should not deflect our attentions totally away from the valuable functions sports have served – and probably still serve – in the capitalist enterprise at home and abroad. This gives a different slant to the variety of Marxism that sees sports in a one-dimensional way: as politically safe channels, or outlets for energies that might otherwise be disruptive to capitalism. Yet, it clearly complements it in identifying the main beneficiary of sports as capitalism.

WEBER'S MODEL: RATIONALIZATION AND THE PROTESTANT ETHIC

Max Weber's theories are typically seen as either a direct challenge to Marx's or an attempt to augment them with additional ideas. Unlike Marx and his followers who emphasized the role of material, economic, or productive factors in shaping all aspects of social life, Weber believed ideas and beliefs played a significant role; not in isolation, but in combination with the kind of material factors Marx had played-up. In particular, Weber argued that the rise of modern capitalism is, in large part, a result of the diffusion of Protestant tenets throughout Europe and America. Protestantism did not cause capitalism, but its principles and values and those of early capitalism were so complementary that Weber detected an "elective affinity" between them. The attachment is what Weber, in the title of one of his major books, called *The Protestant Ethic and the Spirit of Capitalism* (1958).

The Protestant ethic that emerged in the sixteenth century and, over the next 300 years spread through Europe and the United States, embraced values, attitudes, and behaviors; it encouraged rational asceticism (or austerity), goal-orientation (ambition), constancy (determination), thrift, individual achievement, a consciousness of time, and work as a "calling." In other words, the ethic encouraged the very beliefs and action that were conducive to the rise of business enterprises and, eventually, capitalist economies. While it was originally a religiously-inspired protocol, the Protestant ethic transferred to everyday life, promoting human labor to a central position in the moral life of the individual and elevating the business entrepreneur to an exalted status. Laboring in one's chosen vocation was extolled in sermons and in popular literature (for example, the writings of Cotton Mather, Benjamin Franklin, and Thomas Carlyle) as both a duty and a vehicle for personal fulfillment.

To understand how all this ties in with the growth of sports, we need to go back to the time before the Protestant ethic had risen. The Renaissance was a period beginning in the early fifteenth century, in which individuals seemed to find release. Starting in Italy, then spreading throughout Europe, creativity, self-expression, and imaginative construction became watchwords. Europe underwent an extraordinarily fertile period of cultural rebirth in which many great masterworks in art, architecture, and engineering were produced.

One of the effects of this was a growth in play and recreation. As artists and scientists were released to exercise their imaginations on new, previously undreamed-of projects, so others were released to express themselves in playful physical activities. Ball games in particular enjoyed a surge in popularity. Elementary forms of tennis and handball emerged, known as *palo della mano*, *racchetta*, and *paletta*. A rough and often dangerous version of football called *calcio* was also played. These and other games had none of the organization or regulation of contemporary sports and they were played in a rather different spirit: the object was to take pleasure from the activities – not necessarily to win.

As playful games gained in popularity, they fostered occasions for spectators to watch. Not that this made them any more competitive. For example, fencing contests were closer to acrobatic exhibitions than outright conflicts: opportunities to express one's physical abilities in front of audiences. In this sense, they had some resemblance to the ancient Egyptian games of the second millennium BCE. Of the latter, J. Sakellarakis writes: "The sole purpose of such displays of athletic prowess was to entertain a spectacle-loving people rather than to serve an ideal similar to that expressed by the later Greek Olympic Games" (1979: 14).

In the Renaissance, no higher values of glory or honor were embodied in games: they were to be enjoyed and watched, plain and simple. Urban festivals and tournaments became popular throughout Europe in the fifteenth and sixteenth centuries. Inter-town rivalries were friendly, if raucous. The predominant Roman Catholic Church at first tried to outlaw the carnival-like activities; they had no obvious utility, either practically or spiritually. Faced with a gathering momentum of interest in games such as *calcio*, the Church eventually conceded and actually recognized such pastimes by allowing them to played on Holy Days, a tradition which has endured in one way or another.

Catholicism's influence waned as the belief that human beings could shape their own destinies gained currency. Among the most influential Protestant reformers was John Calvin, who lived between 1509 and 1564, and taught that humans, rather than remain subservient to papal dictates, could save their own souls and change the world around them in the process. Human conduct should be ordered according to divine ends, asserted Calvin: discipline, abstinence and the avoidance of pleasures of the flesh were among the many principles he laid down. So, the playful activities about which the Catholic Church had been reserved, were quite definitely opposed. Those accepting the ethic of Protestantism were forbidden from taking part in anything so frivolous and cheerful as game-playing.

The Catholic Church's response to the challenge of the Reformation was to reinterpret tournaments, festivals, and carnivals at which games were played as representations of the Catholic faith, performed for the greater glory of God and serving the added purpose of maintaining a healthy body. But, as Protestantism grew and the science it encouraged developed, magic, mysticism, and many theological doctrines were driven out in a process Weber called the "disenchantment" of the natural world. Catholicism came under attack, as did all activities that involved expressive human movement.

In his book *The Influence of the Protestant Ethic on Sport and Recreation*, Steven J. Overman pays close attention to the consistency between the ethical principles and the impulses that led to the rise of what he calls "rationalized sport" which was "built on the prerequisite that sport was to be taken seriously" (1997: 161). Activities that were once regarded as useless and trivial were rationalized in a way that made them agreeable to Protestants. By this, Overman means that the casual, impromptu and hit-or-miss nature of games and sport-like activities were turned into pursuits that bear much closer resemblance to today's regulated sports.

Older cultures, including Spartan and Roman, had exploited the utilitarian potential of sport, linking training and competition to military purposes. The athletic field was a perfect preparation for combat. In *Max Weber: From history to modernity*, Bryan S. Turner notes that, while never enthusiastic about athletic contests in themselves, nineteenth-century Protestants were prepared to interpret athletic activities as having a rational motive: they promoted healthy bodies, strengthened "character" and assisted the production of a hale and hearty population that was habituated to discipline and hard work (1992: 120–21).

In other eras, athletic competition or games might have been pleasurable escapes from the grind of everyday life. But the Protestants preferred to stress their pragmatic value. The seriousness of purpose that directed action toward goals, the stress on calculable outcomes rather than sheer chance and the avoidance of pleasures of the flesh were features of the Protestant ethic;

but they were also features of the newly-rationalized athletic contests that emerged in the late eighteenth and nineteenth centuries.

The labor-intensive character of sports and recreation had been recognized years earlier. The late seventeenth-century scientist Robert Boyle observed that "tennis . . . is much more toilsome than what many others make work"; and the philosopher John Stuart Mill mused "many a day spent in killing game includes more muscular fatigue than a day's plowing." Such views chimed well with Protestants who championed hard work: they denounced monks as lazy parasites because their lifestyle did not count as work. Early settlers in North America were even suspicious about Indian males who hunted, while females did the real physical work – laboring in the fields, rearing children, and preparing food.

The conception of athletics as paid work goes way back before 1869 when the Cincinnati Red Stockings became the first salaried club, or 1864 when the English instituted the "gentlemen *vs* players" distinction to ensure that the working-class players who were paid were not genuine "sportsmen." But, after the 1860s, professionalism began to change sports. For example, an old practice first used in fifth-century BCE Sparta was revived: employing a specialist person to supervise training. The coach, or trainer, was given the responsibility of ensuring that athletes prepared adequately for their event; this meant taking sports seriously, using rational planning, systematic routines and, perhaps most importantly, exercising self-discipline. All had analogous features in the Protestant ethic.

If the devil makes work for idle hands, there was no room for his enterprise in sports. Work and productivity replaced pleasure and recreation in several sports, a notable exception being the Olympic Games, which were re-introduced in a modern form in 1896. The Olympic movement strove to create a tenuous and largely artificial link with the ancient games that ceased in AD 393. As such, it prohibited professional competitors and allowed only those who participated in athletics for the honor and pride of competing. Early games were not the spectacles we have become used to in recent decades: programs of events were smaller and competitors were poorly-prepared – training was frowned on by amateurs.

Yet, by the 1924 Olympics, a more goal-directed approach had begun to appear. Hugh Hudson's 1981 film *Chariots of Fire* captures the emergent trend nicely. Leading up to the games, the two central athletes, Harold Abrahams and Eric Liddell, are steadfast in the training, Abrahams actually using a professional coach Sam Mussabini (who is not even allowed into the stadium because he has been paid) to oversee his regimen. Yet a third competitor, Lord Andrew Lindsay, presents an alternative portrait of the English gentleman competitor of the 1920s: he places champagne flutes on the edge of his hurdles during practice runs to deter him from clipping them and spilling his favorite tipple. After training (and, occasionally, before) he partakes in a few glasses of champagne. He is the complete gentleman-amateur, with no trace of the single-mindedness, less still the ruthlessness that gradually takes hold of his fellow Oxford student Abrahams.

While amateurism – from the Latin *amorosus*, pertaining to love – was not sacrificed by the International Olympic Committee until much later, the elevation of winning over just competing became a more prominent feature. And winning required hard work, discipline in training and efficiency in performance. A further point of symmetry between the Olympics and the ethic that guided society into industrial modernity was the exactitude of its record-keeping. Quantification was absolutely vital for industrialism, of course. The Olympic Games, like their ancient predecessors, kept strict registers of results. With the technological benefit of accurate timepieces, the modern games were able to log times and distances, setting in motion a quest for record-breaking performances.

This is one of the characteristics Allen Guttmann believes marks out the traditional from the modern society, the others being secularism (decline of religion), equality, specialization, rationalism, and bureaucratic organization. In his book *From Ritual to Record: The nature of modern sports*, Guttmann argues that, while sports, or at least their progenitors, were originally intended as alternatives to work, they became reflections of it (1978). Overman goes even further: "The Protestant sport ethos succeeded in transforming sport into a regimen of goal-directed behaviors which are the antithesis of pure play" (2000: 338)

By the end of the 1920s, the meaning and purpose of sport had completely changed: sports had become organized, regulated, and subject to rules. The rational planning that Weber had analyzed as a major feature of modernity had supplanted the spontaneity and freedom of earlier forms of play. The focus of sports narrowed: to coin a phrase, winning was the only thing. And this was consistent with a Protestant ethic that praised and honored the accomplishment that derives from exertion, perseverance, abstinence, and self-control. Rewards are not given; they are earned.

In presenting a model of the Protestant ethic and its pivotal role in the rise of capitalism, Weber did not intend to explain the mutation of sports into the rational activities we witness today. But his analysis offers a way of recognizing how the ethic that conferred on work a positive status, stressing its benefits and condemning idleness, made a considerable impact on reshaping sports.

AN ETHOLOGICAL CONCEPTION: MORRIS

While he dismisses most of the Marxist approaches to sport as "political clap-trap," Desmond Morris discerns a "small grain of truth" in the idea that events that fascinate, excite, and entertain people also distract them from "political terrorism and bloody rebellion." But, on examination, this aspect of sport "is not political after all, but rather has to do with human nature" (1981: 20). Morris, as a student of animal behavior and who affords humans pride of place in his perspective, has turned his sights to sport in his book *The Soccer Tribe*.

Morris begins from an observation of the 1978 soccer World Cup Final between Argentina and Holland, an event comprising 22 brightly clad figures "kicking a ball about in a frenzy of effort and concentration" on a small patch of grass, and watched by something like one-quarter of the entire world's population. "If this occurrence was monitored by aliens on a cruising UFO, how would they explain it?" asks Morris. His book is a kind of answer.

Morris adopts the role of the puzzled, detached observer, recording notes in the ship's log in an effort to discover "the function of this strange activity" and, while his sights are fixed on soccer, his records have relevance for all sports. His rejection of the Marxist "social drug" approach is understandable, for Morris's ethology follows that of Konrad Lorenz, who believed that aggression is instinctive in all animals, including humans (*On Aggression*, 1966). Sport is truly a "safe" diversion from violent behavior. But were political systems to change, the aggression would still exist and would still need an outlet. Political frustrations may aggravate aggressive tendencies, but they do not cause them. This removes the need for any detailed social or psychological theory: sport in general and soccer in particular are grand occasions for venting instinctively violent urges.

Morris goes on to expose several interesting facets, the first being the ritual hunt. Morris's initial premise is much the same as the one offered in this book: that the predecessors of sport were activities that "filled the gap left by the decline of the more obvious hunting activities." The activities passed through a series of phases, the final one being symbolic in which players represent hunters, the ball is their weapon and the goal the prey. Football players "attack" goals and "shoot" balls. Sport is a disguised hunt, a ritual enactment.

Morris calls today's athletes "pseudo-hunters" whose task of killing the inanimate prey is deliberately complicated by introducing opponents to obstruct them, making it a "reciprocal hunt." Goalkeepers of a soccer team resemble "claws" of a cornered prey "lashing out to protect its vulnerable surface." Its parallels with hunting have given soccer global appeal. Some sports, such as archery, darts, bowling, billiards, snooker, skeet, skittles, curling, croquet, and golf, all concentrate on the climax of a hunt in the sense that they all involve aiming at a target. They lack the physical risks and exertions of a headlong chase and the necessary co-operation between members of the hunting pack. Tennis and squash are more physical, but, unless played in doubles, lack teamwork. Some sports, especially motor racing, capture the chase aspect of hunting and also retain dangers.

Basketball, netball, volleyball, hockey, cricket, baseball, lacrosse, and rugby football have plenty of fast-flowing movement and a climactic aiming at targets. Yet the risk of physical injury is not too high. Morris believes that, apart from soccer, only Australian rules football and ice hockey approach what he calls the "magic mixture." The former has been isolated geographically and the latter suffers because the small puck (the "weapon") makes it difficult for spectators to follow the play (while Morris does not mention it, attempts have been made to resolve this by experimenting with a luminous puck that is easier for television cameras to pick up). Soccer seems to capture all the right elements in its ritual and has the potential for involving spectators to an intense degree, which makes watching all the more satisfying.

For all its ritual, soccer – and for that matter many other sports – has a tendency to degenerate into what Morris calls a stylized battle. At the end of play there is usually a winner and a loser, and this is not a feature of hunts. Soccer caricatures many other sports in arousing its spectators; fans seethe and fight, they are outraged at bad play or decisions, and euphoric at good results. Other sports engender similar reactions, but at a milder level. At least one piece of research has put this to the test, focusing on hooliganism at football stadia as "ritualized aggression" in that it is not typically violent in a destructive way, but conforms to an "order" with unwritten rules and codes of behavior. As befits an ethological approach, comparisons are made with non-human species which use ritual displays of aggression for various purposes, but do so without transgressing boundaries. The stylized war for Peter Marsh and his co-writers, Elizabeth Prosser and Rom Harré, is bounded by *The Rules of Disorder* (1978).

In a similar vein, Morris argues that sport serves as a safety valve through which people vent their spleen in a way which would be unacceptable in many other contexts. But attending an emotional event, as well as providing an outlet for anger and frustrations built up during the week's work, may add a new frustration if the result is not satisfactory and so make the spectators and players feel worse than before. So, the fan (who happens to be male in Morris's example) "goes home feeling furious. Back at work on Monday, he sees his boss again and all the pent-up anger he felt against the soccer opponents wells up inside him" (1981: 20). So, every game is therapeutic and inflammatory "in roughly equal proportions."

Another ambiguous function of sport is its capacity to act as a status display. Again, Morris writes about soccer, but in terms that can be adapted to fit other sports: "If the home team wins a match, the victorious local supporters can boast an important psychological improvement, namely an increased sense of local status" (1981: 20). Soccer, like most other organized sports, developed in a period of industrialization; as we have noted, many British clubs began life as factory teams. A successful side conferred status not only on the team, but on the firm and even the area. Winning teams and individuals are still held in esteem locally because a victory for them means a victory for the community or region.

The conferment of status is quite independent of objective material positions. Since the publication of Morris's book, this aspect of his argument has become more relevant, as depressed areas in which local manufacturing industries have collapsed or in which communities have been destroyed have yearned for success through sport. The troubled West Midlands city of Coventry was boosted by the local football club's first-ever English Football Association (FA) cup win in 1987. Northern Ireland gained respite from destruction and bloodshed on fight nights when boxing occupied center stage in the sports world. On a national level, staging a major sports event can have an uplifting effect economically and politically as well as culturally on a whole country, as Hugh Dauncey and Geoff Hare show in their collection of essays *France and the 1998 World Cup*.

Morris's fourth function of sport as a religious ceremony is arguably the most underdeveloped in his assessment, but others before him have expanded on this concept. Like a religious gathering, a sporting event draws large groups of people together in a visible crowd; it temporarily unites them with a commonly and often fervently held belief not in a deity but in an individual sports performer, or a team. Sport is a great developer of social solidarity; it makes people feel they belong to a strong homogeneous collectivity which has a presence far greater than any single person. Morris equates the rise of sport with secularization: "As the churches . . . emptied with the weakening of religious faith, the communities of large towns and cities have lost an important social occasion" (1981: 23). The function has been taken over by sport.

This argument has been expressed by a number of writers, perhaps most famously by Michael Novak, whose book *The Joy of Sport* is a reverent acknowledgment of the ecstatic elements of sport (1976). Certainly, the general view that sport has assumed the position of a new religion is a persuasive one and is supported by the mass idolatry that abounds in modern sport. (For the most complete study of the relationship, see Shirl Hoffman's *Sport and Religion*, 1992.) We need look no further than the opening or closing ceremonies at the Olympic Games, or half-time at the Super Bowl, to see the most stupendous, elaborate displays of ritual and liturgy. These are precisely the type of rituals that have been integral to mass religious worship in the past.

The purposes they serve would be similar. In measurable terms, one could suggest that sport is more popular than religion: far more people watch sport than go to church; sport gets far more media attention than religion. Sports performers are better-known than religious leaders. In all probability, people discuss sport more than they do religion. So, it seems feasible to say that sport occupies a bigger part of people's lives than does religion.

But religion is intended to provide transcendental reference points beyond everyday experience; it gives moral guidelines; it instructs, informs, and enlightens. Some fanatics may believe sport does all these things. Realistically, it does not, though this is not the thrust of the argument. Do religious believers follow the guidelines or learn from the enlightenment? Some might respond that sports fans do. Otherwise, why ask Mika Hakkinen to tell people to wear TAG Heuer watches, or Mario Lemieux to appear in Old Spice ads? People follow sports with much the same zeal and commitment as active church-goers follow religion and, although it might seem insulting to religious adherents, sports fans do pursue a faith, albeit in their own way.

The comparison between sport and religion extends beyond superficial resemblances when we recognize that sport has become a functional substitute, supplying for the follower a meaningful cause, an emblematic focus, and a source of allegiance, even belonging. But there is still another way in which sport fills a vacuum left by religion and here we move on to the concept of sport as a social drug. Morris, who is dismissive of Marxist theories of sport, fails to make the connection between the two functions. The "opiate thesis" we encountered earlier, when applied to sport shows how sport can function to keep workers' minds off political revolt and so preserve the status quo – which is, according to Marx, what religion was supposed to do. Morris, in rebutting this, states the argument rather crudely, making sport seem a "bourgeois-capitalist plot," a conspiracy orchestrated by the bosses. As we saw in previous sections, this isn't quite the intention of Marxist writers.

There are two residual functions, both of which Morris concedes are exaggerations. As big business sport is commercialized and run effectively as if making money was the sole organizing principle. This is partly true, but misses the reason for the involvement of the "vast majority" which is because they "love" sport. "Money is a secondary factor," according to Morris. As theatrical performance, showbusiness influences are very evident in sport nowadays and the suggestion is that sport has become a mass entertainment. This is true for football, boxing, baseball, and other sports, but not for bowls, netball, judo, and many other minority sports. Even then, sport, by definition, can never be pure entertainment for as soon as the unpredictable element of competition is gone, it ceases. It then becomes pure theater.

THEORY	Marxist	Figurational	Weberian	Ethological
DYNAMIC	Class conflict	Social configuration	Rationalization	Human nature
CENTRAL TREND	Hegemonic control	Civilizing process	Growth of capitalism	Instinct suppression
SOURCE	Economic power	Control of violence	Religious beliefs + economic change	Innate aggression
REASON	Distraction	Quest for excitement	Reflection of social organization	Symbolic hunt
EFFECTS	Pacification of working class	Stress-tension release	Rationalization of sports	Outlet for violence

theories of sports

Morris's treatment is not a formal theory, but a catalog of functions which soccer serves, as indeed do all sports at various levels, from the psychological to the political. There is no attempt to link the functions together, nor much evaluation of which functions are most effective. Its minor strengths lie in drawing our attention to the many ways in which sport has embedded itself in modern culture and the modern psyche. Try thinking of something that can simultaneously function as a stylized battle, a religious ceremony, and a status display. Morris offers what is really no more than a preamble to his "dissection" (as he calls it) of soccer, but even in this he dismantles the notion that sport is "only a game" and indicates that a match is "a symbolic event of some complexity."

So much for attempts to make sense of sport through grand theories, all of which have merits yet none of which is without problems. At least they provide frames of reference within which we can operate when investigating some of the more specific issues concerning sport. In the following chapters we will do exactly that, in each case looking at popular ideas that circulate in sport and exposing some of their shortcomings.

FURTHER READING

Sport Matters: Sociological studies of sport, violence and civilization by Eric Dunning (Routledge, 1999) provides an elegant defense of figurational theory while remaining alive to the contributions of Weber, Marx, and several other theoretical approaches to the study of sports.

Leftist Theories of Sport: A critique and reconstruction by William J. Morgan (University of Illinois Press, 1994) is a challenging evaluation of the major tendencies in critical theories of sports. After examining the varieties of Marxism, Morgan offers a "reconstructed critical theory." Morgan argues that the "mass commodification" of sports amounts to "the capitulation of the practice side of sport to its business side."

The Influence of the Protestant Ethic on Sport and Recreation by Steven J. Overman (Avebury, 1997) is a brilliant Weberian analysis of the development of contemporary sport in North America. As the title suggests, Overman is concerned with identifying the ways in which religious ideas impacted on the emergence of sports.

Sport and Leisure in Social Thought by Grant Jarvie and Joe Maguire (Routledge, 1995) is an interesting attempt to select a number of traditions in social thought and examine what light they shed on the development of sports. Many of the classical social theorists had little or nothing to say about sports, so the authors try to explicate.

ASSIGNMENT

Consider ways in which sport reflects almost perfectly changes in technology, patterns of work, and people's values and attitudes in a manner not suggested by any of the theories covered in this chapter.

behind on points

why black sports stars
are symbols of failure

A MILLION DREAMS, ONE STAR

In March 1995, two of the most potent black sporting symbols were released, one from prison, the other from baseball's backwaters. Mike Tyson and Michael Jordan were the most successful African Americans in sports. They earned more money, more respect and, in Tyson's case, more notoriety than any previous black athlete in history. Their absence from sport's big league was agonizing. Tyson's was enforced: he was found guilty of raping a beauty queen contestant in an Indianapolis hotel room and banished in ignominy. Jordan quit the Chicago Bulls with the plaudits ringing in his ears; he wanted to conquer his second sport, baseball, but fared poorly with the Chicago White Sox. Their returns had promoters rubbing their hands and advertisers reaching for their check-books. It was a unique return to action of two black males who had defined their sports and inspired the dreams of millions.

But, are they realistic dreams, or just dangerous fantasies? In this chapter, we will address not only this question, but, perhaps more importantly, why we should be asking it at all. After all, whose business is it if someone wants to channel all his or her energy into the pursuit of an ideal? Sports themselves thrive off the zeal and ambition of millions of "wannabes," the vast majority of whom never approach the level where they can make a living, let alone a fortune, out of sports.

Tyson's cases

On September 19, 1991, heavyweight boxer Mike Tyson was indicted by a Marion County grand jury of raping Desiree Washington, a contestant at a Miss Black America pageant, who claimed Tyson had forcibly had sex with her in an Indianapolis hotel room. Tyson had attended the pageant. On February 10, 1992, Tyson was convicted of rape and sentenced to six years in prison. Washington later alleged that Tyson had given her a venereal disease. During his imprisonment, the boxer converted to Islam. Tyson was released from prison in March 1995, and resumed his professional boxing career five months later under the guidance of Don King. Richard Hoffer believes: "He [Tyson] was the perfect man for King's purposes, though, smart enough to be actively complicit in the con, but emotionally disorganized enough to defer to King in its execution" (1998: 266). The "con" was a series of easy fights spread over two years which earned Tyson $135 million. By 1998, Tyson was back in prison again for assault, having served a suspension from boxing for the infamous ear-biting incident with Evander Holyfield.

Tens of thousands of young African Americans and African Caribbeans who grew up in American and British inner cities in the 1970s are now reflecting on a sports career that never was. They, like literally millions before them, had watched television, listened to radios and read newspapers and magazines. There was the evidence before their eyes: black sports stars lauded all over the world, winning world titles, gold medals, and making the kind of money that qualifies you for a place in *Fortune* magazine.

But appearances are often deceptive and these highly unrepresentative superstars unwittingly create an illusion. As American sports writer Jack Olsen observed in his 1968 book, *The Black Athlete*: "At most, sport has led a few thousand Negroes out of the ghetto. But for hundreds of thousands of other Negroes it has substituted a meaningless dream."

While the time and effort demanded in trying to become another Jordan or Tyson is so great that it may ruin a young person's prospects of doing anything else, the actual chances of emulating them are infinitesimally small. Failed sports performers have quite frequently destroyed any other career possibilities they might have had. No sports performer can avoid making sacrifices; the black performers' sacrifices are just greater than most.

But, the gains are greater too, the reader might argue. Even the black sports performers who do not spring to mind when we talk of riches are multi-millionaires. Ato Bolden (the sprinter), Andy Cole (soccer), Stephon Marbury (basketball); sport is such a lucrative area, nowadays, that even modest success earns a lot of money. And, no matter how you interpret the evidence, many blacks achieve success relative to the number of blacks in the total population. African Americans account for about 13 per cent of the total US population; African Caribbeans are, by the largest estimate, only 3 per cent of the British population. Yet, the NBA has 80–90 per cent majority of black players, and one in five professional soccer players in Britain is black. Ninety per cent of world boxing champions are black. We could marshal other figures to support what is an obvious fact: black people over-achieve in sports; it's also a fact that far more leave sport in failure and disappointment. We need to uncover some of the processes at work beneath these facts.

There are also questions to be asked about women, not a minority group in a numerical sense, but certainly a minority in terms of top jobs, wealth, income, and political influence. The position of women in sports is, generally speaking, quite unlike that of black people, for they have been discouraged from participating, often by means of convenient fallacies about their being physically incapable of withstanding the pressures of competition and naturally unsuited to the demands of sport. Their results have – certainly up to quite recently – shown this to be so. Women do not, by and large, compete head to-head with men (and when they do, they are invariably beaten) and where performance can be measured, women are some way behind their male counterparts. Again, this is deceptive for there have been concealed processes at work for many decades and these have served to suppress women's success in sport.

Cast in a different light, women's experience is comparable with that of blacks. Being minorities, both have marginal positions, meaning that they are largely excluded from many of the key areas of society. Neither features prominently in politics, the professions, or other areas of society where important decisions are made that affect people's lives. Their exclusion is usually the product of an "-ism": as blacks are discriminated against and their accomplishments diminished through racism, so women are prohibited from competing on equal terms with men through sexism. Both remain on the underside of a lopsided structure of inequality and this has affected the involvement of both in sport in quite different ways, as we will see in this and the following chapters.

> ### Racism
>
> A set of beliefs or ideas based on the assumption that the world's population can be divided into different human biological groups designated "races." Following on from this is the proposition that the "races" are ordered hierarchically, so that some stand in a position of super-ordinacy, or superiority, to others. This is a classic type of racism; nowadays, ideas of superiority are often veiled in arguments concerning culture, nationalism, and ethnic identity. Quite often, these contain connotations of racism that are not specific, but only inferred. When ideas, or beliefs, about racial superiority are translated into action, we speak in terms of racial discrimination, or simply racialism. Racism is the idea; racialism is the practice.

ESCAPE ATTEMPTS

There is quite a story to blacks' involvement with organized sport in the West. It begins in the late eighteenth century during the American War of Independence, when General Percy of the British forces captured the town of Richmond. Impressed by the fighting prowess of a slave who worked on the plantations there, Percy took Bill Richmond – as he named him – under his tutelage and groomed him for prize-fighting. While it could not have been an easy life, prize-fighting had its perks (like extensive travel in Europe) and must have seemed far preferable to plantation work. Richmond was something of a prototype, his modest success encouraging slave owners and merchants to scour for potential fighters whom they might patronize.

The celebrated Tom Molineaux was one such fighter. Once a slave, he was taken to England and trained by Richmond, eventually winning his freedom. Molineaux built on his predecessor's success, rubbing shoulders with the nobility and generally mixing with the London beau monde. It was in his classic fight with all-England heavyweight champion Tom Cribb that he created his niche in sports history. Moulineaux was beaten and died four years later. He is the subject of George MacDonald Fraser's historical novel *Black Ajax*, which takes the form of eyewitness "reports" of the epic fight in 1811.

Peter Jackson was born on the Caribbean island of St. Croix and travelled to Sydney and San Francisco before settling in England in the late nineteenth century. He, more than any pugilist of his day, embraced fame, though world champion John L. Sullivan's refusal to fight him denied him the ultimate title. Yet his decline was abrupt and he became a habitual drinker and was made to play in a stage version of Stowe's *Uncle Tom's Cabin*.

Some slaves continued to leave America to campaign as prize-fighters in Europe, but the majority were pitted against each other locally. The years on either side of emancipation in 1865 saw blacks filtering into other sports; they were most successful at horse-riding and baseball. In the latter, they were not permitted to play with or against whites. Ninety-eight years after the first Molineaux–Cribb clash, a black man ascended to the apogee of sporting achievement. John Arthur Johnson in 1908 challenged and beat Tommy Burns, a white man, to become the heavyweight champion of the world. Fighting as "Jack Johnson," he broke the "color line" which segregated blacks from whites in all areas, including sport. In fact, after Johnson eventually lost the title in 1916, the line was redrawn and no black man was allowed to fight for the world title until 1937 when Joe Louis started a succession of black champions interrupted only by Rocky Marciano (1952 5), Ingemar Johannson (1959–60), and Gerrie Coetzee (1983–4).

Johnson and, in an entirely different way, Louis were black icons of their day, Johnson especially cultivating a reputation as a "bad nigger," a moral hard man who, as Lawrence Levine puts it in his *Black Culture and Black Consciousness*, "had the strength and courage and ability to flout the limitations imposed by white society" (1977: 420). Johnson's image was based as much on his penchant for the company of white women as his boxing. This was a time when the Ku Klux Klan was in its ascendancy and blacks were lynched for far lesser deeds than consorting with white females. Far from being "bad," Louis was obsequious, apolitical and exploitable – as his poverty, despite vast ring earnings, demonstrates. Yet, he too was a potent symbol for black Americans who were short of heroes or role models on whom to style their own lives. Both were anomalies: conspicuously successful black men in a society where success was virtually monopolized by whites.

The other outstanding black sportsman of this period was Jesse Owens who, like Louis, was "a credit to his race" – which meant he was self-effacing and compliant to the demands of white officials. Well, not totally compliant: after returning a performance of theatrical proportions at the 1936 "Nazi Olympics" in Berlin (covered in Chapter fifteen), where he won four gold medals and shamed Hitler into a walk-out, he was expelled from the American Athletics Union for refusing to compete in a Swedish tour. Owens was eventually reduced to freak shows, racing against horses and motorcycles.

Other black sports performers were similarly brought to reduced circumstances. Johnson suffered the indignity of imprisonment, of fighting bulls in Barcelona, of performing stunts in circuses, of comically playing Othello, and of boxing all-comers in exhibitions at the age of 68. Louis ended his days ignominiously in a wheelchair, welcoming visitors at a Las Vegas hotel.

The careers of all three followed a comet's elliptical path, radiating brilliance in their orbit, yet fading into invisibility. Plenty of other blacks have followed the same route. Sports history is full of dreams turning to nightmares. But black sportsmen seem particularly afflicted. Not even "The Greatest," Muhammad Ali, could maintain his dignity in later years.

While boxing was the first sport in which blacks were able to cross the color line and compete with whites, others followed the form. In 1946, when Joe Louis was nearing the end of his reign as heavyweight king (and the year in which Jack Johnson died), Jackie Robinson became the first black person to play major league baseball. He was sent death threats and his teams, Montreal and the Brooklyn Dodgers, were sometimes boycotted by opponents. The hostility of his reception may have initially daunted administrators from recruiting black players, but by the 1950s the numbers entering major league were multiplying.

Nowadays, basketball is dominated by black players. The trend began in 1951 when Chuck Hooper signed for Boston Celtics and precipitated a rush: within 16 years, over half the National Basketball Association (NBA) players were black. The specter of freak show that had hung over Owens and the others visited basketball in the shape of the Harlem Globetrotters whose goals were more in making audiences laugh than scoring hoops. The comic Globetrotters' popularity with whites was probably because of the players' conformity to the image of blacks as physically adept, but too limited intellectually to harness skill to firm objectives. James Michener, in *Sports in America*, wrote of the Globetrotters: "They deepened the stereotype of 'the loveable [*sic*], irresponsible Negro'" (1976: 145).

Stereotype

An image or depiction of a group based on false or, at best, incomplete information, which can be used as the basis for gross generalizations about members of such groups. Typically, a stereotype extracts alleged features of a culture or a "race" and elevates these to prominence, making them into defining characteristics. The stereotype is usually insulting, frequently demeaning, and occasionally hostile.

Civil rights legislation in 1964 and 1965 erased the color line, in a *de jure*, or legal, sense at least. As the segregationist barriers in education tumbled down, so black youngsters began to mix and play competitively with whites. College football came within reach of more blacks and this, in turn, translated into more black professional players. By 1972, African American players comprised 40 per cent of the NFL.

In Britain, the historical developments were similar, though compressed into a shorter timespan and with considerably fewer numbers, of course. The old prize-fighters Richmond and Molineaux were followed by a succession of prize-fighters, one notable being Andrew Jeptha, who migrated from Cape Town, South Africa, in 1902 and became the first-ever black boxer to hold a British title in 1907 (this was before the formation of the British Boxing Board of Control). On the track, sprinters from the British Caribbean, like Arthur Wharton, Jack London, McDonald Bailey, and Arthur Wint established reputations from the end of the nineteenth century to the 1950s.

Wharton transferred to professional soccer with Preston North End, thus becoming the first-ever black player; though the person popularly credited with that distinction is Lloyd Lindbergh Delaphena, who played for Middlesbrough and Portsmouth in the 1950s. This period was one of mass migration from the Caribbean and, as a consequence, many migrants, such as Trinidad's Yolande Pompey and Guyana's Cliff Anderson, were active in British rings. Hogan "Kid" Bassey, originally from Nigeria but based in Liverpool, won the world featherweight title in 1957.

But one boxer embodied all the elements of the black sportsman in this period. Born in the Midlands town of Leamington Spa in 1928, Randolph Turpin had a Guyanese migrant father and an English mother. Inspired by the example of his older brother Dick, who in 1948 won the British middleweight title, Randolph had a shimmering boxing career that came to a climax in 1951 when he upset Sugar Ray Robinson to become the world middleweight champion. Lacking any financial acumen, he ran into trouble with the Inland Revenue which filed a bankruptcy petition against him for unpaid tax on his considerable ring earnings. His career plunged to humiliating depths when he engaged in "boxer *vs* wrestler" bouts and even consented to a fully fledged comeback in an unlicensed boxing promotion at the age of 35. On May 16, 1966, he committed suicide by shooting himself, though rumors of a gangland murder were rife, according to his biographer Jack Birtley (1976: 140–53). His fall resembled that of other black champions.

Marilyn Fay Neufville broke the world's 400-meter record in 1970 when she was 18. Born in Jamaica, she ran for Cambridge Harriers, a London club, and became the first black female to make an impact on British sport. Sprint events were later virtually dominated by black women, but less conspicuously, judo and volleyball also benefited from the growing participation of black women.

Unlike the USA, Britain has never had formal segregation, so black school children have competed in sport with peers from a variety of ethnic backgrounds. Soccer, as the nation's most popular game, has been played in high schools throughout the country; so it was not unexpected when, in the late 1970s and early 1980s, black players began appearing in Football League teams. First, the trickle: Albert Johanneson, a Leeds United player in the 1960s; Clyde Best, who played for West Ham United in the 1970s. Then the flood: dozens of professional players, including Viv Anderson, who in 1979 became the first black footballer to represent England, began to appear, prompting reactions from the racist fans, who frequently pelted them with bananas and targeted them for abusive chants. Through the 1980s, black footballers continued to make their mark on British soccer often to the ambiguous rejoicing of newspapers whose "Black Magic" and "Black Power" headlines were more than faintly reminiscent of a London paper's banner after a promotion in June 1946 when five black boxers posted wins: "Black Night for British Boxing" (quoted in Henderson 1949: 340).

At the close of the 1980s, a "second generation" of British-born blacks was established in British sport. Over half the British boxing champions were black as were more than 40 per cent of the Olympic squad of 1988, and virtually every Football League club had two or three black players on its books. It is no coincidence that the major sports in which blacks have excelled – boxing, track and field, football, and basketball – are ones which demand little in the way of equipment. They can be practiced away from any formal organization and with minimal resources. A strong pair of legs, fast hands, sharp reflexes, and a desire to compete are basics. Much more than this is needed to progress in the club-oriented sports, like cricket, golf, and tennis, which tend to be accessible only to the middle class. It might be argued that cricket has some possibilities for players of working-class backgrounds – and blacks in the main come from such backgrounds – but the very structure of the sport and the educational institutions in which it is encouraged make it more available to the more affluent class. The same argument applies to Rugby Union.

In the more accessible sports, blacks have grown to a prominence that belies their numerical minority status in both the USA and Britain. Their sometimes overwhelming success in certain sports is quite disproportionate to their numbers within the total population. The ratio is most pronounced in boxing, track and field, and basketball. But in sports in which blacks have either been allowed to compete or have been attracted to, they seem to approach a mastery that is difficult to match. Blacks' apparent predilection for sport, and the high orders of success they have achieved, has been the subject of bar-room discussion and academic controversy. Why so many in sport and why so many champions? The answers are intertwined.

SECOND NATURE

One of the simplest and most influential explanations of black excellence has been supplied by Martin Kane in an article entitled "An assessment of black is best" in the magazine *Sports Illustrated* (January 18, 1971). At the center of Kane's argument is the "insight" that blacks are endowed with a natural ability that gives them an advantage in certain sports. Around this lie a number of other related points, many culled from Kane's interviews with medical scientists, coaches, and sports performers. An important, though oddly dated, point is that there are race-linked physical characteristics. Blacks as a "race" have proportionately longer legs to whites, narrower hips, wider calf bones, greater arm circumference, greater ratio of tendon to muscle, denser skeletal structure, and a more elongated body. Typically, they have power and an efficient body-heat dissipation system. Kane inferred these features from a small sample of successful black sportsmen – that is, a minority with proven excellence rather than a random sample from the total population. And he concludes that blacks are innately different and the differences, being genetic in origin, can be passed on from one generation to the next.

So, cold climates are said to affect all blacks badly, even ones who are born and brought up in places like Toronto. Weak ankle bones would account for the relative absence of black ice-hockey players. The disadvantages are transmitted genetically, as are natural advantages which equip blacks to do well in particular sports where speed and power are essential. Kane argues that blacks are not suited to endurance events. Since the publication of the article, hundreds of African distance runners have undermined this point, though Kane tries to cover himself by claiming Kenyans have black skin, but a number of white features.

Kane's arguments border on the absurd, especially when we consider anthropologists' dismissal of the concept of race itself as having any analytical value at all. Black people are descended from African populations, but, over the centuries, their genetic heritage has become diversified and complicated by various permutations of mating. There is no "pure" race. Kane ignores this when he examines the area of psychology, emerging with a set of personality traits that are supposed to be determined by race. Blacks have the kind of yielding personality that puts them, as one coach told Kane, "far ahead of whites . . . relaxation under pressure" (1971: 76).

This has a common-sense authenticity about it, for coaches and spectators seem to associate black sports athletes with a cool approach to competition, never stressing-out, or growing tense. But competitors themselves actually work at portraying this: they consciously try to convey an image that reflects coolness. That is all it is – image. Beneath the surface, black performers are as tense and concerned as anyone else. Possibly more so: sport for many blacks is not a casual recreation (as it may be for white youths), but a career path, and every failure represents a possible sinking to obscurity. Every event has to be approached as if it were the most demanding of one's life; defeat is not easily assimilated as a result. Kane mistook impression management for deep psychological profiles.

Slavery is the key to the third part of Kane's argument. "Of all the physical and psychological theories about the American black's excellence in sport, none has proved more controversial than one of the least discussed: that slavery weeded out the weak" (1971: 80). Here Kane introduces some home-spun Darwinism, his view being that, as only the fittest survived the rigors of slavery, those best suited to what must have been terribly harsh environments passed on their genes to successive populations, who used them to great effect in sport. There are two drawbacks to this. First, it is preposterous to suggest that blacks bred for generations in such a controlled way as to retain a gene pool in which specific genes related to, for instance, speed, strength, and agility, became dominant. Second, these properties were probably of less significance in matters of survival than intelligence, ingenuity, and anticipation and Kane considers none of these as essentially black features.

All three categories of Kane's theory gel into a formulation that states that blacks' achievements in sport are linked to their so-called race. Sport is seen as "second nature" to a black person. This implausible suggestion belongs in the realms of racist folklore and not scientific inquiry. Unfortunately, its simplicity and comprehensiveness have made it appealing to many who want to explain the success of blacks in sport as due to race. US writer Harry Edwards has even suggested that the explanation itself has effects for white competitors who, believing blacks to be innately superior, start off at a psychological disadvantage. "The 'white race' thus becomes the chief victim of its own myth" (1973: 197).

But its appeal disguises something more sinister because, if we accept as proof of the natural-ability argument the outstanding results recorded by black sports performers, then what are we to infer from the under-achievement of blacks in formal education? That they are naturally limited intellectually? If so, it could be argued that they should be encouraged to develop their gifts and possibly neglect areas in which they haven't much aptitude. Sadly, this is what has happened in the past and it gives us the first clue in answering the question of blacks' sporting success all over again, this time with an entirely different approach.

LOSERS AND STILL CHAMPIONS

History alone tells us that sport has been one of the two channels through which blacks have been able to escape the imprisonment of slavery and the impoverishment that followed its dissolution; the other being entertainment. In both spheres, blacks performed largely for the amusement of patrician whites. This holds true to this day: the season-ticket holder or cable television subscriber, no less than old-time slave masters, have decisive effects on the destinies of sports performers. For this reason, slaves were encouraged; the incentive might be freedom or at least a temporary respite from daily labors.

There is an adage that emerged during the 1930s depression in Yorkshire, England, a county famed for its cricket and its mining industry: "Shout down any coalpit and half a dozen fast bowlers will come out." The theme is similar: that material deprivation is an ideal starting-point for sporting prowess. "Hungry fighters" are invariably the most effective. As we have seen, many fight their way out, only to return to indigence; but they are not to know that as they are striving for improvement. Blacks' supposed predilection for sport is more a product of material circumstances than natural talent.

Whether or not sport is a viable avenue from despair is not the issue: it has been seen as such by people who lacked alternatives. And the perception has stuck, and probably will continue to stick as long as obstacles to progress in other avenues remain. The argument here is that the early slave prize-fighters began a tradition by setting themselves up – quite unwittingly   as cultural icons, or images to be revered and copied; in today's parlance, role models The stupendous success of blacks in such sports as boxing and athletics has clearly been inspirational to countless young blacks over the decades.

Icons

The term "icon" is from the Greek *eikon*, meaning Image. Its application to culture refers to the image that is conferred, granted, or attributed to an individual by a collection of others. In a sense, the cultural icon exists almost independently of the individual, who may be a sports or rock star: popular perceptions, expectations and beliefs define the icon much more powerfully than the person. Jack Johnson, for example, "was not merely a fighter but a symbol," as Levine puts it (1977: 430). In 1912, it was widely believed that Johnson had been refused passage on the doomed *Titanic*, and this enhanced his status even further. Contemporary cultural icons also have beliefs built around them that contribute to their status; there is a willingness to believe almost anything about either of them. Similarly, some contemporary black sports stars command iconic status.

Racism and racial discrimination have worked to exclude blacks from many areas of employment, restrict their opportunities and, generally, push them toward the "marginal" or least important areas of the labor market. Experiencing this at first hand or anticipating it through the stories of others has set young people thinking about alternative sources of employment. "There aren't too many successful black tycoons, professionals, or politicians, so where should I look for an example?" black youths might ask themselves. Answers spring to mind readily. Kevin Garnett: six-year contract worth $125 million (£76 million); Lennox Lewis: estimated career earnings of $100 million (£61 million); Sheryl Swoopes: status on par with a movie star; Terrell Davis: stellar NFL player; the list goes on. Blacks can make it, but only in certain areas. Evaporating into insignificance are the millions of other aspirants whose fortune never materialized and whose career ended shabbily. No matter how remote the chances of success may be, the tiny number of elite black sports stars supply tangible and irrefutable evidence that it can be achieved.

By their early teens, black youths showing potential become draught horses, drawing along the displaced ambitions of parents, siblings and human cargo of others who, for some reason, have had their own ambitions blighted and remain fixed in the underclass, their only hope of redemption lying in the success of the would-be champion. Encouraged, even cajoled, by physical education teachers at high school who might subscribe to the popular if mistaken view that blacks have "natural talent," young persons might, while running or fighting, discover new dimensions of themselves. Zealous scouts for colleges pump up the youths with inflated claims when they attempt to woo them into their programs. Many youths understandably find comfort in the view that they do possess natural advantages. The fact that such views are based on stereotypes, not realities, does not enter into it: beliefs often have a self-fulfilling quality, so that if you believe in your own ability strongly enough, you eventually acquire that ability. I can illustrate the point.

A few years ago, I received a call from a journalist from the British *Sunday Times*. He was writing a story on black over-achievement in sports and wanted to know why no one actually expressed what he felt was an evident truth: that there is a natural edge that blacks possess. Was it because of political correctness? he asked. Partly, I answered, but also because it has racist implications and mainly because it is just wrong. Then, I qualified my response: the fact that a journalist, who happened to be black himself, writing for a prestigious newspaper was prepared to entertain the idea was testimony to its power. It is not only whites who have bought the myth of black natural talent in sport: black people have accepted and, in some cases, even clung to a defective theory that has actually performed a disservice. Actually, it's not the myth itself that has performed the disservice so much as the culture in which it has stayed credible; that being one in which blacks have been regarded as unsuited to or just unwanted for work that demands intellect and imagination – cerebral rather than physical skills.

Study after study in the USA and Britain – and, more recently, in parts of continental Europe – has chronicled the extent and intensity of racism in today's society. We need not dwell on specific examples; suffice it to say that in the post-war years in Britain and for many more years before that in the USA, blacks have been systematically squeezed out of education and employment opportunities for reasons that derive from, in its rawest form, racist hostility.

The origins of this hostility lie in the European colonial expansion of the seventeenth century, the settlement of the West Indies, or Caribbean, and the expansion of trade in slaves, gold, and sugar between Africa, the Americas, and Britain. Slavery meant that whites maintained their domination over blacks and so kept a rigid inequality. The inequality has been modified and lessened in the decades following emancipation, but blacks have never quite shed the remnants of their shackles and whites have passed on their colonial mentality. Seeing blacks as great sports performers might seem a compliment, but, as Harry Edwards memorably observed in his *The Revolt of the Black Athlete*: "The only difference between the black man shining shoes in the ghetto and the champion black sprinter is that the shoe shine man is a nigger, while the sprinter is a fast nigger" (1970: 20).

Historically, sport, along with entertainment, was one of the areas in which blacks were allowed to maximize their prowess, and circumstances have not changed sufficiently to permit a significant departure. Blacks still approach sport with vigor and commitment at least partly because persistent racism effectively closes off other channels. Even if those other channels have become freer in recent years, black youths have become accustomed to anticipating obstacles to their progress. So that, by the time they prepare to make the transition from school to work, many have made sports as a career their first priority.

With sights set on a future filled with championships, black youths fight their way into sports determined that, slim though their chances may be, they will succeed. And they usually do, though mostly in an altogether more modest way than they envisaged. Few attain the heights they wanted to conquer and even fewer surpass them. An unstoppable motivation and unbreakable commitment are valuable, perhaps essential, assets to success in sport and this is why so many possessors of these achieve some level of distinction. But titles are, by definition, reserved for only a very small elite and, while blacks are always well-represented among the elite of all sports in which they compete, there are never enough championships to go round. The majority inevitably fail.

Stacking

This refers to the disproportionate concentration of ethnic minorities in certain positions in a sports team. In American football, black players were traditionally allocated to running-back and wide-receiver positions; in baseball, they have been stacked in outfield positions. This tends to exclude them from, for instance, quarterback and starting pitching positions – which are the most prestigious – and compels them to compete against other blacks for their team position. It could be argued that stacking is based on stereotypes and that such stereotypes have been dismantled by quarterbacks such as Shaun King and Steve McNair, who show intelligence and judgment rather than power and speed in their play. Evidence from baseball suggested that the stereotypes operated into the late 1980s (Jiobu 1988). (In the 1970s, Eitzen studied stacking, both with Sanford, 1975, and with Yetman, 1977; see also Curtis and Loy 1978.)

Blacks' success in sports may look impressive, but, compared to the numbers of youths entering sport, their interest primed, their success is not so great, even when their chances are affected by "stacking" and other racialist maneuvers. Sheer weight of numbers dictates that a great many African Americans and African Caribbeans will rise to the top of certain sports. When the phenomenon is approached this way, the reasons are less opaque. There is no need to resort to imprecise ideas such as natural ability: blacks' sporting success is actually constructed in history and contemporary culture. Let me summarize.

Cultures on both sides of the Atlantic have fostered strains of racism that, while less virulent now than 20 years ago, are still bitter enough to convince young black people that their future in mainstream society may be curtailed by popularly held stereotypes about their abilities. Weighing up the possibilities of a future career, many opt for a shot at sports, where it has been demonstrated time and again that black people can make it to the very top and command the respect of everyone, whites included. Respect is a sought-after commodity by people who have been denied it historically. Ideas of the "White Men Can't Jump" variety are conveyed to young black people by possibly well-meaning, but mistaken, coaches and high school teachers who enthuse over a career in sports. Then the story separates into two contrasting plots. Some tread the road to respectability, even stardom, making a living they can be proud of from professional sports. Others dissolve into oblivion, never to be heard of.

What this scenario does not seem to account for is the scarcity of black competitors, let alone winners, in certain sports. Their exclusion from more expensive pursuits like golf, shooting, skiing, and so on, is obvious: you need money to get started. But swimming, tennis or some field events pose more of a mystery. One might reasonably suppose that, over the years, a percentage of young blacks would gravitate toward areas not traditionally black-dominated. Perhaps they will, but so far the pull of the icons has been irresistible. Black stars today have been recast into idols by corporations, watchful of an emergent black middle class with plenty of disposable income. Having their products endorsed by successful blacks can help them gain a piece of the developing African American market.

Eitzen and Sage reported that, in the 1980s, world-ranked tennis players Lori McNeill and Zina Garrison were missing out on sponsors to inferior white players (1993: 339). Since then there has been a steady march of blacks into higher tax brackets. By 1995, it was possible for the Wall Street value of stocks in the five companies endorsed by Michael Jordan to swell by $2.3 billion (£1.4 billion) amid rumors that he would return to basketball. The endorsement of a recognizably successful sports performer can add enormously to the marketability of a product. Advertisers have been guided less by fine spirits, more by the argument that affluent blacks can be persuaded to part with their money by other, more successful blacks.

The result is the transformation of the likes of David Robinson and Marion Jones into something much more than sports performers: they have become representatives of an aspirational culture in which people are prepared to emulate them in nearly every respect. If they chase the same dreams and seek the same praise, they might eat the same breakfast cereal or wear the same sneakers. If those dreams have long since gone, they might still buy the products they endorse. Whatever the logic behind the advertisers' ploy, the effect is to create a televisual pantheon for living sports stars. The majority of young blacks will structure their ambitions around the icons of success they see before them, all but deified by tv culture.

BETWEEN MIND AND MUSCLE

But there is a heavy cost and one which John Hoberman emphasizes in his book *Darwin's Athletes*, which bears the subtitle "How sport has damaged black America and preserved the myth of race" (1997). Hoberman's thesis is that the "fixation" on the athletic achievements of African Americans has led to a glorification of the physical aspects of black people, a glorification that degenerates, as Orlando Patterson once put it, "into a vulgar exoticism" and "inverted racist claims of superior sexual potency and greater zest and passion for life" (1997: 303).

Hoberman believes there exists what he calls the Law of Compensation which states that there is "an inverse relationship between mind and muscle, between athletic and intellectual development" (1997: 225). America has perpetuated falsehoods about black people's biological propensities; and "black athleticism has served . . . as the most dramatic vehicle in which such ideas can ride in public consciousness" (1997: 225).

Prominent black sports performers have been used as living evidence of a not-so noble savagery: virtually every sports star embodies concepts of racial evolution that are enthusiastically accepted by both white and black populations as support for the view that blacks are naturally good athletes, but not much good at much else. Among Hoberman's examples are Joe Louis "who was granted messianic status by his fellow blacks [and] was also depicted as a savage brute to his white audience" (1997: 115–26) and Mike Tyson whose "well-publicized brutalities in and out of the ring have helped to preserve pseudo-evolutionary fantasies about black ferocity that are still of commercial value to fight promoters and their business partners in the media" (1997: 209).

Black boxers are bit-part players in a "Darwinian drama par excellence, in that portraying the black male as an undisciplined savage confirmed both his primitive nature and his inevitable failure in the competition with civilized whites in a modern society" (1997: 209). They are joined by an all-star cast that includes all top black athletes and the millions more who want to follow in their footsteps.

Hoberman argues that black people in the States and, to a similar degree in Britain, have been depicted in an unending series of images that have contributed toward a social pathology. Whites are society's stewards. The typical image of blacks in the media is that of a violent physical people, habitually involved in criminal activity, entertainment or sports. In the late twentieth century, the slayings of black musicians and the vulgar misogynist material of rap artists contributed to a "merger of the athlete, the gangster rapper, and the criminal into a single black male persona" that the sports, entertainment, and advertising industries have made into the dominant image of black masculinity – a single menacing figure. The high-profile sports figures who have courted ambitions in music and movies supports Hoberman's point.

The power of Hoberman's argument is not so much in its dismantling of the myth of athletic prowess, which has been done before, nor in discerning the racist implications of exalting black athletic accomplishments; but in analyzing the ways in which the cost of black success, whether in sports or entertainment, far outweighs its benefits. In 1997, I was spending a sabbatical at the University of Massachusetts, Boston, when Tiger Woods became the first black player to win the US Masters. As a Fellow of the William Monroe Trotter Institute, I was in the company of several distinguished African American scholars, many of whom greeted Woods's success heartily. But, why? After all, how badly does black America need yet another sports champion? For Hoberman, this is not liberation, but entrapment.

Woods, no less than Joe Louis, Willie Mays, or Michael Jordan, was a symbol of black potential that has been continually adapted to changing circumstances. The media visibility of successful black sports stars discourages thinking about what blacks have accomplished in areas such as education, politics, the professions; perhaps, more pertinently, what they have *not* accomplished in these areas.

There is a scene in the movie *Hoop Dreams*, in which a basketball coach addresses his protégés with some sobering statistics (directed by Steve James, Fred Marx, and Peter Gilbert, 1994). Each year, 500,000 boys play high school basketball, he tells them. Of the 14,000 who progress to intercollegiate basketball, fewer than 25 per cent ever play one season in the NBA. No need to reach for your calculator: it works out at about 1:143. Some American writers, like Jack Olsen and Nathan Hare, have looked at the underside of this "shameful story" (as Olsen calls it) which begins with visions of wealth and glamor but frequently ends in poverty, crime, and, sometimes, insanity. Their conclusions concur with those of Hoberman in the sense that they believe that young blacks are seduced into sport and, in the process, ignore their formal academic and vocational studies. They invest so much energy in sport that little is left for other pursuits. So, by the time dreams fade, they are left with few if any career alternatives and join the gallery of "also-rans."

Sports that attract blacks are always expensive in terms of people: wasteful, profligate even. If it takes 143 ambitious kids to make one NBA player for one season, how many to produce a Jordan? Entering sports is less a career choice, more a lottery. As I noted earlier, the idea of recruiting bowlers from Yorkshire coalpits might have proved workable in the 1930s. Now, young whites are told to enjoy their cricket, but, first, get a degree and qualify as a lawyer or a doctor. The same piece of advice does not reach as far as London's Brixton, or South Central LA.

There are always a small number of outstanding performers with naturally endowed faculties, but there's no reason to suppose that the black population has a monopoly or even a majority of them. Success in sport is due much more to non-physical qualities such as drive, determination, and an ability to focus sharply. Given that blacks see the job market as a maze of dead-ends, they may well accrue more than their fair share of these qualities. Failure has potentially direr consequences for them than for their white, working-class counterparts who, while still having limited opportunities, at least escape racialism.

Returning to *Hoop Dreams*, we hear the familiar cliché from one of the school players: "Basketball is my ticket out of the ghetto." One can almost hear a chorus of others saying the same thing. It is explosive motivational fuel.

Add the "push" of outsiders, the magnetizing influence of black icons and you have a heady mixture – one which sends young blacks into sport year after year. If and when this slows, it's been suggested that this would reflect a quickening of the rate at which opportunities arise in the job market. In other words, if racialism disappeared completely there would be only a few black sports stars. That is not the case at present and, while discrimination persists, sport is bound to prosper from the contributions of blacks.

BEFORE AND AFTER

When Minnesota Vikings failed narrowly to make it to the Super Bowl in 1999's NFC championship game against Atlanta Falcons, the club's head coach Denny Green missed out in his attempt to become the first African American coach to take his team to American football's ultimate prize. Despite the high percentage of black players, Green was one of tiny number of African Americans who successfully transferred to senior coaching positions. Tony Dungy was head coach at Tampa Bay, and Ray Rhodes worked with Philadelphia Eagles and Green Bay Packers at the time.

This situation proved so embarrassing for the NFL that, in 1998, the governing organization hired a recruitment agency to stage and video interviews with other black coaches and aspiring coaches and distribute the tapes around the league. This is part of an effort to raise club owners' awareness of the abilities of black coaches and stimulate more enlightened hiring policies. Players like Doug Williams and, later, Warren Moon helped destroy the fiction that black football players did not have the intelligence to play quarterback, so needed to be "stacked" in other positions. Green's success may have helped dispel the similar fiction that existed about black coaches.

We know about the "before" part of the black experience in sports, how and why athletes make it to the pros, or fail in the process. The "during" phase can be read about in the sports pages of any newspaper. But, what happens "after"? Green *et al.* are exceptions. More usual are rags-to-riches and back-to-rags stories. Boxers especially have a knack of earning and blowing fortunes: Razor Ruddock was one of many millionaires-cum-bankrupts when he was declared financially insolvent in 1995. Others go on to become sportcasters, movie stars and all-round media personalities; the most successful of these combined all three and became the most famous black sports star ever – but for the wrong reasons, of course.

Considering the heavy investment of black people in the playing side of sport, one might expect many to stay in sport and serve in officiating or administrative capacities. Here there is an unevenness. Although there has been a steadily growing number of black game officials since 1965 (when Burt Tolar became the NFL's first black official), the number of black coaches and administrators has been few. Green was the first African American head football coach when he joined Northwestern University in 1981. Art Shell was the first black NFL coach when he joined Los Angeles Raiders in 1989. In Britain, Viv Anderson successfully transited from playing to managing, first at Barnsley, then as assistant manager at Middlesbrough. Black people are certainly appearing in the front offices, but not in the numbers one might expect from a glance at the number of active players.

One of the main reasons why owners and general managers have failed to appoint more black people is highlighted by Douglas Putnam, in his book *Controversies of the Sports World*: "Team owners and general managers, as businesspeople, prefer to hire candidates who are similar to coaches who have already achieved success or are similar to coaches they have known personally and admired" (1999: 27). If so, they might think in terms of a Parcells, a Jackson or, in Britain, a Ferguson. "Consequently," writes Putnam, they "often pass over qualified blacks and hire whites with whom they are familiar . . . and to conform to their long-held ideal about what a successful coach should be" (1999: 27).

This is sport's equivalent of what the sociologist Alvin Gouldner once called the "Rebecca Myth," after Daphne du Maurier's famous novel. In the book *Rebecca* and Alfred Hitchcock's 1940 film of the same name, a young woman marries an English aristocrat, but, after moving into his mansion, meets an unfriendly housekeeper, Mrs Danvers, who idolizes the late mistress of the mansion, Rebecca. Entranced by the thought of the dead Rebecca, Mrs Danvers makes her new mistress's life a misery. In his *Wildcat Strike: A study in worker–management relations*, Goulder transposes this theme to an industrial setting and shows how the succession of personnel in senior positions can be impeded by the expectations of colleagues. "The successor may fail to show the old lieutenants proper deference, willfully or through ignorance of their expectations, but in either event making them dissatisfied," writes Goulder (1965: 158). They resist the new boss as a "legitimate heir" to the position once held by someone they knew and trusted and withhold legitimacy unless he conforms to their ideal (Goulder's study was an all-male affair).

The "Rebecca Myth" has obvious applications to players' responses to a newly-appointed coach or manager, but it also helps clarify why owners and chairs fail to hire more blacks in senior positions: because they have what Putnam calls a "subliminal perception." Consciously or unconsciously, they desire to appoint someone who resembles a past manager/coach, who has brought success to their organization. And the historical chances are that this person will be white. This creates special difficulties for aspiring managers/coaches from ethnic minorities who need to convince prospective employers of their capabilities, but may also need their approval as someone who resembles a successful predecessor.

Interestingly, there are (literally) one or two African Americans who have bypassed the salaried positions and headed straight for the seats of power. Beginning as a boxing promoter in the 1970s, Don King became one of the most powerful figures in sport: a man at the center of an extensive web of business interests stretching over a range of sports and sports-related areas. Peter Bynoe and Bertram Lee aspired to King-like powers in 1989 when they bought the Denver Nuggets of the NBA for $50 million (£31 million); they were the first African American owners of a major sports club. The deal went sour when Lee had cashflow problems and was made to sell his share. Bynoe also sold out in 1992, leaving the sports without a black owner, though Evander Holyfield and entertainer Hammer were once prepared to spend $80 million (£50 million) on Houston Rockets.

Don King

The world's leading sports promoter has summed up his own rise thus: "I was an ex-numbers runner, ex-convict who received a full, unconditional pardon. I am, what they would say in America, what everyone's supposed to be – when coming from the wrong side of the track to the right side of the track" (quoted in Regen 1990: 115). After serving a prison sentence for manslaughter, King's first promotional venture was in 1972 when he staged an exhibition by Muhammad Ali in an African Americans' hospital in Cleveland. His first major promotion in 1974 (when aged 43), also featured Ali, when he regained the heavyweight title from George Foreman in Zaïre. After this, King kept an interest in the heavyweight championship, either by promoting bouts or managing the champions. Mike Tyson left his manager Bill Cayton and entered into a business relationship with King. Tyson refused to criticize King, even when many of his boxers, like ex-champion Tim Witherspoon, turned against him. King has also co-promoted rock stars, such as Michael Jackson, and began his own ppv tv system, KingVision. His biggest promotion never materialized: Tyson's conviction and imprisonment for rape meant that a fight with Evander Holyfield (originally scheduled for November 8, 1991) fell through. It was expected to gross more than $100 million (£62 million), with the ppv operation alone drawing $80 million, foreign sales $10 million and the promotional fee from Caesar's Palace $11 million. Former heavyweight champion Larry Holmes once said of King: "He looks black, lives white and thinks green." See Jack Newfield's Only in America: The life and crimes of Don King (1995).

These are success stories and, while there are only a few of them, there will be more in the years to come. Hoberman would be ambivalent about this: good news – blacks breaking ground by demonstrating intellectual abilities; bad news – they stay in sports. However many success stories emerge about blacks in sport, whether on the field or in the front office, they should not disguise the practices and processes which effectively produce the black sports star, who is both a champion and a loser. From the 1770s to the present, sport has been a route to fame and material fortune for thousands of blacks and will continue to be that in the future. For tens of thousands of others it will be only a route to nowhere.

Sport conceals deep inequalities and, for all the positive benefits it yields, it remains a source of hope and ambition for blacks only as long as those inequalities remain. Sports co-opt black people into the racist belief that they do have some natural aptitude for sports, while convincing whites that the success of a few counts as proof that they are right. But perhaps sports' vilest function is in persuading whites that, as long as blacks continue to succeed athletically, the American dream is still alive, and race poses no barrier to achievement.

FURTHER READING

A Hard Road to Glory: A history of the African-American athlete 1619–1918 Vol. 1; 1919–1945 Vol. 2; Since 1946 Vol. 3, by Arthur R. Ashe (Amistad Warner, 1993) is a three-volume history of the participation of African Americans in sports. Ashe himself, during and after his tennis career, was a constant advocate of academic study over sports and spoke publicly on the need for black children to temper their sports ambitions.

Darwin's Athletes: How sport has damaged black America and preserved the myth of race by John Hoberman (Houghton Mifflin, 1997) includes the insight that both blacks and whites have bought into the "myth" and how identifying with black sporting success has made black professional achievement "a seldom-noticed sideshow to more dramatic media coverage of celebrities and deviants." Also worth reading in this context: Marek Kohn's "Can white men jump?" which is chapter four of his book *The Race Gallery* (Vintage, 1996).

Glory Bound: Black athletes in a white America by David K. Wiggins (Syracuse University Press, 1997) critically examines the achievements of black Americans in sport against a historical background of racism and segregation.

Winners and Losers by Gajendra Verma and Douglas Darby (Falmer, 1994) is based on a two-year study in Manchester, England, designed to explore the orientations ethnic minorities have toward sports and the responses of providers of sports facilities. The study focuses mainly on South Asian youth. It is complemented by the broader focus of *All in the Game? Sport, race and politics*, which is a special edition of the journal *Race and Class* (vol. 36, no. 4, April–June, 1995).

Taboo: Why black athletes dominate and why we're afraid to talk about it by Jon Entine (Public Affairs, 2000) exhumes the ghost of Kane's early theory about the origins of black excellence in sports and treats it to a lengthier, more systematic treatment, though without questioning the premise that genes not culture lie at the source of black people's sporting success.

ASSIGNMENT

In 1947, psychologists Kenneth and Mamie Clark conducted a famous experiment: they asked 253 black children to choose between four dolls, two black and two white. The result: two-thirds of the children preferred white dolls. Conclusion: that black children had internalized the hatred society directed at all black people and so suffered from poor self-esteem. But this was before the rise of so many African American and African Caribbean sports icons. Repeat the experiment using a smaller sample of children, but use dolls in the likeness of famous sports stars: two black and two white. Document the results and draw out the implications, taking note of major social changes over the past 50 years.

leading QUESTIONS

q: Who was the best pound-for-pound athlete ever?

a: Wayne Gretzky.

That is the answer if you make an assessment based solely on objective, quantitative data and minimize subjective evaluations. Opting for a strictly measurable approach clearly has limitations, but its advantage is that we can marshal incontestable evidence to support arguments. Sports differ in the way excellence is measured, of course; and statistics are never timeless indicators, especially when stripped of their context.

To take two examples from the 1920s: Babe Ruth's career total of 714 home runs, including 60 homers in 154 games (in 1927) provides a case for ranking him among the greats; as does Jack Dempsey's seven-year reign as the world's heavyweight champion (1919–26). But, both athletes operated in an era of segregation and did not compete against African Americans, a fact that invalidates comparisons with athletes from other eras. Further complicating the assessment is whether the individual's overall career performance was enhanced by being a member of an exceptionally good team. Taking these factors into consideration and taking note of the number of years in which the athlete maintained peak performances, we can arrive at an appraisal that concludes that there are ten possible contenders – plus an emerging claimant to all-time greatness.

When he retired in 1999, Gretzky was the National Hockey League's all-time leader with 2,857 points, 894 goals, and 1,963 assists with four teams. In scoring his 1,072nd point (in 1994), he passed Gordie Howe's record to become the top goal scorer of all time. With Gretzky, the Edmonton Oilers won four Stanley Cups in a four-year span (1984–5, 1987–8), all in the club's first nine years as an NHL franchise. In 1981/2, he scored 92 goals (the previous record was 76) and an unprecedented 212 points. The only player to reach 200 points, Gretzky did it four times over five years, including his record 215 points in 1985/6. Gretzky moved to Los Angeles Kings in 1989. Among his other achievements was 50 goals in 39 games, smashing the previous mark of 50 in 50. He was also the NHL's top scorer nine times (1981–7, 1990–1). Gretzky played in every All Star game between 1980 and 1998 and was voted Most Valuable Player (MVP) ten times (1979–87, 1989).

They are statistics that tower over those of fellow hockey players and are unlikely to be challenged in the years ahead. The Oilers won another Stanley Cup without Gretzky, in 1990, but became a largely 0.500 team. The Kings, on the other hand, were transformed by Gretzky, winning their first playoff series since 1982. When evaluating any athlete, consideration must be given to the length of time he or she spent at the peak of their game. In Gretzky's case, this was a relatively long (15 years) stretch between 1979 and 1994.

Gretzky's superiority over other NHL players, past or present, strengthens his candidature over Michael Jordan, who won six National Basketball Championships, all with the Chicago Bulls, ten scoring titles and five Most Valuable Player awards. Jordan finished the 1986/7 season as only the second player after Wilt Chamberlain to score 3,000 points in one season. In an unbroken spell between 1987 and 1993, he led the NBA in scoring – a feat that is unlikely to be equaled.

The factor that undermines Jordan's credentials is the depth of quality in the Chicago team during his 12 peak years, 1986–98. Jordan's Bulls dominated the NBA in the 1990s; as soon as he retired, the team collapsed. But, at the time of his retirement, two of his key colleagues, Scottie Pippen and Dennis Rodman, also left. It is at least arguable that Jordan's record-breaking feats were made possible by an exceptional supporting team.

The same might be said of Pelé, who is universally acknowledged as the best-ever soccer player and who scored a career total of 1,200 goals in 1,253 games, a barely believable average of 0.9577 that will never be bettered. In 1972, he scored his 1,000th goal to become the most prolific striker in history. During his 16-year peak (1958–74), he led the Brazilian national team to three World Cup victories (1958, 1962, 1970) and was the first – and, so far, only – player to win three World Cup Championships. He completed his active career playing for New York Cosmos and led the team to the North American Soccer League title. Pelé played for the Brazilian club Santos, which won the first World Club Championship in 1962; he never played in the arguably more competitive European leagues which have longer and more physically taxing schedules and, in some cases, play in severe weather conditions. So, we will never know how he would have fared in more demanding circumstances.

Pelé's great reputation was forged in international competition in periods when the Brazilian national team had an *embarras de richesses*: players like Garrincha, Gerson, Rivelino, and Tostao were each outstanding in their own right and made a significant contribution to Pelé's success. As with Jordan, Pelé's calculable accomplishments possibly mask the degree to which the player depended on a singularly strong team.

Some team sports allow competitors to demonstrate individual excellence: in cricket and baseball, for instance, a batsman or hitter stands alone while the ball rushes toward them. Australian cricketer Don Bradman amassed statistics and broke records that stand up to any scrutiny. His overall career average was 95.4 runs per innings; he made 100 in every 2.9 innings and just failed to average 100 (99.94) in full Tests (the next best Test average is 60.97 achieved by Graeme Pollack, of South Africa).

Bradman hit a record number of six triple centuries (300+ runs) and a record number of 37 double centuries. His aggregate runs: 974 at 139.14 in a Test series of eight games. Twice (1930, 1938) he scored 1,000 runs by the end of May, a feat no other batsman has achieved. In 1929/30, he made 452 not out, then a record individual score – subsequently beaten. He scored a total of 6,996 runs (including 29 centuries) in 52 Tests. To gauge the magnitude of this, we should note that it took Australia's Greg Chappell an additional 30 Test matches to pass that total (and Sunil Gavaskar more than 100 Tests to beat the 29 centuries).

Personal accomplishments aside, Bradman led Australia in 24 Tests for an overall record of 15–3–6. He was 40 when he made his final tour of England and still in good form, averaging 89.92 runs and hitting 11 centuries. Bradman's peak years extended from 1927, when he started playing for New South Wales, to 1948, but the 21 years were interrupted by the 1939–45 war. So one can only imagine what Bradman's already impressive statistics would be like had he not been deprived of six years of activity. It is probable that every record would stand in perpetuity.

Willie Mays led the National League (NL) in home runs in 1955, 1962, 1964, and 1965 and in stolen bases between 1956 and 1959. He was the first player to hit 300 home runs combined with stealing 300 bases in his career and the first NL player to score 600 home runs. He completed his career with a total of 660 home runs and a batting average of 0.302, leading many to believe that he was the consummate baseball player. Mays played center for the New York Giants and led the team to the NL pennant. After serving in the military 1952–3, he returned to the Giants in 1954 and became the NL's leading batter with a 0.345 average. He also won the season's MVP award while leading the Giants to a World Series victory.

Mays maintained consistently excellent form throughout a 16-year peak (1950–66), but was past his best when, in 1972, he made a late career move to the New York Mets at the age of 41; he retired at the end of the 1973 season. Reservations such as those made about Jordan and Pelé do not apply to either Bradman or Mays. Certainly, both played in strong teams, but, given the individuality of their playing positions, it is reasonable to suppose that both would have excelled in other teams.

Playing in a team is a skill in itself and, while we should strive to contextualize the achievements of individuals, we should also acknowledge that operating as an integral part of a unit demands a discipline and selflessness that is beyond some otherwise accomplished athletes. Yet, there are sports where the ability to perform as an isolated individual, often in pressure situations, is paramount. The next selection of contenders have all distinguished themselves in such sports.

We have seen elsewhere in this book how women have been either excluded from or pushed to the margins of many sports. Yet, the record of Martina Navratilova and the manner of her dominance for much of her 11-year peak (1976–87) amply justifies her inclusion in this evaluation.

Czech-born Navratilova defected to the USA in 1975 after having already won four doubles titles (with Chris Evert), played in the singles finals of seven major championships and won the Junior Girls Championship at Wimbledon in 1973. She was 19 at the time of the defection. In 1976, she won the doubles title (with Evert). But her ascent truly began the following year when she won the official women's tour and took the Wimbledon singles title. She successfully defended the title in 1979 and finished the year as the number one ranked women's player.

Between 1982 and 1987, her supremacy on grass was beyond question and she won six straight Wimbledon singles titles; her nine Wimbledon singles titles remain a record that is unlikely to be bettered. In the same period, she prevailed at the US Open four times (1983–4, 1986–7), three times at the Australian Open (1981, 1983, 1985) and twice at the French Open (1982, 1984). In doubles, she won ten US Open championships, eight Australian, seven French, and six Wimbledons (with various partners). Unlike many players, she could adapt to different surfaces and still triumph.

Navratilova's career total of 167 singles titles are the most won by any player, female or male. She won 18 Grand Slam titles and held the record of 109 consecutive doubles wins (with Pam Shriver). Between 1982 and 1987, she held the number one ranking for all but 22 weeks of a 282-week stretch – almost five and a half years. All in all, she was ranked number one for 332 weeks, or a cumulative six years five months, suggesting a dominion unsurpassed in tennis or any other sport. Her 11-year peak was between 1976 and 1987, though her decline thereafter was very gradual: in 1993, a year before her retirement, Navratilova, then in her 37th year, beat the number one ranked player Monica Seles.

Another all-conquering athlete born in Czechoslovakia (as it then was) was Emil Zatopek whose track achievements over a range of distances will probably never be emulated. The highlight of Zatopek's career was at the 1952 Olympics at Helsinki, where he won three gold medals at 5,000 meters, 10,000 meters, and the marathon – the cumulative distance of which is over 35 miles (an extent of three and 26+ miles, respectively). In the previous Olympics, Zatopek had won gold at 10,000 meters and silver at 5,000 meters. He also won European titles at 10,000 meters (twice) and 5,000 meters.

Between 1949 and 1951, Zatopek was unbeatable, winning 69 straight races over various distances. His career total was 261 wins from 334 races, giving him a win percentage of over 78 per cent. In the process, Zatopek broke a career total of 18 world records over several distances. His six-year peak (1948–54) was relatively long for a middle-distance runner, especially one who opted for such a variety of distances.

Vying with Zatopek for the premier athlete of the immediate post-war period was Detroit-born Sugar Ray Robinson who won the world welterweight title (limit: 147lbs, or 66.68kg) in 1946 and the middleweight title (160lbs, 72.58kg) in 1950 before being defeated by heat exhaustion in his attempt to win the light-heavyweight title (175lbs, 79.38kg) – fighting in 96°F, Robinson was leading on all judge's cards against Joey Maxim at the time of the stoppage in the 14th round (it was the only time he was beaten inside the distance).

Like Zatopek, Robinson's range was formidable. Boxing in a period when there were no intermediate titles (such as junior middleweight, or supermiddleweight), Robinson often gave away over ten pounds to opponents. Also like Zatopek, he was, for a while, invincible: between February 1943 and July 1951, he fought 91 consecutive contests without defeat (two draws, one no-contest). From the start of his pro career in 1940 until 1955, he avenged his only three losses. Robinson's nine-year peak (1943–52) was a fiercely competitive period with boxers such as Jake LaMotta, Rocky Graziano, and Kid Gavilan vying for titles.

Robinson announced his retirement in 1952 after the Maxim fight, but returned 16 months later and declined, at first gradually, then more sharply until his final retirement in December 1965. Sixteen of his defeats came in his comeback phase, his overall record of 175–19–6 being distorted by the 13-year extension beyond his prime. Few pundits dissent from the view that Robinson was the most complete boxer ever, combining finesse with punching power (63 per cent of his wins were by knockout).

None of the athletes considered thus far featured in sports that are reliant on technology. Clearly, advances in training apparatus, techniques, nutrition, etc., need to be considered when making an evaluation. But there are even more complicating factors when we appraise athletes whose performance is directly linked to technology: how would they have fared with today's advanced equipment. It is too trite to state simply that they would have been even better. Björn Borg towered above opposition in the late 1970s using a wooden tennis racket. Nowadays, players favor rackets with a frame of graphite, a light material that absorbs less energy when the ball is hit and so allows for faster, stronger returns with less effort and minimizes vibration in the arm (limiting the chances of injury). Borg made an abortive comeback in 1991 and could not adapt to the lighter racket; he continued to use a wooden version. It could be argued that, at 34, he was unlikely to have recovered his best form, anyway. But the example at least suggests that particular athletes excel because of the equipment available and there is no guarantee that they would have been as dominant using other technologies.

In the case of Eddy Merckx, it is likely that the athlete would have triumphed regardless. The Belgian cyclist's habit of devouring the competition earned him the nickname of "The Cannibal" and his five Tour de France wins (1969–72, 1974) included wins in a record 35 stages. His supremacy was underscored with five wins in the Giro d'Italia (1968, 1970, 1972–4) and one Vuelta a Espana (1973). He also won two tours of Belgium (1970–1), one tour of Switzerland (1974) and three world road championships (1967, 1971, 1974). In 1972, at Mexico City, Merckx covered 30.717 miles (49.432 km) in 60 minutes to break the world one-hour record. He finished his career with 32 major classics for a career total of 525 wins in 1,800 races.

While Merckx's statistics alone are sufficient to warrant contention among the world's all-time elite athletes, it was the manner of his victories that set him apart from other cyclists, such as Bernard Hinault, Miguel Indurain, or Jacques Anquetil, all of whom dominated professional cycling for periods. Merckx's pro career spanned 1965–78, his 6-year peak (1969–74) seeming short compared with competitors from other sports, but not for cycling which exacts a punishing toll.

Juan Manuel Fangio is regarded as the finest racing car driver ever, and his record endorses this: five times Formula One champion (1951, 1954–7), including an astonishing victory in 1951 achieved while dropping only five points in the whole season. The blip in his form in 1953 was the result of a crash at Monza. Born in Argentina, Fangio did not move to Europe until he was 38 and, in his first season driving for Alfa Romeo, came second in the world championship. Between 1951 and 1953, he drove for Ferrari, BRM and Maserati, before switching to Mercedes. Apart from his track victories, he won many long-distance road races. Fangio's six-year peak (1951–7) did not start until he was 40 (he retired at 47). Many have speculated that Ayrton Senna, who was killed in 1994 when aged 34, having won four world championships, would have eclipsed Fangio had he lived. But, would Senna have handled the relatively primitive technology Fangio had at his disposal? Would Fangio have controlled the extra power Senna had to command?

Who will stake first claim to be the best athlete of the twenty-first century? Marion Jones, of Thousand Oaks, California. Her accomplishments can be best placed into perspective by considering the scarcity of her defeats. In September 1997, she was beaten into second place by Merlene Ottey over 100 meters; it was Jones's last defeat over the distance until the end of the century (when she was 24). Over 200 meters, her invincibility was even more consummate: unbeaten from 1994, when a college student. Imperious on the track, Jones amassed world, Olympic and Grand Prix titles, though without ever threatening the sprint world records held by Florence Griffith Joyner (see Chapter seven for possible explanations why). Jones's defeats in the long jump were more common, though she generally claimed a top three place among the world's best.

More questions . . .

- Today's athletes have the benefit of high-tech training as well as psychologists, dietitians and other specialists. Is it not logical to presume they are better than their counterparts from the past?
- Are achievements across sports commensurable?
- Which are the greatest teams ever?

Read on . . .

- Blue, A., *Martina: The life and times of Martina Navratilova* (Birch Lane Press, 1995).
- Fangio, J. M. and Carrozzo, R., *Fangio: My racing life* (Thorsons, 1990).
- Halberstam, D., *Playing for Keeps: Michael Jordan and the world he made* (Random House, 1999).
- Mays, W. and Sahadi, L., *Say Hey: The autobiography of Willie Mays* (Pocket Books, 1989).
- Messier, M., Gretzky, W., and Hull, B., *Wayne Gretzky: The making of the great one* (Beckett Publications, 1998).
- Page, M., *Bradman: The biography* (Pan Macmillan Australia, 1988).
- Pelé and Fish, R., *Pelé: My life and the beautiful game* (Doubleday, 1977).
- Robinson, R. S. and Anderson, D., *Sugar Ray: The Sugar Ray Robinson story* (Robson Books, 1992).
- Sandrock, M., *Running with the Legends* (Human Kinetics, 1996).
- Vanwalleghem, R., *Eddy Merckx: The greatest cyclist of the twentieth century* (Velo Press, 1968).

building bodies

science, sex, and

natural-born losers

BEAUTIFUL IN MEN, UGLY IN WOMEN

The human body has changed physiologically over the years: improvements in nutrition, better sanitation, healthier living conditions, and better understandings of its structure and functions have made an impact on the body. These physical changes have cultural counterparts: changes in popular comprehensions of the body. The story of Bernarr Macfadden reminds us that the way we make sense of our and other people's bodies is open to sometimes quite considerable changes.

Macfadden was, among other things, a publisher, an advocate of vigorous exercise and campaigner for the relaxation of censorship. In 1893, Macfadden watched a demonstration of strength by Eugen Sandow, in Chicago. Sandow pulled a few strongman stunts and posed in a way not unlike today's bodybuilders. Macfadden was so inspired, he went away and invented an exercise machine consisting of cables and pulleys. He also wrote a manual on how to use "The Macfadden Exerciser," as it was called.

Macfadden toured the United States and Britain, exhibiting himself as evidence of the machine's efficacy. He lectured on the benefits of physical exercise and struck up poses, much as Sandow had done. Soon he became a rival to Sandow, who had made money from a mail order training

program. Macfadden's manual changed into a free-standing magazine with articles on training and diet. In 1899, he published a second magazine, *Physical Culture* (retailing at five cents). Later, he launched the first women's physique magazine *Women's Physical Development*, which was changed in 1903 to *Beauty and Health*.

One of the premises of Macfadden's philosophy of physical culture was that a oneness with nature is absolutely vital to a healthy life. It followed that a natural act like sex should be practiced as often as possible. He encouraged sex in his publications – much to the annoyance of censors who objected particularly to the illustrations that accompanied his articles on sexual activity. According to Macfadden, a healthy sex life was highly conducive to physical fitness. What's more, he publicized this through his magazine.

The magazine was so successful that, in 1919, Macfadden expanded his business interests with another publication, this time more of a tabloid venture specializing in confessions. Again the magazine was decried, especially by censorious church groups, which insisted that sexuality and the body were private issues and should be kept that way.

Macfadden published copious articles about physical beauty, how to achieve it and how to show it off to your best advantage. A sedentary life was the worst enemy of beauty: good looks came through exercise and plenty of sex. Macfadden was years ahead of his time, of course: the prevailing wisdom was that women were naturally fragile and ill-equipped for the kinds of activities applauded by Macfadden. In fact, Macfadden's training prescriptions were seen as downright dangerous for women.

The popular view of the day was that women were naturally beautiful the way they were: the kinds of physical changes brought on by regular exercise were liable to make women unsightly. "To men and women in the first half of the nineteenth century, any sort of muscular development on women was seen as useless and unattractive," writes Jan Todd in her article "Bernarr Macfadden: Reformer of the feminine form" (1987: 70). "Strength was beautiful in men and ugly in women."

Todd traces how the ideal female form was in the throes of change. "Ethereal frailty," as she calls it, was on its way out in the 1870s and, by the turn of the century, the hourglass figure had evolved into an "S" shape, with more prominence given to women's busts. The prettiness associated with women during the Victorian era "had given way to height, grandeur and sturdiness." The emerging ideal women was described as a "Titaness."

Macfadden set out to find his perfect woman in 1904, when he promoted a contest eventually won by Emma Newkirk, of Santa Monica. Run like a beauty pageant, but with quite different criteria, the contest was augmented with other competitions, all featuring women. Foot races, wrestling, and, bizarrely, fasting competitions were held. As expected, in an age when the role of women at sports events was thought properly to be ornamental, Macfadden's project proved controversial.

One of Macfadden's particular dislikes was the Victorian corset, which was both a harmful and constricting article of underwear and a symbol of female captivity, confinement, and downright servitude. Even when playing tennis, women were obliged to wear corsets under their full-length skirts, long-sleeved blouses, and boater hats. And tennis was one of the few sports in which women were allowed to compete in the early years of the century.

Todd points out, that while Macfadden was campaigning, unprecedentedly high numbers of American women were going to work: "The number of women who entered the work force increased at a rate faster than the birth rate" (1987: 74). So, conceptions of women were changing. The time had not yet arrived when women could enter a full team at the Olympic Games. But, it was alright for a woman to work a full day in a factory.

Popular understanding of the purposes and limits of a woman's body was in the process of change and, while Macfadden may not appear in anybody's "Who's Who?" of feminist reformers, Todd believes he made a "significant contribution" to the aesthetic shift that encouraged a more energetic, active role for women. By projecting images of strong, fit, and vigorous females, he paved the way for a reconsideration of women. Specifically, he initiated new perspectives on women's bodies. For Macfadden, firm, healthy, and toned bodies were not simply for decorative purposes; they were active, agile, mobile, and could perform as athletically as men's.

We will never know Macfadden's intentions. Maybe he was a shrewd entrepreneur with an eye for an opportunity; having witnessed Sandow's success, he set about improving on it. Courting controversy as he did served to improve his business position. But, even if his motives were tainted, the effect he had on provoking discussions on the female body is undoubted. Subsequent popularizers of what we might call the cult of the body beautiful borrowed from Macfadden's portfolio. Angelo Siciliano a.k.a. "Charles Atlas" made his fortune through his "dynamic tension" system of bodybuilding. A champion bodybuilder himself, Atlas's claim that "You too can have a body like mine" was featured in mail order advertisements the world over.

In the 1940s, Joe and Ben Weider tried to extend bodybuilding from its exhibition format to a fully-fledged competitive sport. This was quite an innovation as it carried no connotation of strength. Unlike, for example, weight-lifting, bodybuilding focused solely on the look of the human body, its symmetry of shape, the sharpness of muscle separation, the tone of the skin and so on. The brothers' intention was to create bodybuilding as the legitimate competitive sport it now is.

BEYOND NARCISSISM

Introducing their collection of essays, *The Making of the Modern Body: Sexuality and society in the nineteenth century*, Catherine Gallagher and Thomas Laqueur observe of the human body:

> Not only has it been perceived, interpreted, and represented differently in different epochs, but it has also been lived differently, brought into being within widely dissimilar cultures, subjected to various technologies and means of control, and incorporated into different rhythms of production and consumption, pleasure and pain.
>
> (1987: i)

Their point is that there is no single understanding of the human body that holds good for all cultures at all times. Of course, every body is made of flesh, blood and bones, and, nowadays, the odd piece of metal or plastic. But, the significance of the body and the purposes it serves change as our interest in it broadens, or narrows. The way we care for it, nourish it, adorn it, display it, represent important statements about our culture. The space it occupies, the curves it defines, the manner of its regulation, the methods of its restraint, its fertility and sexuality: these and other features make the body a potent instrument for understanding ourselves and our culture.

From today's standpoint, Macfadden's ventures appear to be ludicrously tame. After all, what was he saying? That beauty and fitness go together and that sex can be healthy. His infamous magazines featuring the partially-clad female form that incurred the wrath of the censors were as innocuous as a DC comic and probably less exciting. Macfadden, though, was doing something more than peddling mags and exercise machines: he was pushing people to a new awareness of their own and others' bodies. He was urging women in particular to experience their bodies differently.

In many ways, Macfadden anticipated the changes that came about during the growth of what historian Christopher Lasch, in the title of one of his books, called *The Culture of Narcissism* (1979). As the promise of the 1960s radicalism waned and the anti-Vietnam movement gradually wound down, people looked for a therapeutic intervention in their own lives, rather than theirs *and* others. A new movement in the 1970s was driven by a quest for self-understanding or self-perfection; in other words, personal growth. Lasch argues that people became preoccupied with themselves: they admired themselves, pampered themselves, attended to themselves. Like Narcissus who fell in love with his own reflection, people became emotionally and intellectually fixated with their own images.

The almost obsessive self-centeredness translated into a demand for physical perfection; an avoidance of substances that were obviously harmful; and a fascination for any new product that promised youth. If maintaining the body was once a privilege, it became a binding duty. The preoccupation intensified, giving rise to an industry dedicated to the requirements of keeping in shape and attending to body maintenance.

The term body maintenance itself reveals how we came to regard the body as analogous to a machine, particularly a car which requires regular servicing and repairs to perform efficiently. The analogy works both ways: diagnostic checks are now advised for cars between major services.

But, if the term itself is relatively new, the concept behind it is not. "In traditional societies, religious communities such as monasteries demanded ascetic routines with an emphasis upon exercise and dietary control," writes Mike Featherstone in his "The body in consumer culture" (1991: 182). Denying the body more earthly gratifications meant that higher, spiritual purposes could be pursued. The whole Christian tradition emphasized the primacy of the soul over the body, which needs to be repressed. It was, after all, the body not the soul that succumbed to temptation.

Perversely, one of the main intentions of body maintenance is to maximize the opportunities to succumb to such temptation. People restrain and care for their bodies in order to feel good about their appearance. In other words, they want to believe they look attractive to others. The often unstated purpose of cultural imperatives to become fit, healthy, and toned is sexual. An athletic body is a sexy one; a dissipated one is definitely not.

We have now entered a stage that we might call "the culture beyond narcissism." Lasch was writing of a period slightly before the body became such a focal point of people's lives; when we were less absorbed about the status and appearance of our bodies. Now, we have idealized forms to which we are supposed to aspire. Television commercials, magazines, movies, videos, and many other media heave with images of supermodels and hunks, who, three decades ago, would have been regarded as freaks of nature and muscle-bound monstrosities, respectively. Now many people want to mimic them.

Macfadden was hounded for publishing pictures of women and men who would be overdressed by today's magazine standards. Pick up any copy of a respectable publication, like *GQ* or *FHM*, and you will find about a dozen pictures of women in swimwear or underclothes, the kind of shots that would have embarrassed Macfadden himself.

The culture beyond narcissism has fostered a self-awareness of our own bodies that has produced its own corollary: we are interested in other people's bodies, not for licentious reasons, but just out of curiosity. This is part of the same mentality that allows us to declare often highly personal details about ourselves in the interests of security, but fires our interest in the lives of others

– as the success of confessional tv programs suggests. We do not mind disclosing more of ourselves just as long as we can inspect more of everybody else. Their bodies included.

The 100 years or so after Macfadden first saw Eugen Sandow's act saw changes of such enormity in the way people related to and experienced their own and others' bodies that it is laughable to imagine how his projects caused offense. The fact that they did and that Macfadden was forced to operate like an early Larry Flynt reminds us of an important point: that when people thought and looked about bodies in Macfadden's day, they were thinking and looking very differently than we do today. So differently in fact that we might as well say they were thinking and looking about two different things.

How about the bodies of female sports performers? After Florence Griffith Joyner in the 1980s and Gabrielle Reece in the 1990s, we have a generation of women athletes who are often indistinguishable from fashion models or rock stars. But, never mind their looks: they perform to standards and have capacities that are not far behind – and are, in some cases, ahead – of men's. Rarely, if ever, do we doubt their durability, resilience, or downright toughness. We are probably not sure why we ever wondered at these features. There are reasons.

LIKE A MAN

Macfadden flew in the face of popular wisdom when he maintained that women not only could, but should, do vigorous physical exercise. This was in stark contrast to what most felt was appropriate to women, who were simply not naturally suited to such endeavors. It was a matter of scientific fact established by an intellectual tradition in which women's bodies were defined by scientists as objects of sexuality and reproduction.

Nelly Oudshoorn's extraordinary book *Beyond the Natural Body: An archaeology of sex hormones* analyzes how this conception of the female body dominated medical discourse through the eighteenth and nineteenth centuries. In this period, intellectual curiosity centered on the dissimilarities between men and women: in what respects were they different? This may strike us as perfectly obvious; the fact that it does illustrates again just how dramatically understanding of the human body can change. Oudshoorn's work underlines that new knowledge does not just make the body more transparent: it actually alters its nature – nature being the order we impose on our physical environment to help us make sense of it.

Oudshoorn acknowledges that her account was influenced by the work of two scholars, Thomas Laqueur and Londa Schiebinger. Laqueur's studies of medical texts indicate that the concept of a sharp division between male and female is a product of the past 300 years and, for 2,000 years before that, bodies were not visualized in terms of differences. In other words, there were people, some of whom could have children, others of whom could not; sexual difference was not a concept, so it was impossible to conceive of a distinct bifurcation of types based on sexual identity. Even physical differences we now regard as obvious were not so obvious without a conceptual understanding of sexual differences. In some periods, a woman's clitoris was thought to be a minuscule protuberance, an underdeveloped version of the equivalent structure in men – the penis.

For most of human history, the stress was on similarities, the female body being just a "gradation," or nuance of one basic male type. Needless to say this vision complemented and bolstered a male-centered world-view in which, as Laqueur puts it in his *Making Sex: Body and gender from the Greeks to Freud*, "man is the measure of all things, and woman does not exist as an ontologically distinct category" (1990: 62).

The tradition of bodily similarities came under attack, particularly from anatomists who argued that sex was not restricted only to reproductive organs, but affected every part of the body. Anatomists' interest in this was fired by the idea that even the skeleton had sexual characteristics. Schiebinger's medical history *The Mind Has No Sex: Women in the origins of modern science* shows that anatomists in the nineteenth century searched for the sources of women's difference and apparent inferiority. Depictions of the female skull were used to "prove" that women were naturally inferior to men in intellectual capacities. In the process, the concept of sexual differences was integrated into the discourse; so that, by the end of the nineteenth century, female and male bodies were understood in terms of opposites, each having different organs, functions, and even feelings.

Oudshoorn's work picks up the story by identifying how the female body became conceptualized in terms of its unique sexual essence in the 1920s and 1930s. In these decades, sex endocrinology created a completely new understanding of sexual differences based on hormones. Eventually, hormonal differences became accepted natural facts. Knowledge, on this account, was not discovered but produced: research on hormones created a different model of the sexes which was adopted universally and served to re-shape our most fundamental conceptions of human nature. Women were different to men in the most profound, categorical, and immovable way.

So, women were not only discouraged from participating in sports and exercise, but were warned against it. "Medical advice concerning exercise and physical activity came to reflect and perpetuate understandings about women's 'abiding sense of physical weakness' and the unchangeable nature of her physical inferiority," writes Patricia Vertinsky in her article "Exercise, physical capability, and the eternally wounded woman in late nineteenth century North America" (1987: 8). In this and her later book, *The Eternally Wounded Woman: Women, doctors and exercise in the late nineteenth century*, Vertinsky explores how physicians' interpretation of biological theories of menstruation led them to discourage taxing physical exertion.

Menstruation – the eternal wound – was seen as a form of invalidity and its beginning meant that young women would need to be careful in conserving energy. Growing up had quite different meanings for young males and females, as Vertinsky observes: "Puberty for boys marked the onset of strength and enhanced vigor; for girls it marked the onset of the prolonged and periodic weaknesses of womanhood" (1987: 17). Remember, this was the popular view at a time (the 1880s) when the full ramifications of sexuality were the subject of great debate.

Disabled by menstruation women were less-than-perfect when compared to men. Their physical inferiority prohibited them from competing against each other, let alone men. As in so many other instances of exclusion, the justification was based on patronage: it was for women's own sake. If they tried to emulate their physically superior male counterparts, they would be risking damaging themselves.

Scientific studies of how menstruation defined and delimited a woman's capacity for physical activity shaped popular thought, their credibility enhanced by their apparent symmetry with folk beliefs and taboos concerning impurity and contamination. Vertinsky notes that scientific and medical theories were "strongly colored by these traditional beliefs" (1987: 11).

Women were thought to be so handicapped during monthly periods that they were prone to accidents and hysteria, making sport and exercise unsuitable areas of activity. Another scientific view was that women possessed a finite amount of energy and, unlike men, were "taxed" biologically with special energy demands necessitated by menstruation and reproduction. Women could never aspire to the kind of intellectual and social development pursued by men because they were simply not built for that purpose: they were naturally mothers.

There were some schools of thought that held that the enfeebling effects of menstruation could be offset by cold baths, deep breathing, and mild exercising, such as beanbag-throwing, hoops, or golf. Especially appropriate, according to Alice Tweedy, writing in *Popular Science Monthly* in 1892, were "homely gymnastics," i.e. housework. Other physicians prescribed rest and energy-conservation. While these may sound like (if the reader will pardon the phrase) old wives' tales, they had the status of scientific fact in the period when organized sports were coming into being. Sports were intended for men only.

Vertinsky quotes a passage from influential physician Henry Maudsley who, in 1874, wrote that "women are marked out by Nature for very different offices in life from those of men ... special functions render it improbable

---

Pregnancy

While scientists once cautioned that exercise might damage a woman's reproductive functions, the potential benefits of the hormones produced in early pregnancy were realized in the 1950s. During the first three months of pregancy, the mother's body generates a natural surplus of red corpuscles rich in hemoglobin. These assist cardiac and lung performance and improve muscle capacity by up to 30 per cent. A pregnant woman also secretes increased amounts of progesterone to make muscles more supple and joints more flexible. In 1984, Evelyn Ashford, of the USA, broke the 100-meter world record and 40 weeks later gave birth; Ingrid Kristiansen, of Norway, did it in reverse order, first giving birth, then returning to the track to record the world's best times for 5,000 and 10,000 meters.

Olga Karasseva (now Kovalenko), a gymnastics gold medal winner at the 1968 summer Olympics, later revealed that she had become pregnant and had an abortion shortly before the games to prepare her body. She also claimed that, during the 1970s, females as young as 14 were ordered to have sex with their men friends or coaches in an effort to become pregnant (reported in the British *Sunday Times*, S1: 23, November 27, 1994). Suspicions that female athletes from the former Soviet Union planned abortions to coincide with competitions first surfaced in 1956 at the Melbourne summer Olympics, then eight years later at Tokyo. One estimate at the time suggested that as many as ten out of 26 medal winners may have manipulated their pregnancies, though no conclusive proof ever came to light.

---

she will succeed, and unwise for her to persevere in running over the same course at the same pace with him ... women cannot rebel successfully against the tyranny of their organization" (1987: 25). The same natural tyranny that dictated women's exclusion from sports and exercise restricted women's activities in all other areas of social life. "Scientific definitions of human 'nature' were thus used to justify the channeling of men and women ... into vastly different social roles," writes Schiebinger in her article "Skeletons in the closet: The first illustrations of the female skeleton in eighteenth-century anatomy" (Gallagher and Laqueur 1987: 72). "It was thought 'natural' that men, by virtue of their 'natural reason,' should dominate public spheres of government and commerce, science and scholarship, while women, as creatures of feeling, fulfilled their natural destiny as mothers, conservators of custom in the confined sphere of the home."

One can imagine why Macfadden's startling ideas caused such a stir. In proposing a more active capability for women, he was unwittingly undermining a whole set of roles that had been reserved for women and which supported an entire configuration of social institutions. Even the most tremulous suggestion about activities for women was likely to incense those whose interests were best served by passive women.

For example, toward the end of the nineteenth century, cycling was a popular pastime in North America and Europe. Both men and women cycled, though to mixed reactions from the medical community. While the advantages to men's health were acknowledged, there was a suspicion about whether women's bodies were up to the rigors of cycling. Many doctors believed that the pedaling motion when operating a sewing machine gave women sufficient exercise, according to Helen Lenskyj (1986: 30). One wonders what those doctors would have thought about the six-day, 274-mile Hewlett-Packard International Women's Challenge pro biking race, or the women's Tour de France (and particularly about Canada's Linda Jackson, who competed regularly in and won some of these events when approaching her 40th birthday).

As we have seen, up till relatively recently, women's bodies were seen as ill-equipped to cope with the physical and mental demands of sports. An entire discourse devoted to the subject of the effect of exercise and competition on the body and minds of women threw up all manner of reason why women should not enter sports. The same discourse served to justify women's subservient position in society generally.

This did not stop women who wanted to get involved in sports, and in her *Out of Bounds: Women, sport and sexuality*, Lenskyj provides examples of competitors in several sports and women's organizations that would cater for them. She also points out that sportswomen were generally seen as odd. Labeled as tomboys or hoydens, they were thought to lack "femininity" and even represent a moral degeneracy that was thought to be creeping into society. Macfadden, incidentally, had pointed out that almost all beautiful women had been tomboys in their youth.

"Although some doctors advocated exercise therapy in the early 1900s, a time when rest, not exercise, was the accepted medical treatment for virtually all diseases and injuries, they rarely made the connection between exercise therapy and women's full sporting participation," writes Lenskyj (1986: 30).

Despite the fears, women were cautiously admitted to the more demanding track events of the Olympics, though the sight of exhausted females fighting for their breath as they crossed the line of the 800 meters in 1928 was so repugnant to Olympic organizers that they removed the event from women's schedules. Not until 1960 was the distance reinstated for women.

Yet, women continued to steal their ways into competition, giving rise to a different scare. Contemporary biologists Lynda Birke and Gail Vines use a cautionary quotation from a 1939 book on women and sport: "Too much activity in sports of a masculine character causes the female body to become more like that of a man" (1987: 340). Virilism is the term that describes the development of secondary male sexual characteristics in women; and there is evidence that continued use of synthesized testosterone-based products is responsible for facial hair, deep voice, broad shoulders, muscle mass, and other typically male features. In the 1930s, this evidence was not available. The assumption was that exercise and competition in themselves would cause female genital organs to decay and so pervert woman's true nature.

Virilism

This referred to the theory that exercise affected a woman's endocrinal system, possibly leading to virilism – the development of secondary male characteristics. The idea was based on the fact that testosterone, the hormone responsible for facial hair, deep voice, broad shoulders, muscle mass, and other typically male features and which is produced primarily in testes, is found in both sexes, though significantly less in females' adrenal glands. Prolonged exercise, it was speculated, induced an imbalance in women's hormones, causing an overproduction of testosterone and a resultant "de-feminization."

Not only was a woman's body regarded as too weak and liable to serious hormonal dysfunction if she went into sports, "but the competitive mentality was antithetical to her true nature," reported the respected *Scientific American* journal as late as 1936, adding that women had an "innate tendency to shun competition." By this time, women were already showing competence in a variety of Olympic sports, including track and field, swimming, and many team sports. Yet, fears about the long-term effects persisted and physical prohibitions were reinforced by social ones.

Lenskyj's study reveals how sneering comments about tomboys added to alarm over the masculinizing effects of sport grew into fully-fledged condemnations of sporting females' alleged sexual proclivities. Women aiming to succeed in sports were freighted with scientific and popular beliefs and images about the rightful place of women. Any achievement of note was a subversion of established wisdom. Lenskyj's thesis is that, in all other social contexts, women's femininity served to validate male identity and male power at both individual and social levels. A woman who defied scientific orthodoxy and excelled in areas defined by and for men was a threat.

Women who managed to negotiate a successful passage into sports, or any other traditionally male domain, for that matter, were snagged in a paradox. Lenskyj argues that male heterosexual standards were applied to sports and women who succeeded were immediately suspected of being lesbians. If they were not lesbians before they went into sports, they would be before long. Their achievements were undermined by the presumption that they were not natural women at all; or, as Lenskyj puts it, by "the equating of any sign of athletic or intellectual competence with masculinity, and by extension, with lesbianism" (1986: 74).

Those who failed escaped allegations, especially if they had conventionally good looks (as defined by heterosexual males, of course). "Thus, the unathletic or unintelligent woman suffered no handicap in men's estimation as long as she was attractive. Although beauty redeemed a lack of intellectual ability, the reverse was not true," writes Lenskyj. "Moreover, it seemed that athletic ability did not redeem any feminine inadequacies. Beating a man at golf was hardly conducive to a harmonious relationship" (1986: 74–5).

No culture that promotes masculinity could surrender one of its bastions of masculine pride to women. But, preaching conformity to male standards requires a transgressive influence as an example of otherness. It appeared that women athletes might fill that position; their transgressions being punished with the stigma of homosexuality, or the stain of virilism. All this would be grossly offensive today; but, as mid-century approached, it was nothing of the sort. In fact, it was common sense and rested on a scientific discourse that had been in progress for a couple of centuries.

Barr bodies sex test

This was designed to establish unambiguously whether contestants were male or female. The test required that a sample of cells be scraped from the inside of a competitor's cheek, or hair follicle, and subjected to a laboratory examination to determine whether a minimum number contain what are called "Barr bodies" (collections of chromatins). Although the exact number of these chromatins varies from woman to woman and may change over time for any given woman, usually about 20 out of 100 cells contain this characteristic. If the count dropped below a minimum percentage, the athlete would be disqualified from competition.

The thought of female sports performers functioning within these kinds of restrictions was not a promising one. Yet, women showed that their talents were more supple than they may have appeared. Struggling through the fears and prejudices, women showed that their bodies were sturdier than they appeared and their minds as competitive as any man's. Besmirching sportswomen remained commonplace through the 1940s and 1950s. At the 1952 summer Olympics, the achievements of brawny Soviet field athletes and tenaciously competitive Japanese volleyball players were regarded with skepticism: were they women at all? Appeals for sex tests followed.

Actually, the calls for some standardized sex-testing had been growing since 1946 when three female medal winners at the European Athletic championships declared themselves to be men. They had "male-like genitals" and facial hair as well as chromosomal indicators of maleness. In 1952, two French female medalists were later exposed as males. The cries for testing reached full pitch in 1955 when it was revealed that the German winner of the women's high jump at the 1936 Berlin Olympics was in fact a man who had been pressured into competing for the glory of the Third Reich.

Other individual competitors, like Stella Walsh, the Polish-American track and field athlete, was the subject of widespread discussion in the 1930s and 1940s. It was not until her death in 1981 that it was discovered that she had male-like testicles. The innuendo about Walsh was mild compared to that about Irina and Tamara Press, of the former Soviet Union. They both disappeared suddenly from active competition soon after the introduction of mandatory sex-testing in 1966.

Prior to this, certificates from the country of origin were sufficient proof. But visual examinations from gynecologists replaced this at the European Athletic Championships in Budapest. Chromosomal testing was introduced in 1967, when Polish sprinter Eva Klobkowska was disqualified from competition after failing such a test. To her apparent surprise, she was found to have internal testicles (a condition that is not as uncommon as it sounds).

At the time, knowledge of the extensive performance-enhancing programs that were being pursued in Soviet-bloc countries, especially the Soviet Union and East Germany, was obscure. The connection between taking anabolic steroids and the acquisition of male features was not widely known. In retrospect, it is probable that many of the female athletes who were suspected of being men had been inducted into steroid use, probably at an early age.

Lenskyj's comment that "it has served male interests to stress biological differences, and to ignore the more numerous and obvious biological similarities between the sexes" returns us to where we were before the emergent scientific discourse of the eighteenth century started kicking in (1987: 141). The implication of Lenskyj's statement is that women's experience in sport would have been radically different if they had not been the subject of an intense yet tortuous debate on the precise nature of the woman's body.

Historically, sports, particularly those that involve strenuous competition, have certified masculinity: by providing the kind of unmediated athletic challenge rarely encountered in working days, sports made possible a strong and assertive proclamation of men's strength, valor, and, above all, physical superiority over women. Industrial society brought with it, among other things, a less physical life, one in which manual labor, while still essential in many spheres of work, was less dangerous and taxing than in pre-industrial times.

The proliferation of organized sports toward the end of the nineteenth century is due in large part to the desire for an expression of canalized aggression to counteract what was becoming an increasingly sedentary lifestyle. Sports had the added benefit of providing a sense of traditional masculinity which was in the process of erosion as the seas of industrial and urban change swept against it.

The developing scientific discourse over the female body elevated two themes that fitted perfectly the masculine purposes of sports. Lenskyj summarizes them as: "Women's unique anatomy and physiology and their special moral obligations" (1987: 18). Both derived from nature and were immutable; both effectively disqualified women from sport. As we have seen, the perils of competing in sports lay not in the effects of exercise on women's bodies, but in the reaction of society to their achievements. Jennifer Hargreaves summarizes the wider relevance of this when she writes: "The struggle over the physical body was important for women because control over its use was the issue central to their subordination: the repression of women's bodies symbolized powerfully their repression in society" (1994: 85).

A CONSUMMATE SYMMETRY

In Chapter three, I examined the body as a collection of about 60 billion cells, organized into substances like muscle and tissue, flesh and bone. In this chapter, I am presenting an alternative way of approaching the same thing: not as a physical entity, but as the subject of a discourse, the center of scientific debate, and public discussion. Women's bodies in particular have fascinated scientists and philosophers for the past 300 years: the search for the "true nature" of women led to the female body becoming something of a terrain on which competing versions of truth contested their claims.

Overwhelmingly, favor swung toward a conception of the female body that was capable of certain types of function but either incapable or unsuited to others, usually those that were regarded as male undertakings. These included not only sports, but, to repeat Schiebinger, the "public spheres of government and commerce, science and scholarship." The symmetry was consummate.

Think for a moment about the ways in which men have sought to restrain women. The ancient Chinese practice of footbinding was ostensibly to prevent women developing large and therefore (in Chinese males' eyes) ugly feet: small feet were the epitome of beauty in Chinese culture. It also effectively confined them to the boudoir away from the gaze of men other than husbands. As feet were generally first bound when the woman was seven years old, she would be hobbled. The custom was abolished by imperial decree in 1902; it had lasted for more than 1,000 years.

As cultures define physically appropriate shapes for women, so women have been obliged to conform. Witness the neck brace used by Ndebe women, or the plates that are wedged between the lower lips and the mandible of Ubangis in equatorial Africa. Neither practice has the practical utility of footbinding, which restricted women's physical mobility so that it was virtually impossible to escape servitude. In these cases, women voluntarily mutilate their bodies for the pleasure of men.

Cliteridectomy is widely practiced in many parts of the Middle East and in the North and sub-Saharan desert. About 74 million women have currently undergone this procedure, which involves excising part or all of the clitoris. The catalog of infections, complications, and long-term effects of this mutilation is immense. It reminds us of how far men will go to reaffirm the subjugation of women through the control not only of their reproductive functions, but of their ability to experience sexual pleasure. (In one form of cliteridectomy, the clitoris is excised, as is the labia minor, before the sides of the vulva are sewn together with catgut, to be ritually opened with a dagger on the eve of the woman's wedding.) The process is defended as an integral part of some sections of Islamic faith, but, as Linda Lindsey writes in her *Gender Roles: A sociological perspective*, "Regardless of how it is justified, it is a grim reminder of the subjugation of women" (1990: 104).

What we must ask ourselves is: are those kinds of gory activities so different from the things women do to themselves even today? Victorian women and their daughters self-destructively squeezed themselves into whalebone-lined corsets that were so tight that they stopped blood circulation and distorted the spine. Now, women have swapped this contraption for liposuction (vacuuming fatty tissue from the epidermis), rhinoplasty (slicing open the nose and filing down gristle) and all sorts of cosmetic surgery designed to bring women's bodies into alignment with men's expectations (silicone breast implants being a supreme example; the American Federal Food and Drugs Administration severely restricted these after the damaging effects of them became known, though they are still widely available in Britain).

Then we still have to reckon with the less invasive, but no less disabling, attempts women make to meet with men's approval. By defining ideal shapes in ways that please them, men actually force women into near-starvation diets or, worse still, chronic eating disorders like anorexia nervosa and bulimia. The burgeoning popularity of aerobic classes and their progeny, step classes, boxercise, etc., are related to changes in how men define the perfect shape. The 1950s Monroe model looks podgy by comparison with the busty but slimmer supermodels of today. Women remain willing to connive with men: they are still prepared to risk their health to chase what Naomi Wolf calls *The Beauty Myth*. But, the myth is "not about women at all," argues Wolf. "It is about men's institutions and institutional power" (1991: 10, 13).

Anorexia nervosa and bulimia

Research has shown that anorexia nervosa and bulimia are more prevalent in certain sports than in the general population. Sports that emphasize the importance of physical appearance, such as gymnastics, ice dancing, and synchronized swimming, harbor more eating disorders, and competitors have been encouraged by coaches and trainers to restrict food intake, use purgatives, or induce vomiting in an effort to maintain nymph-like bodies.

While it may contradict popular expectations of healthy young people with, one assumes, a keener sense of their own bodies than most, several studies in Europe and the USA have indicated that they are more rather than less prone to eating disorders. Since the early 1980s, researchers have reported an increase in clinically diagnosed eating disorders and eating disordered tendencies (like faddish dieting, diuretics abuse, and overdosing on diet pills). The rates have varied between 1 and 4 per cent in the general population, with an increase in anorexia occurring primarily in white females between the ages of 15 and 24 years. In 1983, Puglise, Lifshitz, and Grad coined the term *anorexia athletica* to indicate the particular eating disorder that affects competitive sports performers. Estimates of the prevalence of eating disorders in the female sporting population vary between 4 and 22 per cent, with gymnasts, long-distance runners and synchronized swimmers being most affected.

Monitoring weight is normal in most sports: in some, leanness is considered of paramount importance. Sports that are subject to judges' evaluation, like gymnastics, diving, and figure skating, encourage participants to take care of all aspects of their appearance. About 35 per cent of competitors have eating disorders and half practice what researchers term "pathogenic weight control." In some sports, looking young and slender is considered such an advantage that competitors actively try to stave off the onset of menstruation and the development of secondary sexual characteristics; or to counterbalance the weight gain that typically accompanies puberty. Menstrual dysfunctions, such as amenorrhoea and oligomenorrhoea, frequently result from anorexia.

In endurance events, excess weight is generally believed to impair performance. Athletes reduce body fat to increase strength, speed, and endurance, though they risk bone mineral deficiencies, dehydration, and a decrease in maximum oxygen uptake (VO_2max). The Norwegian biologist Jorunn Sundgot-Borgen suggests that the training load typically carried by endurance athletes may induce a calorific deprivation which, in turn, elicits "certain biological and social reinforcement leading to the development of eating disorders" (1994). But the prevalence of bulimia is more difficult to explain.

Sundgot-Borgen also argues that competitors most at risk tend to be characterized by "high self-expectation, perfectionism, persistence and independence." In other words, the qualities that enable them to achieve in sports make them vulnerable to eating disorders. The same researcher reports that a change of coach can trigger an eating disorder, as can an injury that prevents the athlete training at usual levels. A further finding of Sundgot-Borgen and several other scholars is that coaches actually recommend the use of pathogenic control methods, including vomiting, laxatives, and diuretics.

Coaches and trainers in weight-sensitive sports need to keep an eye on their charges' eating habits in preparation for competitions. For example, lightweight rowers and jockeys must meet weight restrictions before competition. In their article "Weight concerns, weight control techniques, and eating disorders among adolescent competitive swimmers," Diane Taub and Rose Benson write that: "Excess body fat and body weight in both males and females are widely considered by coaches, parents and participants to hinder performance." See also: Chapman (1997), Petrie (1996), and Ryan (1998).

In her essay "Femininity as discourse," Dorothy E. Smith reminds us that: "We must not begin by conceiving of women as manipulated by mass media or subject passively to male power . . . when we speak of 'femininity'" (1988: 39). Femininity, she argues, is more a matter of self-creation, not just imposition. This allows for a conception of femininity, or, perhaps, more accurately femininities, that is not fixed but always in the process of redefinition. No one is suggesting that there is an equally weighted balance of power with men and women trading ideas on how the body should look. Men have had their own way in most areas of society and this is no exception. But, where the female body is concerned, they have had either to resort to coercion (footbinding, cliteridectomies) or secure the complicity of women themselves.

As we have seen, transgressive bodies have been liable to penalties, whether through the application of stigma, or disqualification. Rewards went to the soft and weak. The unwritten rules or codes of the discourse dictated that women whose bodies and exploits did not conform were not "real" women at all. The 1980s witnessed the emergence of a number of women athletes who defied the coded expectations and, in the process, began to re-write a different code.

CROSSING NATURAL BOUNDARIES

Almost as newsworthy as Ben Johnson's expulsion from the 1988 Olympics, was the spectacular performance of US sprinter Florence Griffith Joyner. "Flo-Jo," as the media dubbed her, had risen from the relative obscurity of a so-so track athlete in a couple of years; her personal best times for the short sprints tumbled and her physical appearance altered visibly. Not only was she bigger and more conspicuously muscular, but her outfits were more suited to a catwalk than a running track.

Had she not won a bagful of medals, detractors would no doubt have dismissed her, perhaps in the way they did Mary Pierce, the 1990s tennis player: as a bellwether of fashion who looked aesthetic enough, but could not compete consistently at the highest level. If that had been the case, there would have been no violation of the popular image of female athletes: the ones that look like women have limited athletic ability.

Griffith Joyner's egregious track presence challenged the media: would they concentrate on her record-breaking speed, or her flamboyant appearance? In the event, they escaped the double-bind by integrating sexuality and athleticism. Anne Balsamo calls the media's treatment of Flo-Jo "the process of sexualization at work" (1996: 44). Hard-bitten newspaper hacks were forcibly turned into fashion correspondents as they prefaced reports of her track triumphs with detailed fashion itineraries, right down to the color of her nail varnish.

Of course, sports history is full of unconquerable females. Yet none had resisted type as much as Flo-Jo. Far from being a delicate-looking creature, she was a chunky, strong, and radiated power; *and* she still managed to conform to heterosexual standards of female attractiveness. It was as if she was stamping out the message that women can be big, good-looking, well-dressed, and still produce in the competitive arena.

In her *Coming on Strong: Gender and sexuality in twentieth-century women's sport*, Susan Cahn argues that: "A reservoir of racist beliefs about black women as deficient in femininity buttressed the masculine connotation of track and field" (1994: 138). African American achievers not only in track and field but other sports, were regarded as "mannish" and, as Cahn calls them, "liminal figures."

There was some ambivalence about Griffith Joyner even before the 1988 games. Linford Christie, the men's 100-meter winner at the 1992 Olympics, reacted to her win in the US trials in which she took a massive 0.27 seconds off the existing world record. "No woman can run 10.49 legit," he pronounced. "I know what it feels like to run 10.49 and it's hard" (quoted in the British *Sunday Mirror Magazine*, September 4, 1988). She further astonished the world by breaking the 200 meters world record twice at the games. Slurs faded when she retired with a lucrative portfolio of modeling contracts. Despite the gossip, she never failed a drugs test. Her world records remained intact a decade later, Marion Jones's 10.71 in 1998 being the closest time.

She retired with her "real woman" status intact, having changed some of the rules of the discourse irredeemably. Gone was the quality of otherness usually afforded big, strong women. Griffith Joyner herself may have elicited confusion by mixing the athletic with the erotic, but subsequent women in track and many other areas of sport, normalized the image of the powerful female body. Almost immediately after her death in 1998, journalists turned rumors into claims: Griffith Joyner's body and her track performances were almost certainly enhanced by drugs, many writers charged, presumably in the safe knowledge that they could not libel a dead person.

Four years before Flo-Jo's triumph, the film *Pumping Iron II: The women* was released. Directed by George Butler, who had co-directed the Schwarzenegger vehicle *Pumping Iron* (1976), the docudrama focused on the lead-up to the 1983 Caesar's Cup bodybuilding competition in Las Vegas. The film introduced the world to the astounding Bev Francis, an Australian woman whose body pullulated with "manly" characteristics. Tall, flat-chested and square-shouldered, Francis was so vasculated that snakes seemed to be crawling beneath her skin.

Female bodybuilding had been around for years before. As a sport, female bodybuilding began in 1979, a product largely of Doris Barrilleaux who was formerly a physique photography model. Barrilleaux started the Superior Physique Association which set down competition rules for female bodybuilding contests. In 1980 she was asked to head a national American Federation of Women Body-builders. Butler's movie not only took the sport to a global audience, but it dramatized one of the questions that had tormented the sport since about 1980. The Francis model was clearly transgressive: she had a woman's body that for intents and purposes looked like a man's, not just any man's, but one of a latter-day Hercules.

In technical terms, Francis was an obvious winner: her body fulfilled all the criteria of muscle development, separation, symmetry, etc. She had also made it her avowed intention to take women's bodybuilding to its next level. The problem was: she just did not look like a woman. Neither were her nearest rivals feminine in the traditional sense; but Carla Dunlap – an African American who was the ultimate winner – and Rachel McLish were recognizably women.

In terms of strict bodybuilding critieria as applied to men's competitions, neither Dunlap or McLish came even close to the extraordinary, imposing Francis. But, the debate in women's bodybuilding was whether to reward someone who, while superior in terms of musculature and skin tone, would be seen widely as a steroid-pumped malformation or a raging dyke, or both.

In all probability, most female bodybuilders were seen in the same way. To date, they are the mightiest transgressors of the traditional feminine ideal. The fragility, vulnerability, and passivity of the eternally wounded woman are effaced. Instead, female bodybuilders present powerful signifiers of strength, resilience, and activity. Linda Hamilton famously prepared for her role in the movie *Terminator 2* (1992) with a specially designed training program that left her with a hard, yet lean physique, complete with the now *de rigueur* corrugated abdominals. Looking at the video now, Hamilton seems very ordinary; yet, in the early 1990s, her look was something of a breakthrough – an example of how a woman's body can be masculinized while still looking unmistakably female. Bodybuilders did not manage to do this.

When they first came to public attention, women bodybuilders were derided as freaks by men, who found them repulsive. Anne Bolin suggests why when she writes that bodybuilding "exaggerates Western notions of gender difference – muscles deonoting masculinity and signifying 'biological' disparity between the genders" (1996: 126).

Women bodybuilders were encroaching on the domain historically defined as male. Men are supposed to be the ones with the muscles. Putting their male colleagues to shame did them no favors: the typical male response was to reject them as "unnatural." And, in a sense, they were: after all, natural, as coded by a discourse that had been in operation for the previous three centuries, meant weak.

It would be tempting to regard the women who paraded their striated bodies in the 1980s as *ur*-feminists. For instance, in their paper "Pumping irony," Alan Mansfield and Barbara McGinn write: "Because muscularity has been coded as a fundamentally masculine attribute, its adoption by women has offered a threat and a challenge to notions of both the feminine AND the masculine" (1993: 65).

As head of a research project based in Tampa, Florida, and Birmingham, England, I, with my co-researcher Amy Shepper, interviewed competitive female bodybuilders. The pattern that emerged from the case studies was that most had taken up the sport after a personal trauma, such as the breakup of a relationship, a bereavement, or a serious accident. Changes in the body wrought by intense training and strict dieting occasioned a change in self-assurance. Their confidence up after competing, they immersed themselves more deeply into what might warrantably be called a bodybuilding subculture. Here the reactions of fellow bodybuilders were important and the often hostile responses of outsiders were disregarded. Standing on line at a supermarket checkout, one woman heard the sarcastic question of a male behind her: "Is that a *woman*?" he asked his friend rhetorically. She turned, looked at him, and asked no one in particular: "Is that an *asshole*?"

But, while their bodies may have been transgressively masculine, their behavior when not training was not. Away from the gym, most slid comfortably into traditional roles as carers and houseworkers. The majority were involved in heterosexual partnerships and cooked, laundered, cleaned, and performed the whole panoply of duties associated with the natural woman. Some of those who were not involved in heterosexual relationships functioned in traditional ways for their brothers. Gaining control over one's body, it seems, does not imply gaining control of one's life. This tells us something about the pervasiveness of male hegemony: a woman can release herself in one very important sphere, while at the same time retaining attachments, identifications, and dependencies in another.

Balsamo believes there are other ways in which female bodybuilders are domesticated. In her *Technologies of the Gendered Body: Reading cyborg women*, Balsamo reasons that, while their bodies transgress gender boundaries, they are not reconstructed according to an opposite gender identity. "They reveal, instead, how culture processes transgressive bodies in such a way as to keep each body in its place," she writes, suggesting that, for white women, their bodies are subjected to an idealized "strong" male body. "For black women, it is the white female body" (1996: 55).

Women who tread on the hallowed male turf of bodybuilding do not have their bodies "recoded according to an oppositional or empowered set of gendered connotations," Balsamo writes. In other words, they are seen less for what they are and more for what they are not. So, any threat they might appear to pose has been rehabilitated and the gender hierarchy remains intact.

On this account, sport inscribes dominant narratives of gender identity on the material body by providing the means for exercising power relations on female flesh. It does this in two ways. (1) By intervening in the physiological functioning of female bodies: scientific theories and experiments on sexual differences had the effect of opening up women's bodies to surveillance, as we have seen. (2) By institutionalizing subordinate status for women's events and competitions: women's sport has been separated from men's in all but a very few contemporary events. Both confirm that while the female is more durable and capable of exertion than once thought, there is still a natural state, corporeal boundaries that cannot be crossed, at least not safely.

The reaction to French tennis player Amélie Mauresmo's rise to prominence at the 1999 Australian Open could have been designed to hold up this argument. "*Sie ist ein halber Mann,*" said Martina Hingis of Mauresmo, her opponent in the final: "She is half a man." Mauresmo had already been stung by Lindsay Davenport who reflected on her, "I thought I was playing a guy." The then 19-year-old French player was tall and muscular but hardly rippled and she spoke freely about her relationship with another female. The old appellation "mannish" looked set for a return once the media got involved. "OH MAN, SHE'S GOOD" declared the Melbourne tabloid *Herald Sun* in its headline; the paper's story featured two photographs of Mauresmo, including one shot from the rear that showed off her musculature.

The body is neither natural nor unnatural. Sports show us that we are constantly redefining the limits of the body. Not only can we re-make our bodies in ways that we consciously control, but we can move them faster, higher and longer, lift heavier weights and propel objects farther. The whole project of sport is based on the assumption that there are no natural confines of the human body; and if there are, we have not yet approached them. Watching sports reminds us that there is no such thing as the natural body: the body is what we make it.

FURTHER READING

Out of Bounds: Women, sport and sexuality by Helen Lenskyj (The Women's Press, 1986) traces the massively hindered progress of women into mainstream sports from the 1880s, paying special attention to the various ways women's achievements were discredited, typically by accusations of impropriety or unnatural status. It can profitably be read in conjunction with Patricia Vertinsky's excellent *The Eternally Wounded Woman: Women, doctors and exercise in the late nineteenth century* (Manchester University Press, 1990).

The Making of the Modern Body: Sexuality and society in the nineteenth century edited by Catherine Gallagher and Thomas Laqueur (University of California Press, 1987) is a collection of essays all devoted to exploring different aspects of the body's changing meanings.

Beyond the Natural Body: An archaology of sex hormones by Nelly Oudshoorn (Routledge, 1994) is a detailed exploration of how the "discovery" of sex hormones established as a scientific fact the precise natural differences between men and women.

Technologies of the Gendered Body: Reading cyborg women by Anne Balsamo, (Duke University Press, 1996) focuses on the cultural meanings of body-technologies: quite apart from performance-enhancing substances and other aids to competition, we have bionic technology that was once thought fanciful when featured in television shows like *The Six Million Dollar Man* and *The Bionic Woman*. Now, the artificial reconstruction of the human body is under way.

ASSIGNMENT

The most celebrated transsexual in sports is Renee Richards who played on the women's tennis tour before it was discovered that she was formerly Richard Raskind. Hastily, the United States Tennis Association and the Women's Tennis Association introduced a Barr bodies sex test, which Richards refused to take. She/he was excluded from competition. In 1977, the New York Supreme Court ruled that requiring Richards to take the Barr test was "grossly unfair, discriminatory and inequitable, and violative of her rights" (see Renee Richards's biography *Second Serve* (with J. Ames) Stein & Day, 1983; and Susan Birrell and Cheryl Cole's "Double fault: Renee Richards and the construction and naturalization of difference," in *Sociology of Sport Journal*, vol. 7, 1990).

Construct a narrative in which it is revealed that several members of the current tennis circuit, the WNBA, the US track and field team and some beach volleyball players have undergone similar surgery to Richards'. Take careful note of Balsamo's reminder that "gender is not simply an effect of the circulation of representations and discourse, but also the effect of specific social, economic, and institutional relations of power" (1996: 162).

the secondbest sex

how women are devalued and diminished by sports

LADIES FIRST

Imagine we have a DeLorean car like the one in the *Back to the Future* movies. We blast off, travelling backwards through time until we arrive at 1880, right in the middle of the period when most sports are acquiring sets of rules and institutional bodies to govern them. It is 32 years since Elizabeth Cady Stanton and Lucretia Mott met at Seneca Falls to launch the American Women's movement and two years since the 19th Amendment, which proposed votes for women, was first rejected by Congress. It will continue to be rejected in every session up till 1920.

In Britain, women are poised to step up their campaigns: in 1903, they will become more militant in their attempts to secure political recognition for women. Emmeline Pankhurst's suffragettes will suffer indignity and violence in their ultimately successful efforts, but their only excursion into sports is horrific: in 1913, Emily Davidson will throw herself under a horse owned by King George V at the Derby race. It will take until 1918 before the franchise is extended and the shackles of Victorian Britain are left behind.

Women have no genuine involvement in sports save for watching men or playing somewhat gentle games such as skittles, quoits or croquet and their tennis seems relaxed and

playful compared to the more competitive endeavors of men. But we are going to change all that through a historical intervention: we have brought back a VCR and tapes of 6′ 3″ Venus Williams to show how the game should really be played. And there's more: we have a video of Tegla Loroupe, of Kenya, crossing the finishing line of a marathon with the clock showing 2:20.47. A game of women's rugby is a clincher, but, for good measure, we show the television show *RollerJam* in which women on rollerskates flex their well-vascularized biceps and go head-to-head in combat. This, we argue, is proof that women, contrary to the Victorian ideal, are not as fragile, dainty, or timid as they are made out to be by medics, scientists, and a variety of other interested groups.

Sports' various governing organizations are convinced and immediately allow women admission into their activities, but not in separate events. Hingis and the others look capable of playing and beating men, they say. This is not quite what we had in mind, but we let it pass. In one stroke, women are transformed from spectators to competitors: they run, play tennis, golf, football, they even venture into prize-fighting. We witness the first few contests. The female competitors get iced time and again. Yet, as we leave to return to the early 2000s, we notice a slight but discernible improvement. What is happening in the present by the time we get back?

One answer to this is: no difference. Women will always come second and, usually, a very poor second to men. An alternative is: they are able to hold their own in virtually every sporting matchup in which raw physical strength is not the sole determining factor; that is most sports, of course. I have a definite answer, but, to arrive at it, need to explain the logic guiding the argument.

Just as we asked why so many black people are involved in sports and why they achieve proportionately so much success, so we could invert the questions and ask of women: why so few and why so little success compared to men? Both may draw objections on the grounds that women, nowadays, enter sport in considerable numbers and their achievements are many. But sportswomen are still a numerical minority and, in measurable terms at least, their performances do not match those of men.

Pressed to offer an immediate explanation we might take the simple, but misleading, natural ability argument, suggesting that women are just not equipped to handle sports and are always carrying a physical handicap. But the argument has much the same failings as the "black is best" theory; it exaggerates physical factors and ignores social and psychological processes that either facilitate entry into or halt progress within sport. Constructing a narrative about blacks' evident superiority in sports had the effect of crafting a view of the world in which blacks were naturally inferior in virtually every other sphere.

We have seen in the previous chapter how a scientific discourse about the natural state of the female body gave rise to popular beliefs about the dangerous effects of vigorous exercise on women. For the moment, we should take note of three significant implications of this discourse. First, women were not regarded as being as capable intellectually or physically as men; second, their natural predisposition is to be passive and not active; third, their relationship to men is one of dependence. All three statements are sexist and have been strongly challenged since the late 1960s, of course, but their impact on the entire character of sport is still evident today.

Sexism

Like racism, sexism is a set of beliefs or ideas about the purported inferiority of some members of the population, in this case, women. The inferiority is thought to be based on biological differences between the sexes: women are naturally equipped for specific types of activities and roles and these do not usually include ones which carry prestige and influence. Much of the scientific support for this type of belief derives from scientific and medical debates from the 18th and 19th centuries.

BREAKING THROUGH

The first female sports champion was Cynisca, who won the quadriga (a chariot with four horses abreast) race in 396 BCE. In their book *Crossing Boundaries*, Susan Bandy and Anne Darden praise Cynisca for owning, training, and entering the horses, but note that "she was barred from attending and competing in any of the Panhellenic festivals of ancient Greece" (1999: 2). "Her victory then was from a distance, from the outside." Cyncisca was acknowledged as the winner of the event but, as Bandy and Darden put it, "Cynisca's experience as an outsider, not a participant, foreshadowed the role of spectator that women were to play for centuries in sport" (1999: 2)

Athletic contests were part of young women's education in ancient Sparta and Crete. In ancient Greek and Roman cultures, women would hunt, ride, swim, and run, but not (usually) engage in combat. Yet, they were not allowed to compete, nor, in Cynisca's case, even watch competitions. Women were assigned roles as spectators and outsiders.

In the medieval period, women were still seen not as active agents but as objects to be placed on a pedestal, protected and revered and, if necessary, fought for. But, there were exceptions in the Age of Chivalry: some women, certainly noblewomen in parts of Europe, jousted. In his book *The Erotic in Sports*, Allen Guttmann gives examples of women, not only jousting, but fighting men with staffs. He also cites "a titillating contest between two naked women armed with distaffs, one upon a goat, the other on a ram" (1996: 41). And, apparently, foot-races between women were common attractions in parts of Europe in the thirteenth century, the condition of entry being that the competitor must be a prostitute (1996: 43).

Typically, these races took place after men's archery contests. It is also probable that women competed in a forerunner of the modern game of darts which involved throwing 18-inch hand weapons at a barrel. Certainly, many women were adept archers and, by the eighteenth century, shot on level terms with men. Peter Kühnst's book *Sports: A cultural history in the mirror of art* includes a plate of a 1787 fencing match between a female and male (1996: 199). Returning to Guttmann, accounts from eighteenth-century England suggest that female pugilism, often of a brutal kind, existed and sometimes resulted in women with faces "covered with blood, bosoms bare, and the clothes nearly torn from their bodies" (1996: 53).

Activities before the nineteenth century, while resembling sports in content, were not strictly sports in the contemporary sense of the word. By the time of the emergence of organized, rule-bound activities we now recognize as sports, women were effectively pushed out of the picture. Frail of body and mind, women could not be expected to engage in any manner of physically exerting activity, save perhaps for dancing, horse-riding, bowling, and the occasional game of lacrosse. Out of the discourse on sexual difference (examined in the previous chapter) came an image of the female as very distinct from the male, with totally different propensities and natural dispositions – a sexual bifurcation.

The Victorian ideal of the woman was gentle, delicate, and submissive. Women might let perspiration appear on their alabaster complexions, "glow" during exercise, but should never succeed in sport which was customarily associated with ruggedness, resilience, assertiveness, and a willingness to expend "blood, sweat, and tears." The occasional woman who would attempt to emulate men was risking harm to her body, particularly her reproductive organs.

Women, it was thought, were closer to nature than men: their duties should be confined to those nature conferred on them, like child-bearing and child-rearing. Their role was to nurture. Far from being the product of a male conspiracy, this view was widely held and respected by men and women alike. Accepting that anything resembling strenuous exercise was detrimental to their well-being, women actually contributed, in a self-fulfilling way, to sexist beliefs about them. "The acceptance by women of their own incapacitation gave both a humane and moral weighting to the established scientific 'facts,'" writes Jennifer Hargreaves in her *Sporting Females* (1994: 47).

True, many women were campaigning forcefully and sacrificially in their quest for political suffrage, but their quest did not extend into sports. Women, particularly upper-middle-class women, sat ornamentally as they watched their menfolk participate in sports. But a closer inspection of women involved not so much in competitive sports but in active leisure pursuits, such as rock climbing or fell walking, would have revealed that women were as robust as men and their equals in endurance. And Bernarr Macfadden, whose philosophy and activities were covered in Chapter seven, had confederates, such as Concordia Löfving, of Sweden, and her successor Martina Bergman Österberg, both of whom dedicated themselves to training women in gymnastics during the late nineteenth century.

Pierre de Coubertin, to whom so much is owed for his vision of the modern Olympics, embodied Victorian sentiments when he urged the prohibition of women's participation in sport. The sight of the "body of a woman being smashed" was, he recorded, "indecent." "No matter how toughened a sportswoman may be, her organism is not cut out to sustain certain shocks" (quoted in Snyder and Spreitzer 1983: 155–6). The Olympics were to be dedicated to the "solemn and periodic exultation of male athleticism . . . with female applause as reward," said de Coubertin. Despite his reservations, women were included in the 1900 Olympics, four years after the inauguration, though in a restricted number of events and not in competition with men. (Even as recently as 1980, Kari Fasting notes how women were not allowed to run a 3,000-meter event [just under two miles], the reason being that "it was too strenuous for women," 1987: 362.)

A year after women's inclusion in the Olympics, there was a second, this time relatively unsung trailblazer for female sports. Wealthy Frenchwoman Camille du Gast was the first to challenge male supremacy behind the wheel. In 1901, she competed in the great 687-mile race from Paris to Berlin. Because her 20 horsepower Panhard was the smallest car in the race, she had to start last of the 127 entrants, but went on to finish ahead of many of the larger cars driven by some of Europe's top drivers.

Capital-to-capital races were popular in Europe in the early years of the twentieth century, but they often resulted in deaths and serious injuries and were discontinued, leaving Madame du Gast to pursue a different sport – motor-boat racing – though not before she had inspired other women to take up competitive driving. Over the next 30 years, women made their presence felt at all the major European circuits. Gwenda Hawkes, of Britain, in the 1920s, and Australian Joan Richmond and Canadian Kay Petre, in the 1930s, were among the several women to campaign regularly on the racing circuits. Their involvement was curtailed by the cultural pressures on women to return to the home after the Second World War effort. Women were largely absent from motor racing until their re-emergence in the 1990s, when the social changes made it possible for women to assert themselves in areas, including sports, that made been dominated by men.

Golf was a sport considered appropriate for women, at least ladies (as opposed to working-class women): it made minimal physical demands and could be played in full dress. The languid elegance of swing made the sight of female players pleasing to men's eyes; women were not expected to strike the ball with any force. England's Cecilia Leitch changed all that: she brought to the sport a power and competitive spirit that had previously been associated with only men's golf. In 1910, she played a highly-publicized game against Harold Hilton, a renowned amateur who had won two Open championships. Leitch, having practiced hitting balls into the wind, won and was acclaimed by suffragettes. Although she went on to win many titles, her legacy was the style and sense of purpose she introduced to women's golf.

Style was also a hallmark of Suzanne Lenglen, the French tennis player; though it was the style of her outfits rather than her play that made most impact. Tennis was actually one of the few areas where women were allowed to compete, though only those of means could afford to. As well as full skirts, they wore tight corsets, high-necked, long-sleeved blouses, and boaters. It was a convention of Victorian society that women should appear decorative at all times, of course. Like golf, tennis was a seemly sport for women.

In the early 1920s, Wimbledon was the preserve of the elite, to whom even training was considered vulgar, if not outright cheating. Women were expected to be clothed head-to-foot. Lenglen, who dominated Wimbledon between 1919 and 1926, shocked traditionalists when she appeared in loose-fitting, pleated skirts that finished just below the knee. Defying custom, she swapped the blouse for a tee-shirt-style top that left her arms exposed. She also spurned the corsets and the hats, preferring a bandana not unlike those favored today. In 1931, Lili de Alvarez of Spain caused a rumpus when she appeared in shorts.

Tennis's related sport, table tennis, or ping-pong, was not thought befitting for women: too much scurrying about and aggressive bursts of activity. The breakthrough player in this sport was Maria Mednyanszky, a Hungarian, who became the first women's world champion and went on to win 18 world titles. Her all-backhand style which saw her crowd the table was strikingly different in its day. In the 1920s, Mednyanszky elevated what was once a parlour game into a serious competitive sport for women.

Baseball has never been considered suitable sport for ladies. "Unlady-like" is one of those words with a certain ring to it: the many activities to which it refers are to be avoided by any female who favors keeping her dignity. In the nineteenth century, the application of the term to behavior that involved some degree of physical exertion was commonplace, unless the behavior was performed by females out of necessity. Washing, cleaning, fetching coal, and emptying chambers were activities performed by working-class women, but they could have few pretensions to being ladies. These were typically the kind of women whose daily duties were so draining that they would not have the inclination to add to their physical workload. Gentlewomen and the wives of the emergent bourgeoisie would have time for croquet, tennis and perhaps archery, were self-consciously "ladies."

But, as the nineteenth century passed and women were made to play a vigorous role in the 1914–18 war, the flimsy illusion of women as delicate creatures in need of men's protection was eroded. A vocal and effective suffragette movement was prising open new areas in politics and education for women. The Second World War effort also drew women to factories, trucks, and areas of work traditionally reserved for men. The war periods also left a gap in sports that women filled. One famous example of this was the All-American Girls Baseball League, which was started in 1943.

The brainchild of Philip K. Wrigley, of the chewing-gum company and owner of the Chicago Cubs, the league was made up of women's teams. Major League Baseball's ranks were depleted by the number of male players who were drafted into the armed services in the war effort and it was feared that a substandard competition would drive away fans. Women had been playing baseball and softball at a competitive level at colleges from at least the turn of the century and possibly before. The war demanded that many women leave their traditionally-defined domestic duties and work in factories or other parts of industry; it seemed perfectly consistent for women sports performers to occupy positions previously held by men too. The league's popularity waned when men returned home from war and resumed playing, though attendances were poor in the post-war period. But, there was a legacy, as Susan Cahn points out in her *Coming on Strong: Gender and sexuality in twentieth-century women's sport*: "Women ballplayers offered the public an exciting and expanded sense of female capabilities" (1994: 163). The women's league is the subject of the Penny Marshall film *A League of Their Own* (1992).

While women were allowed to enter the Olympic Games from 1900, their track and field competitions were regarded as a side-show, lacking the intensity and vigor of men's. This perception persisted regardless of the quality of competition. The woman who more than any other was responsible for changing this was Fanny Blankers-Koen, of Holland, who amassed four gold medals at the 1948 Olympics when aged 30 and a mother of two. It is probable that she would have won more honors had her progress not been interrupted by the war.

As we saw in Chapter seven, one of the typical strategies used to discredit female sports performers was to defeminize them either through innuendo or allegations of homosexuality. In the 1930s and 1940s, Babe Didrikson, the American track and field star and golfer, worked hard at presenting a feminine and heterosexual front in spite of suspicions – suspicions that were not actually confirmed until years later with the publication of her biography, which contained details of her friendship with Betty Dodd. By contrast, Blankers-Koen's public persona was enhanced by her motherhood and, in this sense, she was an important harbinger: a heterosexual woman with children who could also break world records (and at several events).

Swimming prefigured later fusions of sports and showbusiness. Johnny Weissmuller, who won a total of five gold medals at the 1924 and 1928 Olympics, went on to a successful film career after landing the part of Tarzan in 1932. He played the part 12 times. The man who broke Weissmuller's 400-meter freestyle record at the 1932 Olympics, Buster Crabbe, also played Tarzan, though he became better known for his portrayals of Flash Gordon and Buck Rogers. Hollywood repeated the success with swimmer Esther Williams who made her debut in the 1942 movie *Andy Hardy's Double Life* and went on to become a fully-fledged star, though mostly in swim-related roles. Like Lenglen before her, Williams visibly embodied a popular, male-defined image of femininity. While they had their detractors, both helped to change perceptions of women: freer, possessed of great exuberance, and unafraid to display their bodies. Yet, there were other women who were uninterested in conforming to men's expectations and made forays into sports for which they were considered hopelessly unsuited.

In the 1930s, women from provincial badminton and tennis clubs in New Zealand got together and played rugby. It was planned to coincide with a men's matchup played on the same day and had no serious intentions: it was a sort of exhibition, almost a spoof of the men's game. Although women had played a version of rugby football in Wales in the nineteenth century, the NZ game was the first recorded competition played according to rugby union rules and, as such, was something of a breakthrough for women's sports.

Rugby had traditionally been a byword for macho sport, the type of game for which women were thought ill-suited. After the Kiwi women had broken the taboo, women all over the world set about doing likewise. Organized matches in the USA and France started in the 1960s, leagues sprung up in Canada and all over Europe in the 1970s, and a Japanese women's league was established in 1983. The Women's Rugby Union was founded in 1983 in response to growing enthusiasm for rugby from women in Britain. It staged its first World Cup competition in 1991, Wales hosting a 12-nation tournament which was won by the USA "Eagles" who beat England in the final game.

At various points over the past 100 years or more, there have been women or teams that have broken new ground in sport. Whether wittingly, or not, they became feminist emblems. We have surveyed just a few of the more conspicuously influential figures in women's sport. But, as the 1960s drew to a close and a vital new form of feminism known as "Women's Liberation," surfaced, sportswomen who were prepared to challenge male traditions were immediately re-cast as political icons. This was not because of who they were, nor even what they did, but because of the perfect sychronicity of their timing. Of the two most prominent feminist sports icons of the two decades from 1967, one was an averagely talented marathon runner who was never championship material; the other was one of the most consummate champions of her generation. We will examine them and their impact next.

FEMINIST CHAMPIONS

On April 19, 1967, a 20-year-old Syracuse University student entered the Boston Marathon as "K. V. Switzer" and was given the number 261. About four miles into the race, a race official noticed that K. V. Switzer was a woman; as women were not allowed in the race, Jock Semple tried to remove her from the field He was stymied and Switzer went on to complete a historic marathon. Her well-publicized run demonstrated to the world that women were capable of competing in an endurance event that had, up to that point, been officially men-only. Women, it was thought, were not physically able to withstand the rigors of over 26 miles of road-running.

The International Olympic Committee did not even include a 1,500 meters event for women until the Munich Olympics of 1972 – the same year as the passing of Title IX. It was 1984, 17 years after Kathrine Switzer's historic run, before there was a women's Olympic marathon. Switzer maintained that she was unaware that women were not legally admitted to the event in the 1960s. She filled out her application form and signed her usual signature, enclosing this with a medical certificate. "I wasn't trying to get away with anything wrong," Switzer later insisted. "I wasn't trying to do it for women's rights." But, her impact on women's sports was immense. Her disingenuous use of initials, she claimed, was due to the fact that: "I dreamed of becoming a great writer and it seemed all the great writers signed their names with initials: T. S. Eliot, J. D. Salinger, e e cummings, W. B. Yeats."

Switzer became world famous for her run, which grew in symbolic terms over the next several years. The picture of Semple attempting to abort her run took an almost iconic status: a male vainly trying to thwart a determined woman trying to break into male territory. Switzer ran eight Boston marathons in total and used her success as evidence in her campaign to have a

> ## Title IX
>
> In 1972, the United States Congress passed Title IX of the Educational Amendments and so instituted a law that would seriously affect all educational institutions offering sports programs. The law specified that: "No person in the United States shall, on the basis of sex, be excluded from participation in, be denied the benefits of, or be subjected to discrimination under any educational program or activity receiving federal financial assistance." At first, this was unpopular among the male-dominated sports officials of schools, colleges, and universities. In 1979, three women athletes from the University of Alaska sued their state for failing to comply with Title IX in providing better funding equipment and publicity compared to the male basketball team. This set in train more actions, so that, by the end of 1979, 62 colleges and universities were under investigation by the Office for Civil Rights. The resistance to offering equal opportunity to women has continued to the present day.

women's marathon established as an Olympic event. She also approached the cosmetics company Avon, which sponsored a series of high-profile marathons for women from 1978–85.

There is often special providence in an event. Seven months after Switzer's run, the United States National Organization for Women (NOW), under the presidency of Betty Friedan, held a conference which drew publicity from all quarters in its attempt to create an agenda for women's issues. Although it was actually the second annual conference of NOW, the inaugural meeting had nowhere near the same impact. News of the conference reached Britain at a time when legislators were debating reforms and stimulated interest in the incipient women's movement.

Among the eight-point "Bill of Rights for Women" there were demands for the endorsement of laws banning sex discrimination in employment, more day-care centers, equal educational and training opportunities and the right of women to control their reproductive lives. This final demand effectively called for greater contraceptive facilities and for the repeal of laws that limited abortion – demands that were already satisfied, at least partially, in Britain.

The conference functioned as a clarion call for the feminist movement which was to have resonances in every sphere of cultural life, including sports. Switzer may not have been self-consciously feminist, but, in practical terms, her contribution to the feminist cause was extremely valuable. As well as attracting media attention, she effectively undermined sexist myths about the fragility of women and their inability to complete marathons without incurring physical damage. Because of the circumstances in which she made her run, she was virtually forced into becoming a spokesperson for feminism, a postion she filled with growing assurance.

The marathon is rather an instructive case-study. Between Briton Dale Greig's first official run in 1964 and today, the world record for women has improved by 1 hour 6 minutes and 58 seconds. In the same period, the men's record has been reduced by 5 minutes 2 seconds. The difference in the world's bests was 15 minutes 05 seconds in 2000 (or about 12 per cent). The moral of this would seem to be that, when women are allowed legally to compete in an event, they can perform at least on comparable terms with men. One wonders how great or small the marathon time differential would be had a women's event been allowed in the Olympics at the time of Violet Percy's first recorded run. "The same as it is today," might be the skeptic's answer, marshaling the support of significant differences in all women's and men's track records. But marathons, though separate events in major international meets, regularly pitch men and women together and, in this sense, they provide a meaningful guide. From the 1970s and the boom in popular marathons and fun runs, women have mixed with men, competed against them, and on many occasions beaten them. The gap shown in the marathon figure would surely have been narrower had television not intervened and insisted that women started their races prior to the men, thus removing the opportunity for females to test their mettle against the world's fastest males.

It is misleading comparing performances in male and female events which have developed separately. Tennis has for long been open to at least those women of resources sufficient to afford it. Only in the most playful mixed doubles have they been allowed to confront male adversaries. One-off exhibitions between the likes of an aged Bobby Riggs and Billie-Jean King (and, before her, Margaret Court) owed more to theater than competitive sport, though "The Battle of the Sexes," as it was hailed by the media in 1973, was a victory of sorts for King. But, it was a minor struggle compared to the one she faced eight years later.

"My sexuality has been my most difficult struggle," King reflected on her conflict-strewn career. It had been known in tennis circles that many of the world's top female players engaged in lesbian relationships, though few had come out voluntarily. In 1981, King's former hairdresser and secretary Marilyn Barnett took legal action against her to ascertain property rights; in other words "palimony." King at first denied that she had an intimate relationship with Barnett, then acknowledged it. The case was thrown out after the judge heard that Barnett had threatened to publish letters that King had written her.

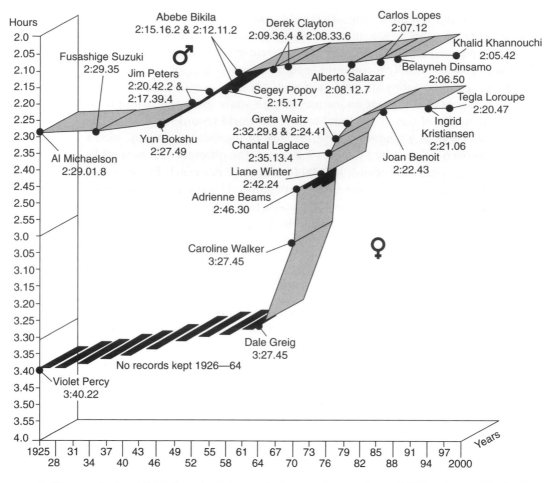

Hours

Abebe Bikila
2:15.16.2 & 2:12.11.2

Derek Clayton
2:09.36.4 & 2:08.33.6

Carlos Lopes
2:07.12

Khalid Khannouchi
2:05.42

Fusashige Suzuki
2:29.35

♂

Belayneh Dinsamo
2:06.50

Jim Peters
2:20.42.2 &
2:17.39.4

Alberto Salazar

Segey Popov 2:08.12.7
2:15.17

Tegla Loroupe
2:20.47

Greta Waitz
2:32.29.8 & 2:24.41

Ingrid
Kristiansen
2:21.06

Al Michaelson
2:29.01.8

Yun Bokshu
2:27.49

Chantal Laglace
2:35.13.4

Joan Benoit
2:22.43

Liane Winter
2:42.24

♀

Adrienne Beams
2:46.30

Caroline Walker
3:27.45

Dale Greig
3:27.45

No records kept 1926—64

Violet Percy
3:40.22

Years

* The year before Violet Percy's first recorded women's marathon, Al Michaelson, of the USA, set the men's world best time with 2hrs 29mins 01.8secs. Since then, the men's record has progressed evenly, the only exceptions being 1952–54, when Britain's Jim Peters lowered the time four times for a total of almost 7 minutes, and 1967–69, when the Australian Derek Clayton sliced 2mins 23.6 off the record, then reduced it by a further 1min 2.8secs. It took until 1981 before Alberto Salazar, of the USA, was able to improve this by less than 21 seconds.

* Official records of women's times began in 1964 and, over the next 34 years, the times improved on average by 1 minute 57 seconds compared with an average increment of 9.1 seconds for men. After Norway's Ingrid Kristiansen's 2: 21.6 seconds in 1985, Joan Benoit, of the USA, ran 2:21.21 seconds, but it was then nine years before another woman broke 2.22 and, even then, Uta Pippig's 2:21.45 was assisted by a drop of 152 yards (139 meters) in the course. Significantly, Loroupe's 1998 world's best was set when women and men started together; many other marathon's have separate start times, effectively removing the head-to-head challenge that helped Loroupe.

The graph does not show every marathon record: only representative runs.

the progression of men's and women's marathon records

King won her first Wimbledon title in 1966, when aged 22. Her prize was a £45 ($30) gift voucher for Harrods. She went on to win 39 Grand Slam titles. Echoing the remonstrations of "women's liberation," King began demanding prize monies for women players. Professionalism was already under consideration in tennis. Although ostensibly an amateur (she worked as a playground director), King was "professional" in her approach to the sport. Her preparations were careful and disciplined and her on-court behavior was often belligerent. It was she rather than John McEnroe who introduced the histrionic protests against umpires' decisions. Admired for her ruthlessness in some quarters, crowds turned against her.

King's major professional initiative was to organize an exclusively women's tennis tour which began in 1968. Operating outside the auspices of "official" organizations, King's tour was openly professional in much the same way as pro men's tours such as the Kramer Pro Tour. BJK was able to recruit fellow player Rosie Casals, but few of the other top players. Interestingly, Wimbledon allowed professionals within three months of the start of the King/Casals tour; and the rest of the world's tournaments went open soon after.

Having taken charge of her own career, King aligned herself with the pro-abortion campaign that had grown in momentum and the Title IX legislation of 1972. And, as if to cement her position as a feminist champion, she negotiated a deal with the Philip Morris tobacco company to set up the women-only Virginia Slims tour. Virginia Slims cigarettes were marketed in such a way as to appeal to newly-independent women. King had no compunction about accepting sponsorship money from a tobacco company, in fact very few people considered the combination of sports and tobacco sponsorship objectionable. The United States Tennis Association (USTA) set up a rival women's tournament, though it was clear that King's ascendancy during 1972–5, her most prodigious championship-winning period, and her sheer notoriety made the Virginia Slims the major attraction in women's tennis.

After BJK's sexual proclivities had become a matter of public record, her finances collapsed: heavy legal bills and the withdrawal of sponsorship money forced her into resuscitating her playing career. Actually, she made quite a fist of her comeback, progressing to a Wimbledon semi-final at the age of 40.

The zeal with which King prised away control of tennis from the grip of men was almost matched by her initial reticence about her homosexuality. Her first ineffectual denials gave way to a reluctant admission of her affair, though she maintained she was not a lesbian. In the 1980s, outings were not yet in vogue. After King, they became commonplace, especially among female tennis players; though, less frequently among male sports performers. (See *leading* QUESTIONS – "Why don't more gay sports performers come out?" page 298.)

The question we asked of marathons stands with tennis: how would Venus Williams fare in a head-to-head with Pete Sampras had women been playing competitively against men for the past 50 or 60 years? Again, the skeptic might argue that the results would be basically the same, the support this time coming from the copious amount of evidence on the physical differences between the sexes – that is, differences which do not refer to social or cultural influences.

We can gain some measure of the rate of women's progress in sports over the past couple of decades by glancing back at what was once a standard text, *Social Aspects of Sport*. In the 1983 edition of their book, Snyder and Spreitzer wrote about the types of sport women have been encouraged or discouraged from pursuing. "The 'appropriateness' of the type of sport continues to reflect the tenets of the Victorian ideal of femininity," they wrote (1983: 156). They went on to identify three types.

1 *The categorically unacceptable* includes combat sports, some field events, and sports that involve attempts to subdue physically opponents by body contact, direct application of force to a heavy object, and face-to-face opposition where body contact may occur.

2 *Generally not acceptable* forms of competition include most field events, sprints, and long jump; these strength-related events are acceptable, the authors believe, only for the "minority group" women, particularly, we presume, ethnic minorities.

3 *Generally acceptable* for all women are sports that involve the projection of the body through space in aesthetically pleasing patterns or the use of a light implement; no body contact is possible in sports such as swimming, gymnastics, figure skating, and tennis.

Types (1) and (2) no longer exist. Professional women boxers appear regularly on major boxing bills; some, like Christy Martin in the late 1990s, made over a million dollars from boxing. Taekwondo, an exhibition event at the 1988 Olympics, will be featured as a competitive event in the 2000 games. And there are hundreds of female kick boxers operating all over the world.

The inclusion of marathons and 10,000-meter races in the Olympics indicates that women are now seen as capable of handling endurance and strength events as capably as men. Nor are these events dominated by black women. Leadership has circulated among Europeans, Africans, and Asians. Of course, black women, especially, have achieved excellence, for reasons advanced in Chapter six.

Over the years, women have not achieved as much as men; yet the conclusion that women cannot achieve the same levels does not follow logically from the original premise that they are biologically different. In fact, it could be argued that, if women had been regarded as equally capable as men physically, then they would perform at similar standards, and that the only reason they do not is because they have been regarded as biologically incapable for so long. In previous editions of this book, I have included a section on the physical differences between men and women and how these affect sporting performance. I highlighted the areas of skeletal and cardiovascular systems and body composition, comparing the typical woman's body with the typical male's.

It would be ridiculous to deny that there are differences, though I now believe they are of significantly less importance than our conceptions about them. As we have discovered in this and the previous chapter, the body is a process, not a thing: it is constantly changing physically and culturally. Sporting performance promotes changes in terms of muscular strength and oxygen uptake; changes in diet and climactic conditions induce bodily changes too, of course. In our particular culture and this stage in history we understand women and their association with men in one way; in another place and at another time, this relationship may be understood quite differently. It is a matter of convention that we organize sports into women's and men's events.

It seems contradictory then to itemize the differences in adipose tissue, respiratory volumes, activity of sweat glands, etc. To do so would fall into the same trap as those who went to so much trouble to "prove" that women were simply not capable of sporting endeavor.

There can be no argument about the fact that the experience of women in sports virtually replicates their more general experience. They have been seen and treated as not only different to men, but also inferior in many respects. Historically, women's position has been subordinate to that of men. They have been systematically excluded from high-ranking, prestigious jobs, made to organize their lives around domestic or private priorities, while men have busied themselves in the public spheres of industry and commerce. Being the breadwinner, the male has occupied a central position in the family and has tended to use women for supplementary incomes only, or, more importantly, as unpaid homeworkers, making their contribution appear peripheral. Traditionally, females have been encouraged to seek work, but only in the short term: women's strivings should be toward getting married, bearing children, and raising a family.

Since the late 1960s and the advent of legal abortion and convenient female contraception, women in the West have been able to exercise much more choice in their own fertility and this has been accompanied by feminist critiques of male dominance. Empirical studies showed wide discrepancies in earning power and this prompted legislation on both sides of the Atlantic designed to ensure equality in incomes for comparable jobs.

One of the loudest cries of feminists was about the abuses of the female body: women, it was argued, have not had control over their own bodies; they have been appropriated by men, not only for working, but for display. "Sex objects" were how many women described themselves, ogled at by men and utilized, often dispassionately. Against this, they recoiled. Even a respectable magazine like *Sports Illustrated*, ostensibly interested in what women do as opposed to what they look like, devotes an annual issue to photographs of women posing in swimwear.

Women are under-represented in politics compared to their total number in the population. They consistently earn less than their equivalent males and are increasingly asked to work part-time. Despite recent changes in the number of places in higher education occupied by women, they tend to opt for subjects (like sociology and art) that will not necessarily guarantee them jobs in science and industry. When they do penetrate the boundaries of the professions they find that having to compete in what is, to all intents and purposes, a man's world, has its hidden disadvantages – what many call the glass ceiling.

Some argue that this state of affairs has been brought about by a capitalist economy geared to maximizing profits and only too willing to exploit the relatively cheap labor of women who are willing to work for less than men, mainly because they have been taught to believe that their work is unimportant and subsidiary to that of men, and that their "real" work is domestic not industrial. Others insist that women's subordination has a larger resonance that transcends any political or economic system and is derived from patriarchy, a state in which men have continually sought to maintain the grip they have had on society and have found the deception that "a woman's place is in the home" a great convenience which they wish to perpetuate. Whatever the motivation behind the successful effort to keep women subordinate, its effects have been felt in sport, where women have for long been pushed into second place.

Like it or not, women who succeed in sport do not always succeed in the popular imagination: where are the female Bryants or Favres? In recent decades, only Nancy Kerrigan, Mia Hamm, and Gabrielle Reece have generated enough interest to guarantee portfolios of endorsements and, in Kerrigan's case, a movie. For a while she was America's favorite covergirl. Had she been pear-shaped with carious teeth, scrubby hair, and pimples, only skating fans would have ever heard of her. Her athletic ability on the ice alone would have quickly been overlooked. Well, not entirely: her conflict with arch-rival Tonya Harding would have guaranteed headlines. But the soft-focus treatment reserved for Kerrigan, in spite of her failure to gain an Olympic gold medal, indicates that her physical appearance was uppermost in the minds of those who bombarded her with contracts.

Women, like black people, have never managed entirely to shrug off their stereotypes: each group is in the process of redefining itself in a way that suggests they are much more capable than popular images suggest. But old ideas die hard. Blacks in sport have unwittingly contributed to the stereotype of a brawny and physically adept specimen but with little "upstairs." They have grasped the only opportunity they were offered for escaping deprivation and, in the process, have become so brilliant that their prowess appears natural.

Women's experience has been one of denial: they simply have not been allowed to enter sports, again on the basis of a mistaken belief in their natural predisposition. Because of this, the encouragement, facilities, and, importantly, competition available to males from an early age has not been extended to them. In the very few areas where the gates have been recently opened – the marathon being the obvious example – women's progress has been extraordinary. Given open competition, women could achieve parity with men in virtually all events, apart from those very few that require the rawest of muscle power. The vast majority of events need fineness of judgment, quickness of reaction, balance, and anticipation; women have no disadvantages in these respects. Their only disadvantage is what men believe about them. To close this chapter, I want to consider another set of beliefs produced – not entirely, but mostly – by men that purports to explain why, in sports as in life, women will simply never catch up.

MEN'S 10 PER CENT ADVANTAGE

Imagine a man attempting to park a car. He looks at the space, then quickly uses mental imagery to assess whether his car will fit, pulls forward, then backs into the spot. A woman's approach to parallel parking is different: she mentally converts the picture into words, estimating the car's length, the size of the space available, then takes time to evaluate whether one will go into the other. At least that is one interpretation of what happens. According to Anne and Bill Moir, men can form a spatial image easily, while women cannot; they need to reduce the situation to a verbal form. And this constitutes a "fundamental" difference between the sexes. As the Moirs put it, "women are generally more verbal, men are more spatial" (1998: 116).

This has clear implications for sports. Able to assess spaces, judge distances, and co-ordinate hand and eye, men are well-equipped to tackle the demands of athletic competition; they are, as the Moirs say, "good with things." Women, by contrast, are not: they are "good with words" – which is not a great deal of help in sports. In their book *Why Men Don't Iron: The real science of gender studies*, the Moirs pull together a number of studies, all of which purport in some way to confirm the view that the difference between males and females is not a matter of cultural convention, nurturing, stereotyping, or, indeed, anything to do with the environment.

"The truth is that the brains of the two sexes are organized in different ways, and it is this difference which gives rise to the differences in ability," argue the Moirs (1998: 119). The sources of this structural and chemical difference are biological. A typical six-week-old embryo is exposed to a cascade of genes – a sort of hormonal soup – that affect later sexual characteristics. Many of these characteristics are obvious. Others are not. Marshaling support from researchers into brain functionality and morphology, the Moirs insist that we have neglected more fundamental, though less visible, differences between men and women. Brain differences give rise to different abilities. "Real science" shows that permanent differences in brain capacity can never be removed. Men will always be better at some things than women and vice versa.

In itself, this sounds retro, though not especially threatening. After all, "real science" has found genes that predispose some individuals toward homosexuality and others that determine that the person will become an alcoholic. We saw in Chapter six, how one theory sought to explain that differences between blacks' and whites' athletic abilities were due to biological differences. Other theories have used the same approach to explain why African Americans do poorly at school. These have been controversial because they imply that no amount of social change can do much to alter constant differences and the inequalities that turn on them.

For instance, the Moirs believe that the equal sports facilities mandated by Title IX is the "most ludicrous application" of the doctrine of "absolute equality between the sexes" (1998: 144). On their account, it is not surprising that young men are better at physical events: they are more aggressive, impatient, and competitive than young women and they have brains suited to high-speed, high-pressure situations. These are traits likely to be of service in sports. And the reason why men typically have them is not because they are socialized into them; but because they have the right neurological equipment and ten times more testosterone than women. "For boys there should at least be more active and practical learning; more action and stress; a firmer structure and more competitive (virile) tests," they argue (1998: 152).

On this account, the male is an adventure-seeker, attracted to "dangerous sports and physically risky activities involving speed or defying gravity (like parachuting or skiing)" (1998: 161). A woman's "instinct is to avoid risk" (1998: 163). Again differences in the engineering of the brain explain all, including why women underperform compared to men in, well, just about everything that matters, including sports. The Moirs directly answer the question I set at the outset. They cite two marathon times: that of Boston marathon winners Moses Tanui, 2:7.44, and Fatuma Roba, 2:23.21, who were 15.37 apart. "In track and field events, on the whole, males have a 10% advantage, and nature will keep it that way" (1998: 165). In addition to the physical advantages of greater lung capacity, faster metabolic rate and proportionately more hemoglobin, men have a brain with "triggers" that prompt their bodies to pump out more testosterone and "testosterone in competition is what oxygen is to fire" (1998: 166).

This type of argument has been used before (as we have seen in Chapter seven), though the Moirs are careful to support their claims with evidence from studies by, among others, Roger Gorski whose studies demonstated that male rats, if starved of testosterone in fetal stage, become female in later sexual orientation (1991). Other researchers who are cited approvingly include Munroe and Govier: their work on sex differences and brain organization indicates that females use both hemispheres of their brains to process language, while men involved in verbal tasks utilize only the left side of the brain (1993). Ernie Govier, in particular, argues that males who are verbally gifted (one assumes he means professors, like himself) have female brain patterns (in his 1998 essay "Brainsex and occupation"). But, the crucial insight about boys doing better than girls in spatial tests comes from Gina Grimshaw who has worked with several co-researchers and discovered a correlation between exposure to testosterone in the womb and "male-typical brain patterns." Interviewed by the Moirs, Grimshaw confirms that male and female brains are neither the same, nor equal and this has consequences for the way boys and girls learn (1998: 125).

Any number of social scientists agree that there are significant learning differences between young males and females, though most would maintain that the differences are due, not to brain organization, but to cultural determinants. The learning process begins from Day One: the way children are named, dressed, rewarded, punished, taught, in the most general sense, dealt with – these are all influenced by the different expectations people have about males and females. This does not necessarily mean that the research used by the Moirs is misguided or invalid. It just means that it is less earth-shattering than the authors suppose.

Say there are biologically-driven differences in brain structure: a sophisticated social scientist will accept the possibility, at the same time adding that the biggest influences on our lives come not from within but from without. Our parents, peers, and "significant others" bear heavily on us; the institutions that surround us and enter our consciousness induce us to think and behave in ways that strike us as perfectly natural, but which are, in all probability, social. Differences may appear so deep and distinct that they have sources in biology, but it is often the shaping effect of culture that makes us who we are. Culture has a habit of overpowering biology.

In other words it does not take a sledgehammer to crack the Moirs' nut: while their argument exaggerates the effects of biological factors, we do not have to reject out-of-hand the evidence they gather to substantiate it in order to arrive at a different conclusion. Perhaps the reason why men and women are not equal is *not* because they are different biologically, but because they are treated differently. The parallel processes of exclusion that have operated in sports and in society generally should alert us to the possibility that, over time, cultural conventions have a tendency to be accepted as natural inevitabilities.

Women have under-achieved in sports relative to men. We have seen how sports were originally intended exclusively for men and how, for most of their history, stayed exactly that. Women were warned off either forcibly or by medical scares and those who did have the temerity to venture toward the male domain were stigmatized as freaks. So, when they eventually broke onto men's turf, female athletes started from a position of weakness. Even then, they were, and are still, reminded by many that they occupy a secondary status. Paid less, with fewer representatives in senior administrative, coaching, media, and academic positions, women are left in little doubt that they remain interlopers rather than tenants.

FURTHER READING

Sport and the Physical Emancipation of English Women, 1870–1914 by Kathleen McCrone (Routledge, 1988) looks at the entry of women into sport during the Victorian period. It was a crucial time in the development of sport and also one in which myths about women abounded. At public schools, the new sports with rules and time-scales were meant to instill character and decisiveness fitting for future purveyors of the Empire. Women were not seen as purveyors.

Coming on Strong: Gender and sexuality in twentieth-century women's sport by Susan K. Cahn (Free Press, 1994) is a splendid historical and contemporary analysis of women athletes and the changing social milieux in which they competed. Emphasizing the sexuality issue, Cahn concludes: "Sport remains a key cultural location for male dominance, as a site where traditional patriarchal values are upheld." Worth complementing with *Feminism and Sporting Bodies* (Human Kinetics, 1996) by M. Ann Hall.

Women in Sport, edited by Greta L. Cohen (Sage, 1993), is a solid collection with contributions from economists, psychologists, historians, and other disciplines, all organized around the theme suggested by the title. The chapters range from "Understanding nutrition" to "Women with disabilities." The editor's own chapter examines the role of the media in impacting women's developments in sports.

Women and Sport: Interdisciplinary perspectives, edited by D. M. Costa and Sharon Guthrie (Human Kinetics, 1994), is split into three sections: (1) Historical and cultural foundations of women's sport; (2) Biomedical considerations; (3) Psychosocial dimensions. This may profitably be read in conjunction with *Women, Sport and Culture*, a collection of essays from various writers, edited by Susan Birrell and Cheryl Cole (Human Kinetics, 1994).

ASSIGNMENT

It is 1880 and the scenario imagined at the start of this chapter is unfolding. Reconstruct the history of any three sports (you choose) plotting the progress of women and men to the present day. Remember: women are able to compete freely in open competition with men, and sports authorities do not recognize separate gender-based events. Extrapolate creatively from known evidence, which may be drawn from sports and social histories, using statistics where appropriate.

leading QUESTIONS

q: Do cheats epitomize today's sports better than fair players?

a: Yes. It might plausibly be argued that the sports performer who is prepared to risk disqualification and the defeat, shame, and abject humiliation that often follow embodies the very qualities that define competitive sports in the twenty-first century.

To cheat is to act fraudulently, to deceive, swindle, or flout rules designed to maintain conditions of fairness. In the context of sports, fairness may be defined as in accordance with specified rules. As professionalism has crept into virtually every major sport, often irresistlble incentives have been offered to competitors. The temptation to do "whatever it takes" to win has meant that the competitors – as opposed to those who are gratified by participating alone – have broken the rules whenever they believed they could escape being penalized for their infraction.

Cheating is endemic in professional sports, though the actual form it takes changes. There are three main classes of cheating: (1) an intentional infraction designed and executed to gain an unfair advantage; (2) an unintentional infraction that goes un-noticed by game officials and which the offending player fails to report – and so exploits his/her advantage; (3) an instance when rules are observed, but the spirit of competition is compromised, a tactic often described as "gamesmanship." All three feature strongly in today's sport.

(1) Several NFL and British Premiership players have made reputations from their dirty play. As *Sports Illustrated* puts it: "There's a nasty breed of NFL players who follow one cardinal rule: Anything goes, and that means biting, kicking, spearing, spitting and leg-whipping" (October 26, 1998). Kevin Gogan epitomized this type of player. Soccer's Vinnie Jones held a similar distinction. But there are less obvious methods of cheating.

Perhaps the most notorious unpunished instance of disguised cheating was Diego Maradona's "Hand of God" goal, when he palmed the ball into the goal of the England soccer team in a 1986 World Cup game. Video evidence showed clearly that the Argentinian player deliberately used his hand illegally. The referee did not see it and awarded a goal amid much protest. Maradona did not confess his sin to the referee. As his biographer Jimmy Burns wrote: "Neither in the immediate aftermath of the game nor in the years that followed did Maradona ever admit to his folly" (1996: 163). Nor did New York Jets players own up to referee Phil Luckett, whose crew allowed a touchdown call to stand on quarterback Vinny Testaverde's play which finished over a foot shy of the endzone in the Jets' crucial 1998 game against Seattle Seahawks.

Cheating is not confined to competitors. Owners, managers, and coaches want to win just as fiercely as those who play under their guidance. Tall stories of cornermen slipping horseshoes into their boxers' gloves may be laughable, but the most notorious instance of tampering with gloves was the Resto–Collins case of 1983. The unbeaten Billy Collins, then 21, took a terrible pounding from the normally light-hitting Luis Resto, who was 20–7–2 at the time. Collins's injuries were so bad that he did not fight again and was killed in a car accident nine months later. It was found that padding had been removed from Resto's gloves. Resto was banned from boxing and, later, convicted of assault, conspiracy, and criminal possession of a deadly weapon (his fists). His corner-man, Panama Al Lewis was convicted of assault, conspiracy, tampering with a sports contest, and criminal possession of a deadly weapon. They both served two and a half years in prison.

Less serious in its repercussions was the case in 1963 when Henry Cooper was poised at the brink of an upset victory over a dazed Cassius Clay (as he then was). Clay clung on until the end of the round at which point his cornerman Angelo Dundee claimed that a tear in his charge's glove occasioned a replacement. In the several minutes it took to change the glove, Clay's head cleared and he went on to defeat Cooper. Years later it was revealed that the tear was Dundee's own handiwork, posing the question, was this the action of a brilliant, quick-thinking strategist, or a crass cheat? Or both.

Willie John McBride's revelation about the British Lions touring rugby team is a telling illustration of how the pragmatism typically associated with coaches can become wholesale cheating. Players were told to strike members of the opposing teams when-ever they heard a coded instruction from the sideline. The foul tactic was rationalized as a defense against referees who favored the home sides.

(2) It is difficult to imagine an instance when a coach would not condone cheating if there was a guarantee that it would go undetected. In a 1997 game of soccer between two English teams, Liverpool player Robbie Fowler was awarded a penalty after the referee ruled that he had been fouled by Arsenal's goalkeeper David Seaman. Fowler risked censure by insisting to the referee that he had not been fouled by Seaman. The referee was adamant that the penalty stood and Fowler duly took it. While Fowler's spotkick was saved and driven home on the rebound, one wonders what might have happened had the player remained true to his original confession and deliberately sliced the ball wide of the goal. It strains credibility to believe that Liverpool's head coach would have commended him on his uprightness. More likely, he would have been disciplined for failing to act in the best interests of his team. In the event, the player was congratulated by team mates and was hailed as triumphant.

This was a rare case when a player actually owned-up to an official but was overruled in such a way that he prospered. Players are discouraged from making such disclosures, not only by team mates and coaches, but by game officials themselves, who may interpret the player's confession as an attempt to undermine his or her authority. Even if the original intention of the athlete was not to cheat, the structure of the game actually inhibits him or her from doing much else.

(3) Intention is never clear in instances of "gamesmanship": when rules may be observed but the spirit of competition is broken. Exaggerating the effects of low blows

to gain time to recover when under pressure is a stratagem sometimes employed by boxers. Soccer players are so notorious for this that Fifa introduced rules that forced all injured (or pseudo-injured) players to be stretchered off the field of play before they could resume playing. These maneuvers are right at the margins of fair game: strictly-speaking legal, but designed to gain a benefit or relieve pressure. For example, during her losing match against Steffi Graf in the French Open final of 1999, Martina Hingis (a) demanded that the umpire inspect a mark on the clay surface after her forehand landed adjacent to the baseline, (b) went for a five-and-a-half-minute restroom break at the start of the third set, and (c) served underarm when facing match point on two occasions. While the actions did not contravene the rules, they prompted Graf to ask the umpire: "We play *tennis*, OK?"

Instrumental qualities such as prudence and calculation have seeped into sports and one effect of this has been the loss of the abandon with which competitors once pursued their goals – which were gratuitous before the onset of professionalization. The under-pinnings of sport have been destroyed, says William Morgan in his book *Leftist Theories of Sport*. Market norms have come to prevail: sports "practitioners," as he calls them, have no compelling reason to value or engage in competitive challenges save for extrinsic rewards – money. They are provided "with no reason not to cheat and every reason to cheat in order to obtain the external goods they desire."

For Morgan, rules have become little more than technical directives that enable prac-titioners to acquire the external goods they seek. Any moral power the rules of sports once had has disappeared. So, sports performers break every rule they can get away with and comply with every rule they cannot. If a player gets caught, he or she is rightly accused of not being clever or adept enough, or even being plain stupid. This is either a technical infraction or a miscalculation. Morality does not enter into it. Morgan believes that the institutional imperatives of professional sports "underwrite and legitimate such rule breaking."

This explains why track and field athletics found itself in the somewhat precarious position in the 1990s when its authorities discouraged the use of performance-enhancing drugs. After track and field professionalized, promoters, television compa-nies, and an assortment of other interested parties sought to impose a new type of economic logic. Athletes began competing for very high stakes as the prizes for success rose sharply. Many were prepared to take banned substances in the all-out effort to win at any cost. So much so that taking drugs became almost synonymous with cheating in the 1990s.

The discovery of vials of somatotropin, the human growth hormone, in the luggage of a member of the Chinese team at the 1998 World Swimming Championships cast doubt on the integrity of coaches who, it was thought, packed the drugs either with or without the consent of Yuan Yuan, the swimmer concerned. The quantity of soma-totropin involved indicated that this was not the swimmer's personal supply; more likely that of the whole team. Similarly, the Tour de France of 1998, in which performance-enhancing drugs were administered by some team officials, indicated how team coaches, managers, and medical officers were all involved in organized cheating.

More questions . . .

- Should we admire rather than castigate the cheat who escapes penalties?
- Is fair play compatible with professional sports?
- Do coaches/managers influence players' approaches to cheating?

Read on . . .

- McIntosh, P., *Fair Play* (Heinemann Educational, 1980).
- Lüschen, G., "Cheating" in *Social Problems in America*, edited by D. Landers (University of Illinois Press, 1976).
- Leaman, O., "Cheating and fair play in sport" in *Philosophic Inquiry in Sport*, edited by W. J. Morgan and K. Meier (Human Kinetics, 1988).

champs or cheats?

drugs in sports and

attempts to eliminate

them

GOOD AND EVIL

Amid the memories of 1998's sporting calendar, one will remain. Not the astonishing upset win of Denver Broncos, led by 37-year-old John Elway, over hot favorites Green Bay Packers in the Super Bowl. Nor Mark MacGwire's record-shattering 70 slugs, or the Bulls' sixth title in the 1990s. Nor even the mystery illness of Brazilian soccer star Ronaldo on the eve of his team's defeat by France in the World Cup final, or Cal Ripken's first rest after 2,633 straight days.

The story that will remain in the memory in years to come will be that of the Tour de France which disintegrated into chaos after the disqualification of one team, police raids on the hotels of several teams and a go-slow protest by riders at the 17th stage. The reason: drugs.

The expulsion of the entire Festina Watches team from the Tour was unprecedented in the race's 95-year history. On July 23, all nine Festina riders were taken into police custody, along with three more team directors. The specific charge against the masseur was for smuggling drugs, including anabolic steroids and erythropoietin (EPO). Four people connected with a second squad, TVM, were also questioned over a seizure of banned substances.

The Festina manager, Bruno Rousel, told a police inquiry of "the conditions under which a co-ordinated supply of doping products was made available to the riders, organized by the team management, the doctors, the masseurs and the riders. The aim was to maximize performance under strict medical control to avoid the riders obtaining drugs for themselves in circumstances which might have been seriously damaging to their health." Rousel reported that the drug war chest amounted to £40,000 ($65,000) per year, or 1 per cent of the team's £4 million annual budget.

Massacre à la Châine: Révélations sur 30 ans de tricheries

This was the title of a book written by Willy Voet, the Belgian trainer of the Festina team that was disqualified from the 1998 Tour de France. Voet was stopped by French customs on his way to Dublin, the starting-point of the race. It was alleged that the French government had been determined to create a test case and had been watching Voet for months. In his book, which became a best-seller in France, Voet argued that 90 per cent of professional cyclists regularly take banned substances, not simply to enhance their racing performance, but to assist their recovery from perhaps the world's most grueling competition. He named over 100 athletes. Riders are obliged to fulfil excessively demanding commitments agreed by their teams in conjunction with sponsors and television. The publication of the English translation of the book, *Breaking the Chain: How drugs destroyed a sport*, by Yellow Jersey Press, was held up by the criminal trial in France involving rider Richard Virenque, who denied allegations about him made in the book.

Rider Frederic Pontier confessed to the French sports daily newspaper *L'Equipe* that he had used EPO and knew that an "important number" of other cyclists were also using performance enhancers. Police sweeps resulted in a number of other riders and officials being held for questioning. The crisis deepened when competitors sensed they were being, as rider Jeroen Blijlevens put it, "treated like animals, like criminals." Their snail's-pace demonstration forced organizers to annul the Albertville to Aix-les-Bains stage of the race.

Contemporary sports have taken on a Manichean character in which good co-exists with evil: the evil is represented by the spread of drug-use among athletes willing to risk chemical side-effects, or even direct effects, in the attempt to build muscle, steady the hand, flush out body fluids, speed up the metabolism, improve endurance, or spark more aggression. There are drugs available that can assist in all these, but woe for any athlete caught taking them. Before addressing the contemporary issues, let us trace the history of drug use in sports.

HISTORY OF DRUG USE

Taking supplements as a way of improving physical or mental performance in sports is arguably as old as sports themselves. Competitors in the ancient Greco-Roman games were known to eat animals' parts, such as horns or the secretions of testes, which they thought would confer the strength of bulls, for example. It is probable that Greeks habitually used plants and mushrooms with chemically active derivatives either to aid performance or accelerate the healing process.

In the modern era, as sports became professionalized, evidence of the systematic application of stimulants arrived initially through the six-day cycle races in Europe. Riders in the late nineteenth century favored ether and caffeine to delay the onset of fatigue sensations. Sprint cyclists preferred nitroglycerine, a chemical later used in conjunction with heroin, cocaine, strychnine, and others. In his *Journal of Sports History* article, "Anabolic steroids: The gremlins of sport," Terry Todd records "the first known drug related death of an athlete" after a cyclist had taken a "speed ball" of heroin and cocaine (1987: 91).

"The most famous early case of drug enhancement, however, occurred in the 1904 Olympic Games in St. Louis," writes Todd. Marathon winner Thomas Hicks, of the USA, collapsed after the race. "Hicks' handlers, who had been allowed to accompany him throughout the course of the race in a motor car, admitted they had given him repeated doses of strychnine and brandy to keep him on his feet" (1987: 91). Hicks was allowed to keep his medal.

There is irony in the fact that sports medicine's role in contemporary sports was given impetus by the efforts of sports federations to eliminate the use of the very products that medicine gave to sports. This is the conclusion of Ivan Waddington, whose article "The development of sports medicine" shows clearly that medicine was originally invoked by sports to help improve performance (1996). It did so, of course. Medicine's largess included pharmaceuticals, many to treat sports-related injuries, but many others to promote competitive performance. In the 1950s, colleges in Germany and the United States were established to exploit the applications of medicine to sports.

The Male Hormone, a book by Paul de Kruiff, which was published in 1945, covered research into the impact of testosterone on the endurance of men involved in muscular work; and this alerted some coaches to the potential of what was supposed to be a medically-prescribed treatment. After returning from the 1952 Olympics convinced that the successful Soviet weight-lifting team had used "hormone stuff," US coach Bob Hoffman sought something similar for his own squad. The product he obtained was Dianabol, an anabolic steroid first produced by the CIBA company in 1958 and intended for patients suffering from burns. The gains in weight and strength were impressive enough to convince him and observers of the value of medical science in sports. During the 1950s and 1960s, there were no rules forbidding the use of pharmaceuticals and, as news of Dianabol circulated in the sports world, strength-reliant performers, like field-eventers and football players, started using steroids. Other sports were not slow to realize the importance of testosterone and, through the 1960s, it was commonplace for cyclists, skiers, and an assortment of other athletes to use the substance.

Testosterone

From *testis + o + sterol + one*, this is a steroid androgen formed in the testes. The basic function of testosterone is to control the natural production of sperm cells and this, in turn, affects the male's masculine appearance. A feedback control system is at work involving the hypothalamus; this secretes a hormone called LHR which stimulates the pituitary gland to secrete luteinizing hormone (LH) and this, in turn, stimulates the testes to produce the testosterone. A high concentration of testosterone inhibits the secretion of LHR by the hypothalamus which causes a drop in the level of testosterone, triggering the hypothalamus to release more LHR, LH, and ultimately testosterone in a smoothly regulated system.

If there was a turning-point in attitudes toward the use of drugs in sport, it was on July 13, 1967, when Tommy Simpson, aged 29, collapsed and died on the 13th stage of the three-week-long Tour de France. Simpson, a British rider, was lying seventh overall when the race set off from Marseilles. The temperature was well over 40°C (105°F). Simpson fell and remounted twice before falling for the final time. Three tubes were found in his pocket, one full of amphetamines, two empty. The British team's luggage was searched and more supplies of the pills were found. At the time, the drugs element did not cause the sensation that might be expected today: the death itself was of most concern. In continental Europe, there was substantial and open advocacy of the use of such pills to alleviate the strain of long-distance cycling. There is little doubt that many of the leading contenders in the 1967 and other tours were taking amphetamines. Seven years before, in a less publicized tragedy, another cyclist, Knut Jensen, died at the Olympics after taking nonicol, a blood dilatory.

An attempt in the previous year to introduce drug testing was opposed by leading cyclists, including the five-times Tour winner Jacques Anquetil, who told the newspaper *France-Dimanche*: "Yes, I dope myself. You would be a fool to imagine that a professional cyclist who rides 235 days a year in all temperatures and conditions can hold up without a stimulant." Interestingly, Simpson was not denounced as a cheat at the time; his death opened up a rather different discourse about the perils of drug-taking rather than the morality of it.

The IOC had actually set up a Medical Commission in 1950, mainly to investigate the medical effects of the use of stimulants, especially amphetamines, to increase endurance. Simpson's death prompted the introduction of testing, which came into being at the 1968 winter Olympics, though it was, as Barrie Houlihan calls it, a "modest effort" and largely for research purposes (1997: 180). Todd cites an American decathlete at the Mexico Olympic Games of 1968, who estimated a third of the US track and field team used steroids at training camp (1987: 95). Writer Jack Scott reported that drugs were circulated quite freely at Mexico and conversations revolved not around the morality of taking them, but which ones were most effective (1971). At the games, Bob Beamon improved the world's long jump record by 21.75 inches with a leap of 29ft 2.5in (8.90m). In the previous 33 years, the record had progressed by only 8.5 inches; it took a further 23 years before Mike Powell broke Beamon's record. If such a feat was accomplished in today's cynical climate, people would be suspicious.

Beginning in 1960, East Germany had operated a systematic program of inducting about 10,000 young people into sports academies where they were trained, conditioned, and supplied with pharmaceuticals intended to improve their athletic performance. State Program 1425, as it was known, was responsible for some of the world's outstanding track achievements, including Marita Koch's 47.60-second 400 meters record set in 1985 and rarely threatened ever since. After the end of the Cold War, a special team of prosecutors began sifting through captured files of the Stasi secret police and uncovered details of often abusive treatment accorded young athletes. Offenders were later prosecuted.

Drug use in American sports was less systematic: stories of baseball and football players' use of amphetamines, narcotic analgesics, and other substances were escaping via books such as Scott's *The Athletic Revolution* and Paul Hoch's *Rip Off the Big Game*, which concluded "that the biggest drug dealers in the sports world are none other than team trainers" (1972:

122). Ted Kotcheff's 1979 film *North Dallas Forty*, which was based on Pete Gent's account of pro football, showed football players trotting onto the field as near-zombies after taking copious amounts of painkillers and sundry other drugs.

Coaches were doling out amphetamines before a game to pep players up and analgesics to help them play without the sensation of pain while carrying injuries. After a game the players were, as Hoch puts it, "tranquilized to get their eyeballs back in their head – to even get a night's sleep" (1972: 123). Hoch cites two players who filed law suits against their clubs for administering drugs "deceptively and without consent" and which eventually proved detrimental to their health (1972: 123).

Estimates about the amount of drug use are so vague as to be useless, but it is at least suggestive that, in 1983, a *Sports Illustrated* article stated that between 40 and 90 per cent of NFL players used anabolic steroids (May 13). Several deaths were attributed to steroids in the years that followed. In 1987, the International Olympic Committee (IOC) recorded 521 positive tests for steroid use; this was 16 years after the introduction of anti-drugs legislation by the International Amateur Athletics Federation (IAAF).

Recreational drug use was also widespread among athletes. In his 1986 book *Fractured Focus*, Richard Lapchick referred to an "epidemic in American sport" and highlighted several athletes who were either in gaol or fighting addictions. The NBA, in particular, was infamous for the number of cocaine-using players and, as we will see in Chapter fourteen, improved its marketability only after introducing drugs-testing. Michael Ray Richardson was banned by the NBA after his *fourth* positive test for cocaine. A succession of boxers, football players, and other athletes were penalized for cocaine use. While cocaine use was probably recreational rather than performance-enhancing, the term "drugs" was used indiscriminately. Using such an emotive word had the effect of heightening the feeling that sports were adrift in a moral sea with no terra firma in sight.

Unquestionably, the case that converted concern over drug use in sports from concern to hysteria was the ejection of Canadian sprinter Ben Johnson from the 1988 Seoul Olympics after he had won the 100 meters in a world record 9.79 seconds. Stanozolol, an anabolic steroid, was detected in Johnson's urine sample; he was stripped of his gold medal and his time expunged from the records. Overnight, Johnson went from the "world's fastest man" to the "world's fastest cheat." While he was the 31st competitor to be disqualified for drug use since the IOC instituted its systematic testing in 1972, Johnson's stature in world sport ensured that his case would make news everywhere and that he as an individual would carry the sins of all. As well as his medal and record, he instantly lost (at the most conservative estimate) $2 million in performance-related product endorsement fees.

This was the official inquiry headed by Charles Dubin set up following Ben Johnson's ejection from the 1988 Olympics. Among the inquiry's conclusions was the fact that there was a conspiracy of silence among athletes, coaches, and physicians. Dr. Jamie Astaphan, Johnson's physician, referred to "the brotherhood of the needle." Dr. Robert Kerr, author of *The Practical Use of Anabolic Steroids with Athletes* (1982), testified that he had prescribed anabolic steroids to about 20 medalists at the 1984 summer Olympics. At the hearings, IOC vice-president Richard Pound famously answered the question why, with rumors abounding, he did not ask Johnson if he took drugs: "As a lawyer, I felt I was better off not knowing" (Houlihan 1997: 194–5).

Following the Johnson case, the use of drugs to improve athletic performance was universally condemned by sporting authorities. Lists of prohibited substances lengthened so that many prescription drugs and perfectly legal products that could be purchased at drug stores were banned. Alexander Watson, an Australian pentathlete was disqualified from the same Olympics as Johnson, for having an excessive level of caffeine in his system; to have reached such a level he would have needed to have drunk 40 regular-sized cups of coffee a day.

The expulsion of Argentinian player Diego Maradona from the 1994 soccer World Cup was the biggest "bust" since Johnson. Maradona all but had his cleats exchanged for cloven hooves during a media demonization. Like Johnson, he was an exceptional athlete, a world-class performer who had, in the eyes of the world, resorted to cheating. But, there was a suspicion that, in another sense, he was not exceptional at all; he was simply one of countless others who systematically used substances to enhance their performance. They probably escaped detection through a variety of methods, such as coming off the drugs early, taking masking agents, or catheterizing (replacing the contents of one's own bladder with someone else's drug-free urine).

By the time of the Tour de France scandal, drugs-testing procedures were in place in all major sports and each had policies, mostly derived from the IOC's. The list of proscribed substances had lengthened to the point where athletes needed to be careful about reading the labels on over-the-counter headache or cold remedies in case they contained a banned constituent. In the next section, we will examine the prohibited substances.

BANNED SUBSTANCES

The IOC's banned list includes over 4,000 substances which are grouped into five categories. They are anabolic steroids, stimulants, narcotic analgesics, beta-blockers, and diuretics. I will deal with them in that order, before moving to an examination of blood doping, peptide hormones, and procedures for detecting substances in sports performers.

Anabolic steroids. In 1889, Charles Brown-Sequard devised a rejuvenating therapy for body and mind: the 72-year-old French physiologist had claimed he had increased his physical strength, improved his intellectual energy, relieved his constipation, and even lengthened the arc of his urine by injecting himself with an extract derived from the testes of dogs and guinea-pigs. His discovery triggered a series of experiments that led to synthesis of testosterone, the primary male hormone produced in the testes, in 1935. Since then, synthetic testosterone has been attributed with almost magical qualities and become the most controversial drug in sports. For this reason, it is worth reviewing its history.

Anabolic steroids

From the Greek *ana*, meaning "up" and *bole* "throw," anabolism is the constructive metabolism of complex substances for body tissues, i.e. body-building. Steroids are compounds whose molecules contain rings of carbon and hydrogen atoms; they influence cells by causing special proteins to be synthesized. So, an anabolic steroid is a compound considered to be responsible for the particular synthesis that causes the construction of muscle mass. The idea of using an anabolic steroid is to mirror the chemical action of the testosterone in the body and facilitate muscle growth.

There is nothing new about the concept of ingesting animals' sexual organs and secretions: Egyptians accorded medicinal powers to the testes; Johannes Mesue prescribed a kind of testicular extract as an aphrodisiac; the *Pharmacopoea Wirtenbergica*, a compendium of remedies published in 1754 in Germany, refers to horse testicles and the penises of marine animals. These and several other examples are given by John Hoberman and Charles Yesalis, whose *Scientific American* article on the subject is essential reading for students of the history of performance-enhancing drugs (1995).

In 1896, an Austrian physiologist and future Nobel Prize winner, Oskar Zoth, published a paper which concluded that extracts from bulls' testes, when injected in athletes, led to improvements in muscular strength and the "neuromuscular apparatus." Here was the first official recognition of the significance of hormonal substances for sports performers. Zoth anticipated the objection that a placebo effect may have accounted for the change in his sample of athletes and denied it. Around the same time, other scientists were excited by the prospect of finding the active ingredient in the male sex organ and specifying its effects.

Placebo

From the Latin *placere*, to please, this is a pharmacologically inert substance given to patients usually to humor them rather than effect any cure. Yet the substance often works as effectively (if not more so) as an active substance because the patient believes it will. The substance is called a placebo and its result is known as the placebo effect. This has many applications outside the clinical setting. Weightlifters have been told they were receiving an anabolic steroid while, in fact, only some of them received it – the others were given a placebo. Both groups improved leg presses, the first group by 135 lbs, the other (receiving the placebo) by 132 lbs. The sheer expectation of benefit seems to have been the crucial factor. A similar process can work in reverse. For example, subjects may be given active drugs together with information that they will have no effect: consequently the drugs may not have any effect. In other words, the direct effect of drugs alone may not be any more powerful than the administrator's or experimenter's suggestions. More recently, research has shown that high doses of testosterone given to healthy young men can increase muscle size but not necessarily strength. Increases in strength may come about as a result of the extra hard training the subjects were encouraged to do by taking the substance.

Clinical applications were many. In 1916, two Philadelphia doctors transplanted a human testicle into a patient who was suffering from sexual dysfunctions, starting a spate of similar transplants, the most audacious being a mass removal of the testes of recently executed inmates for transplanting into patients suffering from impotence. The commercial potential of this was not lost on the large pharmaceutical corporations which initiated research programs to isolate the active hormone and synthesize it. By 1939, clinical trials in humans were under way, employing injections of testosterone propionate. Early synthetic testosterone was used with some success by women suffering from a variety of complaints, the intention being to alter a female's hormonal balance. One of the problems was that the testosterone virilized the patients: they took on male secondary features, like facial hair and enlarged larynx.

From the 1940s androgens were used to treat wasting conditions associated with chronic debilitating illnesses and trauma, burns, surgery, and radiation therapy. Anabolic steroids' efficacy in acclerating red blood-cell production made it a first choice therapy for a variety of anemia (having too little hemoglobin) before bone marrow transplants and other treatments arrived. Between the 1930s and the mid-1980s, psychiatrists prescribed anabolic steroids for the treatment of depression and psychoses. Most recently, steroids have been used to arrest the muscle wasting that occurs during the progression of HIV infection and Aids. Testosterone treatment is currently in use for strengthening older bodies, rejuvenating an ailing libido and improving a declining memory.

In sports, no one doubts the efficacy of anabolic steroids: they *do* work. Precisely what makes them work, we still do not know. There is, for instance, a school of thought that argues that the critical component in the equation is our belief that they will enhance our performance. If, for some reason, we stopped believing in them, then maybe anabolic steroids would not yield the results they apparently do. At present, so much money is spent on testing for drugs that there is little left for ascertaining exactly what they do to sports performers. If self-belief is the single most important factor, it may be that a placebo is at work. (For a fuller discussion of the purported effects of anabolic steroids, see Yesalis 1993.)

While there was widespread disapproval of anabolic steroids by the world's sports governing organizations, no such agreement existed over androstenedione, a perfectly legal product available over the counter at any health food store. "Andro," to use its more popular abbreviation, had effects that many swore were identical to those of hormones: it stimulated the increased production of testosterone. During his history-making 1998 season, Mark McGwire made it known that he regularly used andro. Unlike several other sports organizations, Major League Baseball did not include it on its banned list (Randy Barnes, the 1966 Olympic shot-put champion, was suspended for two years after andro was found in his sample – his second drugs test in eight years). The rights and wrongs of andro were discussed, but technically it was recognized as a food rather than a drug and McGwire, while criticized by some, used it with impunity. Creatine was another supplement sold legally and endorsed by sports performers that became popular as a result of its supposed muscle-building properties.

Stimulants. Evidence of the systematic application of stimulants arrived initially through the six-day cycle races in Europe. Riders in the late nineteenth century favored ether and caffeine to delay the onset of fatigue sensations. Sprint cyclists preferred nitroglycerine, a chemical later used in conjunction with heroin, cocaine, strychnine, and others to make an explosive cocktail.

The basic effect of stimulants is to get messages to a complex pathway of neurons in the brainstem called the arousal system, or reticular activating system (RAS). This system is ultimately responsible for maintaining consciousness and determining our state of awareness. So, if the RAS bombards the cerebral cortex with stimuli, we feel very alert and able to think clearly. Amphetamines are thought to cause chemical neurotransmitters, such as dopamine, to increase, so enhancing the flow of nervous impulses in the RAS and stimulating the entire CNS. The sympathetic nervous system is stimulated, speeding up heart rate, raising blood pressure, and dilating pupils. In sports terms, the performer is fired up and resistant to the sensation of fatigue, particularly the muscular pain associated with lactic acid.

One problem facing users active in sport who need nutrition for the release of energy is that amphetamines depress appetites. They used to be prescribed to dieters, though less so nowadays because dieters became dependent on the drugs. This came about because the body quickly develops a tolerance, probably through the readiness of the liver to break down the drug rapidly. An obvious temptation is to increase the dose to achieve the same effect. So with increased use of the drug, the user becomes dependent. Weight loss and dependence are the more obvious side-effects, others include irritability (probably due to irregular sleep) and even a tendency toward paranoia. Cyclists Jensen and Simpson demonstrated that the effects can be terminal.

There is another class of stimulants called sympathomimetic amine drugs, such as ephedrine, which, as the name suggests, acts not on the brain but directly on the nerves affecting the organs. (This produces effects in the sympathetic part of the autonomic nervous system: it speeds up the action of the heart, and constricts the arteries and increases lung inflation.) Ephedrine is used commonly as a decongestant and is often prescribed for asthma sufferers.

Narcotic analgesics. Painkillers are used in all walks of life, but especially in sports where injuries are commonplace and a tolerance to pain is essential. Soccer and American football are examples of games involving the "walking wounded." Derivatives of the opium poppy were probably used by ancient Mesopotamians around 3000 BCE; they left instructions for use on wax tablets.

There are now methods of producing such derivatives synthetically. Opium, heroin, codeine, and morphine, along with the newer designer drugs, are all classified as narcotics which relieve pain and depress the CNS, producing a state of stupor. Reflexes slow down, the skeleton is relaxed, and tension is reduced. The negative effects are much the same as those of amphetamines, with the additional one of specific neurons becoming dependent on the drug and so providing a basis for addiction.

The immediate effects of stimulants or narcotic analgesics would be of little or no service to sports performers who rely on fineness of judgment, sensitivity of touch, acuity of sight, and steadiness of hand. Success in sports like darts, archery, snooker, shooting, or show jumping is based on calmness and an imperviousness to "pressure." The Canadian snooker player Bill Werbeniuk was famed for his customary ten pints of beer to help him relax before a game. His CNS would become duller and tensions presumably disappeared. How he managed to co-ordinate hand and eye movements, stay awake, or even just stay upright is a mystery. Alcohol has serious drawbacks, which include nausea and impaired judgment, not to mention liver damage and a variety of dependency-related problems.

Beta-blockers. The Vancouver-based Werbeniuk switched to Inderal, a beta-blocker which helped counteract the effects of an hereditary nervous disorder. After criticism from the British Minister for Sport, the World Professional Billiards and Snooker Association (WPBSA) reviewed its drugs policy and included Inderal on its list of banned substances. Unable to find an alternative, Werbeniuk admitted to the WPBSA that he intended to continue using the drug and was eventually banned from tournaments.

Originally used by patients with irregular heartbeats, beta-blockers relieve anxiety by controlling the release of adrenaline and by lowering the heart rate; they are used by edgy showbusiness performers – and horses. In November 1994, a racehorse, Mobile Messenger, tested positive for propranolol, a beta-blocker, after winning a race at Southwell, England. The effect of the drug on the horse would have been similar to that on a human: to slow down the heart rate and thereby alleviate stress.

Diuretics. Weightlifters and other sports performers who compete in categories based on body weight have to calibrate their diet and preparation carefully. A couple of pounds, even ounces, over the limit can destroy months of conditioning if the performer is made to take off the excess at the weigh-in. Jumping rope, saunas, and other methods of instant weight reduction can be debilitating and may drain cerebral fluid that cushions the brain against the wall of the cranium. Competitors in weight-controlled sports always check-weigh during the days preceding an event and, should their weight seem excessive, may take diuretics. These substances – widely used therapeutically for reducing fluid levels – excite the kidneys to produce more urea and, basically, speed up a perfectly natural waste disposal process. A visit to the bathroom is usually necessary after drinking alcoholic drinks or coffee; this is because they both contain diuretics.

Diuretics inhibit the secretion of the anti-diuretic hormone which serves as a chemical messenger, carrying information from the pituitary gland at the base of the brain to parts of the kidneys, making them more permeable and allowing water to be reabsorbed into the body (thus conserving fluid). Hormones, of course, are carried in the blood. If the messages do not get through, the kidneys move the water out of the body. Continued use of diuretics can damage the kidneys. In recent years, the suspicion has grown that competitors have not only been using diuretics to reduce weight but also to flush out other substances, in particular the above-mentioned drugs.

It follows that competitors found to have diuretics in their urine immediately have their motives questioned. Kerrith Brown of Great Britain lost his Olympic bronze medal for judo despite pleading that the diuretic furosemide, found in his urine was introduced into his system by a medical officer who gave him an anti-inflammatory substance containing the chemical to reduce a knee swelling.

Peptide hormones. The values of altitude training are undoubted. In Chapter three, we recognized the importance of the protein molecule hemoglobin, which is found in red blood cells. It has a remarkable ability to form loose associations with oxygen. As most oxygen in the blood is combined with hemoglobin rather than simply dissolved in plasma, the more hemoglobin present in a red blood cell, the more oxygen it can transport to the muscles. Obviously then, performers can benefit from having a plentiful supply of oxygen to react with glucose and release energy stored in food. The advantage of training at altitude, where the oxygen in the atmosphere is scarce, is that the body naturally compensates by producing more hemoglobin.

The performer descends to sea level carrying with him or her a plentiful supply of hemoglobin in the blood, which gradually readjusts (over a period of weeks). Each day spent at lower altitudes diminishes the benefit of altitude training: proliferation of hemoglobin ceases in the presence of available atmospheric oxygen. One way to "capture" the benefits is to remove a quantity of highly oxygenated blood during intense altitude training, store it, and reintroduce it into the circulatory system immediately prior to competition via a transfusion. This is known as blood doping and is an illegal procedure in sports. It was rumored that the Finnish distance runner Lasse Viren used this method for peaking at the right time, such as the Olympic Games. Viren himself never tested positively and insisted that his great performances were attributable to "reindeer milk."

Viren's compatriot, Martti Vainio, lost his silver medal for the 10,000 meters at the Los Angeles Olympics after steroid traces were found in his urine. The Finn had been careful enough to cease using the drug well before competition to escape detection, but blundered by having himself transfused with blood that had been removed from his body early in 1984 when training at altitude, by having the blood reinfused when at sea level.

The "doping" in this process does not refer to the administration of drugs but to the more correct use of the term, pertaining to a thick liquid used as a food or lubricant. There is, however, a synthetic drug that can achieve much the same effect. Erythropoietin (EPO) facilitates the production of extra red blood cells, which absorb oxygen, and leaves the user with no tell-tale needle tracks. As well as being more convenient than a transfusion, EPO has the advantage of being extremely difficult to detect once it has been administered. The biggest EPO case was uncovered when French police traced a delivery of EPO and some masking agents to a Paris address. Fifteen people including cyclists Frank Vandenbroucke and soccer player Jean-Christophe Devaux were arrested along with Lionel Virenque, brother of French cyclist Richard Virenque who was already under investigation for his alleged part in the Tour de France scandal of the previous year.

Blood doping and EPO, in a sense, copy the body's natural processes and, at the moment, their long-term effects seem to be broadly the same as those of living at high altitudes. Another method of mimicking nature is by extracting the naturally occurring human growth hormone, somatotropin (hGH), which is produced and released by the pituitary gland, as discussed in Chapter three. hGH controls the human rate of growth by regulating the amount of nutrients taken into the body's cells and by stimulating protein synthesis. Overproduction of the hormone may cause a child to grow to giant proportions (a condition referred to as gigantism), whereas too little can lead to dwarfism. hGH also affects fat and carbohydrate metabolism in adults, promoting a mobilization of fat which becomes available for use as fuel, and sparing the utilization of protein. The potential of this mechanism for promoting growth has not been lost on field athletes, weightlifters, body-builders, and others requiring muscle build.

Illicit markets in growth hormone extracted from foetuses have been uncovered, though a synthetically manufactured version, somatonorm, has nearly made this redundant. In 1997, customs officers at Sydney, Australia, found 13 vials of Norditropin, the brand name of somatotropin, in a bag belonging to Yuan Yuan, a member of China's team in the World Swimming Championships. Yuan Yuan, at 21, was the youngest member of the team and ranked 13 in the world for the breaststroke. It was speculated that, as a relatively lowly member of the team, she was a guinea pig intended to ascertain whether hGH could be detected through conventional equipment.

This has led some to believe that drug users can always stay one step ahead of those wishing to identify them: the line between what is "natural" and "unnatural" for the human body is not so clear-cut as testers would like and science finds ways of replicating nature. By the end of the 1990s, substances such as insulin growth factor (IGF) and pfc, a type of highly-oxygenated plasma, were impossible to detect through conventional methods.

Others believe that drug-testing methods are keeping pace and not even the elite can escape detection, given a vigilant team of toxicologists and a sophisticated laboratory. But doubts remain.

THE DOUBTS ABOUT TESTING

Hewlett-Packard, the multinational computer specialists, charged the IOC $3 million (£1.9 million) to set up the scientific testing equipment at the Korean Advanced Institute of Science and Technology. The system of gas chromatography and mass spectroscopy could, according to its makers, "detect concentrations [of banned substances] as low as one part per billion; roughly the equivalent to detecting traces from a teaspoonful of sugar after it has been dissolved in an Olympic swimming pool." A further claim was that it could check a compound found in urine against 70,000 held in a computer's database in "less than a minute."

The entire testing process comprises four phases. (1) Within an hour of the finish of an event, two samples of a performer's urine are taken, one is tested for acidity and specific gravity so that testers can get a broad indication of any illegal compounds. (2) The sample is then split into smaller batches to test for certain classes of drugs, such as anabolic steroids, stimulants, etc. Testers make the urine alkaline and mix it with solvents, like ether, causing any drugs to dissolve into the solvent layer, which is more easily analyzed than urine itself. (3) This solvent is then passed through a tube (up to 25 meters long) of gas (or liquid chromatogram) and the molecules of the solvent separate and pass through at different rates, depending on their size and other properties (such as whether they are more likely to adhere to the material of the tube itself). More than 200 drugs are searched for in this period, which lasts about 15 minutes. (4) Any drugs found are then analyzed with a mass spectrometer, which bombards them with high-energy ions, or electrons, creating unique chemical fingerprints, which can be rapidly checked against the database. Should any banned substances show up, the second sample is tested in the presence of the performer. (Another method is radioimmunoassay, in which antibodies to known substances are used like keys that will only fit one lock; the lock is the banned substance which is found by the key that fits it.)

Encouraged by the Seoul experience, the IOC stated its intention to implement all-year-round testing, and national sports organizations followed its example, though not without problems. By 1999, a catalog of cases involving athletes appealing their dope tests had accumulated. Among the most discussed was that Harry "Butch" Reynolds who tested positive for the steroid nandrolone in 1991, was suspended by USA Track and Field (USATF) with the support of the IAAF. Reynolds challenged the decision all the way to the Supreme Court and was eventually awarded damages totalling $26 million (£16 million) and allowed to compete in the US Olympic trials.

Further doubts about the reliability of testing procedures were cast by the case of British runner Diane Modahl who was banned from competition for four years after failing a drugs test at a meeting in Lisbon, Portugal, in 1994. The test was administered under the auspices of the Portuguese Athletics Federation. From the sample taken at the meet, Modahl's urine showed a testosterone to epitestosterone ratio (T–E ratio) reading of 42:1. Any ratio above 6:1 provides evidence of the presence of an excessive amount of testosterone and thus grounds for suspension. A reading of over six times the permitted ratio suggested that Modahl had taken gross amounts of a prohibited substance – much more, in fact, than Ben Johnson had when he was banned after the Seoul Olympics in 1988.

After being banned, Modahl appealed to an independent panel constituted by the British Athletics Federation and an investigation opening up questions about the testing procedures followed. Lacking conclusive evidence, the panel determined that there was reasonable doubt over whether or not Modahl had taken proscribed substances. The British Athletics Federation (BAF) agreed, the International Amateur Athletics Federation decided not to refer the case to an arbitration panel and Modahl resumed her running career. Her ban lifted on appeal, Modahl sought up to £500,000 ($305,000) in damages from the BAF which became bankrupt in 1997.

Further questions about the reliability of testing procedures were raised when German marathon runner Uta Pippig challenged the finding of her test by pointing out that she had recently stopped using oral birth control and this had affected her hormonal system; she also pointed out that each of her drug tests following her wins in the Boston Marathon from 1994–6 came up clean. Mary Slaney used a similar defense, claiming that the abnormal T–E ratio in her sample may have been attributable to hormonal changes in women in their late 30s and early 40s who were taking the Pill. Slaney, who completed the 1,500 and 3,000 meters double at the 1983 World Championships, was 37 at the time of her test in 1996. After a three-year process, the IAAF arbitration panel discounted the claim.

Petr Korda escaped a one-year statutory ban from the International Tennis Federation (ITF) after testing positive for nandrolone by convincing the ITF independent appeals panel that he did not know how the substance found its way into his body. The ITF itself was not happy with the outcome, but was prevented by a London High Court ruling from appealing to the Court of Arbitration in Switzerland. Perhaps the most original appeal was that of American sprinter Dennis Mitchell, who claimed the high levels of testosterone found in his test sample in April 1998 were the result of having multiple bouts of sex and five bottles of beer the night before. Mitchell was suspended by the IAAF, but later cleared by the USATF drugs panel.

Efforts to stamp out drugs are obviously related to the degree of drug use in sport and, as I indicated earlier, there seems to have been a fairly sharp increase over the past 20 to 30 years. The reasons for that increase are to be found in cultural changes, as we will see next.

DISCIPLINE AND CONTROL

Harsh denunciations of sports performers found to be taking drugs began to appear from the 1980s. The deaths of Jensen and Simpson in the 1960s drew sympathetic responses quite unlike the treatment afforded Ben Johnson in 1988. For ten years after the Johnson discovery, every competitor found guilty of drugs violations was accused of cheating and incurred penalties, ranging from fines to life suspensions. Media opinion became unanimous: drug users were roundly condemned.

During the 1980s and 1990s, there was little disagreement over the use of performance-enhancing substances and recreational drugs in sports: it was wrong and should be eliminated. The position acquired the status of an axiom – a principle that is so fundamental that it is self-evidently true. Statements such as "drug-taking in sports is wrong" did not invite argument; rather they seemed to state fact. Yet this did little to stem the amount of drug-taking in sports and no major track and field championship (where dope testing apparatus is most sophisticated) ever failed to expose drug users. To understand the censure that unerringly meets drug-using sports performers, we need to examine how the modern world has cultivated a wish for us to control ourselves.

The civilizing process, as Norbert Elias describes it, is a historical trend beginning in the Middle Ages (1300–1400) that has drawn us away from barbarism by bringing social pressures on people to exercise self-control (we covered Elias's theories in Chapter five). At one level, this meant increasing our conscience as a means of regulating our behavior toward others. At another, it meant becoming enmeshed in a network of often subtle, invisible constraints that compelled us to lead ordered lives. One important result of this was the decrease in the use of direct force: violence was brought under control and the state became the only legitimate user of physical violence – outside of combat sports, of course (and these were subject to progressively strict regulation).

The civilizing process implicated humans in some form of control over their bodies. Elias focused mainly on the restraint in using physical violence, but notes the simultaneous trend for people to subdue bodily functions and control their physical being. The physical body became subordinated to the rational mind. While Elias did not discuss this, we might point to the literary interest in the potential of science to complete this process. Mary Shelley's *Frankenstein* tells of a scientist obsessed by the possibility of reconstructing a total human being. In *Dr Jekyll and Mr Hyde*, Robert Louis Stevenson imagined another man of science experimenting with his own mind and body. These and other works of fiction suggest a fascination with trying to reshape the body in accordance with the imperatives of the mind.

Pharmacological advances in the twentieth century hastened the probability that the body could be brought under complete control. Not only could maladies be kept at bay, or even vanquished, but moods could be altered and physical well-being could be promoted. As we have seen, the early efforts of Brown-Sequard at the end of the nineteenth century were to find a rejuvenating therapy for body and mind; his work presaged the development of anabolic steroids. Any initial suspicions about introducing chemicals into the body faded with two world wars in which colossal and often horrific injuries were treated or palliated with medicaments.

The desire for good health that followed the end of the 1939–45 war was complemented by the availability of drugs for the treatment of practically every complaint. A visit to the doctor was incomplete without a prescription, if only for antibiotics. An expanding range of over-the-counter remedies often made the visit unnecessary. The impact of drugs on people's self-evaluations was that ill-health, pain, or even mild discomfort became less and less tolerable. The good life, which seemed to beckon in the post-war period, offered both freedom from suffering and access to well-being. The latter became accessible through a variety of non-medicinal options, including supplements, dieting, and exercise – all of which combined in an enthusiasm for the self that Christopher Lasch characterized as *The Culture of Narcissism*.

It was perhaps inevitable that sports performers, themselves embracing aspirations to self-fulfilment through control of the body, would turn to drugs. Many kinds of substances have been used historically to promote performance, though rarely so effectively. One did not need to be a pharmacist to spot how the effects of, say, amphetamines or anabolic steroids, might be of use to a competitor specializing in speed or power.

The unanticipated, often tragic, consequences of pharmacological products were not confined to sports. Thalidomide was given to pregnant women in Australia, Britain, and Germany in the 1960s as treatment for morning sickness and caused thousands of children to be born with deformities. The Jensen and Simpson tragedies, also in the 1960s, alerted the world to the dangers of ingesting chemical substances to affect changes in the body's condition. Yet, ironically, the imposition of controls by the IOC in the 1970s probably enhanced the appeal of many substances. In his book *Becoming*

Deviant, the criminologist David Matza reasoned that banning something immediately makes it more attractive than it would otherwise be (1969).

As the importance of victory became more pronounced and professionalization made the rewards more extravagant, the value placed on winning replaced that of just competing. A success ethic came to pervade sports, making cost–benefit calculations simpler: the benefits of winning seemed greater than the risk of being found out, for many. As Michael Messner writes in his study *Power at Play*: "Many [competitors], because of the 'win at all costs' values of the sportsworld and the instrumental relationships they have with their own bodies, tend to feel that the short-term efficiency or confidence that is gained through drug use will outweigh any possible problems that might ensue from the drug" (1992: 78).

As the stakes in sports have changed, so the orientations of competitors have changed too: winning supersedes all other considerations, including *how* one wins. Today's athletes approach their events with a single-mindedness that would be alien to their counterparts of 50 years ago. They are prepared to train harder, focus more sharply and risk more in the attempt to realize their ambitions. If pharmaceuticals can help, we can be sure many athletes will give only a sideways glance at moral warnings. The crucial edge that many drugs are thought to provide can be the difference between fortune and ignominy.

Advances in science; the growth of drug culture; an intensification of competitiveness. These are the reasons why so many athletes are prepared to use banned substances; and we know from the number of positive tests in almost every sport that even the most draconian measures do not deter them. So, why do sports governing organizations insist on trying to stop drug use? The answer is not quite so obvious as it seems.

BY ACCIDENT OR CHOICE?

The reasons why the IOC and other governing bodies of sport are prepared to go to quite extraordinary lengths in their efforts to solve the supposed drug problem may be self-evident to many. But we will evaluate each reason on its own merits, beginning with the most obvious.

Drugs are not fair. They confer artificially-induced advantages on the user; and competing with such advantages is tantamount to cheating. Fairness is a rather troublesome concept to define, but we can assume, with Peter McIntosh, author of the book *Fair Play*, that: "Fairness is related to justice" and "breaking the rules with intent to avoid the penalties" as a definition of cheating is too simple (1980: 2, 182). He favors the definition of Gunther Lüschen who believes that the "principle of chance beyond differences in skill and strategy are violated" when the conditions agreed upon for winning a contest "are changed in favor of one side" (1976: 67).

Drugs change the conditions for winning. But, then again, so do many other things. Take the example of blood doping for which athletes may draw penalties, including bans. In a strict sense, this is cheating. But, how about athletes born in Kenya or Ethiopia, both several hundred feet above sea level? Such athletes may be fortunate enough to be brought up in an atmosphere that encourages hemoglobin production in the body and they may find the transition to sea level really quite comfortable as a result. Witness as evidence the dominance of Kenyan middle- and long-distance runners over the past 20 years. Equipped with naturally conferred advantages, Kenyans capitalized on the track and cross-country circuits, leaving weary European and American athletes in their wake.

Another accident of birth meant that Martina Hingis was given every available coaching and equipment facility to help her develop his tennis skills since she was old enough to grip a racket. Her parents, being affluent, could afford to indulge their child and, as things turned out, their money was a shrewd investment for Hingis became a teenage world number one and so unlocked a multi-million dollar treasure chest. Imagine tennis produced a ghetto child from Brooklyn, who had the added disadvantage of being black. Were this imaginary figure to play Hingis, would it be a fair match? When they came face-to-face in a matchup, the conditions may appear fair, but one would hardly say they were "fair" in a deeper sense. One player has benefited from social advantages in a similar way to Kenyan runners, who have benefited naturally from being born at high altitudes. It would be a naïve person indeed who believed all is fair in sport and that background, whether social or natural, is irrelevant to eventual success or failure.

Even drug-taking itself is "unfair" in more than one sense: rich countries have more chemists and better laboratories, so athletes from poorer countries suffer disproportionately. But, perhaps drugs and a working knowledge of how to take them are more transferable than the developed world's high-tech facilities, Olympic-size pools and college bursaries that enable full-time training.

Drugs are taken by choice. There is a difference between the advantages bestowed by social background or place of origin and those that are enjoyed by the taker of drugs. Sports performers can, as the slogan goes, "say 'no' to drugs" in much the same way as many say "yes." Swallowing tablets or allowing oneself to be injected are voluntary activities over which individuals have a high degree of control; one presumes – and only presumes – that they realize the potential costs as well as benefits and they exercise volition when doing or agreeing to the action. Obviously, the same performers have no say in where they were born or the state of their parents' bank account. By contrast, using drugs involves procuring an advantage quite voluntarily.

Yet there is more to this: first, because there are many other forms of advantage that are actively sought out and, second, because some are better placed than others either to seek out or eschew them. Were you a Briton following home Daniel Komen in a 5,000-meter race, you might wish you were born in Kenya. Impossible, of course, so you might think about going to high altitudes and engaging in a spot of blood doping. Quite possible, but illegal. Another possibility is just to train in some part of the world high enough to give you some advantage, or at least to neutralize Komen's advantage. Perfectly possible and legal. The probable result is an advantage quite legitimately obtained through voluntary effort. But an advantage is gained all the same.

Not that everyone is able to exercise choice in such matters: a dedication to competition, a determination to win, and an unflinching resolve to withstand pain are needed and these qualities are easier to come by if the alternative is a one-way ticket back to the ghetto. If your alternatives look unpromisingly bleak, then choices can be rather illusory. Ben Johnson was born in Jamaica and migrated to Canada in 1980 at the age of 19, his ambition being the same as any migrant – namely, to improve his material life. Lacking education, but possessing naturally quick reflexes (which could not be changed) and fast ground speed (which could), he made the best of what he had, so that, within four years, he was in the Canadian Olympic team. Sport is full of stories like Johnson's: bad news – poor origins, little education, few occupational prospects: good news – physical potential and the opportunity to realize it. There is no realistic choice, here. Countless young people with some form of sporting prowess when faced with the once-and-for-all decision of whether or not to sink their entire efforts in the one area in which they just might achieve success do not want to contemplate the alternatives. Given the chance, they will go for it. And this means maximizing every possible advantage in an intensely competitive world. It's doubtful whether any athlete with a similarly deprived childhood would have any compunction about gaining an edge by any means. The choices they have are often too stark to need much mulling over.

Asking whether choice was exercised in trying to determine whether cheating took place is not adequate. Even if we were to dismiss the claims of a performer (who tested positive for a given drug) that his or her drink was spiked (or similar), the question of whether that person freely exercised choice remains. Returning to Hingis: suppose she was found guilty of something untoward; it is feasible to argue that her choice was less restricted than a Turkish migrant worker's daughter in Germany whose one chance for some material success is through sport. To complicate matters further, compare both cases with that of someone insinuated into State Program 1425 as an 11-year-old.

All this is not intended to exonerate those from deprived backgrounds who have sought an advantage through "foul" means rather than "fair." It merely casts doubts on the hard-and-fast distinction between fair play and cheating. If we want to sustain the distinction, we have to ignore the manifold advantages or disadvantages that derive from a person's physical and social background and which are beyond his or her power to change. We can attempt to get round this by isolating the element of choice and defining cheating only when a person has consciously and deliberately taken some action to gain advantage. This works up to a point if we cast aside doubts about the circumstances in which the decision was made. Again, backgrounds are important in influencing the decision.

So the pedestal on which sport stands when it tries to display itself as a model of fair play is not quite as secure as it might at first seem. Not only are advantages dispensed virtually at birth, but they operate either to limit or liberate a person's ability to make choices.

Drugs are harmful to health. Imagine a new drug is introduced. It has great recreational value, giving pleasure to the consumer; its other alleged benefits include a calming effect on the user and a tendency to curb the appetites of those who want to control their weight. A wide range of sports performers spy advantages: the drug steadies the nerves of those who wish to remain relaxed under pressure and helps others unwind after stressful competition. But it contains a chemical that is extremely addictive, another that is carcinogenic; it also causes heart disease, bronchial complaints, and a number of related physical problems. Conservatively, tobacco accounts for about half a million deaths a year in the USA and Britain.

In contrast, the doses of the anabolic steroid taken by Ben Johnson in the 1988 Olympics was allegedly lower than what the World Health Organization subsequently found safe to administer as a male contraceptive. In fact, many of the substances banned from sport and condemned as harmful to health are condoned, and even prescribed in other circumstances, prompting the thought that the banned drugs may not be so dangerous as some of the legal ones.

Sport's central philosophical point seems to be that, whatever people's backgrounds, if they are given the chance to gain advantages over others, they may fairly do so as long as they stop short of knowingly using chemical substances (at least some chemical substances). Some might counter the argument that supports this by saying that acupuncture, hypnotism, psyching techniques, and – in the case of the England national soccer team in 1998 – faith healing may yet prove to have long-term consequences. And there is a growing school of thought that supports the view that the quantity and intensity of training needed in today's highly competitive sports may depress natural immunity systems, exposing performers to infection. Sports clubs themselves acknowledge that players in need of surgery will often postpone operations in order to compete in key games. They do so with the full consent if not encouragement – and perhaps, in some cases, at the request – of coaches or managers, who are surely aware of the probability of exacerbating a condition by delaying corrective treatment.

This has led some observers to believe that the use of drugs is no better or worse than some other aids to performance. They are certainly no worse than many of the drugs commonly available outside the world of sport. Most sports frown on smoking and drinking too, though some, like motor racing and cricket, have been grateful for sponsorship from tobacco companies. Others, like English soccer, have openly embraced breweries, at the same time committing themselves to clamping down on drugs, both performance-enhancing and recreational. Alcohol kills about 100,000 people a year, probably more if alcohol-related road deaths are included. The positive effects of alcohol in oxidizing blood, making it less sticky, are outweighed by the physical and social consequences of its excessive use.

The dangers of paracetamol and Prozac are well known. Even everyday drugs such as aspirin and antihistamine, which we presume to be innocuous, are not completely without potentially harmful consequences. Caffeine found in coffee, tea, and soft drinks is mildly harmful, but who, apart from governing bodies in sports, would dream of banning its general use? The argument that some drugs are more harmful than others has an *Animal Farm* logic to it and, as such, is fraught with inconsistencies. Even if some drugs were found to be dangerous (and steroids in particular are thought to be responsible for cancers and deaths) it would be something of an intrusion into the lives of responsible individuals to tell them not to take them.

Medical bodies are not averse to doing this as the campaigns or, more properly, the crusades of the British and American Medical Associations against boxing have shown. Prolonged involvement in boxing exposes the boxer to the risk of brain damage and many other less severe injuries, is the claim of the anti-boxing lobbyists. So boxers have to be protected, if necessary from themselves, in exactly the same way as any other sports competitors contemplating actions that may result in harm to their health. The effect on health of many banned drugs is small compared to that of boxing.

But to make boxing illegal because of this, presumes that all the young and physically healthy young men and women are oblivious to the hazards of the sport when they enter. It assumes they are not rational, deliberating agents with some grasp of the implications of boxing – a grasp sufficient for them to do a cost–benefit calculation and weigh up the probable rewards against the probable losses.

Were information about the long-term consequences of boxing or drug use concealed, then the "protector" would have a very strong case. But the results of scientific tests are available, and to assume that competitors are so witless as to know nothing of this is insulting and patronizing. If young people with a chance to capitalize on their sporting potential are informed of the dangers involved in their decision to pursue a line of action, then it is difficult to support a case for prohibiting this, at least in societies not prone to totalitarianism. Boxers may well judge the brain damage they risk in their sport preferable to the different kind of "brain damage" they will almost certainly sustain in a repetitive industrial job over a 40-year period, or in an unbearably long spell out of work.

Other sports performers with few prospects outside sport may evaluate their own positions similarly and, when the Mephistophelian bargain presents itself, the decision of whether or not to box should be theirs. Unless, of course, one believes that superordinate moral agents should guide our thoughts and behavior.

But the crudity and patronage of one argument does not license disingenuousness in the attack on it; which means that we should acknowledge that sports performers of whatever level do not reach decisions unaided. We have noted previously that all manner of influence bear on an individual's decision and, quite apart from those deriving from background, we have to isolate coaches and trainers. Bearing in mind the case of American football in the 1960s when coaches were assuming virtual medical status in dispensing drugs, we should remind ourselves of the important roles still played by these people in all sports. We must also realize that sports are populated by many "Dr Feelgoods" who are only too happy to boost performance without necessarily informing the competitor of all the possible implications. It's quite probable that many competitors are doing things, taking things, even thinking things that may jeopardize their health. But do they know it? Perhaps sports authorities might attempt to satisfy themselves formally that all competitors in sports which do hold dangers are totally aware of them and comfortable about their involvement. This would remove the educational task from coaches and trainers and shift the onus onto governing organizations.

Some drugs certainly are harmful to health – as are many other things. Governing organizations quite properly communicate this, though the distinctions that are often made between harmful substances and activities and apparently innocuous ones are frequently arbitrary and difficult to support with compelling evidence. Further, the assumptions carried by governing organizations in their efforts to regulate the use of drugs can be seen in some lights as demeaning, suggesting that performers themselves are incapable of making assessments and decisions unassisted.

Athletes are role models for the young. It follows that if athletes are known and seen to use drugs of any kind, then young people may be encouraged to follow. There is adequate evidence to support this and, while the substances that competitors use to enhance performance are often different to the ones that cause long-term distress at street-level, the very act of using drugs may work as a powerful example. But the argument cannnot be confined to sports: many rock musicians as well as writers and artists use drugs for relief or stimulus. Rock stars arguably wield more influence over young acolytes than the sports elite. The shaming of a sports performer found to have used drugs and the nullifying of his or her performance is a deterrent or a warning to the young: "Do this and you will suffer the same fate." But the Red Hot Chili Peppers are not disgraced and their albums would not be expunged from the charts if it were discovered that they recorded them while using coke. No one considers asking Pavarotti for a urine sample after one of his concerts. The music of Chet Baker, a heroin addict, the acting of Cary Grant, who used LSD, the writing of Dylan Thomas, an alcoholic, all have not been obliterated; nor has the idolatry afforded them.

Sports performers are different in the sense that they operate in and therefore symbolize a sphere where all is meant to be wholesome and pure. But this puts competitors under sometimes intolerable pressure to keep their haloes straight and maintain the pretense of being saints. Clearly, they are not, nor, given the competitive nature of sport, will they ever be.

An argument advanced by parents of promising athletes is that drug-using champions set a bad example. The counter is that, if the young person progresses in sport, he or she will eventually be disavowed of all innocence. Gone are the days portrayed in *Chariots of Fire* when winners were heroes to be glorified and losers were "good sports" for competing. Nowadays, hard cash has spoiled the purity. A yearning for money has introduced a limitless capacity for compromise, and previously "amateur" or "shamateur" sports organizations, including the IOC, have led the way by embracing commercialism rather than spurning it. Competitors too are creatures of a competitive world and probably more preoccupied with struggling to win than with keeping a clean image. They too were once innocents with dreams of emulating their heroes. Yet ambition and money have ways of re-shaping values.

Drugs are not natural. In an interesting essay, "Blood doping and athletic competition," Clifton Perry (1983) argues the case for and against blood doping, which facilitates sporting performance through the introduction of a natural material that is indigenous to the body – blood. He offers the distinction between "performance enhancers" that do not cause lasting changes to the body of the user and "capacity enhancers" that do have long-term effects.

This means that anabolic steroids are ruled out – not on the grounds that they are capacity enhancers but because they have deleterious effects (there is evidence that they elevate enzyme levels in the liver). But does this mean that blood doping should be allowed as it enhances capacities without deleterious consequences? Perry says no. His reason is based on the body's response to coming off the enhancer. "There is a difference between the loss of performance output through the loss of a mere performance enhancer and the loss of a capacity through inactivity" (1983: 43). After coming off an enhancer, the body returns to homeostasis: "There is nothing the athlete can do by way of performance to retain the former level of performance. This is not the case when a performer simply stops training" (1983: 42).

Perry is also concerned about the implications of blood doping. It could lead to the use of "artificial blood" or other people's; or even the supplement Fluosol-DA, which increases the oxygen-carrying capacity of blood. It's a provocative argument in favor of banning blood doping, but significantly Perry en route to his conclusion dismisses one of the staple reasons for banning performance-enhancing substances. There are many things that are allowed in sports that are deemed acceptable, but which are artificial: if we ran only on natural surfaces performance would be diminished, as they would be if we stripped any sport down to its "natural" basics: archery without sights, sprint cycling without the banked track of a velodrome, etc. Sports utilize any number of devices that do not actually make us faster or better, but certainly enhance performance. Pole-vaulters are not better vaulters when they use a particular type of pole, but they achieve better performances.

These do not just facilitate the exploitation of the body: they supplement it for specific periods of time. We have accepted world record times without dismissing them as due in large part to the wearing of lightweight, air-inflated spikes on fast synthetic surfaces. When pressed, we would have to agree that the same times could not have been achieved in flats on cinders. Blood doping, one might argue, is actually only the reintroduction of our own blood into our systems, albeit by means of transfusion and, in this sense, is more natural than some of the other devices that are commonplace in sports.

We might anticipate that a standard reply to this would be that blood doping and other banned methods of enhancing performance involve the ingestion of substances. This is true; but it does not make them any more or less natural. No one accuses a 300-lb defensive lineman or an Olympic heavy-weight weightlifter of being unnatural. Yet, they have achieved the bodies they have through a combination of resistance training and high carbohydrate diets. The activities we perform – or do not perform – affect our bodies, as do the physical environments in which we live and the cultural definitions we try to live up to (or reject). Biochemical changes are affected by virtually everything we do. There is no natural body state: just living means changing our bodies.

Drugs are bad for business. None of the arguments presented is airtight enough to convince a skeptic. Yet sports-governing organizations' pursuit of drug users has taken on the status of a crusade: all-year-round surveillance, invigilation, regulation, and punishment are now institutional features of sport and their maintenance is costly. Yet athletes continue to take drugs, and testers keep spending more time and money trying to catch them. Why? If none of the previous answers ring true, we may turn to the motives of the IOC, an infamously corrupt organization which was involved in bribery, cover-ups, and various other malfeasant activities under the presidency of Juan Antonio Samaranch.

After the financial débâcle of the 1976 summer Olympics at Montreal, the IOC became much more of a commercial organization. All subsequent games were heavily supported by the likes of Coca-Cola, McDonald's, Panasonic, and a host of other mainly American and Japanese companies. While the IOC continued to present itself as embodying the spirit originally revived by de Coubertin, its ideals became progressively diluted. Samaranch had made clear his intention to extricate the Olympic movement financially from governments and become economically independent. In doing so, he made pacts with companies and the mass media; these, in a sense, surrendered the Olympics' independence to other more overtly commercial organizations and, more generally, to market forces.

Increasingly, the IOC grew reliant on money from not only sponsors, but from television companies. NBC paid $750 million for the Sydney games in 2000. Commercial organizations do not donate their money out of the goodness of their hearts; they do it to attract further business for themselves. By encouraging their potential market to associate their products with a clean and wholesome activity that commands the respect and affection of billions, they hope to promote sales. Once that healthy activity is sullied by "drugs" – and remember: the term suggests no distinction between illicit recreational substances and pharmacological products – sponsors quickly move their money. Johnson lost a fortune overnight; Michelle De Bruin failed to land endorsement contracts despite winning three swimming gold medals at the Atlanta games. Many other athletes have suffered financially after being positively tested. The IOC and other organizations that follow its lead in drug testing realize that the money they receive is always conditional.

Long before the scandal of the Salt Lake City winter Olympics broke in 1999, the writers Vyv Simson and Andrew Jennings had exposed the lengths to which the IOC had gone to conceal wrongdoings (1992; see also Jennings 1996). Simson and Jennings revealed how many positive dope tests at the Olympic Games in the 1980s and 1990s had mysteriously failed to reach the light of day, leaving the image of a squeaky-clean IOC that had almost eradicated drug use.

The big-name catch at Seoul was, of course, Johnson. It is interesting that the female 100-meters winner Florence Griffiths Joyner was declared clean, despite hearsay that she had used performance enhancers to achieve her prodigious 10.47 seconds 100 meters record, set in 1988. After her death

ARGUMENT	EVIDENCE	COUNTER
DRUGS ARE NOT FAIR	Decent corroboration: drugs can supplement, assist or compensate in athletic performance.	a. Historically, other performance supplements (like spikes) have been regarded as unfair. b. Circumstances of birth may confer advantages.
DRUGS ARE TAKEN BY CHOICE	Yes: often on advice and with support of peers, coaches and trainers.	Often, the only alternative is lack of success at the highest level.
DRUGS ARE HARMFUL TO HEALTH	Some have negative effects; others do not.	a. Some sports activities are also dangerous. b. Many legal drugs are more damaging than banned substances.
DRUGS ARE NOT NATURAL	Partial support: many drugs are synthetic versions of natural products.	There is no natural body state: training, diet, environment, etc. elicit biochemical change.
ATHLETES ARE ROLE MODELS	Strong support: young people try to emulate sports stars.	a. Rock stars and actors are also emulated. b. Once a certain level is reached, young athletes realize that drugs are used, possibly by their role models.
DRUGS ARE BAD FOR BUSINESS	Good support: sponsors avoid contracts with athletes who have used, or are suspected of using, drugs.	Sports' governing bodies maintain that commercial motives do not guide drugs policies.

the reasoning behind sport's anti-drugs policy

in 1998, writers around the world were emboldened to declare that she had probably used drugs habitually. Had both winners of the Olympic track program's blue riband events been disqualified for drugs, then it is likely the Olympic movement would have lost credibility with its sponsors and may never have recovered. In the event, Griffith Joyner retired suddenly and unexpectedly, aged 29, in the months following her triumph.

Subsequent Olympics were scandal-free. In fact, the Atlanta games were unbelievably "clean," but, as John Andrews, a writer for *The Economist*, put it: "It would have been commercially disastrous – for athletes, organisers, sponsors and broadcasters – to have them declared anything else" (1998: 14). It is this kind of perception that gives weight to the argument that there is a commercial motive behind anti-drugs policies in sport.

The IOC, for long, paved the way for other sports organizations. Its initiative in clinching lucrative sponsorships acted almost as a template for other sports; but, it also had to lead the way in drugs policies. Most of the world's sports-governing organizations adopt the IOC's banned list and accept the reliability of its methods of detection. While they will never admit that their purposes in trying to eliminate drugs from their sports are anything but pure, the argument has a plausibility that is, as we have seen, conspicuously absent from all other explanations.

These, then, are the main reasons why governing bodies have sought to eliminate drugs from sports and discredit those found using them. The reasons are not as straightforward as they appear and all are open to objections. Whatever argument is chosen, we need to recognize: (1) that drugs are part of contemporary sports; and (2) whatever attempts are made to extirpate them, ways and means will be found to continue to use them. In a decade's time, it is possible that there will be no way of preventing competitors from taking drugs which does not involve prison-like supervision in training as well as competition: inspection, invigilation, regulation, and punishment would become features of sport. This would be costly and punitive.

Debates about drugs and how to eliminate their use and their impact on sports will continue. Discussions about the obligations of athletes, especially celebrity athletes, the impoverishment of sporting ideals, and the loss of simple pleasures will exercise the minds of all interested parties. Typically, the effects of business interests in sports on drug use is set aside, though, as I have suggested in this chapter, they are germane to the debate. What of the future? I will return to this issue in Chapter sixteen.

FURTHER READING

The Steroids Game: An expert's look at anabolic steroid use in sports by Charles Yesalis and Virginia Cowart (Human Kinetics, 1998) traces the history of drug testing, examines educational programs designed to curb drug use and presents some of the legal issues relating especially to steroid use. This makes interesting reading in conjunction with *Running Scared: How athletics lost its innocence* by S. Downes and D. Mackay (Mainstream, 1996).

Mortal Engines: Human engineering and the transformation of sport by John Hoberman (Free Press, 1992) is a masterly thesis on the relationship between medicine, technology, and the human body. Together Hoberman and Yesalis have produced the valuable article, "The history of synthetic testosterone," in *Scientific American* (vol. 272, no. 2, 1995).

Sport, Policy and Politics: A comparative analysis by Barrie Houlihan (Routledge, 1997) has a chapter on "Doping and sport" in which the author compares the policy responses of Australia, Britain, Canada, Ireland, and the USA.

Philosophic Inquiry in Sport, edited by William Morgan and Klaus Meier (Human Kinetics, 1988), has a section "Drugs and sport" that contains five searching (previously published) articles, all of which probe the moral issues underlying drugs policies. Every argument has the kind of bite missing from most standard textbook discussions of drugs in sport. Very helpful reading.

ASSIGNMENT

Imagine you are a researcher for a television documentary on drugs in sport. You have five telephone calls to make. Whom do you call? What are the first three questions you ask each? What answers do you get?

Chapter ten

not for the fainthearted

violence and the legal battlefield

A BALL GAME WITH A PUNCH

None of the players could have expected it when they turned up for practice on December 1, 1997, but they were going to witness an event that *Sports Illustrated*'s Phil Taylor describes as "one of the most outrageous acts on the court or field of play that American professional sports in the modern era has known" (1997: 62).

Latrell Sprewell, then with the Golden State Warriors, threatened to kill his coach, P. J. Carlesimo, dragged him to the floor and choked him for between 10 and 15 seconds. Having been pulled off, Sprewell disappeared, returning after about 20 minutes. Taylor describes what happened next: "According to several Warriors players, he went after Carlesimo again and threw punches at the coach, connecting with one glancing blow before he could again be hauled away" (1997: 62).

Sprewell's assault vied with Mike Tyson's notorious ear-biting as 1997's most vilified sporting action. In June, Tyson had taken a chunk out of the ear of Evander Holyfield during a world heavyweight title fight – from which he was disqualified. Boxing is, of course, an often brutal sport; but the universal condemnation of Tyson's behavior underlined how even the

219

most aggressive of sports is sensitive to violence that occurs outside the framework of rules. Both Sprewell and Tyson were fined and suspended by their relevant sporting organizations and absolutely castigated by the world's media.

The reason sports' governing organizations and media alike are sensitive to illicit violence is because so much of sports competition is in itself very violent. There are plenty of people and groups who have no interest or empathy with sports who are only too willing to decry sports for their excessive emphasis on aggression. Boxing, in particular, has been singled out by the American and British Medical Associations for its alleged barbarism. But several other sports that call for offensiveness prompt criticisms, especially when they result in serious injury to competitors.

Parties with an interest in sport – like governing organizations and the media – are usually quick to point out that serious injuries occur in a minority of cases and that cases like Sprewell's and Tyson's are extremely rare. Actually, anyone with a reasonable memory can recall comparable cases: Eric Cantona's detour into the crowd to fight a fan during a Crystal Palace *vs* Manchester United game in London in 1995; Vernon Maxwell's similar pursuit of a fan during a Houston Rockets game, also in 1995; Scottie Pippen's dangerous hurling of a chair across the court; Deion Sanders's on-field fight with Andre Rison in the 1994 49ers *vs* Falcons game; the near riot after the first Riddick Bowe–Andrew Golota fight. There are too many others to be able to dismiss the Sprewell and Tyson affairs as untypical.

The truth is: sport provides a context for the sanctioned expression of violence; but that same context frequently encourages the unsanctioned expression of violence. The line between them is a fine one. By "context," we must also properly include the surrounding environment in which fans view, cheer, boo, and experience vicariously the same adrenaline rush competitors get when the competition is in progress. No fan wants to attend a game of football, hockey, soccer, or any other sport, and sit quietly for the duration. The whole buzz about being there is to get wrapped up in the emotion of the occasion; to feel the elation, the depression and all the emotions in between. The fan can get all the thrills and still get home without stitches.

Being a fan is a relatively safe experience. Not totally: as the example of British soccer reminds us. In some situations, there is more violence off the field of play than there is on it, much more. The pitched battles in the streets of many French cities during the World Cup tournament of 1998 was no blip: soccer's fandom has a well-earned reputation for violence. Just over a year before the World Cup, a game between the Irish Republic and England was abandoned after mass fighting broke out among the spectators. Soccer the world over seems to elicit peculiarly intense passions among its fans and violence has become a staple feature of the sport.

Why are sports so conducive to violent behavior and why is the law so eager to step in and control it? These are the questions to be addressed in this chapter. We will return to the issue of fan violence later in the chapter. But violence among competitors will be our initial concern.

BY FAIR MEANS OR FOUL

Given the amount of money at stake in professional sports, it is hardly surprising that many competitors are prepared to do what it takes by fair means or foul to get the desired results. A win can mean an awful lot to competitors. Winning or losing a title fight can be the difference between boxing for several million dollars or a dozen or so thousand in the next fight (though it did not for Tyson: in his first fight after the Holyfield débâcle, he earned $10 million – not exactly chump change). Most ball players have bonus agreements built into their contracts. So playing a role in a major championship victory can make a big impression on your bank statement, especially when you have a clause like Ricky Jackson's: he was on an $800,000 (£500,000) bonus for one game if his team won the 1995 Super Bowl. It did.

The exponential growth of commercialism brought about by television, as we have seen, introduced to sports more money than could have been dreamt of 25 years ago. In Chapter nine, I argued that the increase in the use of performance-enhancing drugs by performers is one result of this. Coaches over the years have driven competitors as hard as they could, pushing and prodding them to their peak performances. But the carrot is mightier than the stick. There's no better way to get the ultimate effort out of a performer than to offer irresistible incentives.

The results of this are obvious: perfectly conditioned, highly motivated, tunnel-visioned, win-oriented performers, who continually frustrate critics and sometimes governing authorities with the excellence of their play. One product of the high-stakes culture is Pete Sampras, an athlete so well-trained and charged with the desire to win that he achieved virgin levels of excellence untouched by others. Tennis authorities changed the pressure in tennis balls and considered changing the rules of the game to reduce the advantage the power-hitting Sampras enjoyed. Less visible, but similar, is Geet Sethi, who, in the 1990s, occupied a position of supremacy in billiards to that of Sampras in tennis. He held the world-record break of 1,276,000 and billiard's rule-makers implemented changes to blunt his skills. In both cases, the brilliant efficiency of the players made their games repetitive and tedious.

Tennis and billiards are sports in which the competitors are physically separated. Although they are opposed, the competitors' prowess is exhibited in relative isolation. They do not, for example, break tackles, knock opponents out or dribble a puck around defending players. In sports where contact or collision is inevitable, either by design or default, the effort to win by any means necessary takes on a different complexion. Physical encounters are less restrained than they might have been where only pride was once at stake. Serious injuries are accepted as part-and-parcel of today's sports. Illegal play is seen as permissible as long as it goes unnoticed by officials. When the price of failure is measured in terms of what might have been gained, success is pursued with a fury unimaginable in early periods of sports history.

Objectors will scoff at this suggestion, reminding us of former sports stars, like Jack Tatum, Jake LaMotta, or Nat Lofthouse, none of whom were known for their pat-a-cake styles of play. These individuals stand out for their ferocity, single-mindeness and callous disregard for others. My point is: they *do* stand out. Nowadays, there are so many sports performers with the same approaches that we do not regard them as extraordinary. The qualities that distinguished Tatum and the others are now the norm. This is most evident in contact sports, of course, where players' bodies clash and clatter as a normal part of the flow, such as in hockey and basketball.

It could be argued that the success of the National Hockey League since the 1970s has been based on the frequent eruptions of violence during any game. Watch the hockey played at the Olympics Games, where there is a high degree of technical competence but none of the almost theatrical fighting that punctuates an NHL game: the experience is quite different and, I dare say, not as entertaining for an NHL fan.

The George Roy Hill film *Slap Shot* (1977) is a satire on commercialism and violence in hockey. Manager Paul Newman tries to revive his club's fortunes by drafting-in three goons with limited skill, but a lot of butt-kicking ability. The team's principles are sacrificed; but the results improve and the crowd loves the roughhouse tactics.

The film was made in the mid-1970s, when the Philadelphia Flyers dominated the sport, winning two straight Stanley Cups, with a ferocious brand of physical hockey in which the "hit" was a central weapon (the NHL defines a "hit" as contact that "significantly impedes" a player's progress). The Flyers' expert use of bodychecking changed the character of the game: the crushing hits they put on opponents were calculated to intimidate; though, as with all forms of intimidation, once opponents started to hit back with interest, Philadelphia's superiority was broken.

Basketball is another sport that has benefited from more physical aspects. At the start of the 1980s, the sport lagged way behind hockey in terms of popularity in the USA. It now vies with baseball and football as the most-watched sport in the USA and has a large tv following around the world. Much of its success has been based on marketing strategies that have worked like a charm and a format that suits television perfectly. But, again, compare your experiences: watch a game of basketball from any Olympics before 1992, when an all-professional American "dream team" dominated. The action is fast, nimble, and precise; yet there is something lacking; and I do not mean the climactic slam-dunks. The physical contact is almost polite alongside the bumps, knocks, and shoves we are used to seeing.

Players do not get sent splaying after running into a colossus like Shaq O'Neal. None of the players has the mien of a pro boxer, as does Charles Barkley. The NBA purveys a different game from the basketball played by the rest of the world ten years ago. It is harsher, more physical and brings with it an undertow of violence that has made it commercially attractive. Small wonder that tv networks have clamored to throw money at the NBA, which has in turn plowed it through the clubs which have been able to pay players salaries to rival those of the best-paid boxers and baseball players. This has pumped up the stakes even higher, reinforcing the intensity of competition that characterizes the NBA.

The phrase "only in America" springs to mind when we come to comparing this trend with sports elsewhere in the world. Or, perhaps, only North America, because efforts south of the Rio Grande and throughout Europe have been aimed at eliminating the violence that has been allegedly escalating in soccer. The sport has always been tough, of course; but soccer's world governing organization Fifa (*Fédération Internationale de Football Associations*) in the 1980s became concerned that the pre eminent teams were those that employed particularly physical players, whose specialty was intimidation. This had commercial implications, though they were never spelled out: if the finesse players were succumbing to the "cloggers" as they were known ("clog" meaning to impede or hamper), then the shape of the sport would change fundamentally, skill being replaced by a more robust style of play in which only the strong would survive. Soccer was once described as a game of pianists and those who carry the pianos for them. At a time when Fifa was expanding into Africa and Asia to make the sport genuinely universal and needed television monies to fund its mission, it could ill-afford to lose its virtuosos.

Over a period of years, Fifa issued a series of directives to soccer referees to control not only violent play, but disagreements with referees' calls (classed as "dissent"), time-wasting (the clock runs continuously apart from half-time in soccer), and "professional fouls." The penalties for these and other violations were severe: without the hockey-style sin bins, soccer players were ejected from games for the duration and faced further suspensions as a result as well as heavy fines. Despite attempts to contain aggressive behavior, sports there remains a paradox. For many sports to be effective as competitive spectacles, some element of aggression has to be present. One only needs to

---

Professional foul

This phrase was objected to by many in soccer for dignifying what many thought a gross, inexcusable violation of rules. It involves three players: the goalkeeper (G), the player in possession of the ball (A), and the defensive player (D). A is in an attacking position heading for goal and has only G to beat; D chases from behind. Sensing he is unable to catch him and not wishing to allow him a free strike on goal, he either grabs A around the upper body to drag him back, or, more usually, slide-tackles him from behind, aiming at his ankles rather than the ball. Either way, A loses control of the ball and misses the chance of a shot. There is no obvious equivalent in American football, but pass interference in or approaching the endzone is a comparable violation. The penalties are very different: in soccer, the player is "sent off" for the rest of the game; in American football, the defense loses yardage and the player incurs no specific punishment.

---

see coaches before a game; they are never caught gazing reflectively out of a locker room window, whispering gently to their players, "Chill, we'll win if it's meant to be. Go with the karma." More likely, they'll be roaring with passion, using every device they know to bring their players to an aggressive peak.

Seen like this, sports create a milieu that sometimes endorses or encourages physical violence or at least creates conditions under which the possibility of violence is heightened. It then covers that milieu with a sheltering canopy as if to prevent outsiders interfering with internal affairs. The cases of Paul Smithers and Dennis Wise make the point. Smithers was a hockey player convicted of manslaughter in 1973 after beating an opposing player to death in a parking-lot fight after a game; Wise, a Chelsea soccer player who was charged with assaulting a cab driver and initially sentenced to three months' imprisonment. Change the context and the results would be completely different. While neither players' behavior would have been condoned on the playing area, it's likely that long suspensions and heavy fines would have been the limit of the penalties.

Occasionally, the violence has reached a pitch where redress on the field of play has not been sufficient. Players have claimed that the context of sports affords a protection to other professionals whose conduct would otherwise be punishable by law and that this protection is artificial. Dissatisfied with the penalties imposed by the sport itself, they have taken their complaint elsewhere and with interesting results.

All part of the game

As anyone who has watched the NHL knows, hockey is a perilous sport: sticks are wielded like axes, fists fly furiously and players get slammed with bone-rattling hits. In their *Hockey Night in Canada*, Richard Gruneau and David Whitson write, "hockey actually seems to celebrate fighting outside the rules as a normal part of the game" (1993: 189). Not so, said Ted Green, of Boston Bruins, who almost died as a result of a stick blow to the head that fractured his skull. The game in which it happened took place in 1969. In the following year, both Green and his attacker, Wayne Maki, of St Louis, appeared in separate trials in Ottawa, charged with assault causing bodily harm. It was alleged that Green provoked Maki. Both were acquitted on grounds of self-defense.

Within months of the Green–Maki case, a Canada-wide poll conducted by *Maclean's* magazine indicated that almost 40 per cent of the respondents, male and female, liked to see physical violence in hockey. They were not disappointed over the next several years as the amount and intensity of what Michael Smith calls "quasi-criminal violence" increased – as, incidentally, did the popularity of hockey. The NHL's attendances grew by about 40 per cent over the 15 years from the mid-1970s; tv revenue increased about twelvefold.

Quasi-criminal violence

This is defined by Michael Smith as "that which violates not only the formal rules of a given sport (and the law of the land), but to a significant degree the informal norms of player conduct" (in *Violence and Sport*, 1983: 14). Typically, it will result in some form of injury that brings it to the attention of officials and, later, tends to generate public outrage when the mass media report it. Sometimes, civil legal proceedings follow, though, according to Smith, who it must be remembered was writing in 1983, "less often than thought." Nowadays, court cases are more prevalent.

Violence in sports is not a phenomenon to which Canadians are unaccustomed. "The belief that violence sells and that eliminating fighting would undercut the game's appeal as a spectacle has been the official thinking among the NHL's most influential governors and officers," detect Gruneau and Whitson (1993: 185). Yet, in 1976, the Attorney-General of Ontario ordered a crackdown on violence in sports after a year that had seen 67 assault charges relating to hockey. In the same year, a particularly wild bust-up occurred during a World Hockey Association playoff game between Quebec Nordiques and Calgary Cowboys, whose player Rick Jodzio was eventually fined C$3,000 (US$2,200, or £1,360) after pleading guilty to a lesser charge than the original causing bodily harm with intent to wound. There were also convictions arising from a Philadelphia–Toronto game in 1976: the interesting aspect of this one was that, in legal terms, a hockey stick was designated a dangerous weapon.

Despite the commercial success of the NHL since the mid-1970s and the rise of the Philadelphia Flyers, the league remained mindful that too much on-ice brawling could easily turn television away. Big-hit players threatened to overrun the game, making more skilfull players less likely to survive. The NHL's crackdown on violence did not eliminate fights, but between the 1987/8 season to 1998/9 the average number of altercations dropped from 2.1 to 1.2.

Not all the sports-related court cases in this period were from hockey. The first case in recent history was the 1965 Giants–Dodgers game in which the San Francisco hitter Juan Marichal whacked LA catcher John Roseborough with his bat. Marichal was fined by the league and suspended, but Roseborough sought the retribution through a civil suit that was eventually settled out of court. In basketball, a huge case in 1979 involved not only the fining and suspension of the Lakers' Kermit Washington, but an accusation leveled against his club for failing to train and supervise the player adequately. He was ordered to pay damages. The player whom he attacked, Rudy Tomjanovich, was effectively forced into premature retirement as a result of his injuries.

Boxer Billy Ray Collins was also made to retire as a result of injuries incurred during his fight with Luis Resto. Going into the 1983 fight a hot favorite with a 14–0 record, Collins was surprisingly beaten and finished with his eyes so swollen that he was temporarily blinded. He did not box again and was killed in an auto wreck the following year. In the aftermath of the fight, Resto's gloves were confiscated by the chief inspector of the New York State Athletic Commission (NYSAC), who had them inspected by the manufacturers, Everlast, and a state police laboratory. Each glove was meant to weigh 7.95 ounces, but Resto's right glove was 6.92 ounces and the left 6.96 ounces. The Commission announced that unauthorized changes had been made to the gloves and permanently revoked the licences of Resto's trainer, Panama Al Lewis and Pedro Alvarado, who also worked his corner. Resto was suspended for a year. The fight was declared "No contest."

In October 1986, Resto and Lewis were brought to the criminal court by the state of New York and convicted of assault, conspiracy, and criminal possession of a deadly weapon - Resto's fists. Additionally, Lewis was convicted of tampering with a sports contest. Resto was sentenced to a maximum of three years and Lewis a maximum of six; both served two and a half years. There was, as Jeff Pearlman of *Sports Illustrated* put it, "overwhelming evidence that the boxing career of Billy Ray Collins Jr. was ended by illegal means" (1998: 120).

Collins's estate filed a $65 million lawsuit against the NYSAC, arguing that the inspectors had an obligation not only to look at the gloves but also to feel them on Resto's hands, to look inside them - to do everything to ensure they had not been tampered with. The NYSAC countered that the term "inspection" was broad and added that the responsibility lay not with the Commission, but with the promoters, Bob Arum's Top Rank Boxing, which hired the inspectors. A further action by lawyers acting for Collins's estate was directed at Pasquale Giovanelli, an inspector provided by Top Rank. The case ended in a hung jury.

Another significant case of this kind occurred in an NFL game during the 1975 season. The plaintiff, Dale Hackbart of the Denver Broncos, suffered a career-ending fracture of the spine following a big hit from Charles Clark of the Cincinnati Bengals. Taking his case to the District Court, Hackbart was told that, by the very fact of playing an NFL game, he was taking an implied risk and that anything happening to him between the sidelines was part of that risk. An appeals court disagreed and ruled that, while Clark may not have specifically intended to injure his opponent, he had engaged in "reckless misconduct." This paved the way for his employer, the Bengals, to be held accountable.

This case was to have echoes almost two decades later in England, when a Chelsea soccer player, Paul Elliott, pursued a case against Dean Saunders, then playing for Liverpool. Following a tackle from Saunders, Elliott sustained injuries that prevented him from playing again. The court found that the context of soccer mitigated the offense and that Saunders was not guilty of reckless or dangerous play. Elliott's case was weakened by the fact that the player was not penalized by the referee during the game and so the judge was effectively asked to use a video and other evidence to overturn the referee's decision.

John Fashanu was taken to court twice for play that seriously injured fellow soccer players: one was settled out of court and he was cleared of the other, underscoring the point that guilt in a law court and guilt on the playing field are two different things. It could be argued that a player who directs his or her aggression against another in a wild and reckless way is doing so out of a desire to win rather than malice. The relevant principle was originally stated in English law in the *Condon* v. *Basi* case of 1985, when it was decided that, even in a competitive sport whose rules indicate that physical contact will occur, a person owes a duty to an opponent to exercise a reasonable degree of care. In *Condon*, the court accepted the evidence of the referee in

Soccer – a sport to die for

Belgium, 1985. Thirty-eight fans were crushed to death and over 450 others injured at the 1985 European Cup Final between Liverpool and Juventus, at the Heysel Stadium, Brussels. All English teams were suspended from European competitions as punishment.

England, 1989. Ninety-six Liverpool fans died as the result of a tragedy at the Hillsborough stadium, Sheffield, where Liverpool were due to meet Nottingham Forest in an FA Cup semi-final game. Police were blamed for allowing 658 too many spectators into a section of the stadium.

Colombia, 1994. Andres Escobar, a member of the Colombian team that had competed in the 1994 World Cup in the USA, returned home after his country had been eliminated from the tournament and was shot dead in the parking lot of a Medellin bar. Escobar had scored an own goal in the game against the USA.

China, 1995. A 29-year-old fan of the Jinan Taishan club committed suicide by throwing himself out of the window of his fourth-floor apartment when his team's opponents, Beijing Guoan, scored an equalizing goal.

Italy, 1995. Three Genoa fans died of heart attacks when their team was beaten in a relegation play-off game by Padova. Two fans died at the game, one while watching on television.

Congo, 1996. Eleven fans were killed by lightning while watching a game at Moutamba while perched on the branches of a mango tree.

Turkey, 1996. Two fans of Trabzonspor killed themselves after their team had lost a crucial game 2–1 against Fenerbahce. In a separate incident, a Fenerbahce fan died when adjusting his television antenna to improve the reception of his team's game against Manchester United.

Argentina, 1996. A Brazilian man was murdered in Buenos Aires after rooting for Nigeria when watching that country beat Argentina in the final of the 1996 Olympic soccer competition.

France, 1998. Eric Fraschet-Lentin, a French actor, was murdered while on a train traveling from Grenoble to Paris; the train stopped to pick up English fans who had watched their team lose to Argentina in the World Cup championships. Paul Birch, the man accused of killing Fraschet, apparently thought Fraschet was an Argentinian.

Congo, 1998. All 11 members of a team were killed when lightning struck during a game at Basanga; curiously, the players on the other team emerged unharmed, though 30 other people at the game received treatment for burns. Because witchcraft is often blamed for adverse natural phenomena in western and central Africa, teams sometimes hire witchdoctors either to protect them or place hexes on their opponents.

an amateur football game that the defendant had broken the plaintiff's leg by a reckless and dangerous tackle and damages were awarded.

Despite the experiences of Saunders and Fashanu, professional athletes in Britain were dealt an ominous warning in 1998 when Gordon Watson, a player for Bradford City soccer club, won an unprecedented negligence action in the High Court. He became the first player to win damages in spite of returning to soccer after recovering from a double fracture 18 months before. Bradford's chair insisted that he attempted to settle the matter without going to court, but found no satisfaction with soccer's authorities. The club also brought an action for recklessness against Kevin Gray, the player whose sliding tackle did the damage to Watson, but this was rejected.

In Elliott's case, the referee decided that Saunders attempted to play the ball and accidentally injured Elliott, which was how the game officials called it. In Watson's, the referee punished the violent tackle. This might suggest that officials' decisions are respected, though there are exceptions, the most remarkable coming in the aftermath of the European middleweight title fight between Alan Minter and Angelo Jacopucci in 1978.

A few hours after being knocked out, Jacopucci collapsed and ultimately died. In 1983, after a protracted and complicated series of legal actions, a court in Bologna, Italy, acquitted the referee and Jacopucci's manager of second-degree manslaughter on the basis that they should have stopped the fight before the twelfth and last round. The ringside doctor, however, was convicted, ordered to pay Jacopucci's widow the equivalent of $15,000 (£10,000) damages and given a suspended eight-month prison sentence.

The courts have been wary of intervening in Britain, though the incidents involving Duncan Ferguson, Eric Cantona, and Paul Ince were exceptions that may prove to be the rule in future. Before examining this, let us retreat to 1975 and the case of Henry Boucha who played for the Minnesota North Stars of the NHL. During a home game against the Boston Bruins, Boucha got into

NOT FOR THE FAINTHEARTED

a fight with Dave Forbes, for which they were both sent off for a period in the penalty box. On their way back to the game, Forbes lashed out with his stick, dropping Boucha to the ice. Concussed and bleeding, Boucha was helpless as Forbes leapt on him and, grabbing his hair, slammed his head onto the ice repeatedly.

Forbes escaped with a relatively light suspension of ten games from the NHL, but a Minnesota grand jury charged him with the crime of aggravated assault by use of a dangerous weapon. Forbes pleaded not guilty and the jury was unable to reach a unanimous verdict after 18 hours of deliberations. The court declared a mistrial and the case was dismissed. Boucha meanwhile needed surgery and never played again. Remember: *State* v. *Forbes* was a criminal case and its lack of a definite verdict left several pertinent questions unresolved. Smith believes the main ones revolve around whether Forbes was culpable or whether the club for which he played and the league in which he performed were in some way responsible for establishing a context for his action (1983: 20).

It is also relevant that the actual violent event took place as the players were re-entering the playing area rather than in the flow of the game itself, which is why it bears resemblance to the Cantona affair. At first Cantona committed a foul during his team's game with Crystal Palace; for this, his second serious offense, he was dismissed from play. While walking from the field he was provoked verbally by a fan who had made his way to the edge of the playing area. Cantona turned toward the fan, lurched at him feet first and started to fire punches. Seeing the commotion, Cantona's team-mate Paul Ince ran to the scene and engaged with another fan.

While only Cantona was singled out for punishment by his club and the FA, both players were charged with common assault, Cantona being sentenced to two weeks' imprisonment. More severe was the three-month prison sentence imposed on Ferguson for head-butting a fellow professional soccer player in a game between his club, Rangers, and Raith Rovers in Glasgow in 1994.

These were high-profile cases featuring top athletes. In contrast, Jesse Boulerice was a 19-year-old player for the Plymouth Whalers, an Ontario Hockey League (OHL) outfit from Michigan, when he found himself charged by the Wayne County (Michigan) Prosecutor's Office with a felony: assault with intent to do great bodily harm less than murder – a crime that carries a $5,000 fine and ten years' maximum imprisonment. In a 1998 game, Boulerice had swung his stick into the face of Andrew Long, also 19, a player with the Guelph Storm, who sustained multiple facial fractures, a broken nose, concussion accompanied by seizure, a brain contusion, and a cut across his upper lip. The OHL decided that Boulerice had "used his stick in a most alarming and unacceptable fashion" and suspended him for one year. The incident itself was captured on videotape and observers estimated that Boulerice's stick was travelling between 50 and 75 mph when it made contact with Long. Boulerice denied that he meant to hurt Long.

The questions raised by the Boulerice–Long case are germane to all sports in which violence of some kind is integral. Was there any criminal intent in Boulerice's conduct, or was it simply part of the ebb-and-flow of a sport that trades on aggression? In strictly behavioral terms, was the action any different from the hundreds of other instances in the same game that either went unnoticed or did not result in such serious injuries? Should we consider other factors, such as a chanting crowd, an excitable coach, or even the cash incentives? Jeff MacGregor writes: "What is most surprising about the Jesse Boulerice–Andrew Long matter is not that it happened, but that it doesn't happen more often" (1999a: 114).

One of the usual protections afforded sports performers in similar circumstances is the context: players frequently behave in ways that would be alien to them outside of the sporting arena; they forge rivalries that have no meaning apart from in their sport; they consciously psyche themselves to an aggressive level in order to maximize their effectiveness. In other words, their disposition toward violent action is specific to the sport itself.

It is quite possible that the person might have violent tendencies that are only activated by competition. Or it could be that the player's "normal" character is at odds with the violent persona he or she feels bound to assume during a game. The player could just be aggressive in and out of sports. In a sense, none of this is relevant because the behavior itself is meshed into the context of the sport. Forbes, we presume, held nothing personal against Boucha and, if they met at, say, a party, they may well have got along together. Cantona would almost certainly have never met the man he assaulted had they not been player and fan respectively. If sport has provided a sheltering canopy, we can only conclude that it is wearing threadbare.

Sports are violent, but, as Michael Smith in his study *Violence and Sport* points out: "The fact is, sports violence has never been viewed as 'real' violence" and the public "give standing ovations to performers for acts that in other contexts would be instantly condemned as criminal" (1983: 9). Yet, in the years since the publication of Smith's book, many of those acts are being condemned as criminal and the impression is that governing bodies of sport have lost their ability to police themselves. Lawyers are already moving into areas that were once taboo. We will return to this issue in the concluding chapter. For now, let us stay mindful of the fact that sport cannot be regarded as the sealed-in unit it has tried to be. It is so much a central part of our culture that it would be unreasonable to expect it to remain aloof from the conflict and turbulence that occurs elsewhere. Equally, we cannot expect it not to be affected by the same kinds of legal controls that operate everywhere else.

BLEEDING TEAM COLORS

"You're a fan. You bleed team colors. Live or die on every snap." Not, as you might imagine, the words of a malevolent archfiend in a Bill and Ted movie, but copy from an advertisement for Sierra Sports software. It has a similar ring to ads run by the cable company BSkyB which told fans that "football is your obsession . . . your religion."

For some sports fans, the ads are clearly right. Sports attract followings that support teams or individual players with a near-worshipful devotion and zeal that fully justifies the root word of "fan" – fanatic adj. [< L *fanaticus*, of a temple, hence enthusiasm, inspired <*fanum*, a temple] unreasonably enthusiastic; overly zealous (*Webster's Dictionary*). Or: *a. & n.* (Person) filled with excessive and mistaken enthusiasm, esp. in religion; hence ~AL *a.* (*Oxford English Dictionary*).

Fandom

From fan, or fanatic, and "dom," meaning a collectivity or the ways of (e.g. kingdom, officialdom), this refers to the condition in which whole congregations of people devote parts of their life to following, supporting, or just admiring an individual or sports team. Devotees of Madonna, for instance, have been seen as a fandom of "wannabes," trying to emulate or mimic the rock star. Sports fans exhibit traces of this, though their orientation typically lacks envy and is based more on devotion. Gunther Parche, a devotee of Steffi Graf, in 1993 knifed Graf's rival Monica Seles in the back so that his idol could be number one in the world. Often fandom revolves around loyalty to a club. In recent years, there have been two ball clubs that have generated fandoms far greater in quantity and quality than any others: Manchester United and the Oakland Los Angeles Raiders.

Manchester United. In terms of actual achievements, the club has little to boast about when compared to some other European clubs: United has won the European club championship twice, as against Real Madrid's seven, AC Milan's five, and Ajax's and Liverpool's four each. Yet the United fandom far outstrips these. Its fans travel from all over Europe to Manchester, and there are branches of its official supporters' clubs in virtually every Commonwealth and European country, as well as Japan, Malaysia, South Africa, and the USA. There is even a branch on the Indian Ocean island of Mauritius.

The source of the club's special status probably lies in 1958 when a plane carrying members of its playing and coaching staff from Belgrade where

---

the team had just clinched a place in the European Cup semi-final, crashed on take-off after a refueling stop at Munich. Nineteen died, including eight players, three staff and eight journalists. Sympathy for the club went far beyond the conventional limits of soccer or even sport itself. People who ordinarily had no interest in sports were touched by the scale of the disaster. The sympathy translated into a passive support, which in turn converted into a more active allegiance when passed on to a new generation. A warrantable third generation of United fans now follow the team around Europe; the team's success in the English league in the 1990s guaranteed it entry into prestigious European-wide competitions, which sustained the fandom. Added to this was an aggressive approach to marketing United merchandise.

Oakland Raiders. It is almost impossible to visit a country anywhere in the world without seeing someone wearing the black and silver and the Jolly Roger-style insignia of the Raiders. Yet the team has not won a Super Bowl since 1984 and has detached itself from its original fans by moving the franchise from Oakland, California. The suspicion arises that its roots in Oakland may hold the key to understanding the worldwide popularity of the club. This was the birthplace of the Black Panther movement which began operations in 1965 after the riot in the Watts district of Los Angeles. The movement was radical and militant, committed to the ideology of Black Power, which proposed that the steady progress of the civil rights movement was misguided and that violent means should be used where necessary to break down racism.

The Panthers unwittingly acquired a radical chic: the signature black gloves were worn by Smith and Carlos in the 1968 Olympic gesture; cars were soon adorned with bumper stickers signifying allegiance. In fact, a 1971 study involved 15 participants, all of whom had clean driver's licenses, driving about with said stickers on their cars for 17 days, during which they picked up a total of 33 traffic violation tickets. Raiders had the same kind of chic; like the Panthers they had what we now call attitude, playing no-frills, smash-mouth football. For Raiders' opponents, football was a form of torture. This was the type of football perfectly suited to the radical late 1960s/early 1970s when to be "bad" was a positive attribute; and a generation of fans across the USA warmed to it. Subsequent generations have attached themselves to the same Raiders image, dressing in black and silver to express a different type of radicalism, one that owes more to style than politics and is no doubt enhanced by the number of California based musicians who wear the colors.

In his book *Textual Poachers*, Henry Jenkins (1992) argues that fans are often treated as having immoderate tastes and abnormal likings; this, he argues, justifies elitist and disrespectful beliefs about common life. Fans, in this conception, are "others" unlike "us" in their beliefs and activities; they are also seen as dangerous. The obsessive properties of fans are inspected in the Tony Scott film *The Fan* (1996) in which a fan, played by Robert De Niro, gets his spiritual nourishment only by following baseball: his job as a knife salesman holds no interest for him and he is prepared to sacrifice it in order to pursue his real love. When he discovers that his team's recently-signed superstar is interested primarily in money, he turns viciously against him.

The story has some basis in fact. For example, back in 1949, Philadelphia Phillies player Eddie Waitkus was shot by a fan. In the 1990s, Katarina Witt and Steffi Graf were harassed by stalkers. In 1993, Graf's rival Monica Seles was stabbed in an attempt to prevent her from ousting Graf from the number one spot in women's tennis. The attacker kept a shrine to Graf in his aunt's attic. Less well-known is the case of multiple world snooker champion Stephen Hendry: a female fan became fixated on the Scottish player and wrote him a series of letters which grew progressively abusive. In 1991, she threatened to shoot him, later claiming that her threat afforded her "power over people's lives . . . to know that you can cause such harm to people by doing something as simple as writing a letter" (quoted in the *Sunday Times*, September 29, 1996).

While this is an extreme statement of the sense of empowerment that accompanies fandom, it signals the powerlessness that is in some way negated by following the exploits of others and perhaps displacing one's own perceived inadequacies in the process. In her "A sociology of television fandom," Cheryl Harris argues persuasively that being a fan confers a sort of power; she writes of fandom "as a phenonemon in which members of subordinated groups try to align themselves with meanings embodied in stars or other texts that best express their own sense of social identity" (1998: 49–50).

If we begin from this premise that fans try to align themselves with others as a way of expressing some part of their selves and that this can be experienced as empowering, especially for those who have little material power, then we can move toward an understanding of collective fan violence.

"Effects on the hostility of spectators of viewing aggressive sports" is the title of a study by Robert Arms *et al.* which concluded that "the observation of aggression on the field of play leads to an increase in hostility on the part of spectators" (1987). The kind of relationship Arms has in mind came to life in May 1999 when a game between the two Glasgow soccer teams, Rangers and Celtic, turned into a fearsome battle both on and off the field. A total of three players were ejected from the game and nine others were booked (officially cautioned). The referee was hit by a missile during the game – and, later, had the windows of his house smashed. Violence on the field sparked violence among spectators. The crowd invaded the field and joined in a free-for-all. Arms and his colleagues would have used this as support for their argument that violent play encourages, perhaps even causes, violent behavior among spectators.

Of all the forms of football, only soccer has generated hooliganism in the sense we now understand it: a collective violent activity conducted principally in stadia, but often in surrounding areas, between rival fans. Soccer is the most popular sport in the world and, while the specific form of hooliganism originated in Britain in the 1960s, it quickly spread all over Europe and South America. The title of Janet Lever's (1983) book on the South American game captures the manic enthusiasm of fans, *Soccer Madness*.

The mania aroused by soccer is not new. In 1314, King Edward II of England banned large ball games: "Forasmuch as there is great noise in the

---

Football

Football is a generic term covering the world's most popular team game, known variously as soccer, *voetbal*, *fussball*, and other derivations; American football, sometimes called gridiron; rugby, which is divided into Rugby League and Rugby Union; and Gaelic football and Australian Rules football, which differ only slightly in terms of rules. Accounts of its origins usually include primitive kicking games using the inflated or stuffed bladder of an animal. In the Middle Ages, adjacent English villages would incorporate a version of this into their festivals celebrating holy days. These were, as David Canter and his colleagues call them, mêlées rather than games with no rules: the object being to move the bladder by any available means to the boundaries of one of the villages. The inhabitants of villages near Chester in the English north became so fierce in their efforts to move the bladder that the event had to be abandoned (Canter *et al.* 1989). Lack of transportation and mobility meant that the games remained localized until the mid-19th century when common sets of rules and standards emerged. An unlikely but popular story that purports to explain the division into throwing and kicking games involves a certain William Webb Ellis, a pupil at Rugby school, who in 1823, picked up a ball in what was intended to be a kicking game. Legend has it that rugby was born that day and it was this game that had offspring in the form of American football, Australian Rules, and Gaelic football.

---

city caused by hustling over large balls, from which many evils may arise, which God forbid, we command and forbid, on behalf of the King, on pain of imprisonment, such a game to be used in the city in future." Frequent laws banning ball games followed the English types of football through the centuries, partly because of the violence that often erupted among its fans and partly because it was thought to distract young men from sports such as archery and boxing which, as we saw in Chapter four, were useful for military duty. In 1514, the first published thesis on education in the English language described football, or at least its primitive equivalent, as "nothing but beastlie furie and extreme violence." Football, along with other forms of recreation, was banned under the Puritan regime of Oliver Cromwell in the seventeenth century, only to resurface again at the Restoration in 1660.

The term "hooligan" derives from an Irishman, Patrick Houlihan, who migrated to south-east London in the late nineteenth century and, by all accounts, enforced a reign of terror on the local pubs, many of which employed him as a bouncer. There's little evidence that Houlihan was even vaguely interested in ball sports, though ample to suggest he was a mean fighter and a bully to boot. An undistinguished and disagreeable character, Houlihan had the questionable honor of giving his name to a social problem that was to endure for more than a century after his death.

Early football violence normally took the form of trying to kill the referee. In 1921, a stadium in Bradford, Yorkshire, had to be closed for persistent violence. In the 1920s, fans of Arsenal and Tottenham Hotspur met in the streets of North London with knives and iron bars. Police baton charges on crowds were commonplace. One club took the view that a match should not be stopped unless the bottles being thrown were full rather than empty. In the 1930s, pitch invasions and attacks on players and the police were often the subject of public disapproval. The relative calm of 1945–60 was something of a rarity.

Many of the early eruptions of violence were at meetings between local teams, "derby games," such as Rangers *vs* Celtic in Glasgow, and Everton *vs* Liverpool. The rivalry between fans in these cities was intensified by a Catholic *vs* Protestant edge, Celtic and Everton having Catholic ancestry. At a time when sectarian conflict in Northern Ireland was raging, the soccer "wars" seemed a logical, if perverse, counterpart. Anti-Semitism was thought to be behind the age-old conflict between North London fans of Arsenal and Tottenham Hotspur, the latter being traditionally a Jewish-owned club. But then the violence, or "aggro" as it was called (short for aggravation), became, in the tabloid vernacular, mindless. Every weekend, local stores boarded up their windows, pubs were demolished and hospitals filled up with casualties from the games. Every game of soccer carried with it the threat of open violence between fans, wherever it was played.

A new turn in the 1980s signalled a paramilitary tendency among many fans, who gave themselves names, organized their troops into divisions and orchestrated their attacks on rival fans. Among the more notorious was West Ham's Innercity Firm, which is credited with the innovation of leaving behind specially printed business cards at sites of their fights. Other firms were Arsenal's Gooners, Burnley's Suicide Squad, and Chelsea's Headhunters. Soccer hooliganism reached its peak in the early 1980s.

The government, in response, adopted a number of measures which led to decline in violence at games throughout Britain: it was not reluctant to step into the sports arena and implement what might seem draconian legal measures to halt a problem that many felt had roots far beyond the sports stadium. Alcohol was banned from all stadia in 1985. The 1986 Public Order Act made provision for the exclusion from games of those convicted of offenses against the public order. The 1991 Football Offences Act and the introduction of surveillance cameras also reduced the incidence of criminal behavior at games.

None of these legal measures had too much impact on the behavior of fans travelling abroad, specifically to major European cities. Courts of law were empowered to prevent those convicted of hooliganism from travelling to games in countries outside England. But this type of power was helpless to prevent the free travel of violence-seeking fans who had escaped prosecution.

In some ways, the British did the world a favor by creating, developing, and refining a sport, then taking it to the rest of the world, from Lima to Lahore. Years after it had exported the sport, it exported a grimmer cargo. During the 1980s, hooliganism was rife throughout Europe. British passions were hard to rival; but Italians came very close. So, when the top clubs of each country met on neutral territory to decide which was the top team in Europe, some form of fan conflict seemed inevitable. Few could have anticipated the scale of the disaster at the 1985 European Cup Final game between Liverpool and Juventus, of Turin, Italy, at the Heysel Stadium in Brussels, Belgium: 38 fans were crushed to death and over 430 others injured in one of the worst tragedies in soccer's history. After blame was apportioned, English clubs were suspended from European-wide competition for five years and Liverpool for seven. Juventus and its fans were exonerated. Fourteen years later the specter of violence still haunted European soccer: 10,000 extra police were on duty in Moscow for the 1999 Uefa Cup Final; 66 people were detained.

Explanations

Arms's explanation is one of a slew of theories about the causes of hooligan behavior. Sports journalists, anthropologists, ethologists, historians, psychologists, and sociologists have all advanced arguments as to why only soccer fans are driven to destructive behavior. Or is it destructive? Perhaps not from the hooligans' perspective. Certainly, theorists of Marxist persuasions have discerned a constructive element to hooliganism. I will summarize their position and those of various other contributors to a decades-old debate.

Marxist approach. The 1970s-style Marxists, like Ian Taylor, argued that the behavior was a working-class reflex: as British soccer became more commercialized and removed from the old communities where it had originated, it left behind a body of fans who felt the clubs were somehow theirs. The violence was seen as a symbolic attempt to confirm their control over the clubs. Not only hooliganism, but industrial sabotage, vandalism, gangs, and a variety of subcultural exotica were explained with reference to the breakup of the traditional working class in the post-war period. The argument may have appeared reasonable in the 1970s, but has not worn well and is clearly inadequate to explain the continuing violence and its virtual universality.

Ethological account. Alternatives, influenced by ethological perspectives, focused on the ritualistic elements of the violence, viewing it as part of a huge dramatic performance in which youths acted out their parts without risking life and limb. Examining the sometimes quite elaborate hierarchies around which clubs' fans were organized (into troops, divisions, etc.), Peter Marsh and his associates concluded that, while the belligerent behavior witnessed at football grounds appeared to be chaotic and unplanned, there were, on closer inspection, what he called *The Rules of Disorder*. Anybody who has been to a big game at a British stadium and witnessed first hand, or worse been on the receiving end of, crowd violence will be aware of the limitations of Marsh's approach. Nice idea when you are sitting in your ivory tower in the quiet university town of Oxford, where Marsh *et al.* did their research; ridiculous when you are in the thick of a brawl in London or Glasgow.

Figurational perspective. Norbert Elias's theories have influences far and wide. It was almost inevitable that his colleagues at Leicester University in the English Midlands would apply his concepts to the study of hooliganism. Eric Dunning and a team of researchers undertook a detailed historical and contemporary analysis of football violence in Britain and elsewhere in Europe and produced the most sophisticated and plausible account available. Far from being a recent phenomenon, violence related to soccer has a history as long as the game itself.

The origins of violent behavior lay in the neighborhoods, where status was often the reward for being the hardest, toughest, and meanest – the baddest – character around. Not having the money to acquire prestige through conventional resources, like cars, clothes, and other material possessions, inhabitants of the 'hood would fight their way to the top of the pecking order. Inspired by Gerald Suttles's American analysis of *The Social Order of the Slum,*

Dunning and his colleagues discerned a status hierarchy and fighting was the way to climb it. Habituated to fighting, the slum dwellers, or the "rough" working class as they called them, were the same people likely to go to watch a soccer game.

Risk displacement theory. While he did not cite the Leicester research, Simon Jenkins, a writer for the London *Times*, complemented it with his own version of "risk displacement theory" (*Times*, February 18, 1995). "This states that most people need a certain amount of 'risk' and will find it where they can," wrote Jenkins. "Every visit to a soccer game embraces an element of risk, including the danger of crowd trouble." English soccer's authorities thought they had virtually eliminated the possibility of violence in the early 1990s when they ordered all Premiership and Football League clubs to improve their stadia by installing seats instead of the old style terraces on which fans used to stand.

This worked to an extent: but the violence transferred from the grounds to the streets and the pubs, creating what one writer called "landscapes of fear." The risk element is present in a number of sports and its complete elimination would probably detract from the enduring fascination we seem to have with danger and uncertainty. We will revisit this idea in the conclusion, but for the moment, let us take note of Jenkins's point that spectators at British soccer matches are clearly aware of the risks they take and, presumably, make a kind of cost–benefit analysis, concluding that the thrill is worth the risk. Jenkins goes as far as saying that it is part of the appeal of attending the stadium.

Reversal theory. In a way, psychologist John Kerr has combined elements of the figurational and risk displacement theories in his approach to "the pleasure of being destructive" (*Understanding Soccer Hooliganism*, 1994). "Understanding" is the key word here because Kerr's theory is based on the individual's interpretation of the meaning or purpose of his or her own action. Basically, he argues that young people who get involved in fan violence are satisfying their need for stimulation through forms of behavior that involve risk and novel or varied situations. One of the attempts behind this approach is to get away from theories that offer the impression that we are consistent. Kerr believes that human behavior is completely inconsistent. "This means that a soccer hooligan who on one occasion smashes a shop window may on another occasion do something completely different." This depends on our "metamotivational state": we can "reverse" between them as easily as a traffic light changes from red to green; it all depends on the situation, or contingent circumstances.

"The soccer environment provides a rich source of varied pleasure for those who wish to pursue and enjoy the feelings of pleasant high arousal," writes Kerr (1994: 47). Most regular fans reach a satisfactory level of arousal;

others do not and develop their own extreme variation in their quest for excitement. Ergo destructive behavior, which can, given the right motivational state and a conducive situation, be as gratifying as watching a good movie or poring over a work of art. Kerr detects that one way of achieving a high arousal is through "empathy with the team."

Copycat effect. The copycat effect has been invoked to account for a number of violent episodes over the years. Riots have been a stock favorite. The uprisings in English cities in the early 1980s and the Rodney King incidents of 1992 were thought to have been perpetuated by the mass media which, in transmitting images of rioters, virtually invited people to duplicate them. Two murders in Britain in the early 1990s were blamed on the movie/video *Child's Play 3*, which was watched by the culprits shortly before the crimes. Then President Bill Clinton appealed to America's entertainment industry to review its depiction of violence in response to the shootings at Columbine High School, Colorado, in 1999.

The theory holds that once the mass media get hold of a newsworthy topic their tendency is to amplify or exaggerate it, presenting the impression that the event, or events, are larger, more important, more serious, or more widespread than they actually are. But here the self-fulfilling prophecy kicks in: in creating distorted images, the media are actually establishing precisely the kind of conditions under which those images are likely to become a reality. Let's say a minor incident at, for example, Foxboro, is reported by a local tv station in a dramatic way that misrepresents what goes on. "Serious crowd disturbances at the Patriots' game," announces the newsreader under images of a minor fight between two groups of fans whose inhibitions have been lowered by several cases of Budweiser. But the images have been dramatically edited as if they had been picked off the cutting-room floor after the *Natural Born Killers* team had left for the day. (*NBK* was itself blamed for an outbreak of violence that coincided with its release in 1994 and delayed its opening in Britain.)

Determined not to be outdone, local newspapers, including the *Boston Globe*, join in the misrepresentation and soon the nationals get interested. "Is this the first evidence that the violence that's afflicted soccer for decades is creeping into American football?" they ask. The tempting and thoroughly exploitable possibility has scholars rushing out of their offices, journalists calling frantically for soundbites, church leaders tut-tutting about the collapse of morality, politicians scrambling for the highest moral plateau and, of course, the police chiefs promising that every football game will be subject to more stringent controls than ever.

All this is very exciting for at least a segment of the football-following population who could use a little more action off-field and would welcome the chance to experience the same kind of thrill their European cousins have been

240

enjoying for years. Next Sunday they go to their games ready for action, prepared for the kind of behavior the mass media have been focusing on for the past seven days. And, sure enough, the violence breaks out. The "prophecy," as sagely foretold by the media and an assembly of others, has duly been fulfilled.

An unlikely scenario perhaps; but one that illustrates the self-fulfilling potential held by the media. Events can be created as well as shaped or influenced by the way the media covers them. Those who swear the media is behind all the hooliganism in Europe and Central and South America have a tall order. They would also be hard-pressed to explain why the first events occurred – unless, of course, they were phantoms of an over-keen journalist's imagination. Critics of this type of explanation complain that it reduces the actual incident to an almost motiveless reaction to an image or sound. It heaps blame on a movie or the media for initially showing the image and, in so doing, deters investigation into the more complex issues surrounding the incident. But we should acknowledge that the mass media and the copycat effect that it triggers are certainly parts of a complicated jigsaw.

Theories are like flared pants: they come into fashion, go out, and, just when you think they are gone for good, back they come. Mimicry was thought to be at the back of the first outbreaks of hooliganism in Britain in the 1960s, but it was dispatched when the more scholarly analyses of the subject urged a wider scope than the playing field. History, culture, the economy, the mind of the hooligan: these were all factors that needed to be brought into the picture. But, in the 1990s, after a relatively tranquil period, back came the violence and a new version of the observation approach to explain it. Two weeks before the Ireland–England game, Eric Cantona had leapt at a fan in a manner befitting a card-carrying hooligan. Within a week, a game between two London clubs, Chelsea and Millwall, ended with mounted police on the field to forestall a pitch invasion as fans stormed at each other. It was the first serious disturbance in Britain for years and presaged the more serious Dublin outbreak a week later. Sports writers understandably linked the episodes, citing the increasingly boorish and disorderly conduct of players both on and off the field as poor examples for fans.

Despite being suspended, Cantona drew a certain amount of sympathy from many quarters, including the chair of the Football Association, who defended him after a television journalist found himself on the wrong end of Cantona's boots and ended up in a hospital with cracked ribs. Around the same time, another soccer player, Vinnie Jones, bit the nose of a radio reporter, drawing blood, threw a jug of orange juice over another journalist, and, generally, made a pain of himself. Dennis Wise, a Chelsea player, found himself in court after an attack in a London nightclub. "Fans do have a way of aping their heroes," wrote soccer journalist, Joe Lovejoy, who reported the affair for his newspaper the *Sunday Times* (February 15, 1995, sect. 2, p. 20). But this is by no means automatic: we might also ask why every fan exposed to violence by players doesn't behave in the same way? Why didn't viewers of the scrap between Deion Sanders and Andre Rison, in the 49ers–Falcons 1994 game, rush out and start whaling at each other in emulation of the stars?

There is a relationship between the violent behavior of players and that of fans, but probably not a direct one. Both groups operate in an atmosphere charged with competitive intensity in which rationality is rendered vulnerable to emotion, and self-control is put to the most stringent physical tests. Attachments in soccer are unlike any other sporting ties: they often have a lineage dating back to the nineteenth century; affiliations are inherited like family wealth, except in this case the families, being mostly working class, have no wealth to speak of.

Soccer fandom was once about rank, domain, a collective way of marking one's territory. And, while those features might have been modified over the decades, their essence remains: soccer fans call themselves supporters; they see themselves as representatives of their clubs, defenders of their names, bearers of their traditions. Feeling part of a unit capable of winning national and perhaps international honors, or at least challenging for them, has acted in a compensatory way for millions of soccer fans the world over. Once drawn from the industrial poor and deprived, the sport has never lost its base of support and continues to attract its most passionate following from working-class people whose occupations – if they are employed – are comparatively dull and unrewarding and offer little or no personal or professional gratification. By contrast, soccer does.

In this context, we might view the approval given to soccer hardmen as a type of reward. In *Code of the Street*, a study of Germantown, in Philadelphia, Elijah Anderson writes: "In the inner-city environment respect on the street may be viewed as a form of social capital that is very valuable" (1999: 66). It becomes especially valuable "when other forms of capital have been denied or are unavailable." For many working-class soccer fans, fighting for their team may be one of the few resources they have for gaining respect of their peers. That in itself is "social capital."

Fans do not just watch a game of soccer: they vicariously participate in it; they are part of the overall culture of which the actual 90 minutes of play is but one part. And, as activities on the field of play have become more overtly violent, the responses of many sections of supporters in the crowd have become so. In other words, there is a relationship between the two, but it is mediated by a cultural change that has affected the context in which the link between players and fans exists.

Cultural change has also meant that violence in soccer, or indeed any sport, elicits responses that are not usually welcomed by governing organizations. As we have seen earlier in this chapter, the law has made several decisive moves that seem to shout: "Sport is not a hands-off zone!" If offenses are committed, they cannot always be dealt with internally. A battalion of lawyers are now prepared to contest sports cases in the law courts. The cases we have dealt with in this chapter are but a few of the growing number of cases that have started in a competitive sports context and ended up in a legal one. There are more to come. I will return to this in the conclusion.

FURTHER READING

Sport Matters: Sociological studies of sport, violence and civilization by Eric Dunning (Routledge, 1999) contrasts patterns of sports-related violence in North America with those in Europe, though they have one feature in common: "A hedonistic quest for enjoyable excitement is often expressed in social deviance."

Sport, Physical Activity and the Law by Neil Dougherty, David Auxter, Alan Goldberger, and Gregg Heinzmann (Human Kinetics, 1994) is a source book and has obvious utility for those practically involved in sports. Its value for students lies in its interesting use of case-studies to illustrate its arguments.

Football, Violence and Social Identity, edited by Richard Giulianotti, Norman Bonney, and Mike Hepworth (Routledge, 1994), collects essays from around the world to show the narrowness of theories that attempt to reduce fan violence to a single type of analysis.

Code of the Street: Decency, violence, and the moral life of the inner city by Elijah Anderson (Norton, 1999) is not about sports at all, but is full of insights that can be readily applied to the culture of sports fans, the rules by which many of them live and the way their world confers reward and exacts punishment.

ASSIGNMENT

A bitter rivalry between two NHL teams has been given an extra edge by a facial injury suffered by Crawley, a player for the Saskatchewan Scorpions, after an aggressive encounter with Gaea of the Tacoma Titans. The injured Crawley vows revenge and is reprimanded by his club for inflammatory remarks made to the media. The build-up to the next meeting of the teams is marked by the media's attention to the two players concerned and the "revenge" comments. In the game itself, Crawley is sent cartwheeling by a hard tackle from Gaea. His flailing skate catches Gaea across the throat. Gaea bleeds to death on his way to hospital. While it is a freak incident, there are strong reactions. Examine the fall-out from the point of view of (1) the two clubs; (2) the NHL; (3) the mass media; and (4) the criminal justice system. (The players and clubs in this example are fictitious, though the incident is based on the death of Sweden's Bengt Åkerblöm who died after an accidental collision with a fellow hockey player in a 1995 practice game.)

leading QUESTIONS

q: Which is the toughest sport?

a: It depends on how you define "tough."

Sports in which serious injuries are commonplace, or those that take place in severe or unpleasant environments? Sports that require competitors to endure hardship, or contest with unyielding conditions? Violent sports, including combat and collision sports, involve competitors in vigorous, often explosive, conflict; whereas endurance events tax the durability of competitors. *All* sports make demands on the human being, both physical and mental. Sports with more overtly physical demands usually feature in debates about "which is toughest?" Chess, on the other hand, rarely does; though an argument could be made in its favor – after all, the brain is taxed and this is part of the human anatomy.

Gymnastics is another sport that would not be an automatic choice for a tough sport, probably because its actual performance conceals the grueling preparation that it demands. An elegant, graceful, and aesthetically pleasant activity, gymnastics requires its competitors to surrender their lives to the pursuit of excellence from childhood. The disciplined physical regimes that need to be observed are almost inhuman; and the casualties are many. Gymnasts push their bodies to such extremes that career-ending injuries are likely; and, in retirement, many competitors suffer osteopathic problems.

More conventionally, the toughest sports are those that are demonstrably *hard*: those that require endurance, strength, inner fortitude, those that are conspicuously dangerous, perhaps even life-threatening and those that involve competitors in long-term trials of will-power as well as physical ability.

For punishing sports, the field might be narrowed to heavyweight boxing and rugby union, both of which involve the participants in frequent bodily collisions which inevitably result in injuries, occasionally even death. Boxing involves a maximum of 12 rounds, each of three minutes' duration with a one-minute interval between. The fighters are allowed only the protection of a padded cup covering their groin and allowed to hit each other with padded eight-ounce gloves anywhere in a target region that covers the face and upper body. The accelerated force of 50G from a 230-lb boxer's punch is the equivalent of being hit with a 14-lb hammer at 20mph. As might be expected, boxers usually finish fights with many bruises. Cuts around the eyes are commonplace, nose bleeds are also usual. The cumulative effect of punches to the head may be brain damage, and many boxers have incurred serious brain injuries and have occasionally died as a direct result of ring injuries.

Rugby union was one of the sources of American football and the resemblance is clear. The most conspicuous difference is that rugby players are afforded no protective padding apart from an optional skull-cap to protect their ears. Tackles and hits are allowable below the neck and, as players typically weigh over 200 lb, this often results in injury. Many of the more serious injuries are caused by off-the-ball incidents, such as illegal hits, head-butts, raking (dragging cleats across the face of a felled player) and gouging. A game of rugby union is divided into two halves, each of 40 minutes of continuous play, so the teams are on the field and given no respite for time-outs or other stoppages.

In rugby, the ruck is the single most important weapon in the attacking armory and the phase that provides the sport with a unique continuity among related games, such as rugby league, American football or Australian Rules. The ball remains live even when a player is grounded and opponents and colleagues alike will converge to try to gain possession. Players who go down are often trampled underfoot, the principle being "if you're on the ground, you're part of the ground."

Other sports are tough because of the way they tax the durability of their participants. There are few sports more physically demanding over a sustained period than professional cycling, which takes place over between one and three weeks and in any weather conditions, however extreme. Typically, 155 miles will be covered in seven days, and about 14 mountains, none lower than 1,000 feet, will be climbed. A cyclist will burn about 10,000 calories a day.

Triathlon also involves cycling, though only as one-third of a multi-disciplinary event in which the action is compressed into about six hours. While competitions vary, a typical triathlon comprises swimming for 2.5 miles (4 km) without a break, cycling continuously for 75 miles (120 km) and road running for 19 miles (30 km). As in pro cycling, the event takes place regardless of weather; so rough seas, heat, and humidity pose especially difficult problems for competitors, who are reckoned to lose about 4,500 fluid ounces (225 pints, or 128 liters) of bodily fluids during the race. But competition is only one test for triathletes: training also makes exacting demands. Triathletes usually train six days a week, each session lasting six hours and, to be effective, all activity must be performed above the anaerobic threshold between 80 and 90 per cent of maximum heart rate (most triathletes train with a heart rate monitor).

Most debates on the toughest sport center on human beings; but, of course, many sports feature animals and certain events demand strength, durability, and fortitude from them. The Grand National is a yearly horse race that attracts a world audience of 450 million from 150 countries and is one of the most dangerous sporting events for both horse and jockey. Motor racing is the only other sport in which ambulances routinely follow the participants.

The Grand National has been called the marathon of National Hunt racing: its course is four-and-a-half miles of (usually) rain-soaked natural turf punctuated with "drop" fences (i.e. with uneven levels each side of the fence) that were modified in the 1990s after protests from animal rights activists who objected to the "carnage." The field typically comprises over 30 horses, the vast majority of whom do not finish. Horses carry a maximum handicap jockey's weight of 168 lb (76.2 kg), so that, when a horse falls, its legs often break under the combined weight of about 1,200 lbs. Invariably, the injury is not repairable and the horse is put down.

But, for overall toughness, the Iditarod has no rivals. A 1,149-mile sled-dog race over six to eight days and nights in temperatures of -60 degrees, the competition commemorates a 1925 dog run that brought life-saving serum from Anchorage, Alaska, to diphtheria-stricken Nome in the Arctic north. According to writer Gary Paulsen (in his *Winterdance: The fine madness of Alaskan dog-racing*), the mushers come to identify closely with their dogs, talking to them and sleeping with them through the race, so that both human and animal are implicated in the test of endurance and speed.

More questions . . .

- advances in diet and physical conditioning are making us stronger and more durable; so are traditionally tough sports becoming easier for us ?
- Are fans more attracted to sports that make physical demands on athletes' bodies?
- Old-timers always tell us that today's sports are soft compared to yesterday's; do they have a case ?
- Can any sport really be tougher than another, or are they all just as demanding in their own particular ways?

Read on . . .

- Anonymous, *Cyclist's Training Diary*, 7th edn (Alan C. Hood & Co., 1994).
- Depasquale, P., *The Boxer's Workout* (Fighting Fit, 1990).
- Evans, M., *Endurance Athlete's Edge* (Human Kinetics, 1997).
- Greenwood, J., *Total Rugby: Fifteen-man rugby for coach and player* (A. & C. Black, 1998).
- Houts, T. and Bass, J., *Trilog: Diary and guide for the triathlete and duathlete* (Masters Press/NTC Contemporary Publishing, 1995).

through artists' eyes

representations of

sports

MAKING SPORTS VISIBLE

Sports, as we know, never stop changing and, in the next two chapters, we will examine how visual media have reflected and inspired those changes. Chapter twelve will focus on electronic media, especially television, the function of which was intended to report rather than interpret sports. But, art has a different purpose and, in this chapter, I want to examine how artists have approached athletic competition. In the process, I will show how art provides us with a history of sport somewhat different from the history we have disclosed so far. This is a history as revealed through the eyes of painters, sculptors, and film-makers, many of whom were not interested in the significance of sport as a cultural institution; their interests were with images created in the movement excited by sports competition.

A related aim of this chapter is to recognize a continuity amid the change. Over the centuries, countless artists' impressions of athletic competition are testimony to the centrality of sports in human culture. The organization and content of the compositions have changed dramatically within and between periods. But, the effort to visualize facets of sports has remained strong.

A third design of this chapter is to suggest how representations of sport resonate with values and standards specific to times and places. We will see how cultural approaches to, for instance, violence, gender, and the cruelty, have been apparent in the work of artists focusing on sports. None of this suggests that art provides us with a straightforward document of sports or the cultures of which they were part. As painter Paul Klee once pronounced: "Art doesn't mirror the visible . . . It makes visible."

Klee, who worked in the 1920s using sports images as expressions of modernity, believed that art does not simply reflect reality. For him and, we can be sure, every other artist, art is an exposition, a way of witnessing the world, though not necessarily in a way we find comfortable or obvious. Art provokes and challenges as much as it pleases and reassures. This is not usually the purpose of illustrators, photographers, and camera operators. According to Guy Hubbard: "They are journalists and their purpose is to visually explain to people what happened as clearly as possible." In his article "Sports action," Hubbard distinguishes between this group and "Artists who express themselves through sports events [and who] are likely to be interested in portraying physical action and urge to compete and win." They feel no obligation to report what they see, argues Hubbard: "They are free to use their imaginations when interpreting sports action" (1998: 29–30).

Three aims, then: (1) to relate an "alternative history" of sport as told through the expressions, imaginations, interpretations of painters, sculptors, film-makers, and other artists who have focused on sports as their subject; (2) to understand how something resembling what Nicolaos Yaloris, in his *The Eternal Olympics: The art and history of sport*, calls the "athletic spirit" has stirred artists' imaginations, albeit in quite different ways, for perhaps 4,000 years and to highlight consistency across the ages; (3) to appreciate how art that focuses on sport can, indeed must, contain a record of the particular social milieux in which they were produced.

Faced with a cornucopia of materials, I have been extremely selective in my treatment. But, at the end of the chapter, there are recommended sources where the reader will find detailed accounts of the development of arts specializing in sports in specific periods. Peter Kühnst's *Sports: A cultural history in the mirror of art*, which covers the period from about 1450 to 1986, is a particularly solid collection of (mostly) paintings, graphics, and photography accompanied by an analytical text. While Kühnst does not include film in his analysis, there is strength in his thesis that: "By following the evolution of sports and sports-like physical activities, one can see the degree to which they have been the expression of changes in thinking and feeling. They can be understood as an index of individual and social historical transformation" (1996: 9).

READING THE IMAGE

No genre has an official starting-point, though it is tempting to identify 1766 as the year in which a legitimate art form called sporting art emerged, primarily through the work of the British painter George Stubbs whose landmark portfolio *Anatomy of a Horse* was published in that year and whose work is generally considered to have defined a new direction for artists. While Stubbs – to whom we shall return shortly – lent new shape and clarity to sporting art, he was by no means the first artist to have focused on sports. Indeed, artistic impressions of sporting events and competitors are as ancient as athletic competitions themselves.

Wall paintings and reliefs of men wrestling and lifting weights have been discovered in Egypt and dated to the second millennium BCE. There is evidence of other images showing figures seeming to play ball games and fighting with staffs. In later Cretian and Greek cultures there were engravings and frescos that suggested the presence of an athletic spirit: depictions of bull-leaping and combative activities on seals and walls indicate an interest in dangerous competitions. These tell us that the activities actually occurred, but little of their significance. In his essay "Athletics in Crete and Mycenae," J. Sakellarakis points out that, while there is evidence of combat and other athletic activity in ancient Egypt, "these and other similar sports practised in the East had essentially nothing in common with the Greek athletic contests except for the natural inclination to exercise a strong healthy body" (1979: 13–14). The purpose of the activities engraved on seal stones and rings or painted in frescos was to display athleticism and prowess and entertain spectators rather than convey ideals found in later Greek games.

The object of the earlier games was to exhibit a well-trained and skilled human body in contests against other humans and against animals. The games were performed at festivals in Minoan Crete in the second millennium BCE and had an almost ceremonial function which Nicolaos Yaloris likens to acrobatic display. Representations of bull-leaping – in which the leaper stands in front of an onrushing bull and grabs its horns so that the bull's momentum tosses him (women do not appear in the pictures) in the air – are found in ancient monuments. Scenes from the combat events, also popular in the Minoan period, are found on vases, especially *kraters* which were vases placed in the tombs of the dead, suggesting that the activities held some religious significance.

The lack of written evidence forced scholars to rely on bric-a-brac and artifacts as well as the stylized art forms that survived. Apart from combat sports, which seem to have endured through several different cultures and epochs, racing of some sort is found in the decoration of ceramics; this includes foot-racing, horse racing and chariot racing, all of which in some way continue to the present.

Sculptures were characteristic of Greek art and, in this form, there is a pantheon of heroes, the most celebrated of which is Myron's *Discus Thrower (Discobolus)* in bronze from the fifth century BCE. The model for this work could well have been drawn from one of today's gyms. His body is lithe and cut, a flat midsection and prominent ribs giving him a very contemporary look. The position he takes in readiness of his discus throw is much the same as that of today's discus throwers, discus-holding arm outstretched behind him, other arm across his opposing knee, feet poised to rotate and thrust. It is a genuinely timeless piece.

For Greeks, sport, education, and culture were indistinct: they were all involved in the cultivation of the whole being; the mental and the physical were not dualities as the modern Western conceptions, but part of the same unity. So, sport, at least in the way we understand it, did not exist: it was not a separate sphere of activities sectioned off from many other parts of life. Once this is understood, it becomes clear why so many athletic images adorn Greek art and artifacts. Sport was revered in ancient Greece and found its fullest expression in the Olympic Games.

By contrast the Romans, who subjugated the Greeks in 146 BCE, were indifferent to sport and, indeed, to art. The only sporting endeavors encouraged by Romans were those that contributed to the preparation for war. Whereas Greeks had idealized athletic pursuits and endowed them with spiritual purpose, Romans saw them as a kind of military training and undeserving of the cultural attention Greeks had afforded them in their art.

The Romans' lust for gladiatorial conflict is famous: trained, armed men fought in mortal combat against each other, or against animals. At Naples' National Archeological Museum, there is a fresco from Pompeii showing a Roman amphitheater and a number of other activities, some of which appear to be gladiator fights. While the Romans did not leave a largess of art, contemporary reconstructions of gladiatorial contests have been memorable. Jean Léon Gérôme's 1874 oil on canvas *Pollice Verso* is a frightening, dramatic depiction of the climax of a duel in which the triumphant gladiator, wearing a helmet and arm mail, stands over the fallen *netarius* (net-thrower), his foot on his throat. The viewer sees the scene from the floor of the Coliseum and witnesses the imposing crowd baying for blood. As was the custom, the gladiator looks to the emperor seated in his box; to his left are six vestal virgins, all signaling their wishes as to the fate of the victim – thumbs down.

It is probable that director Stanley Kubrick consulted Gérôme's work when he recreated a gladiatorial contest for his 1960 film *Spartacus*. Gérôme was painstaking in his research, obtaining casts of antique armor and weapons in his quest for authentic detail. In *Spartacus*, the similarities are pronounced, though Kirk Douglas did not wear the formidable headgear of the Gérôme victor. Ridley Scott's 1999 film *Gladiator* also recreates the visceral excitement of the Roman combat sports.

The Roman fascination with gory death manifested again in chariot racing. The floor of the huge Circus Maximus was often strewn with bodies as races progressed. Without doubt the most memorable reconstruction of such a chariot race is in William Wyler's 1959 epic *Ben Hur* in which Charlton Heston and Stephen Boyd lead a field of racers, most of whom come to a bloody end. The race stands the test of time as one of the most exhilarating pieces of dramatized sport ever.

The fall of the Roman Empire in the fifth century ushered in a period of 1,000 years that became known as the Dark Ages and then the Middle Ages. Artistic evidence of *les tournements* was preserved in the forms of great medieval tapestries that held narratives of the chivalric conflicts in which honor, glory, and reputation were at stake. More durable were the woodcuts that proliferated, particularly in what is now Germany, in the sixteenth century. Albrecht Dürer was one of the foremost artists of his time.

Dürer was well-versed in fighting sports, including wrestling and swordsmanship. He illustrated the *Wallerstein Codex*, which was a manual of fighting, first published about 1470. Like some later artists of boxing, he believed that he needed to train with competitors in order to gain the insights necessary to produce his art. Germany led Europe in printing, and woodcuts were used to illustrate manuscripts which could then be duplicated and disseminated. Jost Amman's 1565 *Emperor Maximilian's Tournament at Vienna* produced a celebrated vista that reveals much of the organization of tournaments. Eight jousts take place simultaneously in an enclosed courtyard outside of which are thronged spectators, some on horseback. Overlooking the courtyard are balconies from which the nobility watch in comfort. Guards patrol the area to keep order. In the competition, some of the knights have been unseated and have progressed to a ground battle with swords. The atmosphere of the scene is part sporting and part carnival, suggesting that tournaments were occasions for festivities as well as stark competition.

This type of mixture of activities gains full expression in Matthias Gerung's oil on wood *Melancholia*, of 1558, which features a vortex of activities, some of which resemble sports, others of which seem more like pure entertainment, still others of which appear to be celebrations. Knights in combat are also visible in Gerund's work, as are archers and bowlers, but there is no clear differentiation between the clearly-ordered sport of Amman's work and other forms of recreation.

Contemporary visualizations of tournaments are commonplace thanks to the popularity of films, such as Jerry Zucker's *First Knight* (1994), in which Richard Gere plays the medieval knight Lancelot, and Kevin Reynolds's

Robin Hood: Prince of Thieves (1991) which was one of several films to feature the Nottingham outlaw of yore in the legendary archery contest.

ORDER AND TRANSFORMATION

Europe was in the midst of the Renaissance in the sixteenth century. The profound changes that transfigured the cultural and, eventually, scientific landscape mobilized the desire for creative self-expression which in turn led to new ways of explaining, understanding, and appreciating the world. Some of the activities that we now distinguish as sports had links, however tenuous, with games that were played in Europe in this period. Kühnst detects an early visual representation of a ball game in a Venice ceiling fresco produced in the 1550s: the players wear gauntlets and exchange a leather ball in what appears to be an early type of handball.

At the same time, the rough game *calcio*, which has some similarities with latter-day soccer, rugby, and its derivatives, like American football, was played by the working class. In northern Europe, woodcuts produced around 1520 feature ball games that appear to have been played for amusement. These type of games gradually gained in popularity, superseding the chivalric combat characteristic of the tournaments. Some of the tournament events, such as horse riding, running and spear (later, javelin) throwing, mutated and survived; others, like jousting and vaulting did not, at least not in competitive forms.

But the tournaments rapidly became anachronisms as the Renaissance spirit diffused throughout Europe, stimulating the progress, discovery, and a new sense of wonder with the natural world. This inevitably led to changes both in sports and in the way those sports were represented. In art, we find competitive sports signifying the desire for order, the rationalization of society, and the mastery of the self. The Baroque style epitomized this: competitors define geometrical patterns, suggesting an order and control of space. The work of Johann Christoph Neyffer and Willem Swanenburgh in the early 1600s are works of art constructed like architectural plans, so that fencers and riflemen appear as lifeless points rather than active human beings. Their conduct is not spontaneous, but ordered.

Order was even brought to the chaotic and often violent *calcio*: a 1689 copperplate by Alessandro Cecchini shows a game being played: the field of play is clearly demarcated by perimeter fencing and guards are stationed strategically; even the players occupy set positions, much like they do in contemporary ball games. Sports, like every other aspect of European society, were affected by the new model of knowledge known as science. Far from being mysterious if not unfathomable, nature was becoming comprehensible:

theories about the world could be tested empirically, that is by appealing to human senses of observation, touch, taste, and sound.

Sports are often thought of as diversions from the rational planning and scientific rationality of other areas of life. This is only partly true: in the eighteenth century, as it became clear that the natural world was governed by laws, sports too underwent a revision. Luck, randomness, and a certain ineffability have always been vital ingredients in sports, of course. But some of these could be subordinated or controlled using scientific understanding.

From 1800, sports began to devour the fruits of science. The same technologies that served industry aided sports. Races took place over prescribed distances, times were measured, results were recorded; sports acquired the same rationality as industry. The importance of the stopwatch, which was first used in 1731, can scarcely be exaggerated. We find the scientific impulses to analyze, quantify, and record in the art of the period, art which became known as "sporting art."

All three impulses come together in the art of George Stubbs, who specialized in commissioned portraits of racehorses. As we have noted, Stubbs's *Anatomy of a Horse* was published in 1766: it was not only work of great aesthetic beauty but of scientific precision. As its title suggests, Stubbs's art lay at the borders of medical knowledge: he brought to his subject a surgeon's skill and a thoroughness that few of his peers could match. Stubbs seemed to have investigated the minutest of detail in his quest for the perfection of objective accuracy and his masterwork has been likened to da Vinci's studies of human cadavers 200 years earlier.

George Stubbs

Born in 1724 in Liverpool, Stubbs is generally regarded as the most influential artist of his period. Passionately interested in the study of anatomy in his youth, he was commissioned to illustrate medical textbooks with his engravings. In 1754, Stubbs visited Rome and, on his return, he was commissioned by several members of the English nobility to produce paintings of hunts and studies of horses. So exacting was Stubbs that he spent 18 months dissecting horses in a Lincolnshire barn, producing his *Anatomy of a Horse* collection in 1766. Coombs (1978) describes Stubbs's *The Grosvenor Hunt*, 1762, as: "Arguably, the greatest of all sporting pictures." The scene depicts a dying stag surrounded by hounds and hunters on horseback. Stubbs died in 1806.

Stubbs's work chronicles some of the racehorses of the day, reflecting a desire to record sporting achievements rather than just enjoy them and let them pass. There was also an element of exhibitionism, as Martin Vincent detects in his article "Painters and punters": "This kind of art had the triple advantage of showing off the patron's land, his horses and his sporting prowess" (1995: 32)

In his *Sport and the Countryside*, David Coombs refers to Stubbs and his fascination with horses: "His art sprang naturally from its environment, a prosperous, country-based economy in which the horse was the prime means of transport and a major source of motive power" (1978: 56). The horse was central to eighteenth-century and early nineteenth-century life and commanded the attention of many artists. Their work provides a documentary of Britain's changing society between 1700 and 1900, when agriculture was emerging as the primary industry and sporting customs responded to the changes.

The horse was arguably of even greater importance in America, though it was not until 1822 that it became as embodied in art as it had been in England. Charles Hall, an agriculturalist and breeder, commissioned paintings of thoroughbreds by, among others, Alvan Fisher, whose *Eclipse, with Race Track* is displayed at the National Art Museum of Sport at Indianapolis.

"At the end of the eighteenth century the countryside was becoming softer and more orderly as wild areas were conquered and cultivated," write Anthony Vandervell and Charles Coles in their *Game and the English Landscape* (1980: 61). British sporting art bore a close relationship to the changing context, depicting races and hunts against a landscape that was being prepared for the coming of industry.

Other changes were delineated in sporting art. For example, William Powell Thomas's oil *Derby Day* was created in 1858 and captures the atmosphere of the race track, members of different social classes segregated from each other: sports events were attended by all social classes, though they could not always mix. One area where they were free to mingle was the animal pit. William Hogarth's intimidating *Pit Ticket*, of 1759, shows male patrons, from aristocrats to thieves, huddled together around a cockpit, their devilish zeal for the fight apparent in their grotesquely drawn faces. *The Rat Pit*, by an unknown artist around 1860 (after the prohibition of cock-fighting in 1849), shows members of different social classes stratified as if according to rank from the top of the canvas. The picture bears a striking resemblance to Peter Blake's artwork for the cover of *Sgt Pepper's Lonely Hearts Club Band*, the motley characters looking like lifeless cut-outs congregating around a central attraction, in this a case a pit filled with 50-odd rats and a tenacious terrier (reproduced by Coombs 1978: 186).

Théodore Géricault's *The Derby at Epsom*, painted in 1821, on the other hand, focuses on the thrill of a horse race in progress, the horses speeding toward the finishing line; and this too gives some indication of the changes afoot in society. Kühnst argues that this and other works that communicate speed, tension, and the excitement of competition "show the transformation of physical exercises from static exhibitions of skill to lively achievement-oriented contests" (1996: 140).

This achievement orientation spread across the whole sporting spectrum from the beginning of the nineteenth century, and the stylized poses of earlier art gave way to scenes of action in which competitors strove, not just to compete, but to win. For example, Gustave Courbet's oil *The Wrestler*, painted in 1853, shows two men clearly struggling for all they are worth. Frederic Remington's *Touchdown, Yale vs. Princeton, Thanksgiving Day, November 27, 1890, Yale 32, Princeton 0* suggests a less-than-friendly rivalry between the two teams as the players strain for supremacy. In these and in countless other works of the time, competitors are no longer statuesque, but dynamic and goal-directed. In a sense, the change mirrored the transition in art from Romanticism to Impressionism which animated its subjects with a variety of techniques.

Impressionism originated in and refracted a world agitated by the twin forces of industrialization and urbanization. Advances in the natural sciences, especially chemistry, propelled a move toward the mechanization and other technological processes. The same processes that revolutionized economies all over Europe made their presence felt in sports – and art. In 1896, when Coubertin launched the modern Olympic Games, the factory system was in full swing and populations were herding together in cities. European societies were at pains to restore stability in the face of fundamental economic and cultural shifts. Industry demanded order.

Rational progress, uniformity, and standardization were the hallmarks of industrialism. It is no coincidence that they were also key features of Coubertin's vision: a comprehensive program of sports events carefully organized, each performance being quantified, ranked, and rewarded according to standards of excellence. The effects of modernity, industrialism, and the technology they fostered were felt in sports; they were also felt in the modes through which sports were represented.

In the early 1880s, two artists, one American, one British, both of whom shared an interest in technology, came together at the University of Pennsylvania, their purpose being to apply science to art and produce objectively accurate representations of sports. Thomas Eakins was a celebrated oil painter who created some of the most evocative images of boxing and wrestling of the nineteenth century. His nude and near-nude studies of prize fighters formed part of a tradition of homoerotic sports art that found later expression in the sculptures of Eakins's student Charles Grafly and, later, in the art of John De Andrea, David Rohn, and Bruce Weber, the director of the film *Broken Noses*.

Eakins's collaboration with Eadweard Muybridge, a British photographer who emigrated to the United States in 1852, yielded work that changed artists' conceptions of sports. Exploiting the potential of the relatively new technology of photography, Eakins and Muybridge sought to create the most physiologically precise record of sports action using the most technically efficient methods. *Studies of Human Movements* included over 100,000 stroboscopic photographs, each capturing a moment of sporting action.

To the naked eye, a great deal of sports action is a blur. Artists had no way of knowing whether their work faithfully represented what actually happened. Stubbs and his peers, who were fascinated by horses, always imagined and represented them galloping in what is called the "rocking horse" position, all four hooves planted on the ground. Photography exposed the absurdity of this. Painters made use of photography to achieve a new level of naturalism and photographers innovated with new techniques to steer clear of naturalism.

The art of Eakins and Muybridge had aesthetic beauty, but it also had practical application, enabling an understanding of the mechanics of motion and so establishing a base point for later studies. Their techniques were adopted and refined by photographer Étienne-Jules Marey who used time-exposure experiments to disclose the minutiae of athletic actions. Among his more notable studies were *Fencing*, 1890, and *Mounting a Bicycle*, 1891, which were both educative and picturesque. Similar techniques were used by Harold Edgerton who produced stop-motion studies of, among other sports, pole vaulting and tennis in the mid-twentieth century. These artists brought to sports a punctiliousness and fidelity that was to resurface in later film documentaries, such as *Visions of Eight*, 1973, and *Hoop Dreams*, 1994.

Photography became popular in the twentieth century and artists of sport were adventurous in their use of the medium to portray sports in entirely new ways. The photo-collages of John Heartfield in the 1920s extended earlier work, but introduced satire. For example, his *A Specter is Haunting Europe* features a runner made up of industrial parts, the head a stopwatch, pistons for limbs, and what seems to be a clock card in place of a chest. The work satirizes both the preoccupation with industrial production and its effects on sports, which were becoming joyless affairs, interested in records and measurable achievements. The changes in organization and focus in sports is also a theme in the photo-collages of Laszlo Moholy-Nagy, Irene Hoffmann, and Willi Baumeister. In all their work, there is a concern with the apparent mechanization of the modern athlete and the dehumanizing possibilities it entailed.

We find the same concerns at the core of Jean-Marie Brohm's 1978 critique, the title of which sums up the author's thrust, *Sport: A prison of measured time*.

Modernity and the trends it ushered in continued to have salience with other artists, many either intrigued with or disgusted by its impact on sports. The reduction of what was once a playful, expressive activity to flat-out competition was a popular subject for many members of the avant-garde. Paul Klee, whose insight opened this chapter, produced his *Runner–Hooker–Boxer* in 1920: this aquarelle is structured like geological layers, its figure seeming to run through the strata; the sprinting figure wears a boxing glove on one hand and has an arrow jutting from the other. Robert Delaunay's oil *The Runners*, 1926, visualizes its characters similarly: the faceless athletes run in unison. Even celebrated athletes can do little to distinguish themselves in a post-war culture that renders everyone anonymous, the artists seem to say.

THE GAZE OF HIS LADY

Among the vestiges from fifth century BCE Sparta is a vase decorated with a scene from a woman's foot-race. The barefoot runners wear long skirts and short-sleeved tops. Yaloris records that: "Women's sport was a feature of the education of girls in Sparta and Crete" (1979: 59). The same author also reproduces a mosaic depicting women training with dumbbells, practicing discus-throwing, and sprinting. "Women's sport was quite widespread in the Roman period," observes Yaloris (1979: 279).

Even in the medieval period when it is generally assumed women's presence at sporting events was purely decorative, there are artworks that show women in active roles. There are several illuminated manuscripts depicting women competing in jousts. As Allen Guttmann writes, in his *The Erotic in Sports*: "Robert de Borron's *Histoire du Graal* and the anonymous *Lancelot de Lac* are ornamented with pictures of mounted women wielding distaffs and spindles and charging at obviously disconcerted knights and monks" (1996: 41).

Kühnst includes in his impressive text a reproduction of Nicolas Arnoult's 1698 *Le Jeu du Volant* with three figures, two female, playing "featherball," which was a precursor of badminton. He also has a plate of Jean-Baptiste's oil *Girl with a Shuttlecock and Battledore* from 1741. In both works, the women appear to be middle class. A copperplate by Victor Marie Picot features, as its title suggests, *The Assault or Fencing Match which took place between Mademoiselle La Chevalière d'Eon de Beaumont and Monsieur de Saint Georges on the 9th of April 1787*. The female contestant is seen thrusting decisively at her male opponent.

In the late eighteenth century archery became popular with affluent English women who competed on level terms with men. The etching *A*

Meeting of the Society of Royal British Archers in Gwersyllt Park, Denbighshire by Robert Smirke and John Emes, which is now in the British Museum, shows women archers in competition. In the sense that it allowed head-to-head contests between males and females, archery was unusual, and a more telling picture from the same century is James Seymour's *A Coursing Scene* in which a woman sits side-saddle on her horse while a male inspects a dead hare presented to him by his servant. "This is not a painting for feminists," remarks Coombs. "There is no doubt who is the master, as much from the nature of his expression as the gaze of his lady and stance of his huntsman" (1978: 20).

Hunting scenes in nineteenth-century works continued to depict women riding side-saddle to protect their modesty. Sir Francis Grant's opulent canvas *Lady Riding Side-Saddle with her Dog*, circa 1840, is an example. The idea of women opening their legs to ride in the same way as men was an outrage to Victorians. But, in 1861, Pierre Micheaux and his son Ernest invented a machine they called a *vélocipède*, a riding machine that offered a cheaper, simpler, and more efficient mode of transport than the horse. The mass production of the *vélocipèdes* in France in the 1860s was quickly followed by what became known as the "cycling craze." Curiously, given the time in history, cycling was seen as a safe pastime for women.

Cycling and art

Cycling has held a special appeal for several significant artists, including Henri Toulouse-Lautrec. The coming together of human and machine in competitive racing seemed to offer unique possibilities at the end of the 19th century when races spread across Europe and the USA. Toulouse-Lautrec was drawn to the cycling milieu: he regularly attended velodromes and race tracks and stood at the roadside in an effort to absorb some of the atmosphere that he then translated into his art, much of it commissioned by bicycle manufacturers, like Simpsons. Other significant artists of cycling include Jean Metzinger, Natalia Gontscharova, and the Futurist, Umberto Boccioni, in the early 20th century, Fernand Léger in the mid-20th century, and, more recently, Alex Colville. A great many other prominent artists have pictures of cycling in their portfolios.

Sir John Lavery's *The Tennis Party*, 1885, and Winslow Homer's *Croquet Scene*, 1866, chronicle the more typical sporting endeavors of women in the period and, even then, tennis and croquet were sports of the affluent.

Cycling was relatively inexpensive and available to all classes. By the turn of the century, women all over Europe and America were taking to the road on bicycles. Spurning the reserve associated with side-saddle riding, women made a hugely symbolic gesture by cycling – they opened their legs. Kühnst believes that of all the developments in sports, the bicycle "contributed the most to the emancipation of women by increasing their physical independence and personal freedom" (1996: 208).

Jean Béraud's 1900 canvas *The Cyclists' Café in the Bois de Boulogne* shows women and men sharing drinks and inspecting each others' cycles during a break from their recreations. Bruno Paul's lithograph *Die Frau vor dem Rad: Hinter dem Rad: und aus dem Rad* ("The Woman in Front of the Wheel, Behind the Wheel, and on Wheels") cleverly essayed women's relationship with technology by displaying the same women cycling, working a sewing machine, and pulling an agricultural appliance.

Kühnst includes in his collection an anonymous photograph from 1910 that anticipates the later trend to mix sexual and sporting imagery: the female stands besides her bicycle, her skirt and petticoat caught on the handlebars and saddle so that her bare genitalia is revealed. While usually not as risqué as this study, many later works ventured toward the lewd, showing athletic women more as models than as active performers and often wearing skimpy clothes.

Picasso's gouache *The Race*, 1922, features two running women, each of whom displays a breast, their tops having slipped from their shoulders. Anton Räderscheidt's several studies of naked female sports performers in the 1920s typically incorporated a fully-dressed male voyeur in the background. In the same period, Willi Baumeister depicted naked women running on tracks and diving from rocks, not perhaps for prurient purposes, but with the effect of sexualizing the image of the female athlete. Even the celebrated Canadian artist Alex Colville's paintings of sports performers include *Skater*, 1964, which invites the viewer to inspect the rear of a gliding skater, her arms clasped at her back, right leg raised perpendicular to her left and lycra-clad buttocks conspicuously displayed. There is a minor tradition in art that depicts women athletes engaging in competition but positioned, dressed, or undressed in a way that tempts salacity.

Robert Towne's 1982 film *Personal Best*, in which Mariel Hemingway and Patrice Donnelly play two pentathletes involved in a lesbian relationship, does not entirely escape this convention. As Guttmann remarks: "Although the film does justice to sports as physical *contests*, Towne never hesitates to underscore the erotic element" (1996: 119). Guttmann has in mind slow-motion studies of bare thighs and midriffs of female high-jumpers in mid-air, a bench-press session in which the spotter stands invitingly astride her prostrate training partner, and a bout of arm-wrestling that turns into a bout of sex.

DARK AND LITE

Hailed by some, denounced by others, the film *Olympia* (or *Olympische–Spiele*) was undeniably a monumental work of art. Ostensibly, a chronicle of the 1936 Olympic Games held at Berlin, Leni Riefenstahl's film was a propagandist disquisition that attempted to immortalize Nazi visions of Aryan supremacy. Commissioned to make a film of the games, Riefenstahl, perhaps naïvely, produced a stylistic masterwork with cinematographic innovations to rival those of *Citizen Kane*. Despite its seminal artistry, the film is still an ideological frame to showcase Aryanism: so glaring is the Nazi iconography that the viewer can almost sense Hitler himself at Riefenstahl's shoulder.

Leni Riefenstahl

Famed German director of *Olympia*, which is hailed by many as the greatest-ever sports documentary and reviled by many others as a glorification of Nazism. Riefenstahl was a dancer and actor who turned to directing in 1932 when she made *The Blue Light*. Influenced by Fanck's 1926 silent film *Mountain of Destiny*, she used specially imported lenses and film stock to further her experiments with lighting and composition. Having seen Riefenstahl's work, Hitler commissioned her to film the 1933 National Socialist Party Congress, a film that was released as *Victory of Faith*. Dissatisfied with the results, Riefenstahl filmed the following year's Congress at Nuremberg; this time, the end-product was a visually stunning documentary, *Triumph of the Will*. Riefenstahl's *Olympia*, which was ostensibly the filmic record of the 1936 Berlin Olympics, was another work of brilliance, though its exaltation of Aryan manhood ultimately marred its critical reception. Wagnerian in atmosphere, the film's majesty is in its narrative construction, each scene building toward the thunderous climax. After the Second World War, Riefenstahl was boycotted.

The IOC had encouraged art and, at Coubertin's urging, integrated a program of artistic competition into the games with medals awarded for different art forms. So, a filmic record of the Olympic Games was welcomed. Jacob Lawrence's gouache for the poster commemorating the 1972 games at Munich was one of a series that has been acknowledged as stand-alone works of art. But it is another Olympic-themed work, Claus Mattyes's collage *Olympia*, 1978, that Kühnst singles out as the most revelational piece of contemporary sporting art. In it, a Magritte-style figure, bowler-hatted and wearing an IOC lapel pin, stands in front of a faux Greek statue which someone has defaced with a drawn-on beard and mustache. In the background, there is a bunting, but the flags are not just those of nations – they bear the logos of Coca-Cola, IBM, and the Playboy Club. There is even a dollar bill dangling from the bunting. The significance of these needs no explanation. And, as if to connect his work with that of Baumeister, Hoffmann, and, indeed, the writer Brohm, Mattyes positions a clock centrally between the two figures.

Such cynicism informs much of the art on sport over the past 70 or so years. The age of innocence, when art glorified sports, had been drawing to a close for several years before Riefenstahl's film. Shortly after its release, the Second World War occasioned a re-evaluation of sports' merits. It was not long before virtually every Olympic Games became political as well as other sporting events. Coupled with this came the realization that more and more sports were becoming professionalized and the Corinthian ideals that had once motivated competitors was extinct.

The darker side of sports was explored exquisitely by George Bellows in the first two decades of the twentieth century. His usually grim images, often of boxing matches, feature faces in the crowds that seem to have spilled straight from a Hogarth canvas. Fighters collide viciously, blood spattering their bodies as fans frantically make wagers. A fighter's left hook sends a hapless opponent crashing through the ropes. The dim and dingy atmosphere of boxing halls is a fitting backdrop to a sport that enthralled Bellows in much the same manner that pedestrians are enthralled by car wrecks. For Bellows, boxing simultaneously repels and attracts.

George Bellows

Born in 1882, in Columbus, Ohio, Bellows moved to New York in 1904 where he studied art under Robert Henri, a radical artist of his time. Bellows became associated with what was known as the Ash Can School because of his choice of subjects: in contrast to many studies that emphasized the dignity of competition, Bellows stuck to the sordid, often shameful, side of sports. His characters were frequently rough, common people battling savagely in what often looked like a war zone. He inherited the mantle of art's greatest interpreter of boxing with works such as *Both Members of this Club (A Nigger and a White Man)*, an oil painted in 1918 which pictured a black and a white fighter locked in combat, both literally and metaphorically. His *Dempsey and Firpo*, 1924, remains one of the most stirring works of sports art. Bellows died, aged 42, of a ruptured appendix in 1925.

It was probably only logical that, as film became a more established art form, directors would try to adapt features of Bellows's work for the screen. In the late 1930s and 1940s, films such as *Kid Galahad*, directed by Michael Curtiz and released in 1937, probed the dirtier aspects of the fight game. Robert Wise's *The Set-Up*, 1948, examined how a fixed fight goes wrong when no one tells the fighter he is supposed to take a dive. The short (72 minutes) film, shot in black and white, casts shadows across virtually every scene to evoke the gloomy atmosphere of bleakness and moral uncertainty; a radio commentary punctuates the soundtrack as if to remind the viewer that the media has made its malevolent presence felt on a once-noble sport. Mark Robson's 1949 *Champion* was another portrait of a sport callously corrupted by avaricious businessmen. The familarly dire portrait of boxing continued with films such as *Somebody Up There Likes Me* and *The Harder They Fall*, both 1956, and *Requiem for a Heavyweight* (in Britain, *Blood Money*), 1962.

In these and other films, romanticism was jettisoned and a savage realism was brought to the subject. Like the bronzes of Mahonri Mackintosh Young and Richmond Barthé, boxers are disfigured by the strains of competing in a sport that has long forgotten the principles of fairness and "sportsmanship."

This misanthropic approach was by no means confined to boxing. Paul Cadmus's oil and tempera work *Aspects of Suburban Life: Golf*, 1936, was one of four panels created during the Depression. Here golf is a putrid metaphor for the social inequalities of America: a well-heeled, cigar-smoking golfer sits while his supine caddy holds his clubs. The caddy is poverty personified; his shoes have holes in their soles, his jeans, which are a few sizes too big for his undernourished body, are tied with string. He tends to the needs of the conspicuously rich, all overweight and either ignoring completely or peering down their noses at the caddy.

Other disagreeable aspects of sports are dealt with by A. Paul Weber's *The False Penalty Shoot*. Weber envisions a game of soccer as disintegrating into a horrifying riot with the bodies of hundreds of spectators strewn about the field and thousands more pouring forward. The lithograph was produced in 1964 and bears an eerie similarity with the scenes evidenced at the Hillsborough stadium in 1989 when 96 fans died after the worst tragedy in British sports history.

Sports fans have not escaped the critical attentions of film directors. *The Fan*, 1996, featured Robert De Niro as a knife salesman turning on a baseball star who seems to have sacrificed sporting values for money. Tony Scott's film is a study in how contemporary sports are able to destroy the very things they build: devotion, loyalty, and hero-worship. A playful pitching competition between fan and player is shot like a gunfight in a 1950s western, the duel escalating as the fan vents his wrath. Fanaticism is also the focus of Philip Davis's undervalued account of a British police officer who goes undercover to penetrate a gang of hooligans: *i.d.*, 1994, communicated the dubious attractions of gang affiliation and organized violence. Particularly powerful are scenes in a British pub used as headquarters by the gang: here the *esprit de corps* that fuels the fanaticism is dramatically realized and the viewer is made privy to the attractions of fandom.

The photographer Tom Stoddart used a close-up of the blistered, calloused and cut palms of a female gymnast's hands to convey the punishing effects of training regimes. Regarded by most as a beautiful and edifying sport, gymnastics was exposed by Joan Ryan's book *Little Girls in Pretty Boxes: The making and breaking of élite gymnasts and figure skaters* (1998) as hideously cruel. Stoddart's *Hands of a Seven-Year-Old Gymnast*, 1994, presents this ugly side of the sport and, like most quality sports photography, is capable of prodding viewers to regard sports in new ways.

Film, more than any other medium, has been able to expose the darker side of sports graphically and in often disturbing detail. In the fight films mentioned earlier, the decay of the sport was almost palpable; and, in later works, boxing served as a ungodly background against which to paint a larger human drama. John Huston's *Fat City*, 1972, is a piercingly miserable exploration of two losers and the exploitation of one by the other. *Raging Bull*, 1980, is Martin Scorsese's harrowing, monochrome biography of the middleweight champion, Jake LaMotta.

The very nature of the art form permits much more indulgence in the circumstances surrounding sports; the event itself is often filmed in a way that deliberately avoids *reportage*. Scorsese, for example, shot some fight scenes from the perspective of a boxer rather than a spectator, often dwelling on small effects like blood dripping from a ring rope. Scorsese hurls naturalism away, using LaMotta's fights as parts of a narrative that maps out his personal conflicts, especially with his belittled wife Vicky.

Perhaps the most earnest portrayal of the degradation of sports was John Sayles's film of the scandalous 1919 World Series, *Eight Men Out*, 1988. In it, the poorly paid and virtually indentured Chicago White Sox players are depicted as fodder for greedy owners and corrupt gamblers. Baseball action is shown sparingly, most of the plot centering on the bars and boardrooms where the real "action" is played out. Venality is at the heart of several other films on sports, one of the most celebrated of which is Robert Rossen's 1961 *The Hustler*, which moves in and out of the grimy poolhalls of the time; as its title suggests, gambling provides the mainspring of the plot. Most of the film is shot indoors and the black and white cinematography accentuates the grubbiness of both the sport and its milieu. Gambling and the opportunities for corruption it offers are themes in Norman Jewison's *The Cincinnati Kid*, 1965, in which Steve McQueen plays a hot-shot poker player in the 1930s, and in Stephen Frears's *The Grifters*, 1979, which involves a horse race track scam.

A similar scam forms the nucleus of Stanley Kubrick's *The Killing*, 1956. In these films, the camera dwells on images of dollar bills, being bet, exchanged or, in *The Killing*, being swirled around, the black and white photography making them appear like leaves in a gale.

One of the most underrated attempts to uncloak the malignancy of contemporary sport is *Blue Chips*, a 1994 film by William Friedkin, in which an NCAA basketball coach played by Nick Nolte is pulled into offering money to secure college players. The movie's plot was uncomfortably similar to several real-life incidents involving illegal payments and points shaving. The film is an almost natural partner of the epic, 2 hour 50 minute documentary *Hoop Dreams*, 1994, in which directors Steve James, Fred Marx, and Peter Gilbert track the progress of two African American youths who aspire to be pro basketball players: they are but two of countless young black men who single-mindedly pursue what is for most only, as the title implies, a dream. The *in situ* scenes at the home of the aspirants make the viewer feel like an eavesdropper on a private conversation.

Often neglected is *The Club*, 1980, an Australian film directed by Bruce Beresford which tells of the travails of an Australian Rules football club owner who trades in a star player only to find his man has undergone a conversion and despises the competitive machismo of contemporary sports.

These are but a sample of the ways cinema has ripped away the sentimentality and honor traditionally associated with sports to disclose the grimmer, unethical aspects that are integral to professional sports. They find a kindred spirit in Armand Arman's dissection of football helmets, produced in 1972. Twenty-four helmets split in half are mounted on plexiglass. Gone is the sheen, the insignia and smooth curves that athletes are meant to wear with honor; instead, Arman presents a jumbled mess of dismembered metal, plastic, and rubber parts. By literally deconstructing the helmets, Arman is exposing the innards of American sports.

It is tempting to add the silkscreens of Andy Warhol to this myth-shattering tradition in sports art. In 1978, Warhol produced portraits of Muhammad Ali, Chris Evert, Pelé, O. J. Simpson and several other distinguished sports performers. The work has an ambiguity in the sense that each of the portraits is daubed over and modified, some might say defaced. Much of Warhol's work was intended to distort as a way of revealing hitherto unknown truths that lurk behind the images or façades we habitually confront. The Warhol symbols consecrate and condemn simultaneously.

Several films have used sports as metaphors for other areas of social life. There is a vital British tradition that starts with Lindsay Anderson's 1963 *This Sporting Life* set in the North of England, where Richard Harris's mud-spattered struggle on the rugby field parallels the rest of his life and, in many senses, that of the northern working class in the 1960s. In 1962's *The Loneliness of the Long Distance Runner*, directed by Tony Richardson, cross-country running is a simile for a young working-class offender's gutsy clamber out of a correctional facility. There is a resemblance between this and Robert Aldrich's 1974 film *The Longest Yard*, also known as *The Mean Machine* which features Burt Reynolds as a pro football player who winds up in prison and leads a team of inmates against a team of guards. In all three, images of sport are coarse and unpleasant. Anderson's film, like Aldrich's, makes great use of shots that are unavailable to the spectator: inside scrums and scrimmages, where players spit and trade sly punches.

A big part of our enchantment with sports is their ability to evoke extremes, and for every work of art that exposes dim and recondite areas there is at least another that illuminates the glorious, heroic, and even spiritually uplifting qualities of honest competition. The choice is vast, though some films all but select themselves.

The five *Rocky* films (the first and fifth directed by John G. Avildsen, 1976, 1990; the others by Sylvester Stallone, 1979, 1982, 1985) were collectively a saga of a down-at-heel fighter who is plucked from obscurity to challenge for the world heavyweight title. The fable follows Rocky Balboa, "The Italian Stallion" through his ascent, descent, and beyond. The fight action scenes are outrageously choreographed so that they have a comic book quality: ablaze with color and gravity-defying action, the fights that made the series so successful bore little resemblance to boxing. They are counterpointed by Rocky's delicate relationship with his lover and, later, wife. Boxing's dark corners are never fully explored and the film suggests that human courage and perserverance are the qualities needed to triumph. There are just deserts for those with the will to win; merit never goes unrewarded.

Rocky won the Academy Award for the Best Picture in 1976 and it is no accident that the Oscar winner of 1981 embodied similar ideals about the ethic of competition and the glory of victory. Hugh Hudson's *Chariots of Fire*, 1981, is set in the twilight of the British Empire and has little plot to speak of: it simply traces the build-up to the 1924 summer Olympics through the experiences of two real British track athletes. Harold Abrahams was a Jewish university student at Oxford. Eric Liddell was a Scottish working-class Christian who ran because he believed it was for the greater glory of god. In a sense, both were outsiders and the film rejoices in their achievements, employing slo-mo running sequences and a stirring Vangelis soundtrack to amplify all that is good about clean athletic competition. The famous scene of a joyous training group running along a beach, hair swept by the breeze, ocean waves lapping against their ankles, captures the wholesomeness of sport purveyed by *Chariots of Fire*.

If there is a painter whose work embodies the sentiments of these two films it is LeRoy Neiman. His work, particularly in the 1970s, was straightforward fast-moving narrative action. Neiman's characters seem to scorch the canvas: boxers' punches whiz toward their opponent, horses gallop almost into the viewer, tennis players throw themselves across the court. Compositions appear to occur so rapidly that there is no time for thought, less still criticism. Neiman's art is pure, glorious competitive energy.

Baseball films – and there have been dozens – typically gorge on narrative action. But not so Phil Alden's gently fantastic *Field of Dreams*, 1989. Hearing the mandate "if you build it they will come," farmer Kevin Costner clears a section of his plot in Iowa and constructs a baseball diamond. Sure enough, "they," the ghosts of great baseball players, appear from beyond the grave. Every frame is bathed in autumnal tones of greens and browns appropriate to a film that pines for a bygone age. Costner established himself in part through his sports roles. He also featured in two Ron Shelton films: *Bull Durham*, 1988, another baseball film, and *Tin Cup*, 1996, which was about golf. Other notable Shelton efforts include *White Men Can't Jump* and *Cobb*,

---

Ron Shelton

Born in Whittier, California, in 1945, Shelton is the world's premier director of films with sports themes. His *Bull Durham* (1988) featured Kevin Costner as an experienced baseball player coaching a promising young player (Tim Robbins) who is being seduced by Susan Sarandon. It was followed by *White Men Can't Jump* (1992) in which Wesley Snipes and Woody Harrelson play a couple of basketball hustlers plying their trade around parking lots. Returning to baseball, Shelton made *Cobb* (1994), a biopic of the irascible stand-out player of the period either side of the First World War, Ty Cobb, played by Tommy Lee Jones. *Tin Cup* (1996) centers on a golf pro, played by Costner, who enters the US Open, comes within a whisker of winning it, and blows it by refusing to play safe. Shelton focused on boxing in his *Play it to the Bone* (2000). He also wrote the underrated *Blue Chips* (1994) which tells of corruption in NCAA basketball, and co-wrote the tv movie *The Great White Hype* (1996), memorable for Samuel L. Jackson's portrayal of a Don King-type promoter. In Shelton's work, sports are more than the competitive activities that provide their material substance: they are opportunities for mere mortals to test themselves against mightier forces that challenge eternally, mock insufficiencies, but reward victory – and sometimes valiant defeat – with sublime deserts.

the latter of which used an interview between a writer and the old baseball player, Ty Cobb, as a framing device; the narrative proceeds in a series of flashbacks.

Sports have often supplied raw material for the subgenre of fantasy-comedy, the most influential of which was *Here Comes Mr Jordan*, 1941, directed by Alexander Hall and featuring Robert Montgomery as a boxer prematurely called to heaven due to a clerical error; returned to earth as an angel, the boxer seeks out his incredulous manager and seeks to resume his career. The plot was updated in 1978 and the boxer was replaced by a foot-ball player for Buck Henry's *Heaven Can Wait*, with Warren Beatty playing the deceased athlete. The cinematic conceit was to show the audience the returned player even though he was supposed to be invisible to the cast of the film. Much the same story was reprised again in 1997 with *The Sixth Man*, this time the departed-and-returned being a basketball player.

Slightly less whimsical were two comedies directed by David S. Ward, *Major League*, 1989, and *Major League II*, 1994, which followed the adventures of a baseball team of misfits who somehow contrived to win the occasional game. Another pair of baseball films were based on the real All American Girls' Professional Baseball League which was formed in 1943 to fill the void left by male baseball players who were involved in the war effort. Penny Marshall's *A League of Their Own*, 1992, led to a less successful sequel. The baseball sequences were colorful and exaggerated, lending the films their phantas-magorical quality.

Light comedy became outright farce in Harold Ramis's *Caddyshack*, 1980, Dennis Dugan's *Happy Gilmore*, 1996, and Frank Coraci's *The Water-boy*, 1999, all of which treated sports as a burlesque show. A similar playful mischief is evident in the work of pop artist Red Grooms. His *Fran Tarkenton*, 1979, is described by Louis A. Zona: "Grooms choose to create a 'schtick' right out of vaudeville, as the greatest quarterback of his time tiptoes through a flower patch in search of a receiver ... giving American pictorial art that sense of humor and humanity which has been missing" (1990: 122).

While Riefenstahl's *Olympia* had its ideological shortcomings, there was no doubt about its aesthetic triumph and it is still arguably the benchmark against which sports documentary features are measured. The previously-mentioned *Hoop Dreams* was acclaimed as one of the finest documentaries in recent times: young black males become beasts of burden, laden with their failed parents' vanquished ambitions, as they strive to make it in pro basket-ball. In Leon Gast's *When We Were Kings*, 1997, Muhammad Ali's upset win over George Foreman in 1974 is embellished in a way that enriches the viewer's appreciation of the wider issues surrounding the fight, which took place in Zaïre. Edited in such a way that observers of the fight function like a Greek chorus, the film intercuts footage of the boxers in training with clips of them in unguarded moments and scenes from the James Brown concert that preceded the boxing promotion.

Less inventive but still insightful was George Butler's *Pumping Iron II: The women*, 1984, which was a follow-up to the same director's 1976 *Pumping Iron* (which he made with Robert Fiore), but which is altogether more challenging, as it observed women competing in a ruthless yet sisterly way for the 1983 Caesar's Cup. The viewer seems to be secluded in hotel and locker rooms and made privy to personal conversations; the tight camera shots serve to convey competitor Bev Francis's torture and her trainer puts her through near-Procrustean schedules.

But, in terms of lineage, perhaps the rightful heir to *Olympia* is *Visions of Eight*, 1973, which brought together eight noted directors from around the world, each concentrating on a particular event or athlete at the Munich Olympics of 1972. Only John Schlesinger's segment incorporated the Palestinian terrorist hostage deaths into a sports story, this one about British marathon runner, Ron Hill. Other directors included Arthur Penn (of *Bonnie and Clyde* fame) who examined the pole vault, Mai Zetterling, who dwelt on weightlifting, and Kon Ichikawa, who scrutinized the men's 100-meter sprint. This sports documentary, like some others, shares many aims with the photography of Muybridge and his followers: by scrupulously attending to particularities the artist invites viewers to build their own vista. As in all art, it is the person attending to the work that is actually doing the work: making connections, filling in blanks, comprehending the meanings of the image. And so it has been with all art based on sport.

Were it not for our preoccupation with sports, then the art we have covered in this chapter would have less meaning, less value, and less significance culturally. The fact that the art I have referred to here is only a fraction of a much more formidable corpus of work bears witness to the seemingly perpetual interest in both sport and the art it has in some way inspired. Our fascination is not only with the activities themselves, but with the minute moments of a contest and the larger dynamics of the context in which it takes place. Art has enlarged our appreciation of both.

FURTHER READING

The Eternal Olympics: The art and history of sport, edited by Nicolaos Yaloris (Caratzas Brothers, 1979) alerts us to the vital importance of athletic competition to the culture and civic life of ancient civilizations by examining the evolution of sports and sports-related art from the second millennium BCE to the end of the ancient Olympic Games in AD 510.

Sport and the Countryside by David Coombs (Phaidon Press, 1978) concentrates on the period from the seventeenth century to the middle of the nineteenth, when hunting was virtually synonymous with "sports" and supplied the inspiration for a great many artists, especially painters. This may profitably be read in conjunction with *Game and the English Landscape: The influence of the chase on sporting art and scenery* by Anthony Vandervell and Charles Coles (Debrett's Peerage, 1980).

Sports: A cultural history in the mirror of art by Peter Kühnst (Verlag de Kühnst, 1996) is a marvelous narrative exposition of the story of sports from the Renaissance onwards as told through art. "The artist's vision is a unique clue to historical change," argues Kühnst.

Sport in Art from American Museums, edited by Reilly Rhodes (Universe, 1990), reproduces exhibits from the National Art Museum of Sport, Indianapolis; most of the art is from the nineteenth and twentieth centuries and includes the work of Stubbs, Eakins, and Bellows.

Sport on Film and Video: The North American Society for Sport History guide, edited by Judith Davidson and compiled by Daryl Adler (Scarecrow Press, 1993) is one of a number of reference books on the subject; others include *Sports in the Movies* by Ronald Bergan (Proteus Books, 1982) and *Sports Films: A complete reference* by Harvey M. Zucker and Lawrence J. Babich (HM&M Publishers, 1976); there is an entry on "Films" in my own *Sports Culture: An A–Z* (Routledge, 2000).

ASSIGNMENT

As the curator of a museum, you are charged with the responsibility of organizing an exhibition *Sports: From 1950 to the present*. You may commission glass displays of artifacts, waxwork models, performance art, and other forms of contemporary art (*à la* Damien Hirst, Tracey Emin, or Gillian Wearing), as well as more traditional art forms. Imagine three newly-commissioned works you would include; and select three existing works that you would include. Then write an account justifying the inclusion of your pieces.

Chapter twelve

a match made in heaven

why television and sports are inseparable

SUPER BOWL XXXIV

It is 2010 and you are a sports fan, the kind that used to be called "an armchair fan" but, of course, now, the fans who actually go to games are in a tiny minority. There is so much more to enjoy on the screen. Today is a huge day: World Super Bowl Sunday. This year the rival teams are Tokyo Samurai, appearing in their first Super Bowl, and the Las Vegas Fortune. Vegas is going for its second championship this century, having won three years ago under their old name Las Vegas Buccaneers. The old Tampa Bay Buccaneers owner sold out in 2006 and the new owners, a consortium in which News Corp. has a 36 per cent stake, moved the franchise to Nevada. Now, the city of Tampa has been promised an expansion team and has been granted permission to reclaim its original name. So, the Vegas outfit changed to the Fortune – quite an appropriate name in several ways, including the investment that went into building the franchise and an 85,000-seater stadium which has 70 per cent of its capacity taken up by luxury boxes. Still, the investment has paid off handsomely and the club has been estimated as worth $2.6 billion – almost as much as the super-rich Italian soccer club Juventus.

273

The NFL is much bigger than it was ten years ago. In 2007, it decided to globalize the game by setting up franchises all over the world. The abortive World League and its unsuccessful offspring NFL Europe were never more than job-creation packages for players who did not quite make the cut with the NFL. But today's operation has the backing of several big media interest groups and the television audience around the world is guaranteed.

You will watch the game on your 4 × 3-foot screen, which is actually a portable panel that you can move from room to room as the mood takes you. It is light enough to hang on the wall like a painting and about as thin. Nobody has those old-style television sets, now. All you need is a screen and a receiving box, which is as big as one of those palm-size organizers that became popular at the end of the twentieth century. It has a touch-screen and runs the latest edition of Windows CE. Naturally, it is capable of interacting with your media phone, which is also a pager that takes word messages on an alphanumeric display and receives news and sports updates; and alerts you when you have new email; you wear it on your wrist like a watch; it also tells you the time, of course.

Years ago, television superseded the pc as the main access point for internet-related services. You access the game from the internet, much like radio listeners used to tune into the station of their choice. Media groups own rights to broadcast action from professional sports teams. This is quite a change from the days when the terrestrial networks used to control the broadcasting rights; the Super Bowl used to rotate around the networks. But the pay tv market seemed to present the major challenge to the media: how to exploit it to the fullest degree? Pay per view had never quite realized its potential through cable or satellite; but the opening up of digital television and DIRECTV in the 1990s offered clues for the future. Deal after deal, many of them involving European broadcasting corporations – Deutsche Telecom, Canal Plus, Telecom Italia, and others – produced a *mille-feuille* of business alliances, some permanent, others temporary. The name of the game is to control the broadcasting rights of events, or individual teams, and then sell straight to the consumer via the internet.

The FCC and the broadcasting governing organizations of other countries around the world were predictably against this development: they were powerless to prevent the media conglomerates broadcasting wherever they wanted. Even now, governments are busy trying to formulate laws that will stop games like today's being sent around the world on the internet rather than on conventional tv. Universal distribution used to be the central aim of media organizations, like Time Warner and Disney; but the scramble in recent years has been for control of content. Once you have a product that people want to see and the network through which they can access it, you have a colossal market. Your operator is UMC (United Micro-Cable), which has its origins in a deal between Microsoft and AT&T in 1999.

Today's game will cost you $150. Of course, this is a special event; packages for regular season games are less expensive. If you had the money you could watch every single game in the NFL season (there are now 22 games per team in the regular season and four rounds of playoffs). Because the internet is global, you can access practically any sporting event in the world. Of course, you have to pay for each event; the days when you could get sports free-to-air have long since disappeared.

The British terrestrial networks had dropped most sports by 1999. By 2004, the only events that had not been scooped up by either satellite, cable, or digital pay tv were so minor that advertisers lost interest and the networks decided to concentrate on drama, news, and quiz shows. In the States, Fox steadily upped its stake in the NFL and the other main leagues, at the same time buying into local stations and sports clubs themselves. Fans were weaned off the idea of getting sports for free. It's amusing to talk to your parents sometimes when they reminisce about the old days when they were able to watch sports for nothing. They were probably amused by their parents who could remember the days when there was no tv at all. Now attendances have slipped right down: who wants to brave the elements when you can see more games, from more angles, with informed commentary and analysis in the comfort of your own home?

Today, you will have a choice of commentators, a variety of cameras, some of them actually on the players – fixed into their helmets. Soccer fans love the camera that referees have in their caps; the refs resisted wearing headgear to begin with, but the tv companies insisted. Fans can see the action from the perspective of whoever they choose. Baseball catchers and wicket keepers included. But the camera they built into the hockey puck was a total flop: it made the viewer giddy. As you watch, you can order changes on your voice-activated remote control. For example, you say "reverse angle" or "slo-mo" and you can change the image. Or you might say "tighten" or "widen" and this lets you get either a close-up shot or a panoramic vista. And it takes about 1.5 seconds to change. Just think how long it used to take to download something as simple as a screensaver from the internet.

Is this how we will be watching televised sports in the near future? Technologically, everything in the scenario is already possible; the hard part is in persuading the consumers to part with more of their hard-earned cash. NBC thought it could do it back in 1992 and got its fingers burnt. It offered 24-hour coverage of the summer Olympic Games from Barcelona to those prepared to pay $125 (£78) for a 15-day package, or $19.95 (£12.50) for a single day at a time. The meager number of viewers and the resulting losses did not inspire confidence. But, it was all part of a steady process of gently breaking a habit that television audiences had got used to over the previous four decades, that of getting televised sports for nothing.

If ever there was a marriage made in heaven it was between television and sports. The commercial success of each was almost directly attributable to the other. From the 1940s to the present, sports have grown in proportion to tv. Not only have they grown in scale and popularity, but they have become modified into virtual theater. And television's efforts at dragging sports toward the popular entertainment end of the market have paid off in terms of record-breaking viewing ratings. High-profile sports events draw audiences comparable with televisual phenomena, like the coming-out episode of *Ellen*, the moon landing, or the funeral of Princess Diana.

In this chapter I am going to investigate the origins and development of what became an unexpectedly prosperous liaison. Both television and sports have grown rich and influential as a result of their partnership; in the process, they have transformed each other, television validating its place as the premier communications channel, sports mutating into an entertainment medium on par with showbusiness. The beginnings of this alliance lie in the 1950s, but its sources go back further; to the early nineteenth century, in fact.

LET THERE BE TELEVISION

Founded in 1822, the British news-sheet *Bell's Life in London* found its circulation rising as it included sports reports. Sports were hardly news, at least not in the hardest sense of the word, but reports of them had the desired effect and sales continued to rise. The paper held a monopoly until 1865 when *The Sporting Life* issued what was to be a potent challenge. The success of *The Sporting Life* with its quick and detailed reporting and varied advertising prompted other publications to dedicate sections to sports coverage. The North American equivalent of *The Sporting Life* was *The American Farmer* which first appeared in 1819 and was followed by many others, including *The Spirit of the Times*, founded in 1831.

Newspaper proprietors were interested in selling their publications and sports did the trick; but the coverage also primed interest in sports and, as Tony Mason points out: "It was the press who first elevated a minority of sportsmen and women into national celebrities, whose names and faces were recognized by people uninterested in sport; performers whose mere presence on the pitch would tempt people to the event; the exceptional performer" (1988: 50). Here lay the sources of what we now call the sports icon, whose fame relies as much on the mass media as on athletic performance.

There was a clear symmetry of interests between those with an interest in exploiting the mass spectatorship potential of sports and those who could sell newspapers with stories about sports. Reporting in the press had the useful consequence of raising public awareness, so enlarging the mass spectator market. Newspapers' value to sports was undoubted, but there was uncertainty about radio, which came to the fore in the 1920s, when a warrantable mass spectatorship for sports was emerging.

Radio could relay information on any event, but any advantage it held in terms of boosting interest was outweighed by its immediacy: instead of attending an actual event, fans may have opted for listening to "live" commentary on the radio. Radio's capacity to excite was enhanced by the social atmosphere it generated, listeners huddled together whooping and yelling as the commentator's voice crackled through the airwaves.

Despite possible drawbacks, radio had one big plus factor: it paid, sometimes quite well. For instance, in 1935, the radio rights to the Joe Louis–Max Baer world heavyweight fight were a record $27,500 (then about £9,000). Fears that radio commentary would hurt the gate were unfounded as 88,000 spectators attended the event. By this time, radio coverage of sports was commonplace and, as this involved issues of proprietorship and copyright, it gave rise to an economic relationship between the mass media and sports organizers. Newspapers did not pay to cover events because they were regarded as good publicity. Radio's effect was more ambiguous: it may well pump up interest, but it could also keep people away; so it was asked to stump up money.

Radio still saw a profit in sports: it existed to make money and could attract large listening audiences for its sports programs. This meant that advertisers and sponsors were tempted to pay more to have their products associated with the event and so reach a large potential market. Sponsors of radio shows were among the first commercial companies to realize the financial benefits of linking their commodities with sports. We see evidence of this link all around us every day. But, of course, radio has been eclipsed by television.

Filmed news of sports events occupied a segment of newsreels shown in movie theaters even before radio transmissions, but the films were at least a week after the event and could not compare with the thrill of a "live" radio broadcast. In the USA, a 1912 ban on showing fight films was relaxed in 1939 when the Senate passed a bill to permit the transfer of boxing films from state-to-state. But, by this time, a new medium had crept into the homes of a select few. In 1937, a few hundred Londoners were the first to see the first outside broadcast coverage of British sport, when 25 minutes of a men's singles match was televised from Wimbledon. It was strictly an experimental service from the BBC which had improved on an earlier, unsatisfactory, attempt by CBS to broadcast a fight by "sight and sound."

The main technical shortcoming of televising events was that cameras were fixed and were fitted with lenses that made the performers appear as tiny figures. Boxing, whose action takes part in a small, finite territory seemed reasonably suitable for the new medium and, in 1939, the BBC and NBC both broadcast fights, the BBC being fortunate enough to capture the British light-weight title fight between Eric Boon and Arthur Danahar, which is regarded as amongst the best-ever fights on British soil. In the same year, the BBC, still in its infancy, showed its first FA Cup Final and the NBC telecast baseball, at first with one camera and, later, with two, which was a significant innovation as it permitted close-ups not even visible to audiences watching the game live.

Television was still only a futuristic luxury of the rich, with just 5,000 sets being sold in the USA in 1946. Within ten dramatic years, 75 per cent of the country's households had a set. John Goldlust, in his book on sport and the media *Playing for Keeps: Sport, the media and society*, argues that "The significance of sports for this phenomenal rate of penetration should not be underestimated" and that the televising of major sports events was "a key element in launching the television industry" (1988: 8).

Goldlust cites the transmission of the Melbourne Olympics in 1956 as a key event that greatly assisted the sale of television receivers. After this, the television industry of continental Europe and Latin America developed within the framework of either the BBC, which considered the televising of sport one of its statutory obligations in order to provide as many aspects as possible of the "national culture," or the American companies, which geared their schedules so as to maximize demand from advertisers. If manufacturers had products to sell and wanted exposure for their products, then placing commercials in the "natural breaks" of a high-profile event was rational and effective.

Even with a minute fraction of its potential audience, televised sports were attractive: as early as 1947, Ford and Gillette paid $65,000 (then about £20,000) for the rights to sponsor baseball's World Series on television, despite the fact that less than 12 per cent of US households could receive it. Sports themselves were wary of tv, thinking its impact could only be detrimental. As if to illustrate the point, between 1948 and 1956, the Cleveland Indians baseball team won a World Series and a pennant, yet suffered a 67 per cent drop in attendance. The Boston Braves' crowds plunged by 81 per cent following their National League victory in 1948, immediately after which they signed a tv deal for the next three years. The situation needed drastic remedial action, so the owner Lou Perini moved the franchise to Milwaukee and banned television cameras, apart from the World Series winning games of 1957 and 1958.

The gates stayed healthy, prompting Perini to announce smugly: 'We have come to believe that tv can saturate the minds of the fans with baseball. We would very much like to guard against this." Perini relaxed his strictures after 1962 and eventually sold out to a group which wholeheartedly embraced television by relocating the club in Atlanta where a tv–radio guarantee of $1.25 million (then over £600,000) per year awaited.

Another sport whose gates were hit severely was college football. Between 1949 and 1953, attendance declined by almost 3 million. The National Collegiate Athletic Association (NCAA) formed a special television committee and instituted rigid rules for limiting the number of telecasts. Even then, it took ten years before gates rose to their 1949 levels.

Television feasted on boxing, which it left as a carcass in 1964 after 18 years of the kind of saturation Perini had feared for baseball. In some areas of the States, boxing was on every night of the week, with promoters eagerly accepting television monies to augment profits. Gradually, the tv fees became the profits: live audiences dwindled. As tv was interested only in "name" fighters, the bigger promoters who had the champions under contract were able to capitalize, while the smaller promoters went to the wall. In the period 1952–9 alone, 250 of the country's 300 small boxing clubs shut down. At the height of its power in 1955, boxing was watched by 8.5 million homes, about one-third of the available viewing audience in those days. By 1959, boxing commanded only 10.6 per cent – which sounds much more impressive now than it did then when the market was uncluttered by cable channels. NBC was the first to cut boxing from its schedules in 1960.

The other networks followed suit. Both the sport and the medium had merely obeyed the logic of the market. Yet the signs were clear: many sports were being tempted by a cozy and highly profitable relationship; but, in doing so, they were exposing themselves completely to television and risking becoming totally and possibly ruinously dependent on the networks.

Apart from boxing, North American television's sporting energy in the 1950s came from wrestling and roller derby. From a production viewpoint, these were perfect sports for the technically naïve tv companies of the day, CBS and NBC. All that was needed was a fixed orthicon camera trained on a small finite area of action, insulated from natural weather conditions. The two networks enjoyed a relatively peaceful co-existence, carving up the major sporting events between them. ABC's entrance changed all that. Not having access to the big sports, ABC decided to feature minority sports and activities that were barely sports at all and treat them in such dramatic ways that even those with no interest in sports would be converted.

Rodeos, demolition derbies, and even the bizarre fireman's bucket-filling championships were all fair game for ABC's cameras, which would not just document what happened but would take the viewer to where it happened. Cameras would venture to the tops of cliffs, peer over the edge, then draw back to view a diver hurtling into the seas below, where another camera joined him or her in the water. Sports were drama. Inspired by the iconoclastic philosophies of Roone Arledge, ABC vandalized the established traditions and made an overt appeal to younger audiences who were not bound by the fidelities of their parents. Women viewers were wooed, as they were demographically attractive to advertisers: research showed that women make decisions about household purchases.

Roone Arledge

As ABC television's producer of network sports, Forest Hills-born Arledge mapped out a direction for television in the 1960s and, at the same time, established his tv network as a rival to the USA's then duopoly, comprising CBS and NBC. Instead of following sports events, Arledge believed television should take the initiative. Rather than accepting that sporting occasions had a "natural" appeal that should be reflected in television coverage, Arledge created interest across the widest possible range of the population. He recognized no barriers set by class, gender, or age. His premise was much the same as that of the advertisers on whose patronage ABC ultimately depended: if the demand is not there to begin with, build it. The way Arledge built his was by taking obscure sports and adding something to them, something that only television could provide. Among Arledge's ideas were the weekly Wide World of Sports and Monday Night Football, both of which were instrumental in drawing the hitherto neglected female sports fan to television screens.

ABC's approach was unashamedly populist, projecting personalities, highlighting unusual characteristics about them and reducing almost any competitive activity to its most basic elements. Frog-jumping contests were not out of place in ABC's sports panoply. Gillette, one of television's biggest sports sponsors, hooked up with ABC on a Friday night boxing series and, encouraged by the response, fed in more money, which enabled ABC to capture NCAA football in the 1960–1 season. This was the first of many coups, the biggest being the American Football League (AFL), a second-rate rival to the NFL, but one which, given the ABC treatment, rose in popularity. So much so that, in 1966, the two merged to produce the NFL as we know it today.

One significant innovation in the AFL–ABC deal was the pooling of broadcast rights. By dealing with television as a league, the AFL eliminated the kind of interclub competition that arose when selling local broadcast rights of individual clubs. In his book *The Market Structure of Sports*, Gerald Scully suggests: "One could argue that the survival of the AFL as a league was made possible by access to national television, which helped financially in its own right and brought recognition and fan interest" (1995: 27). Another innovation of the period was the introduction of the television time-out in 1958. This allowed stoppages specifically for tv companies to screen commercials.

In the same year as the NFL–AFL merger, BBC television in Britain screened soccer's World Cup staged in England. It was a prestigious tournament and the BBC beamed its pictures all over the world. It was at this event that the advantage of the camera over the naked eye was fully appreciated. In the championship game, the English team's third goal arrived gift-wrapped for television. The ball thundered against the underside of the West German team's crossbar, appearing momentarily to bounce over the goal line before rebounding into the field of play. If the whole ball had crossed (not just broken as in American football) the plane of the goal line, then it was a goal. The referee said "yes," the Germans said "no." The cameras slowed down the action, freeze-framed it, reversed the angle; and it could still not prove conclusively whether or not the ball had crossed the line. The arguments raged and the footage rolled and rolled.

CONTROLLING THE CONSUMER

Unlike early British television which was once intended to become a "theater of the airwaves," American television has always been a business, like any other: whether they derive income from sponsorship or advertising, from cable subscriptions, from production or from station ownership, for-profit corporations have always dominated the industry in the USA. During its formative years, tv followed the successful formula of radio stations, selling space in its programs to advertisers. Ford, General Electric, Singer, and other giants of the expanding industries of peacetime seized the chance of reaching a genuinely mass market of potential consumers.

British television orginally took a superior attitude, attracting funding not through advertising, but through licenses, which viewers were obliged to buy in order to receive tv signals legally. BBC television even today resolutely refuses to screen commercials, although its rivals operate on much the same lines as their American counterparts. The idea is simple: offer to deliver to advertisers an audience of several million consumers, many of whom will be influenced enough by the "commercial messages" (as they were once politely called) to spend their money on the advertised product, whether it be a soap, a car, a chocolate bar, or whatever. Advertisers pay their money to the tv company, which in turn pays the cost of the production and distribution of its programs. The difference is, of course, what keeps the tv company in business.

Subscription television

Unlike terrestrial television and basic cable, subscription television operates on the principle that viewers will pay extra monthly fees for the privilege of watching movies and events that are unavailable on other tv stations. Home Box Office (HBO) is the leading subscription service in the world. It was founded in November 1972 when it broadcast a hockey game from Madison Square Garden, New York, to 365 subscribers. It now has more than 16 million subscribers across 50 American states and screens 24 hours a day (this is still a relatively small number compared to terrestrial network tv which reaches 90.4 million viewers). Beside being a major screener of international sports events, it has become actively involved in the promotion of events, particularly world title fights. In France, Canal Plus fulfills a similar function. In Britain, BSkyB is the foremost subscription channel.

While viewers are sometimes referred to as the customers of the television companies, the real customers are the advertising agencies who handle the affairs of product manufacturers and do business with the networks. Customers are actually part of the deal: the tv companies are selling several million sets of eyeballs trained on the screen. If they can include programs that command the attentions of several dozen million viewers, then they can raise the price of advertising slots. If the program draws only small viewing audiences, then advertisers are less inclined to part with serious money.

A complicating factor in this concerns demographics: some television shows attract high audience ratings (the measurement of viewers), but not of the right type. In the 1950s, when television was building its following, content did not discriminate too much between audiences; advertisers were eager to have their messages seen by as many potential customers as possible. As market research techniques developed, it became possible to identify which segments of the market watched which programs. General Foods, for example, may wish to target young people with a new cereal; advertising in slots during a show that draws an audience typically aged between 55 and 70 would not be logical. Instead, GF would analyze what kind of programs are watched by their target consumers. So, healthy viewing figures are no guarantee of success: advertisers may opt for smaller audiences of the right type. All of which brings us to sports.

"Sports programming is extremely valued by the television networks," writes Scully. "The demographic profile of viewers is attractive to a certain class of advertisers, whose willingness to pay some of the highest advertising fees in the industry has propelled the growth of network television revenues to the leagues" (1995: 28). It is no accident that early sponsors of television and radio sports programs were manufacturers of shaving products and brewers. Followers of sport were predominantly male and working class. Sports audiences are now more variegated, but the essential point remains: they are likely consumers for a range of goods and services.

Some events draw spectacularly huge viewing audiences. For instance, 175 million households regularly watch at least some part of the Super Bowl. This allows the television company to charge about $1.5 million per 30-second advertising slot, anticipating 56 units that yield a total of $84 million, a figure reduced to $74 million after advertising agency commissions. The ads reach a lot of people, but can they be worth $3 million per minute? An answer of sorts comes from Macintosh, which, in 1989, launched its new computer with a series of spots during the Super Bowl.

The following day, $3.5 million-worth of said computer went over the counter and the sales figure grew to $155 million over the next 90 days. This is impressive, though Jib Fowles does not totally buy it. In his *Advertising and Popular Culture*, Fowles is skeptical about the supposed power of tv ads (1996). He quotes another Super Bowl commercial, this time from 1991. A healthy 70 per cent of the television audience recognized that Joe Montana had appeared in the commercial, but only 18 per cent remembered what the ad was for. It was Diet Pepsi. (See also Rick Burton's "Sports advertising and the Super Bowl," 1999.)

The jury may still be out on the power of tv advertising to influence our shopping behavior, but advertisers and tv execs alike seem convinced that commercials shown during sports events move goods off shelves. This means that, from television's point of view, the fan is a resource; an article used in a trade with advertisers. So, for example, an ABC executive in negotiation with an advertising agent is not going to discuss Ryan Leaf's fabulous 40-yard touchdown pass in last Monday night's game; more likely the conversation will converge on how many people watched it, what were their class backgrounds, sex composition, ages, ethnic identities, incomes, and zip codes? It is as if television companies sell the fans to the advertisers.

No one has understood this better than Rupert Murdoch, whose operations are more fully covered in Chapter thirteen. In 1992, he carved open what had previously been a relatively cozy rivalry between BBC television and Independent Television (ITV – the commercial terrestrial network of British stations). Eager to sell subscriptions to his BSkyB cable/satellite network, Murdoch negotiated a £304 million ($575 million) deal for exclusive "live" coverage of English Premiership soccer. The BBC had to settle for tape-delay highlights, while ITV got nothing.

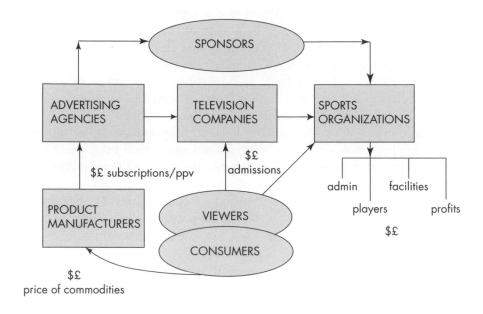

how we pay for televised sports

In the States, legislation prevents collusive arrangements between the leagues and television. Most leagues distribute their product among various television companies. For example, the NFL allocates its games to the major networks and one or two cable companies and draws revenues from Fox, CBS, and Disney totaling $17.6 billion (£10.75 billion). The National Hockey League is unusual in that it signed an exclusive $600 million deal with Disney. This is the type of arrangement the English Football Association favored.

The English soccer contract was one of several seemingly extravagant contracts between television and sports leagues in the 1990s. Major League Baseball negotiated several contracts worth a total of $1.587 billion (just under £1 billion) in 1996; the NBA's 1998 deal with NBC was worth $1.75 billion over four years. And, by the time the FA deal came up for renewal in 1996, the stakes were pushed up to £670 million ($1.1 billion) over the next four years. Scully observes the value of broadcasting rights: "A fourteenfold increase in baseball, a sixteenfold increase in football, and a seventeenfold increase in basketball since the mid-1970s" (1995: 3). This tells us something about how much the tv companies holding the contracts expected to earn from advertising or subscriptions. But expectations do not always square with reality.

The soccer deal worked well for BSkyB: subscriptions soared immediately, then levelled off at about 7 million, or about 8.5 per cent of the population.

Major advertisers like Ford and Carling beer sponsored segments of the soccer coverage. On the other hand, the Murdoch-owned Fox dropped $350 million on its first four-year contract. NBC lost $40 million in the games leading to the Super Bowl in the 1992/3 season and emerged with a profit of between $6 and $10 million derived from spots during the 150 minutes of pre- and post-game analysis plus commercial fees from NBC-owned stations. Few sports events can have the potential to gross $46 million (£65 million) and counting in three hours; but, the Super Bowl has become, as *New York Times* writer Richard Sandomir puts it, "like a luscious *crème brûlée* after a long dyspeptic dinner" (January 26, 1993). Take away the dessert and all you have left is the kind of bellyache that may make certain sports less attractive.

CBS whined about the kind of money demanded by the leagues when reflecting on its estimated loss of $450 million (over £280 million) over the period of its early 1990s contract with Major League Baseball. There are doubters, one of them being Andrew Zimbalist, author of *Baseball and Billions*, who writes: "The [CBS] network's sudden diffidence might arouse some suspicion about whether it is engaging in a public relations game in a bid for smaller contracts the next time round" (1992: 160).

In 1993, with baseball's popularity waning and CBS licking its wounds, rival networks ABC and NBC actually joined forces to reach an agreement with Major League Baseball. For the first time, the league did not receive an up-front tv rights payment, but entered into a package venture with the television companies for administering, marketing, and selling the sport. The following years, disaster struck when the baseball players went on strike and the World Series was aborted. Zimbalist, like Scully, predicts that a prudent sports executive should not expect as much television revenue in the future.

Yet Fox's deals seemed to defy commercial wisdom. It paid MLB a total of $747 million to show its games on its network and cables. It also lashed out $4.4 billion on the National Football League's NFC Eastern division which includes the Dallas, Washington, and New York Giants franchises, despite its losses on the previous deal; this represented a hike of around 30 per cent over the contract Fox signed with the NFL in 1993. There were other huge deals in the late 1990s. In 1998, CBS doubled what NBC had previously paid (on annual average) for the AFC's television rights. The prices the NFL charged ABC and ESPN (both Disney-owned) for Monday Night Football and the Sunday game respectively was three times more than their annual payments under the previous 1993 agreements. Cablevision paid New York Nicks $486 million over 12 years. Despite the familiar grumbles from tv companies that sports are pricing themselves out of the market, there always seems at least one network prepared to cough up.

Advertising revenues remain attractive: there are few safer bets than sports when it comes to pulling in viewers. Even shows like *ER* and *Friends*

ESPN

The all-sports cable tv channel was the creation of Bill Rasmussen, who, in the 1970s, dreamt up an original idea for a regional network of radio stations to broadcast the University of Massachusetts' football games. Cable broadcasting was then in its infancy and Rasmussen was able to buy time on a communications satellite (transponder) inexpensively. He filled the time with small-scale sports commentary, interviews, and analysis. The Entertainment Sports Programming Network operated out of Plainville, Connecticut, and gained permission from the FCC (Federal Communications Commission) to begin broadcasting in September 1979.

Getty Oil sensed the potential of the enterprise and invested heavily; in fact, it assumed effective control and sold out to Texaco, which, in turn, sold out to ABC television. ABC's interest transformed ESPN from a local operation to a national network, reaching 34 million homes by 1984. This was the year David Stern became the NBA commissioner and Michael Jordan made his debut for Chicago Bulls. ESPN had held a contract with the NBA for the previous two years and had shown NCAA games from the start in 1979 – which had the effect of familiarizing tv fans with the players before the transfer to the pro game.

Perhaps inadvertently, ESPN had hitched its wagon to the NBA star, which went into orbit over the next several years. By 1998, ESPN was taken by about 70 per cent of all US television-owning households; of the total televised sports, ESPN carried 23 per cent. In addition, the network's reach extended to 160 different countries around the world; it provided services in 19 languages. In 1996, it set up a second ESPN channel specializing in news items; and, to complement its extensive tv coverage, started ESPN Radio. It is now owned by Disney.

---

lost popularity over time. But, sports are fairly consistent. Fox and BSkyB's motives in paying over the odds were transparent. As marginal players alongside the established giants of the tv industry, they wanted to position themselves more centrally and major sports coverage was an instrument designed to do exactly that. Fox lost money, but it gained an awful lot of prestige. BSkyB won subscribers and a reputation as the leading sports channel in Europe.

CBS's willingness to absorb losses of $450 million on its baseball contract was thought to be based on the assumption that it could use the World Series

> ## Monday Night Football
>
> This has become something of an institution since its inception in the 1970s. ABC's innovation was an attempt to broaden the appeal of football by incorporating elements of drama and popular entertainment into its coverage. Unusual camera angles, personality close-ups, half-time interviews: these were all used to distinguish ABC's football from that of the other networks. It quickly commanded a one-third share of the viewing audience. ABC paid the NFL $8.5 million per year for 13 games and claimed this back by charging advertisers $65,000 per minute during the game. By the end of 1979, it was regularly the eighth most watched program in the USA, enabling ABC to charge $110,000 for a 30-second commercial slot. A British soccer version of this was inaugurated in the 1990s after BSkyB's link with the Football Association.

to include October promotions for its prime-time shows in the crucial fall (autumn) schedule from which ratings are extrapolated. CBS effectively wanted to use sports as a means of generating interest in future programs – from both advertisers and audiences. Not that the leagues themselves care about the motives. Television deals mean that each team can start the season with an assured amount (e.g. $12 million for each MLB club; £10 million for each Premiership club) before a season ticket has been sold. On the other hand, some deals are just flat-out miscalculations. For example, the subscription channel Showtime dropped $8 million when it showed the Evander Holyfield–Michael Moorer fight in November, 1997.

Sports were once cheap production numbers that drew viewers to their screens in millions. Those days have gone. While negotiating various deals with television, major sports governing organizations must have been taking notes. They quickly learnt that the same principles that applied to marketing beer or shaving foam, also applied to sports. Marketing, as Mark Gottdiener states, "has gone from a rather straightforward affair involving the *distribution* of goods to potential customers that existed as a generic mass, otherwise known as 'sales,' to a knowledge-based, purposeful effort at controlling consumer buying" (1997: 70).

From the 1980s, sports began marketing themselves, turning themselves into commodities; not commodities with use-values, but ones with symbolic values. Consumers were sold images they could blend with their personal histories or their identities: sports became a means of self-expression, a statement of lifestyle. While Gottdiener does not refer to sports, his observations about how consumers pursue particular kinds of lifestyles through their consumption patterns has an obvious application. The NBA, more than any other sport, used television not only to re-brand itself, but to offer its followers a lifestyle option. Other sports on both sides of the Atlantic followed suit.

Licensed baseball caps became ubiquitous, replica shirts became staples of leisure wear, endorsed products became mandatory for clued-up youth. It seemed almost serendipity when Nike came on the scene at exactly the right time in history; but, as we will see in Chapter fourteen, the sports goods firm was actually a factor in the whole process through which sports became commodities. None of this was possible without the exposure provided by television. Sports used the same techniques as car makers, soft-drink manu-facturers, and computer companies, attempting to manipulate consumer "needs," using art and design to create agreeable images and packaging their products to make them appealing. Today, it is virtually impossible to find a major sport that does not have a logo.

The evidence of many sports' marketing successes is abundant in the form of players' status and salaries, colossally expensive stadia, and stock exchange listings (for some British clubs), not forgetting the high-priced tv deals. None of this would have been possible without television. Conversely, television may not have become the force of nurture it is without sports. Yet, there has been a price of sorts.

MADE FOR TELEVISION

In 1976, Kerry Packer, the head of an Australian television company, offered the Australian Cricket Board (ACB) a deal for the exclusive rights to screen Australian cricket for five years. The offer was refused. Determined to press ahead and feature cricket on his tv channel, known as Nine, Packer signed up 35 international class players and organized his own "rebel" tournament. Few sports respects their own history as much as cricket: it is one of the oldest and most traditional games and, for most of its existence, worked carefully to retain links with its past.

Packer was a television man; he knew what drew audiences. Horrified traditionalists watched as Packer dressed his players in brightly-colored uniforms, scheduled evening games under floodlights and introduced yellow cricket balls. He used eight cameras, some trained on players' faces, and several microphones strategically positioned to pick up the players' often blasphemous comments. The games were played in a single day, using limited overs, its format being, as John Goldlust puts it, "unabashedly spectator oriented, geared towards providing entertainment, tight finishes, big hitting and aggressive play . . . ideally suited for television" (1988: 163).

The cricket Packer promoted was barely recognizable as the age-old pursuit of English gentlemen, but television fans watched it. After a nervous first season, viewing figures and attendances both rose, enabling Nine to attract more advertisers. Established governing organizations, like England's MCC, opposed the wanton commercialism, but eventually capitulated in the face of the tournament's rising popularity. In 1979, Packer's marketing subsidiary secured a ten-year contract to organize the sponsorship of official cricket. Packer's attempt to capture exclusive broadcasting rights succeeded and, by the mid-1980s, he had virtually taken control of Australian cricket.

Crowds continued to flock to the stadia and, more importantly for Packer, tv audience ratings stayed healthy. The players earned more money, the governing organizations took substantial fees for broadcasting rights and the Nine network increased its advertising revenue by selling more commercial time during the ordinarily quiet summer months. Those who still thought cricket should be played with a straight bat and a stiff upper lip were offended by the changes Packer had instigated, but there was no going back.

Packer acted as a catalyst, instigating changes that were to transform cricket from a sport that might be described as television-hostile (played over five days, often at a ponderous pace) to a shorter and frequently explosive game that provided nail biting finishes. One-day cricket did not replace the more conventional format: it co-existed with it. By the end of the century World Cup cricket was a well-established part of cricket's calendar. It was played over a day, with a white ball, with players dressed in various colors and was watched by television viewers all over the world.

The Packer case gave early evidence of how television could change a sport radically. Cricket was a game that had remained largely unchanged since the formation of the MCC in 1787. Yet it could not resist the challenge of a tv magnate bent on fashioning the sport to his own requirements. Rugby League struck a television deal in 1996, the terms of which obliged the sport to dismantle a 100-year structure and switch to a summer schedule to comply with Rupert Murdoch's plans for a Rugby Super League. The new league was to include European and Australasian teams and culminate in play-offs that could be broadcast around the globe by Murdoch's many media networks. Rugby League agreed, underlining how commercial considerations can supersede those intrinsic to the sport itself.

Murdoch, whose impact on sports will be covered in the next chapter, was decried for instigating this historical change, though he was not the first media magnate to have pushed through changes in sports schedules simply to accommodate television's demands. The length of the NFL season was extended from 1990 after the signing of a $3.6 billion (£2.25 billion) contract. The reasoning behind it is spelled out by Jerry Gorman and Kirk Calhoun in their *The Name of the Game: The business of sports*: "The plan for extension was to sell more advertising over a longer period, that space filled not by more games but by more televised games" (1994: 242).

The additional games, which were broadcast by the ESPN and TNT channels (both featured in the next chapter), earned the NFL about $900 million. In the same year, the play-off format was changed to accommodate ABC television. The net effect was to double the tv network's payments to $225 million, according to Gorman and Calhoun, but "it all amounted to a serious strain on the trust and devotion of the fans" (1994: 242). Then again, fans take low priority when it comes to major issues such as these. As we have seen, the networks are sports' real customers – and advertisers theirs.

Television's influence has not always been so obvious. Boxing's scaling down of championship fights from 15 to 12 rounds was motivated ostensibly by safety considerations, though there was little conclusive evidence that the serious injuries associated with boxing occurred in the final three rounds. A more probable explanation was that boxing changed to suit tv requirements. In its traditional form, a boxing match involved 15 three-minute rounds, 14 one-minute intervals, plus preamble and post-fight interviews, yielding an awkward 70–75 minutes. Twelve rounds gave 47 minutes and, say, 13 minutes for padding, which fitted neatly into a one-hour slot.

The Association of Tennis Professionals (ATP) implemented changes in 1994 that were even more clearly motivated by television's needs. It reduced the time allowed in preparing to serve by five seconds to 20 seconds, so speeding up the game. This followed the introduction of the tie-break, which reduced the chances of protracted games that were difficult for tv to schedule (guaranteeing that there would never be a repetition of the epic 112-game match between Pancho Gonzales and Charlie Pasarell in 1969). The ATP also loosened-up on its strictures concerning specators: they could react freely and spontaneously and wander about during play, instead of sitting still and gasping "oohs" and "aahs" as at Wimbledon. Perhaps the biggest concession was in allowing broadcasters to place microphones on the umpire's side of the court so that conversations between players and officials could be heard by a television audience.

The commercial imperatives of television have led to a proliferation of time-outs, which George Ritzer believes, "alter the nature of some sports, and [may] affect the outcome of a game." For Ritzer, this is just one instance of "the attempts to McDonaldize sports" (1993: 71). Like fast-food chains, television emphasizes speed and quantity over quality. "In basketball this has taken the form of the 24-second clock for professionals and the 45-second clock for college athletes," writes Ritzer about inititatives designed to maximize points-scoring. Ritzer notes other changes in sports, such as baseball's introduction of livelier balls, artificial turf that makes ground balls

BIG FIGHT—BIG EARNERS				
	IN	$m	OUT	$m
TELEVISION COMPANY	700,000 ppv units @ $50	35	Promoter's fee	15
			Other staff costs	5
	Foreign sales	5	Administration	4
			Production costs including communications network, plant and equipment	4
			Advertising and marketing	3
			Commissions	2.5
			Overseas partner services	2
Earnings before tax $4.5 million	TOTAL	40	TOTAL	35.5
PROMOTER	Fee from television	15	Boxers' purses	28
	Ticket sales	13	Publicity	2
	Site fee	6	Legal fees	2.5
	Sponsorship	2.5	Sanctioning fee	1.5
	Merchandise	2.5	to WBA or other governing organization	
			Insurance	0.5
Earnings before tax $4.5 million	TOTAL	39	TOTAL	34.5
BOXER	Champion's purse ($9m for challenger)	16	Manager's commission @33% of gross income	5.9
	4% of ppv gross	1.4	Trainer's commission @10% of purse	1.79
	33% of merchandise sales	0.5	Training expenses	2.5
			Other operating expenses, including insurance cover	0.5
Earnings before tax $7.21 million	TOTAL	17.9	TOTAL	10.69

- The site fee is paid to the promoter for staging the fight at, for example, the Mirage in Las Vegas, the casino owners estimating that the interest generated by a big promotion will draw gamblers, who will collectively lose more than the site fee.
- A manager may take up to 33 per cent commission from a boxer's gross purse (25 per cent in Britain) and a trainer usually 10 per cent; payments to other aides are included in the training expenses in the above example. A big promoter, such as Don King, may also manage one of the main boxers, so that his take is even greater than represented here.
- Financially, the risk is taken by the tv company: if the promotion fails to sell through the ppv agency, the promoter and boxers are still guaranteed fixed fees (though some boxers occasionally prefer to negotiate a commission-only deal).
- The figures represent a typical world title promotion rather than a megabuck heavy-weight extravaganza in which the main boxers might split anything up to $80 million.

big fight earners

travel faster, outfield fences that are closer to the home plate and the AL's designated hitter; all moves that make bigger scores probable.

Television's influence can extend beyond the competition itself and into the ambience. Darts started life as a late nineteenth-century pub pastime. It took place in a confined space, allowed tight shots of the players' faces, and generated plenty of alcohol-fueled passion. Potential sponsors and advertisers became uncomfortable about the habitual smoking and drinking in the crowd and made their concerns known to the British television company which in turn approached the British Darts Organization (BDO). Spectators and players alike were instructed by the BDO to refrain from their normal activities in front of the cameras. Considering that the sport's origins were in pubs, the change must have been tantamount to sacrilege to die-hard fans.

With very few exceptions, televised sports have changed as a result of their relations with tv companies. There are critics for whom "television is a corrupting parasite that latches onto the host body, sport, and draws life support from it while giving nothing back in return," as Michael R. Real characterizes their view (1998: 16). The "corruption" of sports involves the various changes of rules, schedules, and formats instigated by television. It must be saddening for those who mourn the days when sports were real "sports." There again, as Sut Jhally points out: "This seems to imply that before the influence of the media there was something that was pure sports" (1989: 80).

Roone Arledge, who inspired ABC's sports coverage, often defended his network's use of synthetic sports by reminding critics that sports were not delivered by god with rules inscribed on tablets of stone. All sports, even those in Ancient Greece, are in some way artificial. Teams of firefighters competing over how many buckets of water they can carry from point A to point Z is no more or less of a pure sport than 11 men trying to move an inflated ball in the opposite direction to another 11 men. The comparison reminds us that television has not so much corrupted or even transformed sports as extended and reshaped them.

The change is not always so dramatic as many writers seem to think: over the past fiftysomething years there has been a drip-by-drip titration, some sports gradually changing from one state to another. Grand, sprawling, majestic sports, like cricket and golf, no less than the cramped, frenetic basketball, have been changed through their commerce with television, but also just to stay popular with new generations of fans who demand instant gratification. As previous chapters have shown us, all sports are evolving entities, anyway – with or without tv. Rules, durations, start times, methods of evaluation and so on have been changing for decades, centuries even. Sports never stand still. Television has imposed change rather than wait for it to happen. And audiences have responded.

THE CREATIVE ACT OF WATCHING TELEVISION

Sport, for the television executive, is a way of ensuring audience ratings stay healthy and of keeping the advertisers' money rolling in. From the point of view of the consumer, televised sports mean something different: it is a form of entertainment that allows the fan to satisfy personal desires, pursue a type of fulfilment and even reach a form of self-actualization, if writers like Mark Gottdiener are to be believed. In his book *The Theming of America: Dreams, visions and commercial spaces*, Gottdiener argues that, far from being passive consumers conditioned by advertising into behaving as producers wish, television viewers are engaged in "the creative act of consumption" (1997: 158).

So far, I have looked at the industrial processes of production and distribution. Now, I want to turn to the consumers. For years, tv fans were led to believe that they received televised sports for free. In fact, they have always had to pay one way or another, usually by a few more pennies on, for example, the retail price of a bar of soap, the manufacturers of which advertise their products in the breaks of sports programs. Or, a few more dollars or pounds on the sticker price of a car. The cost of buying the broadcasting rights are built into the price the customer pays. But, they surely get something back in return. Consistently high viewing figures tell us how sports vie with soaps as the most-watched genre on television.

Sport in the raw is insufficient for the tv viewer: he or she wants it packaged and presented, just like any other commodity. After all, when viewers are asked to pay for the product, as increasingly seems to be the case, they want more than roving-eye-style presentation. In sports, the action does not speak for itself: it needs the direction and narration that produce drama. If you disagree, try hitting the mute button on your remote control next time you watch sports and see how long you can take it.

There is now a mature second generation of people reared on televised sports, the kind of people who prefer waiting for videos instead of going to the movies and playing computer games at home instead of playing ball in the park. Attendance at sports events must seem pretty one-dimensional to them. Some will insist the tension in the atmosphere of a packed stadium or arena can never be even remotely approximated by watching at home. Yet you can almost hear the groans: "Where are the captions and statistics?" "I missed that piece of action. How about a replay?" "I'd like to see that from a different angle, or slowed-down, or explained to me by an informed commentator."

Expectations and perceptions of sports have changed, as have patterns of viewing. Television has gently encouraged us to *read* sports differently: we may be watching the same piece of action as our grandparents, but we will not necessarily interpret it in the same way. We are also likely to watch more of it, if only because of the volume on the air, or through the cables. Television's facilities for replays allows us to relax our concentration. Missing a touchdown, a goal, a knockdown, a homer, or a hole-in-one is not a disaster when we can see it reviewed again and again from different vantage points. This, plus the comments, summaries, and statistics that accompany the action, encourages a certain detachment and predilection for analysis.

Today's sports-watcher sits like an argus, assimilating all manner of information, auditory as well as visual. One hesitates before suggesting it, but the pre- and post-event features have all but supplanted the actual competition. Analyzing has become an integral part of televised sports and the better-informed viewer can cast a clinical eye on proceedings. The irony is: they can do so with less play-by-play concentration on the activity itself.

But, perhaps I generalize too much: a study by Lawrence Wenner and Walter Ganz found that: "Many sports viewers are active, discerning, engaged and passionate." Yet: "Because sports spectators come to the viewing situation with different levels of sporting interest, knowledge and experience, they look for and receive different benefits from the experience" (1998: 250). Beyond the "engaged" viewer, there are those who value the social dimensions of watching sports, those who use it as emotionally cathartic blow-out and those who just "use sports viewing to kill time." While Wenner and Ganz report on "The television sports viewing experience," they actually discern a series of different experiences and for different sports.

For all the different orientations, there are basic competences that viewers bring to sports shows and rewards they take from them. Whether or not this fulfilment measures up to Gottdiener's self-actualization is not clear, but what *is* clear is that we should not underestimate the amount of critical intellectual work that gets done when watching televised sports, nor the appreciable gratifications derived from the experience. All this suggests that, when we are asked to pay more for sport to be delivered to our home, we will grimace, complain, then pay up. And, it is certain that we will have to pay more directly for our sports.

In the golden years between the 1960s and 1980s, sports were as valuable a commodity as television executives could have imagined: relatively inexpensive (no salaries or heavy production costs) and very watchable, as the ratings bore out. Some sports were elevated to international stature as a result of television. It was a match made in heaven. Now, the relationship is much more conflict-torn and the possibility of a divorce looms.

Established television networks have sought a bigger interest in the cable/satellite systems, giving rise to a compex multi-tiered mesh of alliances, often between rival media corporations. In the US, all the networks have not only cable interests, but pay per view (ppv) links. As major sports find tv money harder to come by, they may buy into cable/satellite themselves or extend the kind of shared risk relationships. Whatever the future, we can anticipate much more interlocking between governing bodies and media groups in sports, rather than straightforward buying and selling of rights. The big leagues and big clubs will want more say in their own destinies. And this means we, the consumers, the fans, the television-watching public, are going to have to pay more for our sports.

Pay per view (ppv)

The first ppv event was in 1980 when the Sugar Ray Leonard–Roberto Duran fight drew 170,000 customers who paid $15 (£10) each. Rock concerts and operas followed sporadically, until the advent of TVKO, an agency owned by Time Warner, which also owned HBO. TVKO struggled to establish itself as an alternative, more selective way of viewing until 1991 when it sold the Evander Holyfield–George Foreman fight to 1.45 million homes at $34.93 (£22). The Mike Tyson–Peter McNeeley fight in 1995 was an even greater success, going into 1.52 million households and grossing $63 million (£42 million) in the USA alone ($96 million worldwide). By comparison, less than a tenth of this number chose to buy a Guns 'n' Roses concert for $24.95 (£15.60) in 1992 and just 34,000 homes took a Pavarotti concert in 1991. NBC's 1992 "Olympic Triplecast," a 15-day event, was the biggest disaster to date. out of a potential 20 million homes equipped with the receiving equipment only 165,000 took the whole deal, with 35,000 taking single days.

Since the 1940s, tv viewers have expected sports for no more than the nominal charge of a few pennies on the price of an advertised product, or the cost of a license in the British case. Sports have been as much a part of television's stock-in-trade as soaps, news, and cop shows. But we have already seen some of the grander sports events either being lured away from the terrestrial networks by competing cable/satellite companies or passed over to the ppv services of the media giants themselves. The ppv route has already been explored by boxing and English soccer, with promoters and clubs sharing some of the risks. It is likely that other major sports will pursue similar packages with media giants rather than just selling rights in bundles.

Digital, or DIRECTV, signal ways ahead, with viewers exercising more individual choice in the market: they can select not only camera angles, replays and so on, but actual events. And, of course, the investments several television groups have made in the internet suggest that the day may not be far off when we can download programs as swiftly and efficiently as we open our email. If this is so, it will be convenient for the consumer, but profitable for the program providers: viewers will pay for their chosen sports directly. There again, in sports, nothing is for nothing. It never has been.

FURTHER READING

MediaSport, edited by Lawrence Wenner (Routledge, 1998), is a collection of essays which "examine how the cultural footprint of sport has grown significantly in the media age"; the essays cover both the production and consumption angles. The book contains the study by Wenner/Ganz referenced earlier in this chapter.

"Sports advertising and the Super Bowl" by Rick Burton in *The Advertising Business*, edited by John Philip Jones (Sage, 1999), is one of several interesting essays in this handbook and may profitably be read in conjunction with *Advertising and Popular Culture* by Jib Fowles (Sage, 1996) which is an intriguing analysis of the power and limitations of advertising and its centrality in contemporary culture.

The Theming of America: Dreams, visions and commercial spaces by Mark Gottdiener (Westview Press, 1997), while not specifically about sports, makes several interesting points about "the powerful compulsions of the consumer society that pressure people to make certain choices in the marketplace"; twenty-first-century sports would qualify as one such compulsion.

The Market Structure of Sports by Gerald W. Scully (University of Chicago Press, 1995) concludes that sports' "rose is fading" and that the "prospects for rapid growth in broadcast revenue are not promising." Scully outlines his reasons and backs them with statistical analyses of the economics of sports.

Fields in Vision: Television sport and cultural transformation by Garry Whannel (Routledge, 1992) focuses on the decades-old debate about the effects of television on sports, "some arguing that television has made sport, some that sport has been ruined, others merely content to bear witness to the unholy alliance." For historical interest, other books dealing with the same debate include: *Games and Sets: The changing face of sport on television* by Steven Barnett (British Film Institute, 1990); *Sports for Sale: Television, money and the fans* by David Klatell and Norman Marcus (Oxford University Press, 1988); *Television and National Sport: The United States and Britain* by Joan Chandler (University of Illinois Press, 1988); and *In its Own Image: How television has transformed sport* by Benjamin Rader (Collier-Macmillan, 1984).

Imagine the kind of futuristic scenario depicted at the start of this chapter – but with a difference. Major sports have come under the total control of the mass media. So much so that there is no need for "live" audiences and events are viewed only via the screen. When people refer to the spectators, they mean the people watching at home. What were once mass open-air sports, like football and baseball, are now played behind locked doors. Indoor sports are performed in studios. How realistic is this? Support your argument with evidence from current trends.

leading QUESTIONS

q: Why don't more gay sports performers come out?

a: Money.

Cultural prohibitions on revealing one's homosexuality may have receded in recent years, but many sports performers, who take part of their income from endorsements, are hesitant about losing lucrative contracts if they come out. But, there are at least two other related reasons: a homophobia that permeates many male-dominated sports; and the spread of popular misconceptions about Aids – both of which we will deal with later. All the reasons have sources in the stigma associated with being homosexual.

Plenty of showbusiness stars have stepped out of the closet and declared their homo-sexuality, suggesting that much of the stigma once associated with being gay has disappeared. But not all of it: commercial companies who sign high-profile celebrities to endorsement and sponsorship contracts are notoriously wary about having their products linked to anything to do with gay issues.

In 1997, the famous "coming-out" episode of the sitcom *Ellen* drew an impressive viewing audience rating; yet the majority of advertisers pulled their commercials, leaving only Volkswagen, a lesbian tour operator, and advertisements for forthcoming films in the breaks. There is no conclusive evidence that advertising in the show would have had a negative impact on sales, but advertising agencies are not typically adventurous and err on the side of conservatism.

Although companies frequently favor using sports performers with "rebellious" images, like Dennis Rodman and Andre Agassi, they rarely opt for genuinely subversive figures. Possessors of remunerative contracts break rules and defy traditions, but only on the surface. Athletes who venture to overthrow traditions are usually penalized by either having contracts cancelled or never getting offered any in the first place.

The first athlete to suffer financially after coming out was Billie Jean King. There was irony in the icy reception she received from fellow women professionals after her outing. King was the single most important figure in the movement that secured prize money comparable with that of men's for women. At a time when the incipient women's movement was making demands for equal pay, reproductive rights, and an end to sexist discrimination, King was a vocal campaigner for women's rights in sports.

Reflecting on her conflict-strewn career, King observed: "My sexuality has been my most difficult struggle." In 1981, King's former hairdresser and secretary Marilyn Barnett took legal action against her to ascertain property rights; in other words "palimony." King at first denied that she had an intimate relationship with Barnett, then acknowledged it. The case was thrown out after the judge heard that Barnett had threatened to publish letters that King had written her.

Despite this and the fact that King was married (she divorced in 1987), King's sexual proclivities had become a matter of public record and her sponsors dissociated themselves from her, leaving her with the task of making a comeback to meet her legal costs. King was the first major sports star to open up about her sexuality. In the 1930s and 1940s, Babe Didrikson, the track and field star and golfer, worked hard at presenting a feminine and heterosexual front in spite of suspicions – suspicions that were not actually confirmed until years later with the publication of her biography, which contained details of her friendship with Betty Dodd.

Martina Navratilova's relationship with writer and lesbian activist Rita Mae Brown was revealed in a 1981 *New York Post* article. Navratilova never concealed her lesbian relationship, though she probably missed out on the kind of commercial opportunities available to other, more conspicuously heterosexual players. By the time of Navratilova's era in the 1980s and 1990s, there had been a liberalizing of attitudes toward homosexuality and a recognition that lesbianism was prevalent among tennis and golf players.

In 1999, Amélie Mauresmo, of France, became famous not only for her world-class tennis and muscular body, but for her candour about her lesbianism: at the age of 19, she talked freely to the media about her relationship with a woman. But, more typically, athletes come out either toward the end of their careers, or even in retirement, or after innuendo. It was something of an open secret for many years before golfer Muffin Spencer-Devlin's announcement in 1996 that she was gay. She chose to do so through the pages of *Sports Illustrated*. In the aftermath of the magazine's revelation, other golfers and officials acknowledged that there were other lesbians on the women's tour.

Mariah Burton Nelson was – and is – one of the most effective advocates of gay pride in sport. A basketball player-turned-writer, Nelson became a self-styled role model for lesbians, who encouraged gay players in all sports to declare their sexual preferences. Despite the limited acceptance of gay female athletes by commercial sponsors, male homosexuality has been a different matter and two examples illustrate this.

In 1998, two Canadian Olympians came out within months of each other. Stung by the cancellation of a contract as a motivational speaker on the grounds that he was "too openly gay," Mark Tewksbury, the gold medal-winning swimmer from the 1992 Olympics, who set seven world records in his athletic career, came out voluntarily in a television interview.

Tewksbury, like other gay athletes before him, suffered financially, and figure skater Brian Orser claimed his career would also be "irreparably harmed" if his homosexuality were made public. Involved in a palimony suit with his former partner, Orser requested to an Ontario Court Justice that records of the case be sealed. When the request was denied, Orser was effectively outed. One immediate consequence was that he lost his job as a television commentator, yet again underscoring the financially ruinous consequences of coming out.

Figure skating is unusual in the sense that it condones or exculpates male homosexuals in a way that many other sports will not. We have seen elsewhere in this book that most contemporary sports were created largely for the purpose of validating masculinity. Inviolable heterosexual norms might be expected to endure even in spite of liberalization outside sports. In many sports, there is a conspicuous zero tolerance of values, beliefs, or behavior that contradict heterosexual standards. For instance, when confronted by the prospect that he would be outed without his consent, Australian rugby league player Ian Roberts chose to foreshadow the news by declaring himself to be gay through the publication *New Weekly*. Roberts withstood the predictably hostile response and continued playing.

British soccer player Justin Fashanu also chose to come out via a news story (in *The Sun*, a sensationalist British newspaper) but with less fortunate consequences. His playing contract was terminated by his club and he moved to several others, including a USA club. He committed suicide in London in 1998 after fleeing the States where he allegedly assaulted a teenage male. Fashanu had earlier claimed he had slept with a Tory party politician, which may not have helped his case. Dave Kopay, the American football star came out in the 1960s toward the end of his playing career, but his decision made it impossible for him to gain coaching positions and he was forced out of the sport.

The reactionary attitude toward homosexuality has been reinforced by the spread of Aids in the last two decades of the twentieth century. While the pandemic was by no means confined to the gay population, fears of the "gay plague" lingered. One of the first gay male athletes to come out actually died with Aids in 1987: Tom Waddell, the Olympic decathlete from the 1968 Mexico Olympics, who was one of the founders of the Gay Games in 1982. He became involved in a legal case with the US Olympic Committee, which refused to let him use the word "Olympics" to describe the gay tournament. Waddell was aged 49 at the time of his death.

Glenn Burke also died with Aids; he was the first Major League Baseball player to declare his homosexuality. After playing in the Dodger's World Series-winning team in 1977, Burke refused to take part in a marriage of convenience to allay rumors of his homosexuality and was traded to Oakland Athletics. He competed at the Gay Games, winning sprint medals, and, later, turned to basketball. Burke died in 1995.

Greg Louganis's public declaration of his homosexuality came through the publication of his autobiography *Breaking the Surface: A life*, which was published in 1995 and contained details of his HIV+ diagnosis. Louganis revealed how, in the 1988 summer Olympics, he cut his head and spilled blood into the pool when attempting a reverse two-and-half pike. The doctor who treated Louganis's wound did not wear protective gloves. Louganis's disclosure came after an acrimonious split with his former partner Tom Barrett who threatened to reveal details of Louganis's medical condition. Louganis came to a court settlement with Barrett and pre-empted any disclosure with his book.

While these are isolated cases, associations between Aids and gays in sport persist and hinder the efforts of campaigners like Burton. It is unlikely that gay male athletes will volunteer information about their sexuality. Despite this, a body of scholarly evidence suggests that at least 10 per cent of men have had some form of homosexual experience and there is no reason to suppose that athletes are exceptions.

More questions . . .

- Does the mass media inhibit or encourage honesty among athletes about sexual proclivities?
- Why are fans so eager to know so much about popular athletes?
- Are sponsors right in assuming gay endorsers would not help sales?

Read on . . .

- Cahn, S. K., *Coming on Strong: Gender and sexuality in twentieth-century women's sport* (Free Press, 1994).
- Festle, M. J., *Playing Nice: Politics and apologies in women's sport* (Columbia University Press, 1996).
- Griffin, P., *Strong Women, Deep Closets: Lesbians and homophobia in sport* (Human Kinetics, 1998).
- King, B. J. and Deford, F., *Billie Jean* (Viking, 1982).

at the business end

Rupert Murdoch and the

commercial world of

sports

THE MOST POWERFUL PERSON IN SPORTS

Josef Stalin's mother had ambitions for him to be a priest. In fact, the young Stalin spent some time in a seminary training for the priesthood. Historians sometimes speculate on whether history would have been different had Stalin pursued the vocation. There is no evidence that Rupert Murdoch's mother had similar aspirations. But it is still interesting to contemplate what sports would have been like had he become a man of the cloth instead of the head of the world's most extensive media group.

Murdoch started the twenty-first century as the most powerful person in sports. There were other contenders, such as Michael Eisner, the head of Disney, and John Malone, the chief of Tele-Communications. But no one came close to Murdoch; his worldwide influence in almost every facet of sports was undoubted. And yet, he had no particular passion for sports. A glance at his career reveals that he only took an active interest in them in the 1990s, when he realized that he could use sports, as he put it, as a "battering ram" to smash down people's doors and install his television services. For Murdoch, sport was strictly a means to an end; a very effective means, we should note.

303

By the start of the century, he had assembled the most formidable combination of sports clubs, production operations, and media outlets the world had ever known. Through his media empire, he had the kind of leverage "undreamed of by bush-leaguers like William Randolph Hearst," as Thomas Frank puts it in his "The new gilded age" (1997: 25). The meshing of media and sports into a combined network was either the masterstroke of a genius or the evil work of a megalomaniac.

It is, of course, no accident that Murdoch conquered both domains of sports and television. At the cusp of the twenty-first century, the two had become so symbiotically attached that virtually any media entrepreneur had interests in sports, almost by default. Sports and the media became convergent fields: Murdoch's ability to unite them into a single business established him as the single most important player in the entire sports business – and I use the term to embrace the whole province of sports.

But, how was it possible for a person such as Murdoch to rise to a position of virtually unrivaled power in sports? What were the conditions under which he rose? And, to return to the original question: what would sports be like if RM had become a priest? To answer these questions, we need to backtrack to a time when sports were exactly that – sports, not businesses. The introduction of money into pursuits or pastimes that were once played for enjoyment only set in motion a series of processes that changed sports irreversibly and, some would say, nefariously. Money corrupts; that much we know. Some misty-eyed romantics will always complain that the filthy stuff has corrupted the ideals that were once integral to sports. Others will point out that the commercialization of sports is only part of an inexorable movement that has affected every aspect of contemporary culture. If people enjoy watching and appreciating something and, in some circumstances, are willing to pay to do so, then there will always be others eager to profit from their willingness.

Murdoch is but one of countless entrepreneurs, competitors, managers, and other personnel associated with sports who have profited handsomely. Where there has been a demand and a raw supply, there has been no shortage of enterprising people with ideas on how to connect the two and appropriate the surplus. This is a business approach to sports and one which conflicts with the cardinal rules of sport as they were originally laid out.

VANISHING AMATEURS

All sports that are watchable have potential for commercial exploitation. An after-dinner game of snooker played in private without even a side-bet would not have this potential. Nor would a one-on-one basketball matchup in the privacy of a high school gym. Take the snooker players Stephen Hendry and

Ronnie O'Sullivan and transport them to Sheffield's Crucible, or the ball players Tim Hardaway and Grant Hill and pitch them together in Madison Square Garden and their games become spectator sports. If contests can draw crowds, they qualify as spectator sports. And, if they are spectator sports, then people are usually willing to pay for the privilege of spectating.

It is perfectly possible to have mass spectator sports without the taint of money that many argue corrupts the central values of competition. The NCAA is strictly amateur and celebrates this fact. The organization's approach to sports is pure in the sense that harks back to an age when sports were for, as the name implies, love (from the Latin *amatorius*, "pertaining to love"). Fondness for the activity itself or the satisfaction drawn from winning fairly were the motivating principles, though participation was, or should have been, regarded as more important than achievement.

Nowadays, "amateur" is almost a pejorative term, implying a lack of refinement or clumsiness – the opposite of professional. In the eighteenth and nineteenth centuries, the reverse was the case and the amateur symbolized all that was good in sport, while the professional was despised as a vulgarian who competed just for money. "Sports had as their ideal aim the production of pleasure," write Eric Dunning and Ken Sheard, "an immediate emotional state rather than some ulterior end, whether of a material or other kind" (1979: 153–4).

It was regarded as "unsportsmanlike" and "ungentlemanly" to show elation in victory and disappointment in defeat. Compare that with today's response to a touchdown or a goal. British public schools and universities were the wellsprings of the amateur ethos and there was concern at the prospect of the dignified ball games practiced at Rugby, Harrow, and other upper-class schools, being copied by the lower classes, whose desire to win rather than just compete amounted to a defilement.

"Subsidized" players who were reimbursed for work time lost while playing, or who accepted straight cash for their services were a threatening presence in some sports, especially rugby. Amateurs could not devote so much of their time to their game as professionals and would be hard-pressed to maintain their superiority. There was also the suspicion that dangling a carrot in front of players would encourage them not only to play harder and forget the joy of it all, but to raise their ability levels through training. In the eyes of the nineteenth-century amateur, this was unfair: it produced a competitive advantage for those who committed themselves to self-improvement. Sports were meant to be about enjoyment, whereas "to train for sport and take it too seriously was," as Dunning and Sheard observe, "tantamount to transforming it into work and, hence, to destroying its essence" (1979: 148).

Of course, sports did eventually become like work: by the second half of the nineteenth century, cricket and other ball games, prize fighting, and pedestrianism (the equivalent of competitive walking) paid contestants. Sports that were played by affluent classes, like golf, were rich enough to employ coaches; while other sports could pay expenses simply because they were popular enough to attract paying spectators. This caused the amateur gentlemen to confound the trend toward professionalism with greater fervor. Mass gatherings of working-class spectators, some of them partisan, posed what was seen as a threat to public order. So much so that such assemblies were outlawed in some circumstances.

Spectators did not benefit from sports in the same way as participants. Quite the contrary: they suffered by degenerating into an excitable, amoral mass. At least, that is what the affluent classes thought. The gentlemen amateurs' reaction to spectator sports presents a type of metaphor for the changes that were occurring in society generally. The industrial working class was getting organized and showing signs of cohesion and solidarity in the face of employers who were worried by the prospect of having their authority challenged from below. Class antagonism, or sheer prejudice, manifested itself in several notable incidents, all designed to cocoon the exclusive elite of gentlemen from others. As well as the landowning English aristocracy, gentlemen would have included *nouveaux riches*, merchants, physicians, lawyers, politicians, and others with new-found prestige rather than inherited wealth.

In 1846 at Lancaster, in the northwest of England, there was a dispute following a Manchester crew's victory in the Borough Cup rowing competition. It was alleged that two of the crew, a cabinet maker and a bricklayer, were not acceptable entrants because "they were not known as men of property." The debate continued until, in 1853, when the category of "gentlemen amateur" was distinguished from just plain amateur, for the Lancaster Rowing Club's purposes. Other clubs followed suit, stipulating that those who worked as mechanics, artisans, or laborers would not be eligible for competition as their employment, being physical in nature, equipped them with advantages.

This may have seemed a subterfuge to members of the working class, but it was perpetuated by the Amateur Athletic Association which, in 1866, officially defined an amateur as a person who had either never competed (1) in open competition, (2) for prize money, (3) for admission money, (4) with professionals, (5) never taught or assisted in the pursuit of athletic exercises, or (6) was not a mechanic, artisan, or laborer. Condition (6) was removed in 1880, but the intent of this typical pronouncement was clear: to exclude working-class competitors and so stave off the evils of professionalism. This applied only to track and field; in other sports professionalism was unstoppable.

By the 1880s, rugby and soccer became so popular, especially in the English north and the Midlands, that spectators were prepared to pay to watch organized games. The money made it possible to pay players. Rugby Union was intractable in its opposition to this and, by 1895, had effectively forced the formation of a professional organization, which became the Rugby League in 1922. Soccer prevaricated, but, by 1885, had agreed to a controlled professionalism, with a maximum wage limit and stipulations about the movement of players between clubs.

This was a similar restriction to baseball's "reserve clause" which prevented out-of-contract players moving on and depressed salaries overall. Baseball itself had much the same matrix as cricket and rugby, but, as Peter Levine points out, in his *A. G. Spalding and the Rise of Baseball*: "Almost from the outset, however, this amateur gentlemen's game was transformed" and baseball became one of the first professional spectator sports (1985). In 1858, fans were charged 50 cents admission to watch a three-game championship series between teams from New York and Brooklyn. In 1862, enclosures were specially built to accommodate paying fans and exclude those who wanted to watch games for free. As gate fees went up, so players began to reap some benefits, though their salaries were to prove a source of dispute for many years.

A. G. Spalding, the subject of Levine's book, was instrumental in the early development of baseball. He had no respect for the "gentlemen's game" and approached baseball as if it were an industry – and he a captain of that industry. Spalding was puzzled by the amateur ethos: "I was not able to understand how it could be right to pay an actor, or a singer, or an instrumentalist for entertaining the public, and wrong to pay a ball player for doing the same thing in his way" (quoted in Levine, 1985).

By 1910 – five years before Spalding's death – attendance had soared to 7.25 million, though players' salaries were still kept artificially low, averaging under $2,500. In Britain, spectators were flocking to sports, and stadia were built to accommodate them. Professionalism was well-established and the business opportunities offered by sports were openly exploited by organizers and promoters. Boxing, for long a pursuit of professionals at some level, whether in fairground shows or streetfighting, evolved into two co-existing organizations, amateur and professional, with boxers transferring from the former to the latter. Other sports refused to condone professionalism.

Prosperous gentlemen of New York, concerned over professionalism, helped organize the National Association of Amateur Athletes of America in 1868. This became the Amateur Athletic Association in 1888. Intercollegiate sports, which gained in currency during the 1880s, were very much amateur affairs and kept a safe distance from the dishonorable baseball leagues. As soccer had emerged as primarily an upper-class sport which was appropriated by the English working class, so American football began life as a derivative of rugby played in the main by sons of the wealthy during their university years. The Intercollegiate Athletic Association (IAA) was formed in 1906 in response to an early-century crisis in college football: players were "moonlighting," playing for money under assumed names. The IAA was a precursor of the NCAA (National Collegiate Athletic Association) which was formed to protect amateurism and regulate college sports.

American football's career was not unlike soccer's: early professional outfits growing out of factory teams and cultivating a working-class following. The Indian Packing Company, of Green Bay, Wisconsin, had its own team in the first decade of the twentieth century; as did the Staley Starch Company, of Decatur, Illinois. Players were paid about $50 per week and given time off to train. In 1920, both companies affiliated their teams to a new organization that also harbored teams from New York and Washington. The teams evolved into the Packers, Bears, Giants, and Redskins respectively. Quite soon it was possible for the teams to divorce themselves from their industrial backgrounds and become independent employers: players who had learnt their skills at colleges could earn a decent living once their years of study were over. This seamless transition from university to pro club has been a feature of American football ever since, the draft being brought into play in 1936.

Some sports were slower than others to accept the inevitability of professionalism. Tennis adamantly refused to allow professionals into its prestigious competition until 1968 when it went "open." From that point, players like Rod Laver, who had previously turned pro and been barred, reintegrated with amateurs whom they dominated so overwhelmingly that amateurism vanished from top levels over the next several years. Track and field for long assumed the ostrich position, burying its head in the sand despite widespread knowledge of "shamateurism" with athletes accepting generous gifts and exaggerated expenses for their services. In 1983, the International Amateur Athletics Federation (IAAF) accepted reality but insisted that payments should go via a subvention into a trust fund and be dispensed later to the athlete. By the end of the century, there were millions to be earned in both sports.

SPORTS ENTREPRENEURS

In some dark and distant age, an enterprising witness to a contest noticed a crowd react excitedly to the sight of competition and thought: "Lo! the gathered masses act as if 'twas them joined in battle!" Inspired by this, the first sports entrepreneur would have brought the same contestants together again, but this time charging a fee for watching – the assumption being that the pleasure taken in just observing was worth a small amount. So, the sports business was started.

No one is officially credited with being the first person to spot the potential for earning money from sports. James Figg was one of the first to establish an organization to exploit the potential when he opened his Amphitheatre in London, in 1743. As we have seen previously, Figg attracted large crowds to watch his combat events which were arranged on a regular basis and supplied him with a successful business. His concept was adopted from that of the ancient Romans, except that his motive was merely to take a profit. His patrons' motives were mixed: to identify with and cheer on their favorite, to extract vicarious pleasure from watching, to wager, or just to meet other members of the "fancy," as patrons of prize-fighting were collectively known (possibly an early form of the word "fan"). This reflects much the same mixture of impulses of fans today.

The correlation between high-caliber athletes and large crowds would not have been lost on early promoters. Figg's natural successors were the prize-fight organizers of America in the 1800s. Some states, such as Massachusetts, outlawed prize fighting and this prompted organizers to stage illicit contests behind locked doors with a small, invited crowd.

In his history of boxing *Beyond the Ring*, Jeffrey Sammons discovers that the first unofficial world heavyweight championship between Paddy Ryan and Joe Goss, in 1880, was "fought in virtual secrecy at Colliers, West Virginia." Sammons explains: "Organizers chose the tiny Brooks County town for its proximity to the Ohio and Pennsylvania state lines: if raided by hostile law officers, participants and followers could scatter across the border to escape arrest" (1988: 6).

In the same period, Richard Kyle Fox, an Irish migrant who was scratching a living by writing about events such as oyster-opening and one-legged dancing competitions, ventured into promoting events that he could then write about for local newspapers. In 1881, he had a chance encounter with John L. Sullivan, a prize-fighter who, as folklore had it, spurned Fox's offer to promote him. Sullivan went on to become the most famous athlete of his day and Fox's determination to secure his services or ruin him drove him to the position of American sports' first major promoter, offering either purses (fixed payments) or percentages of gate receipts to fighters. By the mid-1890s, top pugilists fought for what were then enormous purses of thousands of dollars. Sullivan is known to have charged in the region of $25,000 per championship fight (then worth more than £50,000) – remember, pro baseball players averaged only a tenth of this amount per year by 1910.

The legalization of prize-fighting in New York in 1920 opened up new commercial possibilities for sports entrepreneurs. Sammons notes that, in 1922 alone, gate receipts in New York state totaled $5 million (in those days, about £1.5 million), a sum that made some conclude presciently that boxing was "an industry, financed by banks, and licensed and supervised by state laws and officials just as banking and insurance" (quoted in Sammons 1988: 66).

If this was so, then boxing was a prototype for other sports. Opportunistic entrepreneurs were key agents in the process of establishing sports along business lines. Unquestionably, the most visionary was George "Tex" Rickard, who promoted all but one heavyweight title fight that resulted in a new champion from the reign of Jack Johnson to that of Gene Tunney and whose elaborate publicity stunts and gargantuan promotions (regularly attracting 100,000+ spectators, with receipts of nearly $1.9 million for one show in 1926) established him as *the* sports promoter of his era.

Allegations that many of Rickard's contests were not only run as but actually were showbusiness events complete with scripts and stage directions were commonplace. But the controversy only added to Rickard's notoriety and he was able to exploit the growing enthusiasm for sports which featured not only contestants but a sense of occasion – and atmosphere that drew together the blue-collar and the plutocracy, the anonymous and the famous.

Rickard's promotions were huge but occasional extravaganzas. The market for everyday pro sports was also buoyant. Baseball's National League (NL) was having to stave off the challenges of several rival leagues which were prepared to undercut it with lower admission prices. The most formidable of these was the Western League, which later became the American League (AL). In 1902, the AL attracted 2.2 million fans to its games, compared to the 1.7 million who attended NL games. A truce was signed in January, 1903, and this agreement established the framework of what became Major League Baseball (MLB). By the 1930s, baseball had become America's most popular sport, regularly attracting five-figure crowds. In the midst of economic depression, star players, like Babe Ruth, were able to command staggering salaries of $80,000.

The big-earning athletes were able to command such money not simply because they had more talent than their colleagues, but because (1) they had market appeal; and (2) they were surrounded with entrepreneurs who knew how to capitalize on that appeal. Promoters and owners of ball clubs were about as philanthropic in the 1930s as they are today. In the mid-1970s, Jonathan Brower's research into the subject concluded that they are "neither accustomed to nor comfortable with losing money in business ventures" (1976: 15).

They were and are in sports to make money; to them it was and is a business. Not surprisingly, promoters and owners have run sports organizations as if they were any other business, the only problem being that many ventures fail to make money. Ball clubs in particular are not typically great investments, though, of course there is great prestige and a certain celebrity status that attaches to owners. Ask Wayne Huizinga or George Steinbrenner;

or Victor Kiam, owner of Remington, who apparently liked the New York Patriots so much that, in 1988, he bought the club. "He saw the acquisition as a good way to draw attention to himself and to Remington," suggest Jerry Gorman and Kirk Calhoun, who quote Kiam: "I felt that with any exposure I got, there would be some falloff benefit for Remington" (1994: 30).

Whatever the motives of promoters, owners or any other entrepreneur in sports, their impact has been to transform sports into a unique collective enterprise. Why unique? Because sports may have veered toward but has never become pure entertainment. The packaging and merchandising may be indistinguishable, but sports' abiding appeal lies in an essential unpredictability. The outcome of a competition is never known, at least nearly never. During the 1950s, organized crime had such a stranglehold on North American boxing that the results of a great many title fights were prescribed. Promoters of sports events and owners or chairs of clubs are integral parts of a landscape filled with sponsors, agents, and hard-boiled marketing executives, all seeking to manipulate competitive sports to their own requirements. Yet, they are not simple conveyors of public demand: they originate the demand, shape it, manage it, and, occasionally, destroy it.

Market forces being what they are, it is unlikely that sport would have grown into the massive business it now is without the assistance of the mass media. As things transpired, sports entrepreneurs did enjoy such an assistance. Newspapers, radio, and, later, television were not slow in realizing that they too could turn a penny by extensively covering sports. This both responded to demand and stimulated further interest. As we saw in Chapter twelve, television seized the commercial opportunities offered by sports and quickly extended its interest and influence in ways that would have been considered pure fantasy to any one of the 120,757 people who watched the Jack Dempsey–Gene Tunney fight in 1926.

The complementary nature of interests between sports entrepreneurs and media companies was too obvious to miss. If sports were popular, people wanted to watch them, if not in the flesh, then on the screen. Media magnates were never willing to part with the kind of money demanded by promoters and league commissioners (who represented the interests of clubs), but they usually did. Ever-grudgingly, they paid more and more for every new contract. Then Ted Turner, the head of a media corporation, hit on the novel idea: buy the clubs.

In 1972, the owner of Turner Communications agreed to pay the Atlanta Braves baseball club $2.5 million for the rights to televise games for five years. A year before the end of the arrangement, Turner offered the club's owners $9.65 million for the whole shebang. The new owner was called the Atlanta National League Baseball Club, which was a subsidiary of Turner Communications. The same company acquired a 75 per cent interest in the

Ted Turner

At the age of 24, Turner inherited his father's billboard business and, with it, $6 million worth of debt. After turning the business around, Turner bought two radio stations in Chattanooga and retitled the business the Turner Communications Corporation. He floated the company on the local stock exchange in 1970 to finance the acquisition of Channel 17, an Atlanta television station. At first, he filled its schedules with old movies and tv show re-runs, but, in 1972, he bought the rights to the Atlanta Braves games. In 1976, he bought the ailing club and turned round its fortunes. Turner's flamboyant conduct was despised by the Major League Baseball authorities. In 1976, he was suspended from all baseball activities for a year. But Turner was undaunted and continued to spend more money in the ultimately successful attempt to bring the World Series to Atlanta.

Turner's flagship television network CNN started life in 1979: it was a highly innovative 24-hour all-news cable station. He augmented this with a movie tv cable TNT and, in 1992, split the Turner Broadcasting System (TBS) into five divisions, one of which concentrated on sports activities. In 1996, CNN/SI was launched: this was an all-sports news cable in competition with ESPN's second channel. Turner's mega-deal with media giant Time Warner was one of a number of a series of mergers and transactions in the late 1990s. Turner continued to handle Time Warner's cable networks, including HBO, and ran the Braves, Hawks, and Thrashers.

Atlanta Hawks NBA franchise, in 1977; and, the following year, it bought a partnership in the Atlanta Chiefs soccer club.

An obvious advantage of owning the Braves was that their games had high ratings and gave Turner's tv station a strong presence in the local market. Perhaps more significantly, Turner was able to avoid the hard-fought negotiations that typically accompany a tv–ball club deal. The reciprocity was enhanced by the boost television exposure gave to home game attendance. Eventually, this gave the Braves more money to attract better players and so contributed to the playing performance. Improving performances brought more viewers to their tv screens and enabled Turner to crank up his advertising rates. As the team's W–L record improved, so tv and radio broadcast rights rose, becoming the single biggest source of revenue; in the 1990s, this regularly exceeded $22 million per annum.

The Hawks were a poor team when Turner took over. Its owners were prepared to move the franchise out of Atlanta. As in baseball, clubs received a pro rata distribution of television revenues from telecasts by the national networks, but unlike baseball clubs they received none of the gate receipts from away games. It took only till 1979/80 before the Hawks began averaging 10,000+ for home games and, although this subsequently slipped, attendance picked up again after 1988/9. This was the period when the NBA generally gained widespread popularity. Encouraged by this, NBC paid the NBA $600 million for four years' broadcast rights, 1990–4. The Hawks' share of this was $22 million. TNT (Turner Network Television) retained broadcast rights for the 50-game regular season and, if appropriate, 30 play-off games; for this it paid the NBA $275 million, of which the Hawks saw about $10 million.

Turner's strategy could not be faulted: it was a no-lose situation. And one which other media owners were observing carefully. So that, by the time Turner stepped up to plate with his bid for Los Angeles Dodgers, in 1996, several other media corporations had taken active financial interests in sports clubs and Turner found himself in competition with News Corporation owner Rupert Murdoch. Turner bitterly opposed Murdoch's ultimately successful attempt to buy the Dodgers, though he was outvoted when the 16 National League franchises took the decision in 1998. Turner's enmity was apparent when he promised: "I'll squish Murdoch like a bug." But, Turner must have soon felt like John Goodman who played the bug exterminator in the film *Arachnophobia*, in which a deadly spider finds its way into a small Californian town and lets loose its offspring to wreak havoc (director Frank Marshall, 1990).

VERTICAL INTEGRATION, OR HOW SPORTS BECAME "MURDOCHIZED"

Murdoch's purchase of the 20th Century Fox film and television studio signaled his arrival as a key player in the North American media. But, for many years before, he had been steadily building his interests. He had already assembled a bundle of British newspapers to add to his collection of Australian titles. But, a successful television company escaped him. Having been thwarted in an attempt to buy London Weekend Television, he turned to the States where he had been impressed by the ascent of cable channels, especially ESPN and MTV. In 1983, he bought a struggling satellite operator, Inter-American, which he turned into Skyband. The purchase proved a disaster and Murdoch lost $20 million within six months. In the same year, he tried unsuccessfully to buy Warner, the Hollywood studio (later to merge with Time).

Fox was then struggling and, in 1985, Murdoch took advantage to buy at first a 50 per cent stake and, later, full control from its owner Marvin Davis.

Fox was insignificant in the tv market, but Murdoch grew it into the fourth major network. One of the reasons he was able to do this was by outbidding the established trio of ABC, CBS, and NBC for the rights to screen the plum NFL games. The 1993 deal cost Murdoch what many thought an absurdly high $1.6 billion; Fox lost an estimated $100 million in broadcasts in the 1994/5 season alone. Undeterred, Murdoch also signed contracts with Major League Baseball and the National Hockey League.

Murdoch's logic? By wresting the popular Sunday afternoon games from CBS, he had established Fox as a major network. Many local television stations changed their affiliations as a direct result of the coup and, of course, advertising revenue soared. Solid audience ratings helped Fox advertise its other shows in the commercial spots, thus increasing viewer awareness of the station's menu.

Then, Murdoch changed the formula: he beat off Turner's challenge to buy the Los Angeles Dodgers, admittedly one of sport's astral franchises, but not worth $350 million (£217 million) in the estimation of most market analysts.

On the heels of this deal, Murdoch, through his 50/50 joint venture with Liberty Media, bought a 40 per cent interest in LA's Staples Center, the only arena in the States to house three major franchises, including the Los Angeles Kings, of the NHL. The deal included an option on 40 per cent of the Kings. As the Kings announced their intention to exercise their own option on just under 10 per cent of the Los Angeles Lakers, who also played at the Staples Center, Murdoch became a minority owner in an NBA franchise too.

Over on the other coast, Murdoch's Fox Entertainment Group's 40 per cent ownership of Rainbow Media Holdings Inc., a subsidiary of Cablevision – which held a majority interest in Madison Square Garden, the New York Knicks, of the NBA, and the New York Rangers hockey club – meant that Murdoch had his fingers deeply in the pies of the NBA and the NHL on both coasts. Like Turner's strategy, Murdoch's was to control the media distribution networks *and* the content of the programs to run through them.

His attempt to repeat the strategy in Britain was stymied when a £600 million ($1 billion) bid for Manchester United, though accepted by the owners, was blocked by the Monopolies and Mergers Commission, an official body set up to guard against anti-trust arrangements. Murdoch's BSkyB subscription network had earlier bought the exclusive rights to screen English soccer's Premiership games "live" and was, at the time, experimenting with pay per view transmissions. As Turner had earlier discovered, owning a ball club simplified broadcasting negotiations.

As we have seen, Murdoch was not the only media owner to have sensed the advantages in owning clubs: in the late 1990s, media companies owned at least 20 top clubs in baseball, football, basketball, and hockey. The process was known as *vertical integration*. Time Warner acquired baseball's Atlanta Braves and the Atlanta Hawks basketball club after its takeover of Turner's holdings, which included his several cable channels; it also became owner of the Atlanta Thrashers hockey team. Disney owned the NHL's Mighty Ducks and the Anaheim Angels baseball club; it also owned ESPN. Wayne Huizinga, former owner of Blockbuster Video, owned baseball's Florida Marlins and the Florida Panthers hockey club. *The Chicago Tribune* owned the Chicago Cubs; Cablevision owned the New York Knicks and the New York Rangers (and tried to buy the Yankees); Ascent Entertainments owned the Denver Nuggets and Comcast owned the Philadelphia 76ers. Italian media magnate Silvio Berlusconi owned the AC Milan soccer club of *Serie A*. The French cable television company Canal Plus owned the Paris St. Germain club. These are but a few illustrations of the media–sports cross-ownership patterns in North America and Europe. But, on a global scale, Murdoch's operations had no counterpart.

In addition to Fox in the States and BSkyB in Europe, Murdoch had Star TV that stretched from Saudi Arabia to Australia and included the gigantic Chinese market, as well as Japan (24 countries in total). Think of all the sports Murdoch had access to through his American and British set-ups, then contemplate the size of the sports diet he could offer to markets in the rest of the world. It is estimated by Kevin Maney that, at any one time, Murdoch

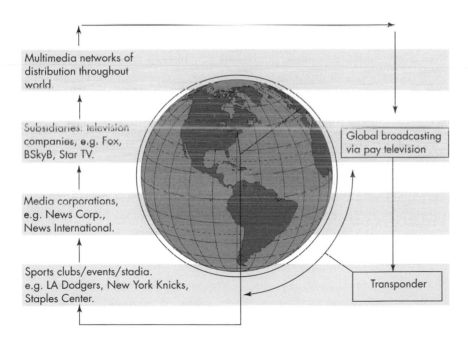

vertical integration

could "reach more than two-thirds of the world's television households and touch yet more people through movies and newspapers" (1995: 173). In his book *Megamedia Shakeout: The inside story of the leaders and the losers in the exploding communications industry*, Maney characterizes Murdoch's "awesome basket of assets" as: "The intertwining of the two trends of megamedia and globalization" (1995: 173).

Apart from the scale of Murdoch's empire, which frightened many, his methods of construction were also alarming. With his cross-ownership of several media, Murdoch would typically sacrifice profits from one medium and underwrite costs from another. An example was the London *Times*, one of four quality national newspapers in a somewhat congested British market. Murdoch also owned the *New York Post*-ish *Sun*, which he had bought cheaply in 1969 and, within nine years, turned into the nation's best-selling daily. He did so by featuring bare-bosomed models, a bingo game, and sensationalist stories, many about the Royal Family. Profits from the *Sun* allowed Murdoch to use the *Times* as a sort of loss-leader by dropping its cover price to about two-thirds of its rivals'.

Could the same tactic be applied to sports? Consider: Florida Marlins' owner Wayne Huizinga split up his 1997 World Series-winning team because the salary demands were too great. Faced with a similar situation, might a Murdoch-owned team underwrite salary costs with money from other ventures just to ensure the team stays ahead of the field and draws more television viewers? (The LA Dodgers' 1999 payroll totaled about $90 million.)

Any club owned by Murdoch was eligible for the *Times* treatment. In other words, it could become the beneficiary of cash from other outposts of the empire. Even with salary caps, the consequence of this would be to weaken rival clubs and media groups by driving up wages. Such possibilities gave rise to the suspicion that Murdoch's goal was not ownership of clubs or media companies, but of sport and the communications industry. His track record suggested that, if he wanted something, he was prepared to pay over-the-odds for it. This is why *Big League, Big Time* author Len Sherman, writing before Murdoch clinched the Dodgers, trembled at the prospect: "Murdoch could, if he gained control of the Dodgers, deploy his newspapers and TV networks to forcefully thrust baseball into the international arena, forever upsetting the power structure of Major League Baseball, remaking the industry and the sport from top to bottom" (1998: 35).

Murdoch revolutionized sports' marketplace by investing for long-term value rather than short-term profits and building globally rather than nationally. If he had begun his campaign ten years, or perhaps even five years, before he did, his *grand projet* may have quickly disintegrated and you would not be reading this much about him in *Making Sense of Sports*. He may still over-reach himself, of course. But, for him to have risen even as far as he has tells us something about the social changes of the past 20 years. In the final part of the answer to the "what if . . .?" question posed earlier, we will look at those changes.

THE PLANET'S CAPTIVATING MEDIUM

Addressing the 1996 AGM of News Corp., Murdoch announced that sports "absolutely overpowers film and all other forms of entertainment in drawing viewers to television." Comforting stockholders with the news that the company held long-term rights to major sports events in most countries, he revealed future strategy: "We will be doing in Asia what we intend to do elsewhere in the world – that is, use sports as a battering ram and a lead offering in all our pay television operations." It was a widely-quoted remark and, as it turned out, an honest one. Murdoch's acquisitive quest for leadership, if not ownership of the sports market, reflects both sports' crucial role in generating television ratings and television's equally crucial role in the healthy cashflow of sports.

As we noted before, during the 1980s, Murdoch became impressed by the ways in which dedicated cable channels, such as ESPN and MTV particularly, were able to isolate specific portions of the population. This was an agreeable development for advertisers; and the enduring commercial success of both of these confirms this. While he had no intrinsic interest in sports, Murdoch realized how effective these were in attracting a particular group of consumers, which he could, in turn, deliver to potential advertisers. At Fox and at BSkyB, Murdoch was prepared to bear brutal initial losses in anticipation that sports would ultimately woo demographically-desirable viewers – the kind that drink alcohol, drive cars, and have pension plans, for example.

The concept of using sports to sell products, possibly products only tangentially connected to sports (like beer, cars, and pension plans) seems blindingly obvious today; but, in the 1960s, it was a daring innovation. Even in the 1970s, the possibilities were never totally explored. Only in the late 1980s and through the 1990s was sport's marketing potential fully realized. In retrospect, the linking of consumerism with sports may be the single most influential development since the advent of professional sport itself in the late nineteenth century.

The link was strengthened by the emergence of a new cultural equation in which sports' stock soared. In the early 1990s, "Sports had arguably surpassed popular music as the captivating medium most essential to being perceived as 'young and alive,'" according to Donald Katz, author of *Just Do It: The Nike spirit in the corporate world*. "Sports, as never before, had so completely permeated the logic of the marketplace in consumer goods that by

1992 the psychological content of selling was often more sports-oriented than it was sexual" (1994: 25–6).

Companies such as Nike, Coca-Cola, and McDonald's in some measure hitched their wagons to sport's star; and profited enormously as a result. While Nike was not the only company to have exploited the new status of sports performers, it did more than any other to enhance the status (we will open this out in the next chapter). The new cultural equation encouraged the interest of all manner of companies in sports, especially televised sports. Car firms, clothes makers, food manufacturers, and other organizations with no particular interest in sports apart from the ability to sell their products began to express interest. This took the form of both signing athletes to endorse products and advertising in the commercial spots that punctuated sports competitions.

The zest with which Murdoch bought television rights, often for sums that other major networks believed to be suicidal, attests to his confidence in the cultural power of sports to deliver its followers to his programs and, by implication, his customers – the advertisers. His ability to deliver grew out of his belief in thinking globally. Murdoch's master plan was never confined to one country, nor indeed one continent. Early in his career, he realized that Australia was simply not big enough for his ambitions. Moving to Britain, then the States, he recognized that markets had no natural boundaries: unlike nations, corporations, especially media corporations, were not confined by government and the limitations of any single polity.

The postcolonial world was one in which old empires had disappeared and new forms of interdependency had grown: nations relied on each other's support, not only militarily, but politically, and, of course, commercially. Advances in telecommunications, particularly in satellite and fiber optic technologies, enhanced the capacity and flexibility of media networks to carry services (data, video, or voice) around the world. No other phenomenon possessed this unique capability.

While no entity could actually *own* a nation's political system or economy, it was perfectly possible to own a telecommunications network that encircled the earth. The power this conferred on the potential owner was unequaled. Owners of the means of communications could exert influences in any number of countries. By the end of the twentieth century, the technologies that could make this theoretically possible were well advanced. They included: digital methods of encoding, transmitting, and decoding; multimedia cable and satellite networks to carry and disseminate information; and a single international collection of computer networks from which users could access information from computers anywhere in the world – the internet. Murdoch's various organizations had invested in all these and more.

Sponsorship

"Sponsorship is the support of sport, sports events, sports organizations or competitors by an outside body or person for the mutual benefit of both parties." This was how former British Minister for Sports, Denis Howell, once serviceably described sponsorship (quoted in Neil Wilson's *The Sport Business*). It is not a new phenomenon: there are examples of commercial companies financing events, especially cycling tours in the late 19th century. But, the significant possibilities of mass exposure through the television opened up new relations between sports and corporations. Breweries were among the first and most enduring sponsors of sports to recognize the potential of televised sports. Pabst Riband, in the USA, and Whitbread's, in Britain, sponsored competitions in the 1950s. Gillette has maintained an interest in sports on both sides of the Atlantic. The majority of leagues and major world competitions have sponsors, sometimes several. Grand Prix, for example, is sponsored by dozens of companies, each with its logo plastered over cars. The Olympics are officially sponsored by a group of blue chip companies which receive in return the right to use the Olympic rings on their merchandise.

Individual athletes often have portfolios of sponsorship contracts, most with companies that have no obvious connection with sports, but wish their products to be associated with a popular and ostensibly wholesome pursuit or person. Athletes endorse products regardless of whether they actually use them. Sponsors seek sports performers with images that signify something about their product. Anna Kournikova's contract with Berlei to endorse the Shock Absorber sports bra is an example: although Kournikova had won only one title (Australian women's doubles) at the time, her youth, looks, and style of dress suggested a perfect match with the bra-makers.

One of the many consequences of the global expansion of the mass and multimedia has been the sharpening of awareness in other cultures. "Awareness" probably understates the case, because there has been a convergence of tastes, consumption patterns, and enthusiasm for lifestyles, many of which have origins in the United States. Witness the eagerness of young people all over the world to follow the NBA, wear replica clothes, and devour any artifact connected with basketball. Yet it is soccer, a sport largely ignored in the States, that has become the first truly global game, capturing the interest of every continent, especially at the time of its World Cup championship. Neither of these sports would have occupied their current status without television.

The global convergence manifests itself in several other areas, of course. Like: the proliferation of fast-food restaurants, the ubiquity of Hollywood movies, and the prevalence of American-English as a language that serves as a medium between different nations – indeed, many of the phrases in the new *lingua franca* derive from a sports idiom. Telstar, the first communications satellite, went into orbit in 1962; since then a miscellany of different transponders have been launched, offering a daily bill of fare of news, sports, and entertainment to a planetary audience. This has been interpreted as part of a generic pattern in which Western powers have sought to conquer and control developing countries and maintain their dominance in a non-economic, non-military way: through the imposition of cultures.

Sport, no less than religion, television, and movies, has played a vital part in this process, occasionally called "Coca-colonization." The meaning of this is that, after the old Western colonial powers ceded their control, multinational corporations took over and introduced a different form of control, this one based on the culture their products carry with them. Coca-Cola is the supreme example: an American product that became arguably the best-known brand in the world. It sourced materials, set up plants, employed labor, and exported its products all over the world. It was also the most prodigious sponsor of sports and one of the biggest beneficiaries of sports' worldwide appeal.

These then are the conditions under which Rupert Murdoch was able to rise to his unique position. His influence developed out of an extraordinary combination of changing global conditions and a corporate set-up flexible enough to be able both to respond to the changes and push them in the direction Murdoch desired. All of which leads us back to the question asked at the beginning of this chapter: were Murdoch not around, would sports be as they are?

The answer is a tentative one: probably. There have been transformations underlying Murdoch's rise, including a technological revolution in the communications field, corporate realignments in the media industry, an expansion of world commerce, a confluence of culture, and a new-found marketability of sports. All of these have established circumstances conducive to the growth of media–sports empires. Vertical integration, as we have seen, was by no means the sole preserve of Murdoch. Turner had turned around his television stations by incorporating sports clubs into his complex. Several other media giants also employed the strategy of gathering clubs and other sources of program content in their efforts to control the entire supply–demand chain. Murdoch's strategy was on a grander scale and perhaps with a higher purpose;

there were those who suspected his efforts to produce, transmit, and sell events were part of a plan to control all sports. Yet, the strategy was not unique.

Coming from a relatively isolated country with a small market probably gave Murdoch a more global perspective than contemporaries, like Disney's Michael Eisner or James Dolan, of Cablevision, both Americans who had little experience or interest beyond the States. Murdoch was also well-versed in other media beside television. His father was a newspaper proprietor and his first few enterprises were in the Australian and British print media. The advantages of cross-ownership were not lost on Murdoch: profits from a lucrative medium could be used to underwrite short-term losses in another. Additionally, newspapers were useful as a way of publicizing other media. So, Murdoch held a competitive advantage when the predacious pursuit began. Were he not around, the other corporate predators would surely have extended their interests though perhaps not at the hellfire pace they did in late 1990s. The power in sports would still be distributed between about four or five media execs, though no individual would reign as supremely as Murdoch.

What we once called spectators or audiences are now markets; what were once measured in thousands are now measured in dozens of millions. The global technological and commercial developments at the end of the twentieth century ensured that the shape and character of sports would be changed more radically than at any stage in organized sports' history. It is possible that entrepreneurs were slow in realizing the genuine commercial potential of sports. If so, they made up for it. They did so by opening out the potential market of those who wanted to sell products with sports and by turning sports themselves into products that could be transported around the world like articles of trade. Nike offers us an object lesson in this. We will look at its development in the globalization process in the next chapter.

FURTHER READING

Big League, Big Time: The birth of the Arizona Diamondbacks, the billion-dollar business of sports, and the power of the media in America by Len Sherman (Pocket Books, 1998) is a fascinating case study of the MLB expansion franchise; as its subtitle suggests, the influence of corporate business and media conglomerates is apparent throughout. Also dealing with the business of franchising, though not as strong as Sherman's account are: *Home Team: Professional sports and the American metropolis* by Michael Danielson (Princeton University Press, 1997) and *Major League Losers: The real cost of sports and who's paying for it* by Mark Rosentraub (HarperCollins, 1997).

The Name of the Game: The business of sports by Jerry Gorman and Kirk Calhoun (Wiley, 1994) is an excellent overview of the different facets of sports business, including licensing, luxury boxes, and salaries. Complemented by *The Business of Professional Sports*, edited by Paul Staudohar and James Mangan (University of Illinois Press, 1991), a somewhat dated, though still valuable collection of essays.

Newszak and News Media by Bob Franklin (Arnold, 1997), *Global Television: An introduction* by Chris Barker (Blackwell, 1997), and *Megamedia Shakeout: The inside story of the leaders and the losers in the exploding communications industry* by Kevin Maney (Wiley, 1995) provide examinations of how the globalized media industry took shape in the late 1990s.

Rupert Murdoch by William Shawcross (Chatto & Windus, 1992) and *Rupert Murdoch: A paper prince* by Georg Muster (Penguin, 1985) are two biographies of Murdoch that have useful background information but few details of his television exploits. Better in this respect is *SkyHigh: The inside story of BSkyB* by Mathew Horsman (Orion Business, 1997).

ASSIGNMENT

You are appointed head of marketing services at a worldwide credit card company, not unlike American Express. For years, your brand has marketed itself on class and privilege. Despite competition from other credit cards, the cachet your company has enjoyed has kept it among the market leaders. Recently, however, your exclusivity has become dated. Even your advertising slogans, such as "never be without it," and "that will do adequately" have become the target of comedians' jokes. Market share has declined sharply. After studying the spending and lifestyle habits of each of your 1 million cardholders your research department has concluded that there is a growing interest in sports among them. Design a series of initiatives that will exploit the sports connection and report the result.

the 〰 that conquered the world

Nike and the

globalization process

DON'T THINK ABOUT IT . . .

You are either wearing or sitting within 20 feet of someone
wearing a product that bears the swoosh symbol. Despite
Nike's fall from grace in the late 1990s, it had built such a
formidable presence in the sports and leisure industry that
its name was almost synonymous with contemporary sports.
It is impossible to find a major sports event anywhere in
the world that does not bear the Nike imprimatur, either as a
competition sponsor, or the supplier of footwear and apparel,
or as an advertiser at the competition venue. The trademark
swoosh, as Nike call the tick or checkmark that is its logo, is
everywhere.

Like sides of a triangle, Nike, the National Basketball
Association (NBA), and its best-known ex-player Michael
Jordan fit together perfectly to form a geometric whole; take
any side away and all you have is an angle. Each owes its
global success to the global success of the other two. Nike
started as an independent sports shoe importer, the NBA an
ailing league with little market value, and Jordan a decent but
unspectacular second-draft pick from the University of North
Carolina. When they all came together, they produced an
international phenomenon. We will focus on Nike, then move

323

Logo

An abbreviation of logotype (from the Greek *logos* for word), this was largely advertising jargon 20 years ago, but has come into popular use in recent years. It describes an unbroken strip of type, lettering, badge, or insignia used by organizations to promote their corporate identities in advertising and publicity material. Today, it is difficult to find a sports performer or team that does not bear at least one, and, more usually, many logos. For example, a pro cyclist, tennis player, or racing driver will typically wear several logos on their uniforms signifying their sponsors. Logos have been especially important in licensing sports-related products. Sports-governing federations strictly control the use of logos by manufacturers and will seek redress from any company using, for instance, the "W" of Wimbledon or the silhouette of the basketball players of the NBA without permission. The growth of the sports logo is, in many ways, a symbol of the corporateness of contemporary sports.

---

to the NBA and Jordan to see how each complemented each other at the close of the twentieth century. In the process, we will show how globalization both affects and is affected by sports.

In a relatively short period of 30 years, Nike's founder, head, and principal stockholder, Phil Knight, broke up the domination of the athletic clothes and shoes market enjoyed by the German brothers, Adi and Rudi Dassler, the respective owners of adidas and Puma. Since 1948, when Rudi had walked out of his father's business and set up the rival Puma (originally called "Ruda"), the two companies had carved up world sales between them. Through the 1970s, a variety of challengers emerged, the strongest of them being Reebok. But, by the late 1980s, Nike had gained a clear edge.

Nike's advantage was based on an apparent understanding of cultural changes, the main one being the shift to consumerism. While others envisaged a market waiting to be exploited, Knight saw new markets waiting to be created; products that were to be displayed rather than just worn; commodities whose value lay less in what they were, more in who was wearing them.

Knight's market was simple: the planet. He wanted – and got – Nike in every corner of the world. He sourced his materials and manufactured his goods in East Asia and sold literally everywhere. Nike was a genuinely global operation. And an extremely profitable one. While its production costs were low, Nike's prices were high: the first $100 sports shoes, in 1986, may have been a flop, but they cleared the way for more extravagant ventures. Knight himself always denied that his company produced anything other than sportswear, but Nike was a fashion item. Nike was worn at the gyms, on the tracks, and in any sports arena; but it was also worn in the clubs and bars, on the streets, and, for a while, in the early 1990s in some boardrooms.

Its slogan "Just do it" had an odd resonance that seemed to appeal cross-culturally. Presumably prefixed by an unspoken "Don't think about it . . ." the phrase was a pragmatic appeal for action. Like other aspects of Nike's corporate persona, it was ideally suited to an age when theory was out-of-vogue, earning money was virtuous, and lunch was for wimps, as the stock-broker Gordon Gecko famously put it in the Oliver Stone movie *Wall Street*.

Right-wing governments under Ronald Reagan in the United States and Margaret Thatcher in Britain in the 1980s promoted a culture in which individualism and the ethic of personal achievement were paramount. Competition was not only healthy, but essential to the well-being of the individual; and this had ramifications at all levels. Cut-backs in welfare payments, affirmative action programs, and other areas of public spending were designed to decrease what many saw as a dependency culture – with an over-reliance on what the British call the "Nanny state."

Nike embodied much of this spirit. Its messages were in sharp contrast to early sporting morals that emphasized the importance of competing over winning. Nike mocked second-placers. Even winning was only one stop on a quest to fulfillment. "There is no finish line," one of Nike's ads reminded its potential customers.

THE SEDUCTION OF SNOW WHITE

Phil Knight was neither a sprinter, nor a marathon runner. The writers J. B. Strasser and Laurie Becklund believe this is significant: when he started his business, Knight was not seeking instant gratification, but nor did he want to wait an eternity for success. He wanted to distribute his energies evenly, pace himself, and exercise strategy – all elements of middle-distance running. Knight himself was no more than an able middle-distance runner on the track; but his application of the elements to industry was devastating.

After working with Bill Bowerman, who became head coach of the US Olympic team at the 1972 summer games (and who, incidentally, was played by Donald Sutherland in Robert Towne's 1999 film *Without Limits*), Knight moved on from the University of Oregon and enrolled at Harvard Business School, where he studied to be an accountant. Here, Knight designed a class project in which he headed a hypothetical company that specialized in sports footwear imported from Japan. His premise was that labor costs in East Asia were far less than those in Europe and the USA.

During the early 1960s, the sports footwear and apparel market was dominated by a sibling rivalry between Adi Dassler, at adidas, and his brother Rudi, of Puma. The Dassler brothers grew ever more competitive in their attempts to establish leadership of the field. American and British manufacturers lagged way behind, specializing in flat-soled sneaker-type shoes, as opposed to the sturdy leather purpose-built jobs with arch and ankle supports that were being produced by the German brothers.

Knight was an admirer not only of adidas' product, but the style in which it promoted its goods. But, he thought he could produce something as good, yet cheaper. His first forays into the industry were tentative: he asked Tiger, a Japanese sports goods manufacturer, to study the adidas design and send him shipments of its version; he would then sell for them in the States. He consulted his ex-coach Bowerman who suggested improvements, particularly in terms of material. Bowerman was a great believer in lightened shoes, his theory being that if you count the number of paces a runner uses, say 880 strides over 1,500 meters and multiply by the number of ounces you can save by making his or her shoes lighter, then the runner carries less weight and can travel faster. Take an ounce off the weight of the shoes and runner is unburdened by 54 pounds.

Japan, in the post-war period, had made significant progress in developing nylon and leather substitute materials, this being made necessary by the lack of land suitable for cattle breeding – and hence no leather. This proved rather beneficial for Knight, who, in 1964, entered into a partnership with Bowerman: Blue Ribbon Sports (BRS) with a starting capital of $1,000. Knight and Bowerman intended to import Japanese-made Tiger footwear made to their own specifications, though modeled on adidas, and sell in 13 western states.

Selling out of a car trunk and taking orders from his father's basement, Knight built his reputation for selling shoes designed by athletes for athletes. The industry giants were warring with each other over big international meetings. It was suspected that adidas was actually giving away its footwear simply to enhance its brand recognition: the distinctive three stripes on either side of the shoe were world-renowned. As Olympic and world championships were becoming global media events thanks to the interest of television, so the athletic footwear market was expanding. Puma responded by taking the unheard of step of paying athletes to wear its products. While this is commonplace today, it was a breakthrough idea in the 1960s, when track and field was ostensibly amateur.

But the matrix for Nike's extraordinarily successful endorsement program was set in 1972 when Blue Ribbon Sports paid tennis star Ilie Nastase $3,000 to use its shoes. Nastase was an interesting choice: a hotheaded and exciting player, he seemed to personify an attitude that Nike shared: always prepared to challenge decisions, often belligerent, and frequently preferring to lose with style rather than win without it. Nastase, while fondly remembered as a baroque character, was never a tennis great; but everything he did, he did with flamboyance. And this made him perfect for Nike. As with many seemingly inspired decisions, its motive was much baser than one might expect. Both Nastase and the then promising teenager but relatively unknown Jimmy Connors had the same agent. Knight was offered both in a sort of package deal. Knight, wanting to save a few dollars, signed only Nastase.

Nike's other key athlete at the time was Steve Prefontaine, a white American middle-distance runner, who missed out at the 1972 Munich Olympics, but who continued to command a following usually reserved for rock stars. Fans wore tee-shirts emblazoned with "Go Pre" and followed him to track meets. Were he alive today, he would have probably have made cds and appeared in movies. Tragically, he died in a road crash in 1975. Nike had subsidized his training, his coach being Bowerman.

After the Amateur Sports Act, of 1978, Nike was able to subsidize athletes: with most major sports abandoning their amateur status, track and field went open, though it had been known for years that under-the-counter payments had sustained the sport and that, in Soviet-bloc countries, athletes were practically full-time professionals, anyway. Nike set up its own track club called Athletics West in Eugene, Oregon, and gave athletes enough support to pursue their sports without having to take part-time jobs. Knight resisted the temptation to include Nike in the name of the club, preferring to allow the worst-kept secret about Nike's financial involvement to circulate. Still, it was a crucial move in Nike's development because it was able both to subsidize and sponsor – which is tantamount to owning – a sport without violating any codes.

The beginning of Athletics West was also the beginning of Nike's transition from a private company worth $28 million to an international public corporation that capitalized, in 1980, at $240 million. Blue Ribbon Sports had been producing goods called Nike for some time, the name being taken from the Greek goddess of victory. In 1978, having disentangled itself from its original Japanese supplier and set up alternative manufacturing sources, it changed its name to Nike.

The whole sports shoe market was buoyant as the health craze of the 1970s swept through North America and Europe. As some measurement of the jogging boom's growth, Strasser and Becklund note that, in 1970, there were just 156 entrants in the annual New York Marathon. By 1977, this had increased more than 32-fold to 5,000. And, to indicate Nike's presence in this boom, Strasser and Becklund point out that 11 of the first 20 finishers in 1977 were wearing Nike shoes. Even then, it would have been impossible to predict the scale of Nike's project over the next several years. Its products had earned a reputation for being runner-friendly: light mesh uppers and the characteristic waffle sole had found favor among joggers and pro athletes alike. But the sportswear market had limits.

Knight's biggest signing in 1978 was John McEnroe whom he paid $25,000. McEnroe was an even better fit for Nike than Nastase: his temperament ensured that even meaningless early round matches of tennis tournaments were likely to become explosive. McEnroe's histrionics gained him the kind of reputation that Knight wanted for his products: insubordinate, brassy, and defiant. With adidas still leading the market, it was Knight's ambition to position Nike as its most audacious contender. In one memorably tasteless sales meeting address in 1978, Knight likened adidas to Snow White. "This year, we became the biggest dwarf," he told his sales team. "And next year, we're going to get into her pants" (quoted in Strasser and Becklund 1993: 271).

A central thrust of Knight's assault was the Tailwind, at $50 the most expensive running shoe to date and a technological innovation, incorporating a sealed module of air in its sole. Launched in 1978, it was a disaster initially, tiny particles of metal in its silver dye rubbing against the shoe's fibers and cutting the uppers. But Knight was undeterred and opened a sports research laboratory with the brief to its staff to come up with concepts like the air module every six months. It will not have escaped any reader's attention that the original idea behind the Tailwind later became the basis for the gargantuan Air Jordan line.

The link with Michael Jordan was forged amid concern about the future of Nike. In 1985, after eight years of market growth and increasing profits, Nike reported two consecutive losing quarters. The market had expanded and new players had entered the fray. While the supremacy of adidas and Puma had been ended, Reebok, a company started in England in the late nineteenth century, had come to the fore. In 1979, Paul Fireman bought the rights to the Reebok name and began a US operation. Within two years, sales were up to $1.5 million and, by 1984, $65 million. Its sudden rise had caught Nike and indeed the whole sector unaware.

Nike's credibility was based on the testimonies of sports performers. If people like Bo Jackson and Andre Agassi wore Nike and spoke on its behalf, then their endorsements carried weight. At least they carried weight with those who played football or tennis – or ran or engaged in any other sports, for that matter. Strasser and Becklund reckon that: "Even in 1980, most consumers were still not aware that many pro athletes were paid to wear shoes" (1993: 258). They probably learnt very quickly over the next few years; but, by then, it did not make much difference, anyway.

Reebok's strategy was different: rather than aim at sports followers, it targeted the apostles of aerobics. Aerobics was a new subsector of the sports market and one that Nike and the others had failed to exploit. For Reebok, the great outdoors did not beckon: its stomping ground was the sprung timber floors of health clubs.

After a shaky start to his enterprise, Fireman did a trading deal with Stephen Rubin of Liverpool and took advantage of Nike's apparent apathy. By 1983, Nike was leading the athletic footwear market, but was not producing any lines designed specifically at women's aerobics. The policy of signing high-profile sports personalities had stood Nike in good stead, but there were suspicions that it had outlived its usefulness. Reebok's campaign included giving away its products to aerobics instructors, whose pupils would take notice.

With profits taking a pounding, Nike needed to cut back its endorsement budget: it opted to go after a few key athletes and offer them money, while just giving away free gear to others. In 1984, the NBA was making gains in the television viewer ratings. It boasted only a small number of stars – Larry Bird, Magic Johnson, Isiah Thomas – and they were under contract to the sports goods maker, Converse. Nike wanted to isolate a name player and tie its colors to him. At one point, it actually released many of its roster, allowing them to find new sponsors.

Nike's ads were blamed for "Sneaker wars" in which young people attacked others and robbed them of their desirable footwear; Nikes were the most desirable. They became the shoes of choice for African American youths, a fact that spurred Jesse Jackson to action. On behalf of his Operation Push (a strategy for securing equal opportunities for ethnic minorities), he protested to Nike that, while it profited from sales to black people and used black people in its advertising, its management structure remained white. In 1990, he warned of a boycott of Nike products if Knight did not promise more contracts with minority businesses and jobs for black people. Jackson claimed, though without evidence, that Nike sold up to 45 per cent of its products to inner-city youths, many of whom were African Americans, though Nike itself estimated only 13 per cent of sales were made to ethnic minorities.

Knight was able to call Jackson's bluff, though he promised to re-evaluate Nike's equal opportunity program. Over the next several years, Nike was criticized for other forms of exploitation. Investigators exposed the menial wages Nike paid to workers in developing countries and compared these to the retail prices of its products in the West. The *New York Times* was swingeing in its attacks of Nike's labor practices. Nike was one of several sports good manufacturers which made use of poorly-paid Asian labor; in fact, it was revealed that some of its products were actually made under the same roof as its competitors', often by the same personnel. Nike's response was to get together with other sports goods manufacturers and draw up a code of practice. Self-satisfied, Nike attached "No sweat" tags to its garments, an allusion to the Asian "sweatshops" it once operated.

And, as if to underline its social conscience, Nike formed NEAT (Nike Environmental Action Team) in 1993. This project encouraged the recycling of worn shoes and created inner-city playgrounds and sports areas and worked as a sop to environmentalists. PLAY (Participate in the Lives of American Youth) was launched in 1994 with Michael Jordan and Jackie Joyner-Kersee as figureheads: this was aimed at reclaiming public spaces for youth. A skeptic might interpret these initiatives as part of Nike's strategy to offset the harm done to its reputation by reports of its labor exploitation in underdeveloped countries.

By 1993, one in every three pairs of sports shoes sold were Nikes. Only Reebok, which was started in England, seemed to have the marketing guile to give Nike a run for its money. Pretenders, like LA Gear and British Knights came and went. Brands such as these made explicit concessions toward fashion, while Knight insisted that Nike was serious sportswear. No one wanted to be seen in a pair of trainers that were not built to train in. Yet, five years later, Nike was under pressure again, not from a rival this time – though adidas was staging a strong rally – but from the market itself.

SEX AND THE MARKETPLACE

In the previous chapter, we took note of Donald Katz's insight about sports' surpassing pop music as a vehicle for selling and how it even eclipsed sex as an orienting consumer theme in the early 1990s (1994: 25–6). In more recent years, the demarcation line between sports and sex has become less distinct, especially in the marketplace where sport and sex permeate, well, everything. The market is not confined to palpable goods and services: it peddles ideas and beliefs, including what Katz and indeed the people at Beavertown called "the Nike spirit."

In the 1990s, sports became "sexy" in more than one sense. Quite apart from the more overt pandering to male libidos by using female athlete models in erotic poses, sport sold itself as inescapably chic: wearing the right label on clothes was a virtual requirement. Sports clothing became leisure-wear. No one was seriously going to spend $200+ on a pair of shoes decorated with all the right appliqués and then wear them for football practice. In the 1970s, people would have balked at the idea of becoming an ambulant advertisement for a sportswear company; in the 1990s, they had to pay extra to have the name and logo plastered across their tops. And not just any name and logo: Hilfiger might have been cool last year, but 12 months on, it could be passé.

Sheryl Swoopes

Swoopes was the athlete Nike tried to turn into a "female Jordan," in the sense that it designed a range of shoes and apparel especially for her and called it "Air Swoopes." Nike had earlier used Gabrielle Reece in an advertising campaign, but her image was used in poses rather than action shots. Unlike Reece, Swoopes was better known for her play than her looks. A formidably productive college player (for Texas Tech), she broke all manner of scoring records and won a gold medal with the USA team at the Atlanta Olympics. She turned pro with the Houston Comets in 1997, the first season of the Women's National Basketball Association (WNBA).

---

adidas was quicker to notice the potential of melding sports and entertainment, but slower to capitalize fully on it. In 1985, the then aspirant rap music entrepreneur Russell Simmons invited adidas representatives to a hip-hop concert featuring his band Run DMC. Unimpressed, the adidas people wondered what Simmons's point was until the impresario turned their attention to the crowd. One of the band members urged the audience to throw their adidases in the air. The result was a volcanic eruption of sports shoes, all bearing the trademark three stripes. adidas realized how its shoes, far from being just sportswear, were now fashion accessories; it signed a deal to sponsor the next Run DMC tour. The band itself responded by releasing its track "My adidas."

Whether Knight himself had prescience and knew sports were going to acquire a new status, or whether he contrived to make this happen, we may never know. Maybe he just happened to have the right product and the right moment in history. One thing we can be sure of: he understood the ephemerality of taste. Never content to let a brand, or a line, succeed, he constantly replaced them with new brands and lines. The changes came with head-spinning speed. No doubt, he learnt this tactic from fashion houses which organized their output in terms of seasons. The label may have been a signifier of quality, but the collection from which it came was also material.

This meant that Nikes became collectible: they could be dated, even cataloged. Connoisseurs – and they still exist – were able to date and value Nike items by just looking at them. A pair of first issue 1987 Air Max's, for example, was eminently collectible; these were the first model to make the air pocket in the sole of the shoe visible. On reflection, they were the shoes that kickstarted Nike's resurgence. With Reebok owning a 30 per cent market share and Nike 21 per cent, Knight gambled with the Air Max, paying Bo

Jackson, who played both football and baseball, $100,000 to endorse them. The ad agency Wieden & Kennedy created the celebrated "Bo knows . . ." campaign to push the product, which was instrumental in Nike's return to market leadership. Hence, the historical significance of the Air Max.

Nike was able to pull through the 1986 crisis and another in 1993. But, in 1998, a third major slump in sales forced the company to issue a profits warning. The problem this time looked less to do with Nike, its products or its advertising; more to do with a structural shift in the market. Jordan's retirement may not have helped, but changes in fashion hurt all sports goods manufacturers. Consumers turned away from athletic gear and toward other brands. Despite Knight's insistence that Nike was a sports goods firm, the evidence suggested differently: some 80 per cent of Nike sales were for non-sports purposes. When sales slumped and Nike profits plummeted to unprecedented depths, Knight's assertion looked especially weak. The fashion that had served him so well for over a decade turned on him. The Nike swoosh that had once signified voguish rebellion changed into a symbol of conformity, the kind of logo that young people would expect to see their fathers wearing.

Knight had made provision for this: knowing soccer, as the most popular sport in the world, offered a mature and prosperous market, Knight wished to establish its presence. Nike contracted the Brazilian Football Federation to a £250 million ($400 million) arrangement which included the right to organize matches, promote tournaments, and sell television rights. The deal formed the core of Nike Sports Entertainment (NSE), the company's event management arm. NSE promoted and produced five Brazil exhibition games per year around the world as well as several other events featuring the company's roster of sports stars. It also promoted the first World Championship of Beach Volleyball. NSE seemed to herald the development of the world's first sports and media conglomerate: the inclusion of the word "entertainment" revealed something of Knight's ambitions.

In some senses, the ascent of Nike is attributable to the gnomic wisdom of Phil Knight, a man who seemed to know more about the mysteries of changes in youth culture and how to exploit them than any other entrepreneur. In another sense, Knight was just part of a new cultural equation that transformed the relationship between supply and demand.

Cultural tastes and fashions may not be totally controllable; but they can be heavily influenced. To take an uncomplicated example from Malcolm Waters's book *Globalization*: "The British taste for tea . . . could not have been cultivated in that damp little island had it not been possible to export its cheap textiles to Southern Asia, albeit to sell them in captive colonial markets, along with common law, cricket and railways" (1995: 66–7).

Nike did not make sports fashionable, though its role in that process is undeniably significant: it extended, expanded, and even exaggerated them in accordance with its own priorities. Sports drew alongside the entertainment industry as one of the most longed-for means through which young, predominantly working-class people imagine becoming successful. Television, movies, and even educational institutions were all parts of a changing cultural configuration in which sports became more glamorous than at any stage in its history. All sorts of products could be sold merely by associating them with sports; which is why endorsement contracts became so lucrative.

Nike emerged after a rude awakening. America had learned that its hitherto unquestioned military and economic supremacy could be questioned after all. Defeat in Vietnam was a hurtful reminder that pride goeth before a fall. America reflected on itself and saw a nation that had gone flabby, a citizenry that ate too much, exercised too little and accepted comfort as if by divine right. Nike's invocation to "just do it" might have been intended for every American who had ever comforted himself or herself in the thought that they were a citizen of the richest, most unassailably powerful nation in history – and had been exposed.

In a sense, the rise of that other colossus of brands, Coca-Cola, might also be seen in the context of the USA's upheaval. In his *For God, Country and Coca-Cola*, Mark Prendergrast writes: "Coca-Cola grew up in a country, shaping and shaped by the times. The drink not only helped to alter consumption patterns, but attitudes toward leisure, work, advertising, sex, family life, and patriotism" (1993: 11). *Mutatis mutandis*, similar claims could be made for Nike in the last three decades of the twentieth century.

In fact, the parallels between Coca-Cola and Nike are inescapable. Both emerged from turbulent periods of change in American society and both became globally recognizable brands (Coca-Cola enlarged its market during the 1930s Depression). Coke, like Nike, seized high-profile stars, in its case from Hollywood, to endorse its products: Joan Crawford, Clark Gable, and Greta Garbo were among Coke's panoply. Coca-Cola's links with sport are well known: it provided soft drinks for athletes in the 1936 Olympics and continued to align itself with a health, vigor, robustness, and fitness, even when it became widely known that the drink itself did not promote any of these.

Jesse Jackson had famous conflicts with both Nike and Coca-Cola in 1981, threatening a boycott of Coke if the demands of African American bottling-plant owners were not met. Jackson reminded Coca-Cola that it had no blacks on its board of directors. It was the second major boycott threatened: in the early 1960s, Jackson's mentor Martin Luther King accused Coca-Cola of using black models in only subservient roles in its advertising and of having no black sales personnel. African Americans formed about 11 per cent of the total US population at the time, yet they consumed 17 per cent of Coca-Cola.

In a similar way, Nike found itself at the center of an equal opportunities embarrassment when Jackson's Push organization revealed what some felt to be an irony – others, an outrage: Nike employed precious few black senior managers at a time when virtually every black urban male under 30 appeared to be wearing Nikes. Both Coca-Cola and Nike were able to schmooze their ways out of embarrassing situations and maintain their popular appeal with markets that were predominantly white.

Racial issues have beset the USA, and sport has mirrored many of them. Nike's adeptness in defusing potentially explosive situations was a factor in its ascent. The NBA too faced a problem. As we have noticed, Nike's destiny was tied to that of the NBA and its star player, Michael Jordan. Each, in its own way, was able to exploit predicaments with racial implications to their own advantage. In the next section, we will discover how the NBA rose to power and how its success both complemented and was fortified by Nike's.

STERN: THE MAN WHO SOLD THE NBA

A key year in the internationalization of sports was 1984, though it would not have seemed so at the time. David Stern took over as the Commissioner of the floundering NBA, Michael Jordan entered the professional league and the then fledgling cable television network ESPN decided to sell out to the ABC network for $237 million. Two years previously, ESPN had broadcast its first NBA game as part of a two-year contract; it had been featuring NCAA games since 1979 and, because it reached (by 1984) 34 million homes, could fairly claim to have primed interest in college and pro basketball. The draft arrangement made it possible for viewers to map the progress of young, aspiring amateurs before they transferred to the pros and grow familiar with the style and personalities of the players.

Since the 1970s, America's (not just North America's) televisual land-scape had become a lattice of cables, some underground, some on poles, all connected to stations which received signals from satellites. Cable viewers all over the continent were able to pick up television shows that originated in the USA. ESPN had exploited America's weakness for sports, serving up competitive action 24:7.

Stern realized the infrastructure was in place to transmit the NBA far and wide, but was also aware that his league lacked the legitimacy of the NFL or Major League Baseball, mainly because it lacked the backing of mainstream corporations. And the reason it lacked them was that, as one advertising agency put it to Stern, "the pro game is too black" (quoted in Halberstam 1999: 118).

The NBA, it was thought, was a sport played by black men and watched by black men. As the United States' black population was over-represented in poorer socio-economic groups and had less disposable income than most, it was not a demographic sector much sought-after by advertisers. Stern's first attempts to persuade ad agencies that the NBA's audiences were not predominantly black, but were as mixed as audiences for the college game, cut no ice.

In his *Playing for Keeps: Michael Jordan and the world he made*, David Halberstam argues that the enthusiasm for NCAA basketball was because: "The college game was perceived, perhaps unconsciously, as still operating within a white hierarchy, under powerful white supervision, a world where no matter who the foot soldiers were, the generals were still white" (1999: 118).

As professionals, black athletes were contractually as powerful as their coaches and able to dictate their own destinies. And this was troubling to white America, especially when coupled with the stories of drug abuse among professional sports performers, many of whom were African American. Overpaid young black males and cocaine seemed to go together in the consciousness of many Americans. Major corporations steered clear and the NBA's few backers were those interested in selling their products primarily to black consumers. Stern addressed this problem by introducing a league drugs policy: he struck an agreement with the Players' Association that allowed players with drug habits to own up without penalty. If they persisted in using illicit drugs, they could get expelled from the NBA. It helped clean up the image of the league.

A second major innovation of Stern's was the salary cap, which was introduced in 1984. The NBA cap was set at 51.8 per cent of the league's "defined gross revenues." While salaries were comparatively meager in early years, by 1998, this translated as $26.9 million (£16.5 million) per 12-man

---

A. G. Spalding

Spalding was the man who started the first sports goods manufacturing and retail industry. In 1876, Spalding opened what was then a unique store specializing in sports goods. Spalding's Baseball and Sporting-goods Emporium was based in Chicago and stocked baseball uniforms and equipment. The firm also manufactured baseball bats, croquet equipment, ice skates, and fishing tackle. Capitalizing on the cycling craze, Spalding published an *Official Cycling Guide* featuring pictures of bicycles, sweaters, and shoes, which he also sold. He anticipated later trends to sign players to endorsement deals and signed three pro cyclists to a contact that required them to use his cycles. Spalding, who had played professional baseball, had several other business interests, though his name is forever linked with recognizing and exploiting the demand for sporting goods and apparel.

team; or an average of over $2 million per player per year. Rather than let franchises operate independently (as, for example, Major League Baseball and, to a lesser extent, the NFL did), the NBA subordinated its members to the central organization and demanded compliance.

His new structure in place, Stern secured the sponsorship of the Miller Brewing Company and aggressively went after other corporations eager to tap into the youth market. The NBA was sold as a fast, exciting game with points racked up at a pace never approached by most other sports. It was also blessedly easy for the uninitiated to understand. Quite unlike the statistically-laden baseball and the intricately-ruled football, basketball was a straightforward game with a playing area that could have been designed as a stage for the more extravagant characters.

Two of the most famous players of the period were Earvin "Magic" Johnson and Larry Bird, whose frequent clashes became a staple feature of the NBA. Both high-class players, Johnson, of the LA Lakers, and Bird, from the Boston Celtics on the opposite coast, had a rivalry that helped the credibility of pro basketball in much the same way as Ali–Frazier and Navratilova–Evert had helped their respective sports. Johnson and Bird first met in the 1984 Finals; three years later when they again met in the Finals, the television viewing share more than doubled to 16 (i.e. 16 per cent of the total viewing population). Johnson was an African American and Bird a white player; they were both intensely competitive and vied for the mantle of the league's best player.

Stern oversaw the early globalization of basketball: a total of 75 different countries received NBA telecasts in 1988. But, by 1989, when Stern was ready to renegotiate a new domestic television deal, the Johnson–Bird rivalry was beginning to lose its potency. CBS had held the broadcasting rights since 1972 and was coming to the end of its four-year $188 million contract. NBC poured out a staggering $600 million to secure rights to the NBA for four years starting 1991. It seemed profligate; but NBC's head Dick Ebersol believed the demographics augured well. The NBA was followed avidly by young people of all ethnic backgrounds: NBC could offer its advertisers a direct route to the youth market at a time in history when young people were becoming the most sought-after consumers (sought-after, that is, by ad agencies and their clients). One of the most revealing acknowledgments of this is an ad for MTV that ran in the business sections of newspapers and was quoted by Thomas Frank: "Buy this 24-year-old and get all his friends for absolutely free," its headline read (1997: 150).

Ebersol may also have sensed the potential selling power of a player who seemed well-equipped to replace any interest lost by the disappearance of Johnson–Bird and whose mannerisms and style were being emulated by young people.

JORDAN: AIRBRUSHING THE ICON

Like the majority of the other players in the league, Michael Jordan was an African American. So, he did not have the same credentials of other American sports icons: Babe Ruth, Jack Dempsey, Joe Namath, *et al.* The reverence in which many now hold Muhammad Ali disguises the fact that, in the 1960s, he was regarded with contempt and described by one sports writer as: "a vicious propagandist for a spiteful mob that works the religious under-world" (Jimmy Cannon, quoted by Thomas Hauser in his *Muhammad Ali: His life and times*, 1997). For all the adulation he received in the 1930s, Joe Louis was accepted as a sports hero in an era when blacks could not vote, attend the same schools or live in the same areas as whites; the fact that Louis did not vocally oppose such arrangements earned him the epithet "a credit to his race."

Jordan had left the University of Carolina in 1984 after his junior year. David Falk, of the ProServ agency, had secured him a deal with the Chicago Bulls worth $3 million over five years and had opened negotiations with adidas and Converse as well as Nike. The emergence of athletes as product endorsers, a process hastened by Nike, of course, meant that pro sports performers regarded their salary as only one and not necessarily the biggest component of their income. Falk demanded that Nike paid Jordan in excess of his salary.

Nike's reply was to offer Jordan a guaranteed minimum plus a royalty. In other words, Jordan would receive a percentage of every piece of endorsed

---

David Falk

Falk is the agent for a fleet of leading sports performers, including many of the best-known NBA players. Because of his influence over so many stars, he has often been portrayed as a puppeteer, pulling the strings of professional basketball. Falk joined the ProServ agency in 1975 and began specializing in negotiating contracts for pro athletes. His major coup was in signing Michael Jordan. Falk was something of an architect, designing a complex structure of corporate links for Jordan: endorsements for the likes of McDonald's, Gatorade, Wheaties, etc., positioned Jordan at the fore of every television viewer's mind. Falk masterminded what might be called the commodification of Jordan, the crucial phase of the process being Jordan's association with Phil Knight's Nike. Falk's own agency, Falk Associates Management Enterprises (FAME), is based in Washington DC.

---

apparel or footwear sold. Not just items bearing his name, but all those in the Air range. That clinched it for Falk: adidas and Converse failed to match the terms and Jordan began the most remunerative commercial relationship with a sports good manufacturer in history.

With sales rising Knight embarked on one of the most aggressive advertising campaigns ever. In the year following his signing of Jordan, Nike's advertising budget leapt from $231 million to $281 million (almost 22 per cent). It seemed like manic extravagance. Even Nike's first toe in British waters was more of a triple pike: in 1992, Knight signed a £4 million deal to supply Arsenal's kit (uniform).

Nike designed a "Jump man" logo for its Air Jordan range and its impact was immediate: $130 million in sales in the brand's first year. As if to underline the sensitivity of the product to Jordan's public appearances, sales dropped off in the second year when Jordan missed 62 games with an injury. Jordan himself said nothing in the first Nike advertising campaign featuring him. "Who said man wasn't meant to fly?" was the question strapped across the screen after a slo-mo clip of him in mid-air.

Another famous campaign featured Jordan with the fictional character Mars Blackmon, who was drawn from Spike Lee's 1986 film *She's Gotta Have It*. Lee also directed the commercial, which was steeped in signifiers of urban street culture, including rap music. The triumph of this campaign was not only in sales, but in its projection of an African American as wholesome and unthreatening and yet still irreverent enough to hold his own on the streets.

At the time, Nike had just slipped behind Reebok in the global trade war. Four years later, Nike had regained the lead and forced Reebok into one of its most embarrassing moves. Recognizing the value of Jordan to Nike, Reebok tried to repeat the trick for itself, signing Shaq O'Neal for $15 million over five years. It was an expensive lesson. Not only did it pass on a renewal of O'Neal's contract after it expired in 1998, but Reebok cut Emmitt Smith for a $1 million buyout fee. In the three years leading to 1998, sales of sports shoes dropped and Reebok trimmed its roster from 130 endorsers to just 20. "Branding" players was no guarantee of cachet, nor of sales. The choice of player, the style of promotion and the social conditions under which the promotion takes place were all important factors that Nike managed to judge to perfection.

"No company enriched Michael Jordan more than Nike or benefited more from his career. Jordan had made around $130 million from Nike over his career by 1998," writes Halberstam, adding: "Not all of Nike's growth was attributable to Jordan's presence, of course, but in 1984 the company had revenues of $919 million and a net income of about $40 million, and by the end of 1997, Nike's revenues were over $9 billion, with a net of around $800 million" (1999: 412–13).

By 1998, Jordan products were estimated to have grossed about $2.6 *billion* for Nike, according to *Fortune* magazine writers Roy S. Johnson and Ann Harrington (1998: 67). The same writers suggest that his value to Nike lay in the power of his name and the ties to the consumer rather than strictly sales and this is worth double the sales amount.

What these bare figures conceal is the work Jordan's agent, David Falk, and Nike put into projecting Jordan, the role played by Stern and the NBA in providing a showcase for the player and the shrewd judgment of Ebersol of NBC television in committing his network to the broadcasting of the NBA. Take any one of these figures out of the equation and Jordan would probably be regarded as a good player; but certainly not as a globally recognizable icon. Take away Jordan and there would be no NBA, at least not a universally popular league that boasts more celebrity players than any other sport. And Nike?

At the time of signing Jordan, Nike had around 20 per cent of the world market in sports shoes and apparel that was led by Reebok. It is possible that Reebok, having ridden the crest of the health wave, would have suffered as the wave broke; it is also possible that another brand might have stolen its way into the hearts, minds, and pockets of young people. Nike picked the perfect intersection of history and personality. At a time when America was still mortified by its never-ending racial problems, it was comforting to know that blacks, however humble their origins, could soar to the top.

Jordan's play could mesmerize audiences, his persuasive advertising could enchant markets. He did not talk politics and his comments about the condition of black people were virtually meaningless. His followers stayed spellbound as long as he did not grow up: while he continued to play the game everyone played in the childhood or youth and acted as a role model of sorts for children, appearing in commercials with young people who sang that they wanted to "be like Mike," his supporters were happy. Were he to have chosen "adult" subjects to talk about in public, or criticized Nike's employment practices or got involved in the kinds of activities typically attributed to black males, then he would have been dropped. Jordan's success was conditional on his remaining a well-behaved man-child in the promised land: a black American who resisted every conceivable negative quality and remained virtuous in the eyes of whites.

And the collective forces of Nike, the NBA, and his agent were involved in this process; so too was NBC, which, as *Sports Illustrated* writer Rick Reilly put it, "airbrushed every Jordan zit into a dimple for 10 years" (vol. 90, no. 2, 1999).

So different was Jordan from the image of the black male that stalks the popular consciousness, that it was almost possible to forget he was black at all. The dread engendered by a virile young black man did not apply to Jordan: he was a symbolic eunuch when it came to women: happily married and strictly unavailable. The goody-two-shoes image took a few knocks when details of Jordan's gambling habit were disclosed, but, if anything, the revelations helped in reassuring the world that this all-too-perfect being had all-too-human failings.

Jordan came to prominence as a black man with no ax to grind, someone who had risen to the top on merit. In a way, he was proof that the civil rights of the 1960s and days of what was once called an American dilemma were gone for ever. Not all black people, he seemed to suggest, were preoccupied with racism and the obstacles it strewed in their paths. White America was in a kind of racial torment in the mid-1980s: the vigilante-style shooting by Bernhard Goetz of black assailants in 1984; the Howard Beach incident of 1986 when white youths assaulted three black men, chasing one to his death on a busy parkway. These had stretched racial tensions. A year later black teenager Tawana Brawley reported that she had been kidnapped and raped by a gang of white men; her story turned out to be a hoax but it added to the mounting psychodrama. The image of Jordan brought comfort amid an atmosphere of challenge and confrontation.

Let us remind ourselves once more: Nike, the NBA, and Jordan owed everything to each other. None of them would have succeeded on a global scale without the others; each was absolutely essential to the success of the trinity. Yet there is still one other factor that made the dominion of the world possible.

The whole phenomenon was made possible by video. I use the term here in its generic sense, referring to the transmission of images via communications technology. Obviously, television has been the most effective and most encompassing form of video technology. By the end of the twentieth century, few, if any, parts of the globe did not have access to television. Since the 1960s, sport and television have existed in a symbiotic relationship, each depending on the other to create revenues. The interest of sponsors, advertisers, and manufacturers seeking endorsements from sports performers is strongly linked to the "videation" – that is, the recording and broadcasting – of sports.

As we have seen in Chapter twelve, sports were appealing to television companies, principally because they were a lot cheaper than drama; when the viewing figures started climbing, the sports organizations began to hike their prices. Television responded by paying the asking prices, but needed to guarantee viewer ratings to make sports a viable proposition. One way was to make televised sports as, if not more, attractive to audiences than actually being there. So, television moved away from the more naturalistic approach of just relaying the contest in the raw and toward what Jay Coakley calls "videated sports," which are "used to create dramatic, exciting and stylized images and messages for the purpose of entertaining viewers and maintaining sponsors" (1998).

To state that Jordan would not exist were it not for television sounds frivolous; Jordan the player would; but not Jordan the icon – the image that has been relayed around the world countless times, plastered across billboards and buildings, stamped onto millions of food packets and even digitally mixed into cartoons. This is a Jordan that exists independently of Jordan the flesh-and-blood man; it is a phenomenon about which followers are prepared to believe almost anything, including the ability to fly.

Halberstam writes of Jordan's "other incarnation" borne of Nike ads: "The commercials were brief, but there were so many of them and they were done with such talent and charm that they formed an ongoing story. Their cumulative effect was to create a figure who had the power and force and charisma of a major movie star" (1999: 183–4). Of course, in contrast to movie stars, Jordan's deeds were not artificial.

So many pieces of information about the world reach our senses via electronic media that we might say we live in a "videated" culture in which entertainment and life have become not inseparable but the same. Images devour life so that our experiences are shaped by tv characters and tv coverage of news events.

The image of Michael Jordan was bigger, immeasurably bigger, than the man. Jordan would simply not have been possible without the cultural and technological transmutations that turned society into one vast network of co-axial cables, with millions of homes in the world connected to all others via some kind of link. And if this incarnation of Jordan was not possible without tv, then the same must be said of the NBA, whose big contract with NBC guaranteed it the kind of exposure it needed to compete with other major league sports; and of Nike which exploited the cultural and commercial possibilities of television in a way no other company had contemplated.

"Circuits of promotion" is David Whitson's term to describe the endless loop-like way in which various forms of "recursive and mutually reinforcing" streams of communications "generate more visibility and more business for all concerned" and in which "cultural commodities, including celebrities, can become vehicles for the promotion of more than one producer's product at once" (1998: 67). The case of Nike, the NBA, Jordan, and, indeed, his club illustrate Whitson's point perfectly. He writes: "Nike . . . attached its corporate persona to images of Michael Jordan, but when Jordan appeared in Nike advertisements in the early 1990s, he was adding to the global visibility of the Chicago Bulls, the NBA, and the game of basketball, as well as promoting Nike shoes" (1998: 67).

There is no distinct effect to speak of; only another cycle, or circuit, popular culture feeding back into an international "economy of signs" in which the symbolic values of products and images replace their use values and a pair of Nikes can fetch ten times more than another pair made of the same materials and under the same factory roof. This was and is the global economy that Nike both helped create and dominate.

FURTHER READING

Just Do It: The Nike spirit in the corporate world (Adams Media, 1994) and "Triumph of the swoosh" (*Sports Illustrated*, August 16, 1993), both by Donald Katz, chart the fortunes of Phil Knight and his company.

Playing for Keeps: Michael Jordan and the world he made by David Halberstam (Random House, 1999) argues that Jordan possessed special qualities that carried him "more deeply into the psyche of the American public than any sports star had ever gone before."

Swoosh: The unauthorized story of Nike and the men who played there by J. B. Strasser and Laurie Becklund (HarperBusiness, 1993) is probably the best account of Nike and the changing social conditions that facilitated its growth.

"Nike's communication with black audiences" by Ketra L. Armstrong (*Journal of Sport & Social Issues*, vol. 23, no. 3, August, 1999) examines the way in which Nike targeted black consumers. Also worth reading in this context: *Nike Culture: The sign of the swoosh* by Robert Goldman and Stephen Papson (Sage, 1999) which also looks at Nike's advertising and marketing.

"Nike" and "Michael Jordan" by Erwin Bengry are entries in my own *Sports Culture: An A–Z Guide* (Routledge, 2000) which also has relevant entries on the "NBA" and "ProServ."

ASSIGNMENT

You are a sports reporter for a local television station in Tulsa which has had an NBA franchise for ten years, yet has won nothing and reached the play-offs only twice. One of the league's most colorful players has recently become a free agent and has expressed a strong interest in joining the Tulsa Tempest, as the club is called. The player is a controversial character who has been the NBA's leading rebounder for the past five years, but who has had several brushes with the law, is in the middle of a stormy marriage with a supermodel, and stars in action movies. Many doubt he will fit in with the conservative suburban style of Tulsa. The team holds a press conference at which the owner announces that the player has signed. The player shows up wearing a glittering ankle-length evening gown which, he boasts, is a Donna Karan creation. You have five questions. What are they and how does the player answer them?

leading QUESTIONS

q: Why do we like to bet on sports?

a: Three reasons.

(1) The obvious one: its adds to the thrill; watching, or listening to, sports events is arousing in itself and it becomes even more arousing if we have money riding on their outcome. (2) Competition lends itself to gambling; it lacks the randomness of games of chance such as roulette and cards, and invites the bettor to measure his or her own judgment against those of another person or firm. (3) Historically, sports and gambling have been interwined; the entire development of sports features a coupling with betting. Many sports would not exist at all were it not for gambling and it could be argued that many others would not be so popular if we could not bet on them, whether legally or illegally. In fact, anthropologist Kendall Blanchard argues that to gamble is one of three prime objectives of sports, the others being to compete and to win prizes (1995: 122).

In all but five American states, betting is illegal. Yet Douglas Putnam estimates that as much as $120 billion is unlawfully wagered on sports every year. He reckons that: "the Super Bowl alone generates about $4 billion in illegal bets each January" (1999: 134). In other parts of the world, where sports betting is legal, particularly East Asia, the figures are much higher. Clearly, the betting is a powerful component of the commercial world of sport. A first step to understanding its appeal is to trace its origins.

Betting's underlying motive probably dates back to antiquity. Two great minds of the seventeenth century, Isaac Newton and Gottfried Wilhelm Leibnitz, inadvertently contributed to our understanding of this motive. Like Einstein who followed them, Newton and Leibntiz were committed to a view of the world as ordered mechanically and moving according to definable principles with potentially predictable outcomes. Like all Enlightenment thinkers, they believed reason and rationalty lay behind all affairs, natural and social. As Galileo had shown in his *Starry Messenger*, first published in 1610, forces that work to render the sky predictable were also at work on earth.

Chance had no place in this ordered universe. Ignorance was merely imperfect knowledge. Everything is potentially knowable; Newton and Leibnitz were both prominent in the advancement of both theoretical and practical science. Given greater knowledge, we could apply the "infinitesimal calculus," a method of calculating or reasoning about the changing world. The seeming mysteries of nature could be comprehended and subordinated to the rational, calculating mind.

Gambling is guided by such reasoning: admittedly, the conscious thought that lies behind rolling a dice or drawing lots is hardly likely to resemble any kind of calculation; these are games of chance, played with the intention of winning money (though many claim to have discovered systems or formulae for winning). But the motive behind betting on sports is very much influenced by a more rational style of thinking – that it is possible to predict the outcome of an event by the employment of a calculus of probability. No one wagers money on a sporting event without at least some inkling that they are privy to a special knowledge about how a competition will end. A suspicion, a taste, a fancy, a "feel"; all these add to the calculus at work in the mind of even the most casual of gamblers when he or she stakes money on a competition.

Orientations of gamblers differ widely: some always feel a tingle or adrenaline rush, whether it is in watching a horse romp home or a dice roll; others observe from a position of detachment, their interest resting on only the result. The sports gambler bets with head as well as heart; the reward is both in the winning and in the satisfaction that he or she has divined a correct result from the unmanageable flux of a competitive event.

The seventeenth-century philosophers' concerns were not with gambling, though they may well have observed the surge in popularity in games of chance in the pre-Enlightenment period. The philosopher Nicholas Rescher locates this popularity in wagering on contests of skill and chance during the English Civil War, 1641–45, and the Thirty Years War in continental Europe, 1618–48. Starved of entertainment, soldiers and sailors killed time by wagering on virtually any activity. Rescher cites a seventeenth-century soldier's remembrance of betting on a race between lice. Returning to civilian society, the militia brought with them their habits and the enthusiasm for gambling diffused, aligning itself quite naturally with the games of skill that were growing in popularity in England.

In the seventeenth century, laws were passed both in England and in the New World to outlaw gambling, principally to restrict the debts that were being incurred as a result of the growing stakes. Some activities had attracted gambling for decades, perhaps centuries. Swordplay, for example, was a pursuit that was viscerally thrilling to watch and stimulated the human passion for prediction. As the military use of swords declined, so the contests continued simply for recreation and entertainment. Engaging in competitive contests simply for the satisfaction they afforded the competitor and observer was exactly the kind of wasteful and sinful behavior despised by Puritans, who passed an anti-gambling law shortly after their arrival in the New World.

Gambling was actually the basis of many early sports, especially blood sports, in which the amusement of watching animals fight or be ravaged was enhanced by a wager. This was by no means confined to the West. Clifford Geertz's classic study of cock-fighting in Bali emphasizes the significance of betting to the meaning of the event (1972). All forms of animal sports were fair game for gaming. Western-style dog racing which has its origins in eighteenth-century coursing (and involved highly bred and trained dogs which chased and – usually – killed a fleeing hare) became an organized sport, complete with its own organization in 1858, when a National Coursing Club was established in the USA. The betting norm became *pari-mutuel*, from the French, meaning mutual stake. In the 1930s, this also took off in on-track British horse racing, though it was known as the totalizer, or just "tote" – betting, in which winners divide the losers' stakes, less an administrative charge.

Appealing as it may be to link the rise of gambling with modern capitalism and the ethos it both embodies and encourages, sports betting is not confined to cultures characterized by materialism and acquisitiveness. Blanchard's work documents the centrality of betting, in some cases as an obligation, to sports in several cultures, many in the underdeveloped world. Yet Western influences brought different aspects. Blanchard gives the example of a Mississippi Choctaw sport to which betting was integral. In the 1890s, "local whites frequented the 'Indian ballgames' and with the whites came a new type of betting, whiskey, and a threat to the safety of Choctaw women" (1995: 175). After appeals from missionaries, the state of Mississippi out-lawed gambling at all the ball games. The sport faded away. While there were other factors, it is believed the elimination of betting from the sport was responsible for the demise. This suggests that the very existence of some sports is predicated on betting. Horse and dog racing are contemporary instances.

In Britain, a form of gambling on soccer came to life in the early 1930s and captured the British public's imagination almost immediately. Newspapers had been publishing their own versions of "pools," as the bets were known, for many years, but the practice was declared illegal in 1928. Dennis Brailsford (1997) notes how the £20 million staked in the 1934/5 season doubled within two years. The outlay was usually no more than a few pence and the bets were typically collected from one's home. The aim of pools was to select a requisite number of drawn games (ties), so it was not clas-sified as a game of chance, but one of skill, thus escaping the regulation of gaming legislation. By the outbreak of war in 1939, there were 10 million players of the pools. The popularity the pools enjoyed with working-class bettors stayed intact until the introduction of the national lottery (modeled on the US state lotteries) in the early 1990s.

In the 1990s, betting on the spread became one of the most popular gambling forms. The bettor could wager not only on the result of a contest but on any facet of it: for example, the number of times Dan Marino used to lick his fingertips, or how often Mark McGwire spat or the total positive drug tests at an Olympic Games. Betting on sports, legally and illegally, was facilitated by the spread of the internet in the late 1990s. Because of the difficulty in regulating it, online betting became attractive where local laws prohibited or restricted most forms of betting, such as in the States, or where gaming taxes were high, as in Britain.

More questions . . .

- Should the USA acknowledge that betting is an integral part of sports' attrac-tion and legalize it?
- Does televising sports make it more possible that people want to bet on them?
- Why are some sports, like jai alai or horse racing, less interesting, if not meaningless without betting?

Read on . . .

- Blanchard, K., *The Anthropology of Sports: An introduction* (Bergin & Garvey, 1995).
- Brailsford, D., *British Sport: A social history* (Lutterworth Press, 1997).
- Rescher, N., *Luck: The brilliant randomness of everyday life* (Farrar Straus Giroux, 1995).
- Shaffer, H. J. (ed.) *Journal of Gambling Studies* (Human Sciences Press, since 1984).

Chapter fifteen

same rules, different game

why sports and politics

mix so well

THE OLYMPIC FLAME AND THE POLITICAL TINDERBOX

"Sport is completely free of politics." So said Avery Brundage in his capacity as president of the International Olympic Committee, in 1956. He was responding to an event that actually undermined his point: the withdrawal of six Olympic member countries from the Melbourne games in protest at the military conflicts in Hungary and Suez. Whether Brundage was being disingenuous, hypocritical, or just naïve, we will never know. But, history has made his statement seem plainly absurd; far from being "free of politics," sport is freighted with politics.

The Melbourne protests were part of a general pattern established long before 1956 and which continue to the present day. Countries absenting themselves from the Olympic Games, either as a gesture of protest, or because of exclusion, have been a feature of Olympic history. They usually make headlines and attract the rhetoric of interested parties who talk regretfully about how unfortunate it is that sports and politics have become mixed up. But, then again, they mix so well. Why?

The Olympic Games have the kind of generic relevance that makes them a perfect theater in which to play out political

dramas. Ostensibly sporting occasions, the games have continually managed grandly to capture tensions, protests, and sometimes atrocities that encircle the world. By celebrating the alleged unity, at least in spirit, of the world's population, the Olympic Games have sought temporarily to suspend terrorism, racism, imperialism, and other "worldly" matters that are the bane of our age. Instead, they have been hijacked by them. The setting and imagery of the games have been used to dramatize events seemingly unconnected with sports. To reiterate: many of the themes inherent in sports have political and ideological potential: nationalism, competition, the pursuit of supremacy, the heroism of victory; all have a wider application. Differences between the contrived competition of the track and field events and the real conflict in the streets have often melted in the spectacle of the Olympics.

When political factions, or even whole nations, consciously manipulate events to make their points decisively and dramatically, they often opt for sports, in the safe knowledge that the rest of the world will be so outraged that it will take immediate notice. For example, a press conference in New York to announce that civil rights in the USA have amounted to nothing and that the majority of African Americans and Latinos are still struggling in poverty will gain a response from the media of "so what?" Announce the same message, this time silently and symbolically, with just two African Americans disdaining the US national anthem and wait for the media to go to work. You have a political event on a near-epic scale.

The difference? In the latter example, the two people in focus are Olympic track medalists and the moment they choose to make their gesture is after being awarded their medals on the victory rostrum at the 1968 Olympic Games in Mexico City. Sport worked as an instantly effective vehicle for what was obviously a political statement. The unspoken protest was louder and clearer than any other in the post-civil rights era. The event itself has a place alongside Martin Luther King's "I have a dream" speech as one of the most potent messages about racial inequality. The image of the two Olympians, their heads bowed to avoid looking at the stars and stripes, their fists pointed upward in an unequivocal act of defiance, is one of most famous sporting representations of the twentieth century.

For Tommie Smith and John Carlos, the US athletes on the rostrum, and the organization behind them that orchestrated the protest, the Olympic Games were perfect: an effective vehicle for publicizing an openly political statement. The massive publicity it received and the fact that people still remember it today underscores the point: sport *is* political, if only because of its proven utility. It draws attention to particular issues, disseminates messages internationally and occasionally eases or exacerbates diplomatic relations.

In this chapter, we will see the diverse – and, to some, perverse – ways in which the development of sports has been and will continue to be influenced by political considerations. We will also see how sports are just too useful not to be used politically. Denials of this slip freely from the lips of those who have interests in presenting sport as an independent, transcendent force, one of few jewels decorating a tarnished crown. But, as we will also see later, those who have argued this are often the biggest culprits and their messages have been subterfuge, covering up their own misdemeanors.

THE OLYMPIC WEAPON

In his book *Sport and Political Ideology*, John Hoberman makes the point: "Sport is a latently political issue in any society, since the cultural themes which inhere in a sport culture are potentially ideological in a political sense" (1984: 20). Nationalism, competition, and segregation are just three of the more obvious themes that spring to mind. They all came together in 1936. If sports ever had an age of innocence, it ended in that year: the Berlin summer Olympics were an occasion for Nazis to flex their Aryan muscles and demonstrate the physical supremacy of the "master race." Adolf Hitler had expressed his doctrine of racial superiority and sought an international stage on which to reveal tangible evidence of this.

In his original conception, Coubertin saw the Olympics as having bridge-building potential. He wanted to bring nations of various political ideologies together in a spirit of healthy competition. Participation was considered to be more important than winning and the only politics that mattered were the politics of unity. Hitler's visions were as ambitious, though less noble. The political ideology he wished to propagate concerned the dominance of one nation, or more specifically, one race, over all others; his philosophy was of the disunity rather than oneness of humanity. While the blatant use of sports as a propagandist tool was roundly denounced, subsequent hosts of the Olympics were not slow to realize the potential of the games and often turned them into jingoistic extravaganzas. Still, it seems fair to suggest that the particular utility Hitler found in sports warrants special attention, if only as the benchmark against which to gauge later expressions of nationalism.

Friedrich Jahn's gymnastics *Turnen* movement of the nineteenth century was partly designed to prepare German youth to wage war against Napoleon. Jahn was a significant figure in fostering the "volkish" thought, which eventually gained political expression in Nazism, with its *leitmotif* of an overarching German essence. This was to be made visible through displays of physical control and strength, "a spectacle of masculine power." Hitler had no interest in sports other than this: to express national superiority and internal unity. The Weimar Republic had assisted the growth of sports in Germany as part of the general morale restoration after the First World War. But, under Hitler's

National Socialism, it came to mean much more. "Fitness was declared a patriotic obligation," writes historian Richard Mandell, author of *The Nazi Olympics* (1971).

Nazism represented an extreme right-wing form of government organized to advance an aggressive brand of nationalism. Its particular virulence was provided by Aryanism, a philosophy of racial purity that informed much, if not all, of Hitler's endeavors. Among its manifestations was a commitment to rid Germany of its Jewish presence and an attempt to propagandize the supremacy of the caucasian "race."

The anti-Semitism that characterized Nazism affected sport: in 1933, when the boycott of Jewish businesses came into effect, the organizing bodies of sport excluded Jewish performers and officials. Two years later there was complete segregation in German sport, something that clearly contradicted Olympic ideals. In the USA, an abortive boycott campaign targeting the proposed 1936 Olympics failed to command support. Avery Brundage, the then president of the American Olympic Committee, warned that: "Certain Jews must now understand that they cannot use these Games as a weapon in their boycott against the Nazis" (quoted in Hain 1982: 233). Germany reassured the world that the extent of anti-Semitism and segregation had been exaggerated and, to underline this, included the fencer, Helene Mayer, who was "half-Jewish", in the national team.

Newsreel depicts Hitler's leaving the stadium in apparent disgust as African American athlete Jesse Owens shook the ramparts of the Nazi's ideological platform by winning four gold medals. Doctrines of racial supremacy seemed ridiculous. Yet Hitler's departure was but one uncomfortable moment in what was in other respects a satisfactory and rewarding Nazi spectacle. Not only did Germans lead the medal table, they "demonstrated to the whole world that the new Germans were administratively capable, generous, respectable, and peace loving," as Mandell puts it (1984: 244). "Hitler, particularly, was greatly emboldened by the generally acknowledged, domestically and internationally, triumph of this festival grounded on the pagan (though very new) rituals of modern sport" (1984: 245). In terms of propaganda, the entire Olympic essay was of value to the Nazis: as the world exulted, Germany stepped up its rearmament program and stamped down on Jews.

Repercussions went beyond the Olympic movement. Before the games, in December 1935, an international game of soccer between England and Germany in London was opposed by Jewish organizations, supported by the Trades Union Congress and the Communist Party. In the event, the match went ahead. In a subsequent international game in 1938, this time in Germany, the England team was instructed to give the Nazi salute as the German national anthem was played before the match. Thanks to newsreel, the moment will live on as one of English sport's most mortifying moments, coming as it did so close to the outbreak of the Second World War.

Only in retrospect was the full resonance of the "Nazi Olympics" realized. No single games since has approached it in terms of ideological pitch. Its sheer scale deserved the posterity afforded it by the openly propagandist film directed by Leni Riefenstahl, *Olympia*, which idealized German sportsmen as *Übermenschen*, or supermen (see Chapter eleven).

After 1936, no summer Olympics meeting escaped political incident. The defeated nations of Germany, Italy, and Japan were excluded from the first games after the war in London in 1948. Holland, Egypt, Iraq, and Spain boycotted the 1956 games in protest at the British and French invasion of Suez. In 1964, South Africa was suspended and subsequently expelled from the Olympic movement (in 1970). Zimbabwe, then Rhodesia, a country which adopted a similar system of stratification to apartheid, was barred in 1972, having made a Unilateral Declaration of Independence from the Commonwealth. New Zealand maintained sporting links with South Africa in the face of world opinion and the fact that it too was not expelled from the Olympics spurred 20 African nations to boycott the 1976 games in Montreal. Boycotts have since proliferated. Taiwan also withdrew after it was refused permission to compete as "China."

The USA team pulled out of the Moscow games in 1980 after the Soviet invasion of Afghanistan. British Prime Minister Margaret Thatcher exhorted British athletes not to go, but the British Olympic Association went ahead. Soviet-bloc countries (except Romania) and their allies replied by steering clear of Los Angeles in 1984, though China sent a limited delegation of 200 athletes. The LA games were the most shamelessly nationalistic Olympics since 1936, though, as Rick Gruneau argues, "in no way a significant departure from practices established in earlier Olympics" (1984: 2).

In 1988, Cuba stayed away from Seoul after the South Korean government refused to share events with North Korea (which itself pulled out). In 1992, the political tensions were primarily internal, Barcelona, the host, being a municipality with a strong conservative tendency and nationalist Catalonian feelings. Its problem was in maintaining its autonomy while seeking the assistance of Spain's central government in Madrid. As Christopher Hill commented in the first edition of his *Olympic Politics*: "The political affinity one might expect it [Madrid] to have with Barcelona seems often to be strained by the rivalry between the two cities, as well as by the different traditions from which the national and local socialist parties spring" (1992: 219–20). Every Olympics has been associated with some form of political issue, which has often prompted boycotts.

Apart from boycotts, incidents internal to the games sometimes led commentators to suggest that the Olympics themselves were hemorrhaging so badly that they would have to be either stopped, or scaled-down drastically. If any single event can be said to have provoked this, it was that at Munich in 1972 when eight Palestinians occupied the Israeli team's quarters and demanded the release of 200 Palestinian prisoners in Israel. Negotiations proved fruitless and gunfire opened up. Ten athletes were killed. There followed a day's mourning before the competition resumed. Brundage, by this stage notorious for his blundering efforts to separate sport and politics, drew parallels between the politically charged incident with the equally political but quite different attempt to force the IOC into squeezing out racist Rhodesia.

The games immediately preceding this, in Mexico in 1968, had under-scored the point made so strongly by Berlin's "Nazi Olympics": that sport, given its world prominence, can be an effective stage on which to make a political point. The point in question was made by two black US track athletes, Tommie Smith and John Carlos, their fists clenched as if punching a hole in the American dream – as we covered previously.

Officials of the IOC have often arraigned politicians for urging their countries to use sporting occasions for political ends. Ascending to the moral high ground, they have stuck to the Brundage line and censured deviations from this. Yet, their bluster has obscured an inner politics of untrammeled corruption, greed, and manipulation at the very core of the IOC. While stories of venality in the ranks of the IOC had circulated since the publication of Vyv Simson and Andrew Jennings's *The Lords of the Rings: Power, money and drugs in the modern Olympics*, in 1992, it was not until 1999 that a true measure of the degradation was revealed. We will return to this later in the chapter.

SOUTH AFRICA'S EXPULSION

In 1968, Basil D'Oliveira, a black cricketer from South Africa's Cape who had settled in England in 1960, reached the peak of his form. Selected for the English national representative team, he scored a triumphal century against Australia at London's Oval and was, almost without question, the most effective batsman in the country at the time. Yet when the national team for the winter tour of South Africa was announced, D'Oliveira's name was missing. The events that unfolded after the announcement presaged one of the longest-standing political controversies in the history of sports.

David Sheppard, a former England captain, later to become Bishop of Liverpool, led a protest, accusing selectors of submitting to the requirements of apartheid, which included the strict separation of those deemed to belong to different "races" (the word apartheid is Afrikaans for "apartness").

D'Oliveira, having relatively pale brown skin, was officially classed by South Africans as "colored" and so had no legal right to share facilities with whites. Needless to say, the South African team comprised only white players. Several England team members threatened to resign as the protest gathered momentum, prompting the selectors to slip D'Oliveira into the squad as a replacement for an injured bowler, Tom Cartwright. It was an act of unheard-of nerve as far as South Africa's premier Johannes Vorster was concerned: he smartly denounced the squad as "not the team of the MCC [Marylebone Cricket Club – the English governing organization] but the team of the Anti-Apartheid Movement, the team of SANROC [the South African Non-Racial Olympic Committee]."

Perhaps wounded by the accusation and certainly refusing to be dictated to, the English team's governing organization, the MCC, called off the tour. Vorster's intransigence and the MCC's pull-out were crucial: the former in hardening South Africa's policy in the face of suspicions that Vorster himself was beginning to soften; the latter in showing the rest of the world's sports-governing bodies how they might in future react to South African policies.

The effects were not immediate and in the following January the MCC actually countenanced a projected tour by the South African cricket team in 1970. This was met with a "Stop the Seventy Tour" campaign and a series of disruptions of the Springbok's rugby tour of the UK, which served as a reminder of what would happen to any attempted cricket tour by the South Africans. The cricket tour did not take place. Progressively, more sports minimized or cut contacts with South Africa, effectively ostracizing that country's sport.

The episode itself was by no means the first to surface: it simply captured the elements more dramatically with a victim-cum-hero, statements from South Africa, and the refusal of the MCC to be dictated to by a regime that had been widely condemned. By grabbing the attention of the world's media, the D'Oliveira case made the sports–South Africa link a significant political as well as sporting topic and one which would press governments into action.

The political significance of South Africa in sports had been realized for at least ten years before D'Oliveira forced it into the open. South Africa had, in 1956, made a formal declaration of its sports policy program, which, it insisted, should stay within the boundaries of its general policy of apartheid. The physical segregation embodied in apartheid was instituted in 1948 and encouraged by pass laws, police brutality, and a repressive state that dealt unsympathetically with any attempt to challenge its authority – as the slayings at Sharpeville in 1960 indicated. Sports performers and teams visiting South Africa were, said the statement, expected to "respect South Africa's customs as she respected theirs" (quoted in Horrell 1968: 9).

Sharpeville

A black township in South Africa that, in March 1960, was the scene of a conflict that ended in 69 deaths (all black) and 180 wounded. It signaled the first organized black resistance to white political rule in South Africa. The Pan-African Congress (PAC) had asked blacks to leave their pass books at home and go to police stations to be arrested. They did so voluntarily, but refused to be dispersed by the police who, eventually, opened fire. Sharpeville triggered nationwide demonstrations. The reaction of the government was to arrest leaders of the PAC and the other main black organization, the African National Congress (ANC), and ban both movements.

Justifications, unnecessary as they were in a country utterly controlled and dominated by the numerically small white population, included the arguments that blacks had no "aptitude" for sport and the alleged potential for conflict in "mixed" teams and crowds of spectators. On the second point: blacks, who constituted over 70 per cent of South Africa's total population, were barred from a new rugby stadium in Bloemfontein in 1955. In the following year, Bishop Trevor Huddleston, who was to become a prominent member of the anti-apartheid movement, observed that sport may be South Africa's Achilles' heel, in the sense that its national teams were so obviously good in certain sports, particularly Rugby Union. To deny South Africa the opportunity to demonstrate its excellence would, as Huddleston put it in his *Naught for Your Comfort*, "shake its self-assurance very severely" (1956: 202).

Another world power in rugby, New Zealand, had traditionally selected Maoris in its national team, but capitulated to South Africa by picking only white players to tour. This opened up a national controversy in 1960, especially when a New Zealand tour went ahead despite the atrocities at Sharpeville. This event crystallized many fears about South Africa, and a cricket tour in Britain in its aftermath prompted demonstrations. Cries that "sport and politics should be kept separate" sounded pathetically weak in the context of 1960 and, in fact, the whole decade that followed was to be filled with examples of the inseparability of the two.

Sporadic protests continued, both at street level and at official levels. The integration-oriented South African Non-Racial Olympic Committee (SANROC) was launched in 1962 with the intention that it should apply for recognition from the International Olympic Committee and officially replace the whites-only Olympic and National Games Association. The government pre-empted matters by banning SANROC. As the 1964 games drew near, the IOC, whose charter forbids racial discrimination, demanded large concessions from South Africa before its entry could be approved. Some concessions were made in the trials, but the South African government maintained its insistence that sport comply with "custom" so South Africa was denied entry to the Tokyo games.

New Zealand continued to send touring rugby sides to South Africa amidst negotiations aimed at allowing the entry of Maoris. But, in a key speech in 1965, the then premier Hendrik F. Verwoerd reaffirmed that no Maori players would be allowed to enter South Africa. Coming from the country's leader, the message was filled with political significance. In 1966, New Zealand finally declined an invitation to tour, but accepted another extended in 1968 under a new South African premier, Johannes Vorster. In the interim, newly independent African states had begun to recognize South Africa's vulnerability to sporting boycotts and were strenuously trying to convince the rest of the world's sports organizations to expel South Africa. The Supreme Council for Sport in Africa, as the alliance was called, reminded the world that, while sport may conventionally have been regarded as trivial or unrelated to politics, "South Africans do not consider it minor" (quoted in Guelke 1986: 128). Outbursts from Verwoerd and Vorster confirmed this. They left no doubt that what was at first glance a sports issue was also one on which nations' premiers were obliged to dispense judgments.

At a different time in history Vorster's conclusion that the MCC's selection of D'Oliveira was designed, as he expressed it, "to gain certain political objectives," may have passed virtually unnoticed by all those cricket devotees and anti-apartheid campaigners. In 1968, an *annus mirabilis* in which conflicting forces of protest gathered and collided all over the world, its effects were more far-reaching. The year had seen student demonstrations and protests from young people from all over Europe and the United States. Vietnam provided a focal point for the protests, though there was a more generic unrest underlying this. It was a time in history when people began to sense that collective efforts by "the people" could change world events. It was thought that not even apartheid was immune from "people power."

The IOC had already withdrawn its invitation to South Africa to attend the Mexico Olympics. A threat of boycott from about 50 member countries and protests from the black members of the American team were factors in the decision. British Rugby Union, a sport reluctant to dissolve its relationship with South Africa, entertained a Springbok touring team in the 1969–70 season and every match was seriously disrupted by mass demonstrations.

The message from the tour was that any future visit by South Africans was likely to be met with a show of force. In May 1970, a planned cricket tour of South Africans to Britain was aborted quickly after the threat of uproar on the D'Oliveira scale in the lead-up to a general election. The same year saw the severance of more links with South Africa: expulsion from the IOC; elimination from the Davis Cup tennis competition; suspension from track and field; and a bar from gymnastics.

Isolation stirred Vorster into action and, in 1971, he announced what he called a "multinational" sports program in which "whites," "Africans," "coloreds," and "Asians" could compete against each other as "nations," but only in international competitions. This rather devious move effectively allowed black sports performers to compete, provided they were affiliated to one of the government's "national" federations. As such it served to divide blacks: some wishing to compete felt compelled to affiliate; others rejected the racist premise of the divisions and refused to affiliate. With international links receding, the government permitted domestic contests between "nations," and later club-level competitions between "nations."

Rugby Union resisted the international trend and, in particular, New Zealand set itself against world opinion by willfully maintaining contacts. During a tour of South Africa in 1976, the near-cataclysmic Soweto uprising (official figures: 575 dead, 2,389 wounded) prompted ever more searching questions. As New Zealand seemed intent on prosecuting links regardless of the upheavals, should it too be isolated? The answer from the black African Olympic member countries was affirmative and New Zealand's admission to the Montreal Olympics in 1976 caused a mass boycott. Thus the crisis deepened.

Commonwealth heads of governments met at Gleneagles in Scotland in 1977 to formulate a now-famous agreement "vigorously to combat the evil of apartheid by withholding any form of support for, and by taking every

Soweto

On June 16 1976, South African police opened fire on protesting students in Soweto, a large African township on the outskirts of Johannesburg, killing two and injuring many. The students retaliated by attacking government property and officials. Police countered and soon violence spread to every part of the republic except Natal. For months, schools were closed. Students forced workers to stay away from their factories and offices in a series of one-day strikes. Some migrant workers refused and a battle between workers and students resulted in 70 deaths. The total number killed as a result of the conflict which began in Soweto was officially reported as 575 with 2,389 wounded – almost certainly an underestimate.

practical step to discourage contact or competition by their nationals with sporting organizations, teams or sportsmen from South Africa." The agreement was between governments not sports-organizing bodies and, as subsequent events were to show, the ability of governments to overrule individual organizations was often tested. Rugby's robust stance against governments gave rise to several anomalies.

In 1979, Britain entertained a "mixed" Barbarians side (eight whites, eight "coloreds," and eight blacks). Critics dismissed the team, which was said to reflect the tripartite structure of South African society, as window-dressing. The British Lions' subsequent tours in which they competed with similarly composed teams, met with much the same skepticism. It was, so the argument went, a case of South Africa using sport to project a distortedly liberal image of itself while preserving its essential tyranny and oppression. The majority of black players belonged to the South African Rugby Union (SARU), which remained outside the aegis of the organization from which sides selected for international competition were drawn. Hence the sides were hardly representative.

It was a period of public relations initiated by Pretorian officials bent on convincing the world that every measure was being taken to desegregate sport – though not education, employment, and housing. For all its promises, South Africa fell short on delivery. Invitations went out to individual players of international repute who were drawn by the love of money to South Africa to engage in what were known as rebel tours. Cricketers, buoyant after the triumph of the individual over governing bodies, courtesy of Kerry Packer, went to South Africa in their scores, both to play and to coach, usually in contexts that were notionally "multi-racial." British soccer players took short-term contracts to coach, some, like Stanley Matthews, working exclusively with blacks. American boxing champions, like Bob Foster and Mike Weaver, both black, defended their titles in South Africa against whites. South Africa made no secret of the fact that it had an embarrassment of riches with which to lure top sports performers.

There were prices to pay, however. In 1981, the United Nations special committee against apartheid published its first "blacklist" (an embarrassing misnomer) of sports performers who had worked in South Africa. This served as an effective prohibition and ostracized South Africa further.

Starved of decent-quality opposition, promising South Africans, like Sidney Maree, a black athlete, and Zola Budd, who was white, left to campaign abroad. Maree took US citizenship, while Budd was rapidly granted British citizenship. Controversies followed both those leaving South Africa and those who continued to flout the prohibition by going there. British cricketer Robin Jackman, who had played in South Africa, was deported from Guyana in 1981 just as a test match against the West Indies was about to begin. The match was abandoned. Others, like Geoff Boycott and Graham Gooch, were banned for a number of years from test cricket.

It was not until 1989 that the International Cricket Conference (ICC) passed a resolution, in defiance of a crucial summons obtained by the right-wing Freedom Association, to formalize sanctions against players, coaches, or administrators who worked in South Africa. Automatic suspensions from test cricket were the penalty. It was the most unambiguous pronouncement on sport and apartheid since the Gleneagles Agreement. The decision was reached after the cancellation of England's scheduled winter tour of India, when Indians refused to play a team that included players with South African connections. "A victory for sport over racism," was how the resolution was greeted by Sam Ramsamy of SANROC. Norris McWhirter, the leader of the Freedom Association, described it as "a crushing blow against cricketers' freedom to trade" and exhorted individual players to take out civil injunctions to prevent the ICC carrying out its ban. It could be argued against this that the freedom of over 21 million black South Africans to trade – and not just in cricket – was of far greater significance than that of a relatively small number of cricketers.

Gleneagles Agreement

The issue of sporting links with South Africa prompted government involvement at high levels, and, in 1977, at Gleneagles, Scotland, Commonwealth heads of government unanimously accepted to override the autonomy of sporting bodies and "take every practical step to discourage contact or competition by their nationals with sporting organizations, teams or sportsmen from South Africa or from any other country where sports are organized on the basis of race, color and ethnic origin." Sanctions were to be applied to those ignoring the agreement. The full agreement was published by the Commonwealth Secretariat, London.

The election of Nelson Mandela to South Africa's premiership in 1993, and the collapse of apartheid which preceded it, effectively ended the isolation of South Africa in all senses and sporting relations were resumed. South Africa was readmitted to the Olympic movement, its rugby teams were allowed to tour and its cricket team was permitted to play test series against the world's other major cricket powers. The West Indies cricket team was the first to tour South Africa after the announcement of apartheid's dissolution in 1991. Black representation in the country's national teams was still scant because of the imprint of several generations of "racialized" sports.

THE CORRUPT MASTERS OF OLYMPIA

In December 1998, Marc Hodler, an IOC member, attended a routine meeting at the Lausanne headquarters of the organization. During press briefings, Hodler, then 81, made allegations about bribery in the IOC. Whispers of bribery and corruption had been heard for some time before Hodler's announcement. But Hodler astonished his colleagues by breaking ranks. There were, he said, four agents who, for a commission of between $500,000 and $1 million, offered to deliver blocks of votes to cities bidding for the right to host the Olympic Games. The agents, one of whom was an IOC member, charged the city that won the vote between $3 million and $5 million. Subsequent inquiries, some by the world's media, others by the IOC itself (which produced a report on the subject within a month of Hodler's accusations) revealed a story that centered on the award of the 2002 Winter Olympics to Salt Lake City, Utah.

Corruption

Some form of deception or fraud has probably been present in all organized professional sports. Even amateur sports in which competitors officially receive no money are vulnerable: gambling has been integral to the sports experience and, while there are observers willing to wager on the outcome of a contest, the probability that they will try to control, manipulate, or determine the desired outcome will persist. In horse racing, this has been achieved through administering drugs to the horses, a tactic known as "nobbling." The most usual way of managing a result in a human sport is by bribing competitors, a practice that has been exposed historically in a number of sports, including baseball (Black Sox Scandal of 1919), boxing (the Jack Johnson–Jess Willard fight of 1916), and soccer (the Tony Kay case of 1963).

After Salt Lake City had been turned down in its attempt to stage the 1998 winter Olympic Games, it began to examine why its bid had failed. All cities vying for the right to host the games give IOC members (whose numbers vary, but usually between 95 and 115) gifts, such as laptop computers, designer luggage, or *objets d'art*. In the run-up to the voting, Nagano, Japan, had employed Goran Takacs as a lobbyist for a fee of $363,000 plus bonuses if the bid succeeded. Goran's father Artur Takacs was a Yugoslavian entrepreneur, and a close adviser to IOC President Juan Antonio Samaranch; he sat near Samaranch at IOC meetings and was influential among IOC members. The meeting to determine the site of the games was held in Birmingham, England, in April 1991. Prior to the voting, Takacs made it known that the president favored the Japanese bid; he later apologized for this impropriety. Nagano won.

Salt Lake City's bid committee set about correcting its mistakes. Over the next four years, it gave away nearly $800,000 in inappropriate "material benefits" to 14 IOC members. The benefits included cash, free housing, medical treatment, scholarships, and jobs. Two rifles valued at $2,000 were given to Samaranch who defended himself by explaining that, as president, he did not take part in the voting. Salt Lake City won the right to host the 2002 games.

The IOC's hastily-assembled report in response to Hodler's statements confirmed that there was evidence that IOC members and their relatives had received "benefits" from Salt Lake City officials, in some cases more than $100,000. The report recommended disciplinary action, including expulsion for members involved. Among them were Jean-Claude Ganga, of the Congo, who was said to have made $60,000 profit on a land deal in Utah arranged by a member of the Salt Lake City bid committee. The committee also gave him $50,000 to help feed children in the war-riven Congo and paid for medical care for him and his mother. Another IOC member, Bashir Mohammed Attarabulsi, from Libya, had his son's education at Brigham Young University paid for by the committee, which also arranged living expenses.

The scandal surrounding Salt Lake City shook a few more skeletons out of the closet. John Coates, the chair of the Australian Olympic Committee and leader of Sydney's bid for the 2000 Olympics, offered inducements estimated at between $35,000 and $70,000 to the Kenyan and Ugandan IOC members at a dinner in Monte Carlo in 1993 – on the eve of the voting which saw Sydney beat Beijing by two votes for the right to host the games. Coates maintained that the money was a contribution toward helping the development of sports in Kenya and Uganda, though he admitted: "We didn't get the Games because of our great facilities or beautiful location" (quoted by Swift 1999: 34).

Melbourne failed in its attempt to host the 1996 games even though its bid committee arranged for the daughter of a South Korean IOC delegate to play with the Melbourne Symphony Orchestra. Atlanta eventually won the vote after high-profile power-broker Andrew Young cultivated links with African IOC members to whom he had the bid committee provide athletic gear and other sports-related aid. The lobbying for this event became intense after Athens had reportedly prepared a dossier with details of IOC members' sexual preferences. Berlin allegedly repeated the operation when bidding for the 2000 Olympics.

Evidence, actual or inferential, was found to tarnish the bidding process for every summer and winter Olympics since 1988. There is no reason to suppose that backroom political deals and dubious gifts were absent from the elections before that date, though the stakes went up appreciably after the stupendous commercial success of the LA games in 1984. The huge costs of running the event are offset by a dozen key sponsors, including Coca-Cola and Kodak, which pay sums in the region of $14 million to use the Olympic five-ring symbol on their merchandise.

Added to this is the extra revenue generated by businesses in the city hosting the games and, importantly, the slice of the television revenues. NBC paid the IOC $3.55 billion for the US tv rights to all Olympics through 2008. The four-year Olympic cycle is estimated to generate some $10 billion. One can imagine, with this kind of money available to host cities, the temptation to leave no stone unturned is great. Perhaps we might also note that the tv deal itself was not completely untainted by controversy: rival networks were not given the opportunity to submit proposals for the games beyond 2000; rumors of multi-million-dollar payments over and above the $3.55 billion circulated, though without substantiation.

It would be too simple to interpret the whole saga of corruption as the product of human avarice and overweening power. Greed has certainly been a factor, but the conditions under which that greed has been fed must be noted. The Olympic movement's embrace of commercialism, the proliferation of logo'd merchandise, the exorbitant television contracts, the bonanzas enjoyed by host cities: these are some of the other factors that made possible the fufilment of individual greed. Being awarded an Olympic Games was like being given a cow that produced money instead of milk for its owner.

The International Olympic Committee was founded as a self-appointed association of ambassadors from national sports-governing organizations. Athletics was amateur and it was thought the best way to protect amateur sports from corrupting influences to insulate its members from outside influences; members were not even supposed to accept instructions from their home countries. The ideal was articulated by the Belgian ex-president Henri Baillet-Latour in a conversation with Hitler during the 1936 games. Baillet-Latour saw notices outside rest-rooms at all the venues warning that Jews and dogs were not allowed in. Hitler refused Baillet-Latour's request to have them removed on the grounds that no one who was invited to a friend's home would tell him or her how to run it. Baillet-Latour's riposte was: "When the five-circled flag is raised over the stadium, it is no longer Germany. It is Olympia and we are the masters here" (quoted in Morton 1999: 23).

The Olympic movement strove to remain independent for much of its history. The débâcle of Montreal in 1976, in which financial losses were punitive and kickbacks from construction contractors were rife, was a turning-point. For a while it looked as if the games had reached an end. The cost of staging what had become a quadrennial extravaganza, each successive host trying to outdo its predecessor, had become too great for even the world's biggest cities to bear. Determined not to let the games disappear, the IOC embraced commercialism, doing deals with sponsors, television companies, and, for many, sacrificing its original ideals. Had such a scandal broke when Brundage was making his pronouncements about sports and politics, it may well have ended the Olympic movement: the hypocrisy would have been too much for the movement to bear. But, at the cusp of the century, it seemed less earth-shattering, though still contemptible.

In a sense, fatigue has set in: we are no longer alarmed when sports are used like political instruments; we are not surprised when individuals get caught up in issues that are far beyond their control; we are not really shocked when we hear that the guardians of sports are themselves debased and dishonest. Perhaps our expectations of sport have changed. No longer do we regard sports as rising above the vileness that dwells in much of political life: sport is part of that political life and cannot help but be affected. Strenuous as efforts may once have been to protect the image of sport as independent and virtuous, the facts tell a different story.

FURTHER READING

Sport, Policy and Politics: A comparative analysis by Barrie Houlihan (Routledge, 1997) selects five countries, Australia, Britain, Canada, Ireland, and the USA, and studies the different relationships between sports and governments; Houlihan takes particular note of how commerce and international sports federations influence policy-making. The book forms a companion to the author's earlier work *Sport and International Politics* (Harvester Wheatsheaf, 1994).

Power, Politics and the Olympic Games by Alfred E. Senn (Human Kinetics, 1999) is an account of the Olympic movement that deals with the controversies affecting many of the games; the author examines the way in which South Africa's apartheid impacted on several Olympic Games. *Trevor Huddlestone: A life* by Robin Denniston (Macmillan, 1999) provides a different perspective on the controversies through the life of the man responsible, perhaps more than anyone, for putting apartheid on the international agenda. Also useful is the second edition of Christopher Hill's *Olympic Politics* (Manchester University Press, 1996).

The Lords of the Rings: Power, money and drugs in the modern Olympics by Vyv Simson and Andrew Jennings (Simon & Schuster, 1992) and *The New Lords of the Rings: Olympics, corruption and how to buy gold medals* by Andrew Jennings (Pocket Books, 1996) were criticized by the IOC when they were first published, but, on reflection, seemed a clear and fair account of the corruption and bribery that pervaded the Olympic movement.

The Revolt of the Black Athlete by Harry Edwards (Free Press, 1970) documents the build-up to the Smith–Carlos gesture at Mexico. What might have seemed to be a piece of rash judgment was actually a carefully prepared and executed operation against a background of civil unrest in the USA. As a case study of the political uses of sports, this stands the test of time.

ASSIGNMENT

You are a national volleyball manager-coach in the final stages of your squad's preparation for a major international tournament to be attended by the world's volleyball powers. In a newspaper feature profiling one of the squad's outstanding attacking players, he/she reveals that he/she is a member of the Order, a group opposed to what it calls ZOG (Zionist Occupation Government) and which, as the newspaper journalist uncovers, has links or sympathies with the Ku Klux Klan, the Posse Comitatus, the Nazi Parties of Britain and the USA, and other anti-Semitic and racist groups. What is the likely fall-out and how will you, as manager-coach, deal with it?

things to come

what lies in the future?

THAT'S ENTERTAINMENT

No matter what romantics tell us, sports are bigger than they ever were. Bigger, that is, in terms of worldwide popularity, awareness, and, importantly, turnover. Never in history, have we spent more time watching sports, mostly on television. We have never been exposed to so many sports images in advertising and marketing. And we now spend much more money not only watching sports, but buying the merchandise related to sports. Major League Baseball alone sells over $3 billion (£1.83 billion) worth of merchandise annually. That is over three times the value of the richest sports clubs in the world.

Our desire to compete and our even greater desire to watch others compete burns as brightly as ever. The difference is that, in the twenty-first century, sports with international appeal are competing among themselves for the attention and loyalty of fans. With the deluge of sports on our televisions, we might expect an imminent saturation. Yet, I doubt it: sports are poised to maintain their universal popularity for two reasons. On the demand side, we want as much sports as we can get; on the supply side, the sports industry is responding with ever more sophisticated ways of delivering the goods.

Len Sherman has an interesting theory of why we are now so devoted to sports. We have lost faith and confidence in the central social institutions of state and government and rescinded our memberships of other organizations that were once regarded as valuable, such as unions, political parties, and volunteer groups. "At the same time our essential organizations and systems have become diminished, the two modern industries of communications and entertainment (whose corporations and personnel are frequently though necessarily one and the same) have increased in autonomy and power," writes Sherman (1998: 188).

In the past, heroes came from the ranks of great political figures, military leaders, explorers, scientists, even philosophers. Now, they have been replaced by pure celebrities, described by Sherman as "the most watched, admired, privileged, and imitated people" (1998: 189). Celebrities are, by definition, famous, but in the twenty-first century they also have a kind of exemplary authority, an influence that they do not usually use to facilitate social change or promote good causes, but to sell commodities. A cynical public, having forsaken and been forsaken by old institutions, "gladly seizes upon this substitute, a substitute that might not provide a lot of benefits, but doesn't require a lot in return either" (1998: 189). Apart from money, we should add.

Professional sports today are constituents of the entertainment industry. The changes wrought in that industry by the twentieth-century revolution of media communications are all about us: the coming of television, the proliferation of film, the advent of digital technologies, the creation of cyberspace: these are some of the key developments that have changed the way we get our entertainment, the way we consume it and the lifestyle patterns we make out of it.

We now consume sports in much the same way as we consume drama, music and other forms of amusement: by exchanging money for commodities. Purists once abhorred the way film and, later, television corrupted live theater; connoisseurs deplored the phonographic cylinders that were used to reproduce music. Traditionalists were more ambivalent over the conversion of sports into packaged goods, though many probably lamented the passing of times when being a sports fan involved more than buying a baseball cap and sitting at home with a six-pack and a big-screen tv. It meant actually going to see competitive action; and, no matter how you analyze the statistics, younger people have tended to go to events less and watch more tv (see Sherman's summary, 1998: 231).

The reader of this edition of *Making Sense of Sports* will be left with an appreciation of the monumental role the media plays in directing sports. He or she should also understand the extent to which international corporations have stepped-up their interests in sports. Both developments are guided by a process in which sports have been turned into global entertainment, controlled, if not yet fully owned, by international corporations.

The trend is a familiar one: a company, say a car manufacturer, starts as a national business, making the cars on home soil and selling them in the home market. In time, the manufacturer buys parts from wherever the best deal can be done, assembles wherever labor is cheapest and sells to a worldwide market. This lucrative arrangement supplied a template: any product could be sold any place on the planet, as long as you had the means to create a market for it. Nike was the first company to show how globalization could work for the sports industry. As we saw in Chapter fourteen, it was aided and generously abetted by television which took the NBA and other pro sports not just to American audiences, but to populations all over the world. Now, everyone in sports thinks and acts globally and corporately, even if this means sacrificing what some see as basic principles. Let me pitch two examples.

Example one. Shortly after the expansion that brought the Colorado Rockies and the Arizona Diamondbacks into Major League Baseball, the *Rocky Mountain News* publication asked whether corporate ownership was good for baseball and invited ex-MLB commissioner Bowie Kuhn to answer. If the trend continued, warned Kuhn, the sport "will be internationalized and the marketing will be intense . . . traditional values may be set aside." By contrast, DBs' owner Jerry Colangelo maintained that the money required to run sports organizations had become so enormous that only large-scale corporations could handle it. Cold-bloodedly, but with perfect accuracy, Colangelo observed: "You see people who recognize professional sports as much more than sport. They're part of the entertainment world" (quoted in Sherman 1998: 233).

Example two: Prior to the start of England's 1999/2000 soccer season, the Football Association announced that it had granted Manchester United an exemption from the yearly competition for the FA Cup, a domestic trophy held by United. The competition had been running for almost 130 years. United had been invited to participate in the inaugural Fifa World Club Championship in Brazil and the dates clashed, so the FA made the unprecedented move. The decision was decried; the tradition of the FA Cup was threatened by the removal of its champions (United also held the European championship). But the FA held firm, reminding everyone of the importance of promoting soccer as a global sport. There was another motive. The English FA was bidding for the rights to stage a future World Cup tournament, which was like being given a license to print money for the host. The decision rested with Fifa, so upsetting that organization by preventing United taking part in its competition would have been ruinous. In both cases, the power of corporate finance in the global marketplace was underscored.

The sports industry has followed and will continue to follow the highly profitable film and television industries: producing internationally for international markets. The consumption of sports is totally international. Diamondbacks and United (which, but for the intervention of Britain's Monopoly and Mergers Commission, would be Rupert Murdoch's property) can be seen pretty much anywhere in the world. Not only that: the clubs' merchandise can also be bought anywhere.

THE CORPORATE INVADERS

We noticed previously that 1956 was a key year in sports history. According to John Goldlust, the televising of the Olympic Games, held in Melbourne, was decisive: not only did the sale of domestic tv sets increase as a result, but the television industries the world over began to recognize the potential of sports for drawing audiences. Less pragmatically, it suggested an obligation to television networks: sports were becoming vital parts of some nations' cultures and, as such, deserved broadcasting to as wide an audience as possible.

If Melbourne '56 was the watershed Goldlust believes it was, then perhaps we are approaching another. Or perhaps we have passed it. Maybe it was when Murdoch bought the Dodgers, or even before that, when Ted Turner purchased the Braves. These deals signaled a new type of arrangement, variously known, as we have seen, as vertical integration, or "murdochization," or the corporate invasion of sports. Whatever we call it, the outcome is clear: the way sports are run and the way we watch them will be affected.

Media corporations have spied the entertainment potential of sports and will persist in their predatory stalking. They will be huge factors in the direction of sports over the next several years. Let us imagine how this direction might lead to a sort of intersection. It has been speculated that media-owned clubs have been able to attract star players not simply because they offer high salaries, but because of movie or television opportunities. Say a club that occupies a small part of Time Warner's vast media empire signs a player. He, or, less probably, she may be lured by the chance of a starring role in the film made by Warners, or maybe a part in a series to be shown on one of a number of cable channels in the corporate stable. To minimize the chances of its being a flop, the film or series can be given recurring promotions on all the channels in which TW has an interest.

The player's profile could be raised by releasing a cd by him or her on the Warner Bros. label; the record would then get worldwide distribution. Toys and clothes and accessories bearing his or her imprimatur could be sold in Warner Bros. stores the world over. Chances are that the player would sign a book contract with a TW-owned publishing house and the eventual book would be marketed in a way that will enhance its chances of becoming a best-seller. If TW is seriously interested in making its investment work, it could make plans for a ride based on his or her exploits at the Six Flags Great Adventure Theme Park The corporation may well regard the signing as the launch of a medium-term commercial enterprise that will yield profit from many sources in many parts of the world. The typical fan may only see the player as a valuable addition to the playing staff.

This presupposes that a corporate giant like Time Warner will have retained the same kind of autonomy it now has. The signs are that media behemoths will coalesce, perhaps for specific periods of time, perhaps for specific purposes. With globalization proceeding at pace, no single media corporation has the reach or resources to spin a web around the world, though, as we have seen in Chapter thirteen, Rupert Murdoch has done more than most to achieve this. In the late 1990s, his companies had Byzantine alliances with media companies in many European and Asian countries as well as his partnerships with North American media outfits.

In Chapter twelve, I described the complex series of media alliances that lies in the future as *mille-feuille*, a confection of layer upon layer of puff pastry. They will become so intricate that it will be difficult to know who owns what rights, what company, what club, what event, and so on. Media corporations specializing in entertainment have already joined forces with telecommunications companies to develop services that were barely dreamt of at the start of the 1990s. We may yet be approaching an inflection point; that is, a moment at which the pace of technological change materially speeds up and perhaps bends in a new direction. The synergy produced by the various alliances is sure to accelerate the pace of change.

I speculated on how we may watch sports in the future in Chapter twelve. It was a vision predicated on the ubiquity of the internet, which will, I anticipate, move from being a personal computer-based instrument to a more extensive tool of communication grounded in a whole range of devices, some fixed, some portable. These include television, cellular phones, and appliances for which we do not yet have a name. The race is already on to plug the net into cell phones. In 1999, Vodafone received the approval of the FCC for taking control of the US telecoms licenses of its AirTouch. The European electronic companies, Ericsson and Nokia — fierce rivals in most marketplaces – joined forces with Psion to form Symbian, a software company designed to take on Microsoft in the effort to transfer software expertise from the PC to portable devices. Imagine the future: a billion computers and portable devices, all sensitive to voice commands, linked to each other through cyberspace.

Over the next several years, telecommunications companies will learn how to adopt existing technology, how to organize cyberspace and, perhaps most importantly, how to sell. It is no coincidence that companies that have an active interest in electronic media have also cultivated an interest in sports.

Soon, all media corporations will have some stake in sports and this will have deep implications not only on how sports are run, but on how we consume. We could soon be sitting in an airport lounge, or in a library or practically anywhere, staring at the space on our wrists that used to be occupied by a watch. The device with which we might replace the watch could be a portable apparatus for receiving sounds and images and we might be viewing a sports competition from anywhere on the planet.

There will inevitably be costs. Subscription television and pay per view have begun the process of accustoming us to paying for televised sports. In Britain and elsewhere in Europe, resistant fans have caved-in and accepted that the only way they can get sports on their televisions is to pay for it. The BBC, which has always rejected attempts to show commercials, has accepted subscription television, in principle, by providing digital-only channels to those prepared to pay extra. It seems that the BBC cannot avoid supporting itself through some form of subscription service. The swiftness with which it descended from the top provider of first-class sports to a scavenger for what scraps BSkyB left over must have alarmed even its most ardent supporters.

In the States, media companies set up specialist ppv arms in the 1990s and cultivated a market, especially among boxing fans, who became used to paying for virtually every decent world title fight. Corporate heads must relish the thought of charging fans to watch football games. The NFL's problem in countenancing this is that the populations of cities have typically had to pay tax dollars to build the stadia in which games are played. The league could hardly rub salt in the wound by making fans pay to watch televised games taking place in a stadium that was built with their tax dollars. Or could it?

MONEY

Pay per view will make already-rich athletes even richer. Glance at any *Forbes* list of top-earning sports performers over the past decade and you will find an average of 20 per cent of them all are boxers. This is despite the fact that boxers' endorsement incomes are consistently much lower than those of players from all the other major sports. The reason is that their income from actual competition is disproportionately great. For example, Oscar de la Hoya, over the last three years of the century, earned an annual average of about $38 million, but only a million of it came from endorsements. Out of $35 million earned by motor racing's Michael Schumacher, a chunk of $10 million came from endorsements. In basketball, the balance is tipped even further. Shaquille O'Neal's average income was just over $25 million, half of which came from endorsements. Were sports that are now largely free-to-air to go over to ppv, or some similar arrangement, the earnings of their athletes would shoot up.

All this presumes that the demand for sports is elastic enough to stretch that far. Sports performers or, more specifically, their performances are exactly the same as any other commodity in the sense that they are only worth what people will pay for them. However much people debate whether the athletes are worth the money and whether the sums involved are beyond the realms of decency, it is the market that will decide. If people are ready and willing to pay for it, athletes – and indeed everyone connected with the sports industry – will earn it.

Sports are already awash with money and, if my prognosis is right, there will be even more money flooding in over the next few years. This makes the incentives to achieve irresistible. If I am the owner of an NHL team that has missed out narrowly on the Stanley Cup for the past couple of years and I have the opportunity of signing a free agent goal tender whose salary demands threaten to break apart my whole wage structure, I have a cost–benefit equation to consider. The goalie's excellent record suggests that, over the course of a season, he will be worth a half-goal advantage per game. If he had been with the team previously, my club would have won two Stanley Cups, the extra money from which would have more than made up for his high salary. The player may not look worth it on paper, but I may think of the small but vital difference he will make to my team and the extra money we will earn as a result.

Actually, this hypothetical example is not so different from the prospects facing Colangelo, the Diamondbacks owner quoted above. Just after Len Sherman's book on the Arizona franchise was published in 1998, premier pitcher Randy Johnson became a free agent. Johnson boasted a 62–17 record over the previous four seasons. Colangelo agreed to pay him $52 million (£32 million) over four years despite having enormous stadium costs to meet. Johnson was a marquee name, but somewhat over ripe at 35. Even so, his salary paled beside the $105 million over seven years paid by Murdoch-owned Dodgers to Kevin Brown, who had gone 51–26 (2.33 ERA) over the previous three seasons, led two teams to the World Series and threw a fastball timed at over 90mph. The Diamondbacks' initiative was rewarded with a successful 1999 season in which they qualified for the play-offs for the first time.

So, the allures for paymasters are powerful enough for them to meet the most exorbitant of player demands, just as long as there is a probable dividend at the end of it. At least it seemed that way before the 1998 NBA lockout, when commissioner David Stern negotiated an agreement that effectively ended the club owners' profligacy. Moaning that they could no longer afford contracts, owners asked Stern to negotiate a salary structure that limited players' earnings. How much brinksmanship was involved we will never know, but Stern emerged having made the NBA the only major sports league with a maximum salary. Had he not done so, wages would have gone into the stratosphere. Possibly mindful of the kind of baseball contracts mentioned above and the one Minnesota Timberwolves signed with Kevin Garnett in 1997 – $126 million over six years, or $40 a minute, awake or asleep – Stern was saving owners from their own excesses. NBA owners will lose no sleep about the prospect of $200 million contracts over the first decade of the twenty-first century; which is more than can be said for some sports.

Bosman case

Jean-Marc Bosman's contract was held by his soccer club FC Liège, of Belgium. At the end of his contract, the club demanded a transfer fee from any other club wishing to sign him. Bosman argued that this was a violation of the Treaty of Rome which allowed freedom of contract for citizens of nations belonging to the European Community. Bosman's club was intransigent, so he took his case to the European Court of Justice which, in 1995, ruled in his favor and ended the necessity for transfer fees in soccer.

In finding in his favor, the court brought the contracts of employment in soccer into alignment with those of any other industry. Transfer fees were traditionally sums of money paid by one club to another for the unused portion of a player's contract. The precise length of the unexpired portion did not typically affect the fee, which was based on the evaluation of the player's skills and possible benefit to the club. Typically, a player could expect to receive the equivalent of 10 per cent of the fee. Post-Bosman, a player was free to move to any club with whom he could agree personal terms. It is no small irony that Bosman himself benefited hardly at all from the ruling which precipitated huge salary increases for many players. His playing career nearing an end, Bosman found himself without a club within three years of the court decision.

European league sports, the principal one of which is, of course, soccer, have never broached salary caps and did not have free agency until 1995, when the Bosman case allowed out-of-contract players to negotiate freely with other clubs. The expectation was that players' salaries would spiral and transfer fees (paid to the club for the players' registration and, if appropriate, the unused portion of his contract) would disappear. In the event, clubs simply started locking players into longer (say, six-year) contracts and renewing them on greatly improved terms about a year before expiry. Some players who were confident of commanding top salaries waited-out their contracts and moved as free agents. But the majority of transferees left before their contracts ended, so enabling their clubs to exact a price for their services. For example, in 1999, the Italian club Lazio received 72 billion lira (£24 million, or $15 million) from Internazionale, of Milan, for the player Christian Vieri.

The type of problem that evidently confronted the NBA may yet visit soccer. The £30 million transfer fee barrier is certain to be broken very soon and wages will soar. Soccer enjoyed its most prosperous period ever at the turn of the century, European clubs feeling most of the benefit. The European Champions League, which was revamped in the 1999/2000 season, is the richest sports league in the world, if the various sponsorships and television revenues are considered collectively. To sustain this kind of transfer inflation *and* ever-increasing salaries, soccer is going to be in serious need of money. This is why soccer will be the next sport after boxing to go totally ppv.

With universal distribution through some sort of pay television system, championship winners would be in a position to name their own price. They will then be able to attract the best players and so strengthen their positions, putting into motion a circulation of elite clubs. The reasoning is straightforward. Whether fans will respond positively to the same clubs perennially dominating remains to be seen. Unlike the US leagues, which have inbuilt mechanisms, like the draft, to ensure a competitive balance, European leagues take a different approach: devil takes hindmost. The prospects for underachieving clubs is daunting.

VALUES AND THE LAW

At the individual level, it is less straightforward. An ambitious player wants success, both athletically and monetarily; the two go hand-in-hand, of course. He or she picks up some locker-room tidbits about how someone is picking up serious money after his performances improved dramatically and how he has been known to take a supplement or two to give him that extra edge. Piousness over drugs is wobbled by this kind of talk; even the most righteous of athletes are tormented by the thought of a less talented colleague reaping a rich harvest on account of his or her readiness to take a few risks. This is basically how athletes' values are changed. Their immersion in a world where competition is ruthless and the stakes are extravagantly high makes them contemplate the difference between success and near-success. You may measure it in millions, or in column inches, or in talk show appearances, or in terms of any other celebrity index.

This is the fundamental reason athletes will continue to take performance-enhancing substances. As testers are becoming more sophisticated and intrusive, so sports performers and their suppliers are becoming more expert in evading them. There is an easy way for sports-governing organizations to eliminate drugs: take away all the financial incentives and go back to amateurism. A non-starter, of course; but, it would soon put a stop to drug-taking. As the future is the exact opposite of this, with more rather than less money becoming available, drugs will stay rampant.

One consequence of this will be to allow lawyers to step up their interest in sports. We have already seen in Chapter ten how the law has stealthily advanced into the heartlands of sports. Despite the best efforts of sports-governing organizations to keep them at bay, law firms specializing in sports issues have made their presence tell; and they will continue to do so in future. Drugs cases will ensure law firms keep healthy bill-able hours. Legally, sports organizations are vulnerable. A tiny mistake in testing procedures, a slightly ambiguous result or an irregularity in conditions are all an athlete needs. With the possibility of catastrophic losses of earnings, athletes are liable to contest positive drugs tests through the courts.

Almost every athlete who tests positive proclaims their innocence. Many have tried to prove it. The cases of Butch Reynolds and Diane Modahl must have shown the financial damage an athlete with a team of lawyers can do to a sports-governing organization. Other athletes, such as Michelle de Bruin and Mary Slaney have been less successful. But we can be sure that there are many more cases to come. Professional athletes have deep pockets and can hire law firms, some of which will specialize in drugs cases.

Most sports-governing bodies take their leads from the International Olympic Committee and will wait to see how that organization responds to the unsettling prospect of having to fight court battles with athletes. A relaxation of penalties is likely. Four-year suspensions can devastate a sports performer's career; two-year suspensions may be easier to take for an athlete who may find it simpler to serve out the suspension rather than get involved in complicated and sometimes lengthy legal disputes.

As head of the IOC, Juan Antonio Samaranch hinted that his organization would have to redefine what exactly "drugs" were. Stung by a few costly court cases, the IOC may well listen to Samaranch, even if it means delicate negotiations with its commercial sponsors. More permissive policies would be viewed warily by sponsors who are predictably reluctant about having their products tainted, if only by implication.

What is absolutely certain is that drugs will continue to dominate headlines and spark controversy. There will be a growing recognition that drug-taking in sport is directly related to the awesome amounts of money sloshing around in sports and this will translate into pressure on the IOC and other organizations to re-evaluate their stances on drugs. By the time of the next edition of *MSS*, most governing organizations will have modified their policies.

The law will also find its way into sports through other avenues. Throughout this book, I have referred to the changes in communications that blur the boundaries between various media. For instance, digital broadcasting's convergence with the internet will lead to interesting questions: most newspapers have websites, but, in future they will feature sound recordings and moving images, prompting us to ask whether we are reading a newspaper or watching a television program. As geographical and technological borders are globalized into oblivion by accessible, versatile systems, national regulatory organizations, such as the USA's Federal Communications Commission (FCC) will be made to struggle with difficult problems over proprietorship and control.

One other area that will keep law firms busy is women's rights. Ila Borders was the first female to pitch in a men's professional baseball league, but she will not be the last. The salary differentials between women's and men's sports are big enough to encourage female players to push for integration. We saw in Chapters seven and eight how women have been excluded from or marginalized in sports through all sorts of means. But, now the toothpaste is out of the tube. The day is not far off when a top-class woman athlete in a team sport will want to stake her place in an all-male team. Major League Soccer (MLS) may be as a candidate. Up to quite recently dismissed as a poor imitation of a man's sport, women's soccer is now at a high point, especially in the USA.

The interesting aspect about this is that the men's game has not progressed in the manner expected after the formation of MLS. Attendances have been up-and-down and the USA national team was disappointing at the 1998 World Cup. Women's soccer will eclipse the men's sport in the States. Early signs of this came in the women's World Cup competition held in the USA in 1999. The teams played in front of sell-out crowds, usually 70,000+ and the quality of the soccer was undeniable. Players like Cindy Parlow and Michelle Akers emerged to join Mia Hamm as sports stars.

Women's soccer will never be accepted fully in most European countries where the man's game is supreme. But, in the States, the MLS is not so strong and women players may well believe they can hold their own in predominantly men's teams. If their advances are spurned, courts will be asked to decide.

Chapters six through eight highlight the different historical experiences of women and ethnic minorities in sports. Despite these differences, both have arrived in the twenty-first century actually sharing a predicament: a paucity of top-level coaching and administrative positions. This situation has been in flux for several years and will continue to change in the future.

Women have advanced into coaching jobs and front offices, though perhaps not at the pace they wanted. Ethnic minorities are making slower progress, though this is likely to speed up now that the "Rebecca Myth" is in the process of being debunked by an expanding number of black coaches and administrators.

PROGRESS AND PERFORMANCE

Arguments about "who was best?" invite false comparisons. "The 1960s Pittsburgh Steelers would have beaten today's Broncos." "The Wolverhampton Wanderers of the 1950s would have seen off the current Manchester United." "Margaret Court, who dominated women's tennis in the 1960s, would have run rings around Lindsay Davenport." "The heavyweights of today would be no match for those of the 1930s." None of these can be proven. No one says "Roger Bannister would have burnt off Noah Ngeny," probably because it can so easily be disproved. Kenya's Ngeny regularly clocks about 15 seconds faster than Bannister's best for the mile. By the same reasoning, we should have accepted that all other sports, including those that rely more on technique and strategy than sheer fitness, improve their standards at roughly the same pace.

The old Steelers team would not register a single win in today's NFL. Davenport would dispose of Court, most likely without dropping a game. Few of the relatively small (Joe Louis weighed just over 200 lbs, or about 14 stones) and immobile heavyweights would last the distance with today's 230 lbs behemoths. If the actual performers of previous eras enjoyed the benefits of better diet, training, and strategy, as well as better social circumstances, the story might be different. Conditions change and these yield improvements, though not necessarily at an even pace.

In the first two editions of *MSS*, I paraphrased former Olympian Sebastian Coe's father and coach, Peter, who once ventured to suggest that there was no limit to how fast the mile could be run. "It's like taking a straight line, dividing it in two, splitting again, then again and again and so on *ad infinitum*," he argued. "The lines get smaller and smaller, but you're always left with something." In other words, there will always be the potential for improvement in competitive performances, but the improvements will be quantitatively smaller each time. I agreed with this prognosis, pointing out that it can be applied to any sport, not just track and field, which are, of course, measurable.

Huge improvements or long-standing records, such as Coe's 2:12.18 for 1,000 meters, set in 1981, Jarmila Kratochvilova's 1:53.28 for 800 meters, set in 1983, Marita Koch's 47.60 for 400 meters, set in 1985, or Randy Barnes's 23.12

Progress

Progress in sports is a uniquely human phenomenon, based more on intellectual abilities than physical ones. For example, today, over 1,500 meters, Hicham El Guerrouj is consistently running about 40 seconds faster than his counterpart of 120 years ago (see Chapter three). Yet, if we compare the Kentucky Derby or Grand National winner over a similar period, today's horses run only about 10 seconds faster. The reason for the difference is that a trained racehorse will maintain between 85 and 95 per cent of its maximum speed, metabolizing anaerobic energy, which is, as we have seen, counterproductive in the long term as it produces lactic acid and retards muscle contraction.

Humans have improved their performances through advances in technique, training, rivalries, and supplements. They will run at between 70 and 75 per cent of maximum speed for most of a middle-distance race, kicking over the final phase: e.g. 5,000m: $11\frac{1}{2}$ laps @ 61.5 seconds + 1 lap @ 56 seconds = 12:43.25. This requires timing, anticipation, and a tactical awareness, as well as the capacity to assimilate stress and discomfort – features that are built into training.

There is also an incentive: a horse has only a whipped flank to motivate it in the final stretch, whereas a human has rewards for which he or she is prepared to suffer pain. Apart from the intellectual stimulus, we should note that humans are physically inefficient at running and have modest locomotion capabilities compared to horses, whose capacity for running is an evolutionary adaptation, probably resulting from their relative lack of defense. The human desire to run fast over distances and, indeed, achieve success in any competition, is a product of self-induced challenge.

meters shot, set in 1990, remain historically aberrant performances, explicable only in terms of freak atmospheric conditions, exceptionally fierce competition or some undisclosed form of assistance. But, records have typically progressed smoothly and by decreasing increments in most events for most of the past century. But, in the mid-1990s, something unusual happened.

In August 1994, Algeria's Noureddine Morceli slashed the world's 3,000 meters record when he ran 7:25.11, which equates to 8:01 for two miles. In other words, very, very fast; nearly four seconds faster, in fact, than the previous world record held by Kenya's Moses Kiptanui. In the 20 years immediately before Morceli's run, the record had been lowered by a yearly average of 0.307 seconds (6.14 seconds in total). Yet Morceli's was a portentous run.

The following year, Haile Gebrselassie, of Ethiopia, began to rewrite the record books. He lopped 1.55 seconds off Tanui's two miles record, which was more than it had been lowered during the entire 1972–94 period. He also destroyed Kiptanui's 5,000 meters record with 12.44.39, an improvement of 10.91 seconds, compared with an average improvement of just under 3.64 seconds every year between 1972 and 1995. The Ethiopian later reduced this to 12.41.86, in 1997, and to 12.39.36, in 1998. But Gebrselassie's most extra-ordinary run was over 10,000 meters, in 1995, when he recorded 26.43.53. In the previous year, William Sigei, of Kenya, had shaken the athletics world when he ran a remarkable 26.52.23, which itself took a gigantic 6.15 seconds off a world record that had been brought down by about 15 seconds in the previous 15 years. So, Gebrselassie's 8.7 seconds improvement seemed to defy rational analysis.

The sequence of events did not stop. Gebrselassie's records were beaten by Daniel Komen and Paul Tergat, both of Kenya, and Salah Hissou, of Morocco, only for him to respond by breaking them again and again. Collectively, the middle-distance records produced a pattern. The athletics equivalent of the law of diminishing returns held good up to around 1995; then the returns started to expand. Even if the pattern has not been replicated in other areas, the sharp and unexpected upturn in performance forces us to reconsider the orthodoxy about athletic progression and ponder on possible reasons for the disproportionate improvement.

Highly-paid athletes often say money is the last thing they are thinking of in the midst of competition. This may be so, but it is tempting to advance cash incentives as at least one factor in the improvement. At the start of the twenty-first century, Gebrselassie would not take his tracksuit off for less than $50,000 a race and sprinter Maurice Greene's asking price was $100,000. Gebrselassie's middle-distance predecessors, like Lasse Viren and Henry Rono – both world record breakers – ran for expenses-only in the 1970s. Money *is* a motivating force, however much people deny it, and it becomes an even greater force when you come from poor African countries. It is, of course, no coincidence that a growing number of soccer players from nations such as Ghana, Nigeria, and Sierra Leone are now playing at the highest levels of European competition and earning millions for their labors.

A second factor is the knowledge we have about how to prepare athletes. We know more about diet and training cycles and, importantly, how to use technology to improve performance. Philosophies of training have changed. The brutal regimes instigated by Franz Stampfl in the 1950s now seem quite modest. Gebrselassie employed a version of Stampfl's philosophy which was to slice up a distance and repeatedly attack just one portion of it during training. He prepared for longer distances by running 400 meters at about 90 per cent of his maximum (e.g. 46 seconds) about 20 times, with a one-minute recovery between reps. This reflects in actual performance. For example, distances up to a mile are now typically run quite evenly at about 96–97 per cent capacity. Runners try to distribute their efforts in a way that replicates hard training. The first three laps of a fast 1,500 meters may each be run at even splits of 56 seconds, with the final three-quarter lap taking 41 seconds (equivalent of a 54.66 lap). This means that all distances up to a mile are likely to be less tactical affairs and more of sustained sprints.

Performance such as this requires training that accentuates quality as well as quantity. Combine better training with better nutrition and the supplementary aid of massage, acupuncture, and assorted methods of modifying cognition and you have potent factors that explain the improvements. But, there is perhaps one other point we need to contemplate.

In no other area of track and field has there been such a dramatic improvement. In some areas, there has actually been a deterioration in measurable performance. Few women's records are challenged nowadays, either in track and field, or swimming. The accepted reason for this is that many, probably most, records set by athletes from the former Soviet-bloc countries were involved in state-run programs which involved taking performance-enhancing substances for which there were no rigorous tests. Anabolic steroids would have had an impact on virtually all strength-related performances, including throwing field events and track races up to 800 meters. Women have only recently begun to contest middle- and long-distance races. In men's events, the deterioration in power-based events is not so marked, though it is worth remembering that the best 21 throws in shot put history were all made before 1991, after which systems of gas chromatography and mass spectroscopy made it possible to check a compound found in urine against 70,000 held in a computer's database.

But, in the late 1990s, when the men's middle-distance records went tumbling, there was no effective test for erythropoietin (EPO – which we discussed in Chapter nine). The genetically-engineered substance is a more convenient and more efficient alternative to blood doping, which was known to be favored by some middle- and long-distance men in the 1970s. The sharp upturn in distance records coincided with the greater availability of EPO. In his *Sports Illustrated* article "Distance thunder," Tim Layden quotes former marathon runner Alberto Salazar, of the USA: "I can believe that there can always be that one great person, that Superman who can run 45 seconds faster than Henry Rono . . . But all these people running so fast? That's incomprehensible to me" (1998: 37). (Gebrselassie's 1998 record for 10K was actually just under a minute faster than Rono's best of 20 years before.)

Perhaps it will become more comprehensible in years to come. Some will hold that the exponential improvement was the product of the genuinely gifted Superman referred to by Salazar, who inspired his rivals to greater and greater achievements. After all, rivalries tend to bring the best out of competitors. Others will dismiss it as a historical deviation. Cynics – and one suspects Salazar is among them – will wish to wait and see what happens when a test for EPO comes into force. If there is a tapering off in times, then we can draw obvious conclusions.

Brendan Foster, the British runner who held the 3,000 meters record, 1974–8, is also quoted by Layden: "You'd have to think these guys are approaching the limits of human endurance" (1998: 34). John Smith, who coached Greene, Ato Boldon, and others, disagrees. "I don't think a limit exists," he said to Mike Rowbottom, of the *Independent* (July 5, 1999). Ben Johnson's now-expunged time for the 100 meters at the 1988 Olympics was 9.79 seconds. It took only 11 years before the same time was clocked by Greene without the enhancement used by Johnson.

It seems my original forecast is in need of revision. The bit-by-even-smaller-bit progression I envisaged may be interspersed with periods of rapid and perhaps explosive improvements. Perhaps we have witnessed them in some sports, but have not been able to measure them. For example, the ascendant Chicago Bulls team of the 1990s may have taken the sport to new heights because of its special combination of coaching and playing staff, and appreciable cash incentives. Without these, it may have taken basketball another ten or 15 years to produce a team capable of elevating the game to the same level.

Historically, we can identify intervals of superabundance in particular sports. The Duran/Hagler/Hearns/Leonard epoch of boxing in the 1970s stands out; there has been no evidence of such a sustained level of competition in the years since. Salazar's Superman theory seems to apply perfectly to Jean-Claude Killy, the best all-round ski racer in history, who glided to previously untouched planes of achievement and whose technical command has probably not been matched since (though fans of Alberto Tomba may wish to argue that point). Technological changes often disguise progress: motor cars have been slowed-up; tennis balls have been deflated; javelins have been made less aerodynamic. The changes have usually been made in the interests of safety or spectacle, but, in both cases, their effect has been to mask quantifiable progress.

In other words, several sports may have passed through the kind of stage that middle-distance running went through in the late 1990s. But, because they are either not objectively measurable in the same way as track or they have changed the conditions of competition, the periods have not been acknowledged as exponential jumps forward.

Perhaps, these are the equivalent of Elias's "civilizing spurts" we encountered in Chapter five: relatively short, but transformative bursts of activity in which human conduct is significantly affected. As we saw, Elias budgets for a reverse gear. Traditionalists maintain that sports also have that facility. It probably only seems that way. While there may be less intense rivalry and/or less talented individuals in some eras, it is unlikely that overall standards reverse; more likely that our retrospective interpretations deceive us. Jordan, Leonard, Killy, and many, many other athletes stand out as parts of "golden ages" in sports and, as I have argued, they were parts of periods of accelerated progress. But, the sports in which they participated would not have remained unchanged by their presence. They defined new standards of excellence in much the same way as Gebrselassie did in middle-distance running.

So, the revision to my prediction is simple. We need to allow for the fact that sports typically progress smoothly without denying the possibility of rapid spurts that violate all accepted criteria. The trick is to identify the conditions under which those spurts take place. A sharp upturn in the financial incentives on offer seems to help. There has always been money to be made in boxing; but in the 1970s, million-dollar purses became commonplace. We have seen in Chapter fourteen how the NBA went from a struggling operation to a mega-billion-dollar sport from the mid-1980s.

The NBA was hardly in its infancy at the time, but, neither was it a mature major league sport. Being in the middle of take-off period also seems conducive to rapid progress. Jordan's NBA epitomizes this, but we should also consider the NFL in the early 1970s, still not the force it is today, but progressing very speedily toward it. The 1973 Dolphins who went 17–0 under Don Shulah represent this phase of the league's development. Sports that are either relatively new or have been reorganized are susceptible to spurts. Women's basketball is due for one. Beach volleyball is probably just coming out of one, right now.

To close, we should consider the subject that obviously occupies much of our attention: you would not have got through 16 chapters unless you had a commitment to the study of sports. Over the final two decades of the twentieth century, sports studies and sports science were, sometimes grudgingly, accepted as legitimate academic pursuits. This reflected a more general recognition of sport as a central institution in contemporary culture. Its historical association with frivolity, recreation, and play is virtually over. A lot of this recognition has grown not so much out of an appreciation of sports, but of a concern with the problems sports seemed to generate. Fan violence, racism, sexism, drugs: these were some of the issues that forced analysts to take sports seriously.

In 1996, I wrote in the second edition of *MSS* that a book such as this would not have been written ten years ago. The fact that it is now in its third edition is testimony to the success of sports as a field of academic inquiry and scholarly endeavor. The proliferation of sports-related degrees and programs of study strengthens the view that the study of sports is as relevant to today's curriculum as studies of crime, education, industry, religion, technology, and any number of other traditional subjects.

There are still areas of bewilderment: the apparent irrationality of some aspects of sports, the near-maniacal following they command, the almost suicidal tendencies of some of its participants and the inexplicable political controversies they are prone to provoke. But, after sixteen chapters, were are hopefully in a better position to comprehend these. For all their supposed lack of reason, sports are too important not to be understood. Making sense of sports is now a matter of obligation rather than choice.

ASSIGNMENT

France, 1558: You are calling for your friend Michel de Notredame on your way to a big *torneiement* in nearby Provence, where a visiting court from Burgundy is due to appear. As he goes to grab his coat, you peer at de Notredame's desk and read his scribbled notes. "Are you making more prophecies, Nostradamus?" you ask. "Yes, those are about the tournaments of the twenty-first century," he replies. You are dismayed: "Not again. Didn't you get into enough trouble when you predicted King Henry's death in a joust?" "I was right, wasn't I?" he says. "Well, you might have got that one right, but all this business about a revolution in France in a couple of hundred years' time and a Great Fire in London and this whatsisname, Hister or Hitler or something in the 20th century . . . it's ridiculous. People are laughing at you. Take that one you wrote recently:

> *In the seventh month of 1999*
> *From the sky will come a great King of Terror*
> *He will resurrect the great King of Angolmois*
> *Before and afterward war reigns happily*

"What was that supposed to mean? The end of the world?" Nostradamus responds: "Not at all: it refers to a type of tournament, except the riders will have mechanical beasts with wheels instead of legs and they will charge not at each other but in unison all over France and with a fury that resembles a war. And when they descend from the mountains, it will seem as if they come from the sky and the swiftest shall be a King." "Yeah, right," you scoff. "So, the tournaments will still be around in 2018." Nostradamus answers: "Not quite. But, the spirit that moves them will be." As you leave, you smile: "You don't seriously think people are going to be reading this stuff in 450 years' time, do you?" He just shrugs. What was Nostradamus writing?

bibliography

Abernathy, B., Kippers, V., Mackinnon, L., Neal, R., and Hanrahan, S. (1997) *The Biophysical Foundations of Human Movement*, Champaign, IL: Human Kinetics.

Adams, J. (1995) *Risk*, London: UCL Press.

Anderson, E. (1999) *Code of the Street: Decency, violence, and the moral life of the inner city*, New York: Norton.

Andrews, J. (1998) "The world of sport: Not just a game," *The Economist* (June 6).

Andronicus, M. (1979) "Essay and education: The institutions of the games in ancient Greece," in *The Eternal Olympics: The art and history of sport*, ed. by N. Yaloris, New York: Caratzis Brothers.

Anonymous (1994) *Cyclist's Training Diary*, 7th edn, Chambersberg, PA: Alan C. Hood & Co.

Arms, R., Russsell, G., and Sandilands, M. (1987) "Effects on the hostility of spectators of viewing aggressive sports," in *Sport Sociology*, 3rd edn, ed. by A. Yiannakis, T. McIntyre, M. Melnick, and D. Hart, Dubuque: Kendall/Hunt.

Armstrong, K. L. (1999) "Nike's communication with black audiences," *Journal of Sport & Social Issues*, vol. 23, no. 3 (August).

Ashe, A. R. (1993) *A Hard Road to Glory: A history of the African-American Athlete 1619-1918 Vol. 1; 1919-1945 Vol. 2; Since 1946 Vol. 3*, New York: Amistad Warner.

Bakhtin, M. (1981) *The Dialogic Imagination*, Austin, TX: University of Texas Press.

Balsamo, A. (1996) *Technologies of the Gendered Body: Reading cyborg women*, Durham, NC: Duke University Press.

Bandy, S. and Darden, A. (eds) (1999) *Crossing Boundaries: An*

international anthology of women's experiences in sport, Champaign, IL: Human Kinetics.

Bane, M. (1997) *Over the Edge: A regular guy's odyssey in extreme sports*, New York: Gollancz.

Barker, C. (1997) *Global Television: An introduction*, Oxford: Blackwell.

Barnett, S. (1990) *Games and Sets: The changing face of sport on television*, London: British Film Institute.

Bauman, Z. (1979) "The phenomenon of Norbert Elias," *Sociology*, vol. 13.

Beck, U. (1992) *Risk Society*, London: Sage.

Bengry, E. (2000) "Nike" and "Michael Jordan," in *Sports Culture: An A-Z Guide*, by E. Cashmore, London: Routledge.

Bergan, R. (1982) *Sports in the Movies*, London: Proteus Books.

Birke, L. and Vines, G. (1987) "A sporting chance: The anatomy of destiny," *Women's Studies International Forum*, vol. 10, no. 4.

Birrell, S. and Cole, C. (1990) "Double fault: Renee Richards and the construction and naturalization of difference," *Sociology of Sport Journal*, vol. 7.

Birrell, S. and Cole, C. (eds) (1994) *Women, Sport and Culture*, Champaign, IL: Human Kinetics.

Birtley, J. (1976) *The Tragedy of Randolph Turpin*, London: NEL.

Blanchard, K. (1995) *The Anthropology of Sports: An introduction*, Westport, CT: Bergin & Garvey.

Blue, A. (1987) *Grace Under Pressure*, London: Sidgwick & Jackson.

Blue, A. (1995) *Martina: The life and times of Martina Navratilova*, New York: Birch Lane Press.

Bolin, A. (1996) "Body building," in *Encyclopedia of World Sport: From ancient times to the present*, vol. 1, ed. by D. Levinson and K. Christensen, Santa Barbara, CA: ABC Clio.

Brailsford, D. (1997) *British Sport: A social history*, Cambridge: Lutterworth Press.

Brill, A. A. (1929) "The why of a fan," *North American Review* pt. 22.

Brohm, J.-M. (1978) *Sport: A prison of measured time*, London: Ink Links.

Brower, J. (1976) "Professional sports team ownership," *Journal of Sport Sociology*, vol. 1, no. 1.

Burns, J. (1996) *Hand of God: The life of Diego Maradona*, London: Bloomsbury.

Burton, R. (1999) "Sports advertising and the Super Bowl," in *The Advertising Business*, ed. by John Philip Jones, London: Sage.

Cahn, S. K. (1994) *Coming on Strong: Gender and sexuality in twentieth-century women's sport*, New York: Free Press.

Canter, D., Comber, M., and Uzzell, D. (1989) *Football in its Place: An environmental psychology of football grounds*, London: Routledge.

Chandler, J. (1988) *Television and National Sport: The United States and Britain*, Urbana, IL: University of Illinois Press.

Chapman, G. E. (1997) "Making weight: Lightweight rowing, technologies of power, and technologies of the self," *Sociology of Sport Journal*, vol. 14, no. 3.

Coakley, J. J. (1998) *Sport in Society: Issues and controversies*, 6th edn, Maidenhead: McGraw-Hill.

Cohen, G. L. (1993) (ed.) *Women in Sport*, Newbury Park, CA: Sage.

Collins, T. (1999) *Rugby's Great Split: Class, culture and the origins of rugby league football*, London: Frank Cass.

Coombs, D. (1978) *Sport and the Countryside*, Oxford: Phaidon Press.

Coren, S. (1992) *Left Hander: Everything you need to know about left-handedness*, London: John Murray.

Coren, S. and Halpern, D. F. (1991) "Left-handedness: A marker for decreased survival fitness," *Psychological Bulletin*, vol. 109.

Costa, M. and Guthrie, S. (eds) (1994) *Women and Sport: Interdisciplinary perspectives*, Champaign, IL: Human Kinetics.

Cunningham, H. (1980) *Leisure in the Industrial Revolution*, London: Croom Helm.

Curtis, J. and Loy, J. (1978) "Race/ethnicity and relative centrality of playing positions in team sport," *Exercise and Sport Sciences Review*, vol. 6.

Danielson, M. N. (1997) *Home Team: Professional sports and the American metropolis*, Princeton, NJ: Princeton University Press.

Dauncey, H. and Hare, G. (eds) (1999) *France and the 1998 World Cup*, London: Frank Cass.

Davidson, J. (ed.) 1993 *Sport on Film and Video: The North American Society for Sport History guide*, compiled by D. Adler, Lanham, MD: Scarecrow Press.

Denniston, R. (1999) *Trevor Huddlestone: A life*, Basingstoke: Macmillan.

Depasquale, P. (1990) *The Boxer's Workout*, New York: Fighting Fit.

Dougherty, N., Auxter, D., Goldberger, A. and Heinzmann, G. (1994) *Sport, Physical Activity and the Law*, Champaign, IL: Human Kinetics.

Downes, S. and Mackay, D. (1996) *Running Scared: How athletics lost its innocence*, Edinburgh: Mainstream.

Dubos, R. (1998) *So Human an Animal: How we are shaped by our surroundings and events*, Transaction.

Dunning, E. (1999) *Sport Matters: Sociological studies of sport, violence and civilization*, London: Routledge.

Dunning, E. and Rojek, C. (eds) (1992) *Sport and Leisure in the Civilizing Process*, Basingstoke: Macmillan.

Dunning, E. and Sheard, K. (1979) *Barbarians, Gentlemen and Players*, Oxford: Martin Robertson.

Dunning, E., Murphy, P., and Williams, J. (1988) *The Roots of Football Hooliganism*, London: Routledge & Kegan Paul.

Edwards, H. (1970) *The Revolt of the Black Athlete*, New York: Free Press.

Edwards, H. (1973) *Sociology of Sport*, Homewood, IL: Dorsey Press.

Eitzen, D. S. (ed.) (1993) *Sport in Contemporary Society*, 4th edn, New York: St Martin's Press.

Eitzen, D. S. and Sage, G. H. (1993) *Sociology of North American Sport*, 5th edn, Dubuque, IA: Brown & Benchmark.

Eitzen, D. S. and Sanford, D. (1975) "The segregation of blacks by playing position in football," *Social Science Quarterly*, vol. 5, no. 4.

Eitzen, D. S. and Yetman, N. (1977) "Immune from racism?" *Civil Rights Digest*, vol. 9, no. 2.

Elias, N. (1982) *The Civilizing Process*, 2 vols, New York: Pantheon.

Elias, N. (1986a) "An essay on sport and violence," in *Quest for Excitement*, ed. by N. Elias and E. Dunning, Oxford: Blackwell.

Elias, N. (1986b) "Introduction," in *Quest for Excitement*, ed. by N. Elias and E. Dunning, Oxford: Blackwell.

Elias, N. and Dunning, E. (eds) (1986) *Quest for Excitement*, Oxford: Blackwell.

Entine, J. (2000) *Taboo: Why black athletes dominate and why we're afraid to talk about it*, New York: Public Affairs.

Evans, M. (1997) *Endurance Athlete's Edge*, Champaign IL: Human Kinetics.

Fangio, J. M. and Carrozzo, R. (1990) *Fangio: My racing life*, Wellingborough: Thorsons.

Fasting, K. (1987) "Sports and women's culture," *Women's International Forum*, vol. 19, no. 4.

Featherstone, M. (1991) "The body in consumer culture," in *The Body: Social process and cultural theory* ed. by M. Featherstone, M. Hepworth, and B. S. Turner, London: Sage.

Featherstone, M., Hepworth, M., and Turner, B. S. (eds) (1991) *The Body: Social process and cultural theory*, London: Sage.

Festle, M. J. (1996) *Playing Nice: Politics and apologies in women's sport*, New York: Columbia University Press.

Fowles, J. (1996) *Advertising and Popular Culture*, Newbury Hills, CA: Sage.

Frank, T. (1997) "Alternative to what?" pp. 145-61 in *Commodify Your Dissent: Salvos from* The Baffler, ed. by T. Frank and M. Weiland, New York: Norton.

Frank, T. (1997) "The new gilded age," in *Commodify Your Dissent: Salvos from* The Baffler, ed. by T. Frank and M. Weiland, New York: Norton.

Franklin, B. (1997) *Newszak and News Media*, London: Arnold.

Fraser, G. M. (1997) *Black Ajax*, London: HarperCollins.

Furedi, F. (1997) *Culture of Fear*, London: Cassell.

Gallagher, C. and Laqueur, T. (eds) (1987) *The Making of the Modern Body: Sexuality and society in the nineteenth century*, Berkeley, CA: University of California Press.

Geertz, C. (1972) "Deep play: Notes on the Balinese cockfight," in *The Interpretation of Cultures*, ed. by C. Geertz, New York: Basic Books.

Geschwind, N. and Galaburda, A. M. (1987) *Cerebral Lateralization*, Cambridge, MA: MIT Press.

Gibson, K. and Ingold, T. (eds) (1993) *Tools, Language and Cognition in Human Evolution*, Cambridge: Cambridge University Press.

Giulianotti, R., Bonney, R., and Hepworth, M. (eds) (1994) *Football, Violence and Social Identity*, London: Routledge.

Goldlust, J. (1988) *Playing for Keeps: Sport, the media and society*, Melbourne: Longman Cheshire.

Goldman, R. and Papson, S. (1999) *Nike Culture: The sign of the swoosh*, London: Sage.

Gorman, J. and Calhoun, K. (1994) *The Name of the Game: The business of sports*, New York: Wiley.

Gorn, E. J. (1986) *The Manly Art: Bare-knuckle prize fighting in America*, Ithaca, NY: Cornell University Press.

Gorski, R. A. (1991) "Gonadal hormones and the organization of brain structure and function," in *The Lifespan Development of Individuals: Behavioral, neurological and psychosocial perspectives* ed. by D. Magnuson, Cambridge: Cambridge University Press.

Gottdiener, M. (1997) *The Theming of America: Dreams, visions and commercial spaces*, Boulder, CO: Westview Press.

Goulder, A. W. (1965) *Wildcat Strike: A study in worker–management relations*, New York: Harper Torchbooks.

Govier, E. (1998) "Brainsex and occupation," in *Gender and Choice in Occupation and Education*, ed. by J. Radford, London: Routledge.

Greenwood, J. (1998) *Total Rugby: Fifteen-man rugby for coach and player*, London: A. & C. Black.

Griffin, P. (1998) *Strong Women, Deep Closets: Lesbians and homophobia in sport*, Champaign, IL: Human Kinetics.

Groves, D. (1987) "Why do some athletes choose high-risk sports?" *Physician and Sportsmedicine*, vol. 15, no. 2.

Gruneau, R. (1983) *Class, Sports and Social Development*, Amherst, MA: University of Massachusetts Press.

Gruneau, R. (1984) "Commercialism and the modern Olympics," in *Five Ring Circus*, ed. by A. Tomlinson and G. Whannel, London: Pluto Press.

Gruneau, R. and Whitson, D. (1993) *Hockey Night in Canada*, Toronto: Garamond.

Guelke, A. (1986) "The politicisation of South African sport," in *The Politics of Sport*, ed. by L. Allison, Manchester: Manchester University Press.

Guttmann, A. (1978) *From Ritual to Record: The nature of modern sports*, New York: Columbia University Press.

Guttmann, A. (1986) *Sports Spectators*, New York: Columbia University Press.

Guttmann, A. (1996) *The Erotic in Sports*, New York: Coumbia University Press.

Hain, P. (1982) "The politics of sport and apartheid," in *Sport, Culture and Ideology*, ed. by J. Hargreaves, London: Routledge & Kegan Paul.

Halberstam, D. (1999) *Playing for Keeps: Michael Jordan and the world he made*, New York: Random House.

Hall, M. A. (1996) *Feminism and Sporting Bodies: Essays on theory and practice*, Champaign, IL: Human Kinetics.

Hannigan, J. (1998) *Fantasy City: Pleasure and profit in the postmodern metropolis*, London: Routledge.

Hare, N. (1973) "The occupational culture of the black fighter," in *Sport and Society*, ed. by J. Talamini and C. Page, Boston, MA: Little, Brown.

Hargreaves, J. (1994) *Sporting Females: Critical issues in the history and sociology of women's sports*, London: Routledge.

Hargreaves, J. (ed.) (1982) *Sport, Culture and Ideology*, London: Routledge & Kegan Paul.

Hargreaves, J. (ed.) (1986) *Sport, Power and Culture*, Oxford: Polity Press.

Harris, C. (1998) "A sociology of television fandom," in *Theorizing Fandom: Fans, subculture and identity*, ed. by C. Harris and A. Alexander, Cresskill, NJ: Hampton Press.

Harris, L. J. (1993) "Do left-handers die sooner than right-handers? Commentary on Coren and Halpern's (1991) 'Left-handedness: A marker for decreased survival fitness'," *Psychological Bulletin*, vol. 114, no. 2 (September).

Harris, M. (1993) *Culture, People, Nature*, 6th edn, London: HarperCollins.

Harris, M. (1998) *Theories of Culture in Postmodern Times*, Walnut Creek, CA: AltaMira.

Hauser, T. (1997) *Muhammad Ali: His life and times*, New York: Pan Books.

Henderson, E. (1949) *The Negro in Sports*, Washington, DC: Associated Publishers.

Hill, C., *Olympic Politics*, Manchester: Manchester University Press, 1st edn 1992, 2nd edn 1996.

Hoberman, J. (1984) *Sport and Political Ideology*, Austin, TX: University of Texas Press.

Hoberman, J. (1992) *Mortal Engines: Human engineering and the transformation of sport*, New York: Free Press.

Hoberman, J. (1997) *Darwin's Athletes: How sport has damaged black America and preserved the myth of race*, New York: Houghton Mifflin.

Hoberman, J. and Yesalis, C. E. (1995) "The history of synthetic testosterone," *Scientific American*, vol. 272, no. 2.

Hoch, P. (1972) *Rip Off the big Game: The exploitation of sports by the power elite*, New York: Anchor Doubleday.

Hoffer, R. (1998) *A Savage Business: The comeback and comedown of Mike Tyson*, New York: Simon & Schuster.

Hoffman, S. (ed.) (1992) *Sport and Religion*, Champaign, IL: Human Kinetics.

Hoggett, P. (1986) "The taming of violence," *New Society*, vol. 36 (October 17).

Holt, R. (1989) *Sport and the British*, Oxford: Oxford University Press.

Holt, R. (1990) *Sport and the Working Class in Modern Britain*, Manchester: Manchester University Press.

Horrell, M. (1968) *South Africa and the Olympic Games*, Johannesburg: Institute of Race Relations.

Horsman, M. (1997) *SkyHigh: The inside story of BSkyB*, London: Orion Business.

Houlihan, B. (1994) *Sport and International Politics*, Brighton: Harvester Wheatsheaf.

Houlihan, B. (1997) *Sport, Policy and Politics: A comparative analysis*, London: Routledge.

Houts, T. and Bass, J. (1995) *Trilog: Diary and guide for the triathlete and duathlete*, Lincolnwood IL: Masters Press/NTC Contemporary Publishing.

Hubbard, G. (1998) "Sports action," *Arts and Activities*, vol. 123 (March).

Huddleston, T. London: Collins, 1st edn 1956, *Naught for Your Comfort*, Champaign, IL: Human Kinetics, 2nd edn 1993.

James, C. L. R. (1963) *Beyond a Boundary*, London: Hutchinson.

Jarvie, G. and Maguire, J. (1995) *Sport and Leisure in Social Thought*, London: Routledge.

Jenkins, H. J. (1992) *Textual Poachers*, London: Routledge.

Jennings, A. (1996) *The New Lords of the Rings: Olympics, corruption and how to buy gold medals*, New York: Pocket Books.

Jhally, S. (1989) "Cultural studies and the sports/media complex," in *Media, Sports and Society*, ed. by L. A. Wenner, Newbury Park, CA: Sage.

Jiobu, R. (1988) "Racial inequality in a public arena," *Social Forces*, vol. 67, no. 2.

Johnson, R. S. and Harrington, A. (1998) "The Jordan effect," *Fortune*, vol. 137, no. 12 (June 22).

Janes, A., Reeves, R. and Weyers, J. (1998) *Practical Skills in Biology*, Harlow: Longman.

Kane, M. (1971) "An assessment of black is best," *Sports Illustrated*, vol. 34, no. 3.

Katz, D. (1994) *Just Do It: The Nike spirit in the corporate world*, Holbrook, MA: Adams Media.

Kerr, J. (1994) *Understanding Soccer Hooliganism*, Philadelphia: Open University Press.

Kerr, R. (1982) *The Practical Use of Anabolic Steroids with Athletes*, San Gabriel, CA: Kerr Publishing.

King, B. J. and Deford, F. (1982) *Billie Jean*, New York: Viking.

Klatell, D. and Marcus, N. (1988) *Sports for Sale: Television, money and the fans*, Oxford: Oxford University Press.

Kohn, M. (1996) *The Race Gallery*, London: Vintage.

Kühnst, P. (1996) *Sports: A cultural history in the mirror of art*, Dresden: Verlag der Kühnst.

Lapchick, R. (1986) *Fractured Focus*, Lexington, MA: Heath.

Laqueur, T. (1990) *Making Sex: Body and gender from the Greeks to Freud*, Cambridge, MA: Harvard University Press.

Lasch, C. (1979) *The Culture of Narcissism*, New York: Norton.

Layden, T. (1998) "Distant thunder," *Sports Illustrated*, vol 89, no. 3 (July 20).

Leaman, O. (1988) "Cheating and fair play in sport," in *Philosophic Inquiry in Sport*, ed. by W. J. Morgan and K. Meier, Champaign, IL: Human Kinetics.

Lenskyj, H. (1986) *Out of Bounds: Women, sport and sexuality*, Toronto: The Women's Press.

Leonard, W. (1988) *A Sociological Perspective of Sport*, 3rd edn, New York: Macmillan.

Lever, J. (1983) *Soccer Madness*, Chicago: University of Chicago Press.

Levine, L. (1977) *Black Culture and Black Consciousness*, New York: Oxford University Press.

Levine, P. (1985) *A. G. Spalding and the Rise of Baseball: The promise of American sport*, New York: Oxford University Press.

Levinson, D. and Christensen, K. (1996) *Encyclopedia of World Sport: From ancient times to the present*, Santa Barbara, CA: ABC-Clio.

Lindsey, L. (1990) *Gender Roles: A sociological perspective*, Englewood Cliffs, NJ: Prentice-Hall.

Lorenz, K. (1966) *On Aggression*, New York: Harcourt, Brace & World.

Louganis, G. (1995) *Breaking the Surface: A life*, New York: Random House.

Lukas, G. (1969) *Die Körperkultur in frühen Epochen der Menschenentwicklung*, East Berlin: Sportverlap.

Lüschen, G. (1976) "Cheating," in *Social Problems in America*, ed. by D. Landers, Illinois: University of Illinois Press.

MacGregor, J. (1999a) "Less than murder," *Sports Illustrated*, vol. 90, no. 12 (March 22).

MacGregor, J. (1999b) "SI view: Air and space," *Sports Illustrated*, vol. 90, no. 13 (March 29).

Malamud, B. (1967) *The Natural*, Harmondsworth: Penguin.

Mandell, R. (1971) *The Nazi Olympics*, New York: Macmillan.

Mandell, R. D. (1984) *Sport: A cultural history*, New York: Columbia University Press.

Maney, K. (1995) *Megamedia Shakeout: The inside story of the leaders and the losers in the exploding communications industry*, London: Wiley.

Mansfield, A. and McGinn, B. (1993) "Pumping irony," in *Body Matters*, ed. by S. Scott and D. Morgan, London: Falmer.

Marsh, P. (1979) *Aggro: The illusion of violence*, London: Dent.

Marsh, P., Prosser, E. and Harré, R. (1978) *The Rules of Disorder*, London: Routledge & Kegan Paul.

Mason, T. (1988) *Sport in Britain*, London: Faber & Faber.

Matza, D. (1969) *Becoming Deviant*, Englewood Cliffs, NJ: Prentice-Hall.

Mays, W. and Sahadi, L. (1989) *Say Hey: The autobiography of Willie Mays*, New York: Pocket Books.

McCrone, K. (1988) *Sport and the Physical Emancipation of English Women, 1870–1914*, London: Routledge.

McGinnis, P. M. (1999) *Biomechanics of Sport and Exercise*, Champaign, IL: Human Kinetics.

McIntosh, P. (1980) *Fair Play*, London: Heinemann Educational.

Messier, M., Gretzky, W., and Hull, B. (1998) *Wayne Gretzky: The making of the great one*, Dallas, TX: Beckett Publications.

Messner, M. (1992) *Power at Play: Sports and the problem of masculinity*, Boston, MA: Beacon Press.

Michener, J. (1976) *Sports in America*, New York: Random House.

Moir, A. and Moir, B. (1998) *Why Men Don't Iron: The real science of gender studies*, London: HarperCollins.

Money, T. (1997) *Manly and Muscular Diversions: Public schools and the nineteenth-century sporting revival*, London: Duckworth.

Morgan, W. J. (1994) *Leftist Theories of Sport: A critique and reconstruction*, Urbana, IL: University of Illinois Press.

Morgan, W. J. and Meier, K. V. (eds), *Philosophic Inquiry into Sport*, Champaign, IL: Human Kinetics, 1st edn 1988, 2nd edn 1995.

Morris, D. (1981) *The Soccer Tribe*, London: Jonathan Cape.

Morton, C. (1999) "The flame that died," *Independent on Sunday*, Focus section (January 24).

Munro, P. and Govier, E. (1993) "Dynamic gender-related differences in dichtotic listening performance," *Neuropsychologia*, vol. 31, no. 40.

Muris, P., Kop, W. J., and Merckelbach, H. (1994) "Handedness, symptom resorting and accident susceptibility," *Journal of Clinical Psychology*, vol. 50, no. 3 (May).

Muster, G. (1985) *Rupert Murdoch: A paper prince*, Harmondsworth: Penguin.

Naison, M. (1972) "Sports and the American empire," *Radical America*, vol. 6, no. 4 (July/August).

Newfield, J. (1995) *Only in America: The life and crimes of Don King*, New York: William Morrow.

Niednagel, J. (1994) *Your Keys to Sports Success*, Nashville, TN: Nelson.

Noble, W. and Davidson, I. (1996) *Human Evolution, Language and Mind: A psychological and archaeological inquiry*, Cambridge: Cambridge University Press.

Novak, M. (1976) *The Joy of Sport*, New York: Basic Books.

Olsen, J. (1968) *The Black Athlete*, New York: Time Life.

Oudshoorn, N. (1994) *Beyond the Natural Body: An archaeology of sex hormones*, London: Routledge.

Overman, S. J. (1997) *The Influence of the Protestant Ethic on Sport and Recreation*, Aldershot: Avebury.

Overman, S. J. (2000) "The Protestant Ethic," in *Sports Culture: An A-Z Guide* by E. Cashmore, London: Routledge.

Page, M. (1988) *Bradman: The biography*, Sydney: Pan Macmillan Australia.

Pass, K., Freeman, H., Bautista, J., and Johnson, C. (1993) "Handedness and accidents with injury," *Perceptual and Motor Skills*, vol. 77, no. 3 (December).

Patterson, O. (1971) "Rethinking black history," *Harvard Educational Review*, vol. 41 (August).

Paulsen, G. (1994) *Winterdance: The fine madness of Alaskan dog-racing*, London: Gollancz.

Pearlman, J. (1998) "Bare knuckles," *Sports Illustrated*, vol. 89, no. 17 (October 26).

Pelé and Fish, R. (1977) *Pelé: My life and the beautiful game*, New York: Doubleday.

Perry, C. (1983) "Blood doping and athletic competition," *International Journal of Applied Philosophy*, vol. 1, no. 3.

Petrie, T. A. (1996) "Differences between male and female college lean sport athletes, nonlean sports athletes, and nonathletes on behavioral and psychological indices of eating disorders," *Journal of Applied Sport Psychology*, vol. 8, no. 2.

Poliakoff, M. B. (1987) *Combat Sports in the Ancient World: Competition, violence, and culture*, New Haven, CT: Yale University Press.

Prendergrast, M. (1993) *For God, Country and Coca-Cola: The unauthorized history of the great American soft drink and the company that makes it*, New York: Collier.

Puglise, M., Lifshitz, F., and Grad, G. (1983) "Fear of obesity," *New England Journal of Medicine*, vol. 309.

Putnam, D. T. (1999) *Controversies of the Sports World*, Westport, CT: Greenwood Press.

Rader, B. (1984) *In its Own Image: How television has transformed sport*, New York: Collier-Macmillan.

Raymond, M., Pontier, D., Dufour, A., and Moller, A. P. (1996) "Frequency-dependent maintenance of left-handedness in humans," *Proceedings of the Royal Society of London*, series B, vol. 263 (December).

Real, M. R. (1998) "MediaSport: Technology and the commodification of postmodern sport," in *MediaSport*, ed. by L. A. Wenner, London: Routledge.

Regen, R. (1990) "Neither does King," *Interview*, vol. 20 (October 10).

Rescher, N. (1995) *Luck: The brilliant randomness of everyday life*, New York: Farrar Straus Giroux.

Rhodes, R. (ed.) (1990) *Sport in Art from American Museums*, New York: Universe.

Richards, R. and Ames, J. (1983) *Second Serve*, New York: Stein & Day.

Rigauer, B. (1981) *Sport and Work*, New York: Columbia University Press.

Ritzer, G., *The McDonaldization of Society*, Newbury Park, CA: Pine Forge, 1st edn 1993, 2nd edn 1998.

Robins, D. (1982) "Sport and youth culture," in *Sport, Culture and Ideology*, ed. by J. Hargreaves, London: Routledge & Kegan Paul.

Robinson, S. R. and Anderson, D. (1992) *Sugar Ray: The Sugar Ray Robinson story*, London: Robson Books.

Rosentraub, M. (1997) *Major League Losers: The real cost of sports and who's paying for it*, New York: HarperCollins.

Ryan, J. (1998) *Little Girls in Pretty Boxes: The making and breaking of élite gymnasts and figure skaters*, Toronto: The Women's Press.

Sakellarakis, J. (1979) "Athletics in Crete and Mycenae," in *The Eternal Olympics: The art and history of sport*, ed. by N. Yaloris, New York: Caratzas Brothers.

Sammons, J. (1988) *Beyond the Ring*, Camden, NJ: University of Illinois Press.

Sandrock, M. (1996) *Running with the Legends*, Champaign, IL: Human Kinetics.

Schiebinger, L. (1987) "Skeletons in the closet: The first illustrations of the female skeleton in eighteenth century anatomy," in *The Making of the Modern Body: Sexuality and society in the nineteenth century*, ed. by C. Gallagher and T. Laqueur, Berkeley, CA: University of California Press.

Schiebinger, L. (1989) *The Mind Has No Sex: Women in the origins of modern science*, Cambridge, MA: Harvard University Press.

Scott, J. (1971) *The Athletic Revolution*, New York: Free Press.

Scully, G. W. (1995) *The Market Structure of Sports*, Chicago: University of Chicago Press.

Senn, A. E. (1999) *Power, Politics and the Olympic Games*, Champaign, IL: Human Kinetics.

Shawcross, W. (1992) *Rupert Murdoch*, London: Chatto & Windus.

Sherman, L. (1998) *Big League, Big Time: The birth of the Arizona Diamondbacks, the billion-dollar business of sports, and the power of the media in America*, New York: Pocket Books.

Simson, V. and Jennings, A. (1992) *The Lords of the Rings: Power, money and drugs in the modern Olympics*, New York: Simon & Schuster.

Smith, D. E. (1988) "Femininity as discourse," in *Becoming Feminine: The politics of popular culture*, ed. by L. G. Roman, L. Christian-Smith, and E. Ellsworth, Philadelphia: Falmer.

Smith, M. D. (1983) *Violence and Sport*, Toronto: Butterworth.

Snyder, E. and Spreitzer, E. (1983) *Social Aspects of Sport*, 2nd edn, Englewood Cliffs, NJ: Prentice-Hall.

Sowell, T. (1994) *Race and Culture: A world view*, New York: Basic Books.

Spears, B. and Swanson, R. A. (1995) *History of Sport and Physical Activity in the United States*, 4th edn, Dubuque, IA: Brown & Benchmark.

Staudohar, P. and Mangan, J. (eds) (1991) *The Business of Professional Sports*, Urbana, IL: University of Illinois Press.

Stoddart, B. (1988) "Sport, cultural imperialism and colonial response in the British empire," *Comparative Studies in Society and History*, pt. 30 (October).

Strasser, J. B. and Becklund, L. (1993) *Swoosh: The unauthorized story of Nike and the men who played there*, New York: HarperBusiness.

Sundgot-Borgen, J. (1994a) "Eating disorders in female athletes," *Sports Medicine*, vol. 17, no. 3.

Sundgot-Borgen, J. (1994b) "Risk and trigger factors in the development of eating disorders in female elite athletes," *Medicine and Science in Sports and Exercise*, vol. 26, no. 4.

Suttles, G. (1968) *The Social Order of the Slum: Ethnicity and territory in the inner city*, Chicago: University of Chicago Press.

Swift, E. M. (1999) "Breaking point," *Sports Illustrated*, vol. 90, no. 4 (February 1).

Taub, D. and Benson, R. (1992) "Weight concerns, weight control techniques, and eating disorders among adolescent competitive swimmers: The effect of gender," *Sociology of Sport Journal*, vol. 9, no. 2.

Taylor, I. (1971) "Soccer consciousness and soccer hooliganism," in *Images of Deviance*, ed. by S. Cohen, Harmondsworth: Penguin.

Taylor, P. (1997) "Center of the storm," *Sports Illustrated*, vol. 87, no. 24 (December 15).

Todd, J. (1987) "Bernarr Macfadden: Reformer of the feminine form," *Journal of Sport History*, vol. 14, no. 1 (Spring).

Todd, T. (1987) "Anabolic steroids: The gremlins of sport," *Journal of Sport History*, vol. 14, no. 1 (Spring).

Turner, B. S. (1992) *Max Weber: From history to modernity*, London: Routledge.

Vandervell, A. and Coles, C. (1980) *Game and the English Landscape: The Influence of the chase on sporting art and scenery*, London: Debrett's Peerage.

Vanwalleghem, R. (1968) *Eddy Merckx: The greatest cyclist of the twentieth century*, Allentown, PA: Velo Press.

Vasili, P. (1998) *The First Black Footballer, Arthur Wharton, 1865-1930: An absence of memory*, Portland, OR: Frank Cass.

Verma, G. and Darby, D. (1994) *Winners and Losers: Ethnic minorities in sport and recreation*, London: Falmer.

Vertinsky, P. (1987) "Exercise, physical capability, and the eternally wounded woman in late nineteenth century North America," *Journal of Sport History*, vol. 14, no. 1 (Spring).

Vertinsky, P. (1990) *The Eternally Wounded Woman: Women, doctors and exercise in the late nineteenth century*, Manchester: Manchester University Press.

Vincent, M. (1995) "Painters and punters," *New Statesman & Society*, vol. 8 (May 19).

Voy, R. and Deeter, K. (1991) *Drugs, Sport and Politics*, Champaign, IL: Human Kinetics.

Waddington, I. (1996) "The development of sports medicine," *Sociology of Sport Journal*, vol. 19.

Wankel, L. (1982) "Audience effects in sport," in *Psychological Foundations of Sport*, ed. by J. Silva and R. Weinberg, Champaign, IL: Human Kinetics.

Waters, M. (1995) *Globalization*, London: Routledge.

Weber, M. (1958) *The Protestant Ethic and the Spirit of Capitalism*, trans. T. Parsons, New York: Scribner & Sons.

Weir, J. and Abrahams, P. (1992) *An Imaging Atlas of Human Anatomy*, by J. Weir and P. Abrahams, St. Louis, MO: Mosby-Wolfe.

Wenner, L. (ed.) (1998) *MediaSport*, London: Routledge.

Wenner, L. and Ganz, W. (1998) "Watching sports on television: Audience experience, gender, fanship, and marriage," in *MediaSport*, ed. by L. Wenner, London: Routledge.

Whannel, G. (1992) *Fields in Vision: Television, sport and cultural transformation*, London: Routledge.

Whitson, D. (1998) "Circuits of promotion: Media, marketing and the globalization of sport," in *MediaSport*, ed. by L. Wenner, London: Routledge.

Wiggins, D. (ed.) (1995) *Sports in America: From wicked amusement to national obsession*, Champaign, IL: Human Kinetics.

Wiggins, D. K. (1997) *Glory Bound: Black athletes in a white America*, Syracuse, NY: Syracuse University Press.

Wilmore, J. and Costill, D. (1994) *Physiology of Sport and Exercise*, Champaign, IL: Human Kinetics.

Wilson, N. (1988) *The Sport Business*, London: Piatkus.

Wolf, N. (1991) *The Beauty Myth: How images of beauty are used against women*, New York: Morrow.

Yaloris, N. (ed.) (1979) *The Eternal Olympics: The art and history of sport*, New York: Caratzas Brothers.

Yesalis, C. E. (ed.) (1993) *Anabolic Steroids in Sport and Exercise*, Champaign, IL: Human Kinetics.

Yesalis, C. and Cowart, V. (1998) *The Steroids Game: An expert's look at anabolic steroid use in sports*, Champaign, IL: Human Kinetics.

Zajonc, R. (1965) "Social facilitation," *Science*, vol. 149.

Zimbalist, A. (1992) *Baseball and Billions*, New York: Basic Books.

Zolberg, V. (1987) "Elias and Dunning's theory of sport and excitement," *Theory, Culture and Society*, vol. 4.

Zona, L. A. (1990) "Red Grooms," in *Sport in Art from American Museums*, ed. by R. Rhodes, New York: Universe.

Zucker, H. M. and Babich, L. J. (1987) *Sports Films: A Complete Reference*, Jefferson, NC: McFarland & Co.

name and subject index

Gramsci, Antonio 93, 96, 97
Grand National 246
Grant, Cary 213
Grant, Francis 260
Gray, Kevin 229
Graziano, Rocky 136
Greece *see* Ancient Greece
Green, Dennis 128, 129
Green, Ted 225
Greene, Maurice 380, 382
Greig, Dale 173, 174
Gretzky, Wayne 14, 133
Griffith Joyner, Florence ("Flo-Jo") 138, 144, 156–7, 215, 216
Grimshaw, Gina 181
Grooms, Red 269
Gruneau, Richard 93, 95, 96, 225, 353
Gulliver, Joseph 69
Guthrie, Sharon 183
Gutsmuths, Johann Christoph Friedrich 75
Guttmann, Allen 69, 80, 104, 166, 259, 261
gymnastics: art and sports 265; forelimbs 18; toughness 245

Hackhart, Dale 227
Hagler, Marvin 25, 382
Hakkinen, Mika 108
Halberstam, David 334, 335, 338, 341, 342
Hall, Alexander 269
Hall, Charles 256
Halpern 25, 26
Hamilton, Linda 158
Hamm, Mia 178, 377
Hannigan, John 10
Hardaway, Tim 305
Harding, Tonya 178
Hare, Geoff 107
Hare, Nathan 127
hare-coursing 66, 345
Hargreaves, Jennifer 152, 167
Hargreaves, John 77, 93, 95, 96
Harré, Rom 106
Harrelson, Woody 268
Harrington, Ann 339
Harris, Cheryl 234
Harris, Marvin 23–4

Hauser, Thomas 337
Hawkes, Gwenda 167
Hearns, Thomas 23, 382
Hearst, William Randolph 304
Heartfield, John 258
Heinzmann, Gregg 243
Hemingway, Mariel 261
Hendry, Stephen 234, 304
Henri, Robert 263
Henry, Buck 269
Henry VIII, King of England 68, 69
Hepworth, Mike 243
Hercules 64
Heston, Charlton 253
Hewlett-Packard International Women's Challenge 148
Hicks, Thomas 191
Hill, Christopher 353, 364
Hill, George Roy 222
Hill, Grant 305
Hill, Ron 270
Hilton, Harold 168
Hinault, Bernard 137
Hingis, Martina 46, 160, 164, 186, 208
Hirst, Damien 271
Hissou, Salah 380
Hitchcock, Alfred 129
Hitler, Adolph 115, 262, 351, 352, 363
Hoberman, John 125–7, 131, 196, 218, 351
Hoch, Paul 93, 94, 95, 193, 194
hockey 106, 133, 222, 224, 225–6, 230–1
Hodler, Marc 361, 362
Hoffer, Richard 112
Hoffman, Bob 192
Hoffman, Shirl 107
Hoffmann, Irene 258, 263
Hogarth, William 256, 263
Hoggett, Paul 91
Holmes, Larry 130
Holt, Richard 51, 52, 70, 80
Holyfield, Evander 23, 112, 130, 219, 221, 287
Homer, Winslow 260
homosexuality: female 150, 170, 173, 175, 261, 298–9; male 299–300
hooliganism: copycat effect 240–3; ethology 238; European Cup Final 237; explanations 237–43; figuration

405

title index